Privatization in the City

Successes, Failures, Lessons

E. S. Savas

Baruch College, The City University of New York

A Division of Congressional Quarterly Inc.

Washington, D.C.

CQ Press
1255 22nd Street, NW, Suite 400
Washington, DC 20037

Phone, 202-729-1900; toll-free, 1-866-427-7737 (1-866-4CQ-PRESS)

Web: www.cqpress.com

Copyright © 2005 by E. S. Savas

All rights reserved. No part of this publication may be reproduced or transmitted in any form or by any means, electronic or mechanical, including photocopy, recording, or any information storage and retrieval system, without permission in writing from the publisher.

Cover design: Brian Barth

Figures 2.2 and 2.4 are reprinted with the permission of the Government Finance Officers Association, publisher of *Government Finance Review,* 203 N. LaSalle St., Suite 2700, Chicago, IL 60601-1210. (312-977-4806; fax: 312-877-4806; e-mail: GFRC@foa.org). Annual subscriptions: $35.

♾ The paper used in this publication exceeds the requirements of the American National Standard for Information Sciences—Permanence of Paper for Printed Library Materials, ANSI Z39.48-1992.

Printed and bound in the United States of America

09 08 07 06 05 1 2 3 4 5

Library of Congress Cataloging-in-Publication Data

Savas, Emanuel S.
Privatization in the city : successes, failures, lessons / by E. S. Savas.
p. cm.
Includes index.
ISBN 1-56802-957-8 (pbk. : alk. paper)
Privatization—New York (State)—New York. 2. Privatization—United States.
I. Title.
HD3890.N7S38 2005
338.9747'105—dc22

2005006199

To my wife Helen, my sons Jonathan and Stephen, and
my grandchildren Christina Anastasia, Elena Andromache,
Stephen Robert, and Andrew James, with love.

Contents

Tables, Figures, and Boxes

Tables

Figures

Boxes

Foreword by Rudolph W. Giuliani

When I campaigned for mayor of New York City, I said that privatization was an important management tool, and that I would use it to improve government performance. I quizzed Steve Savas, Mayor Steve Goldsmith of Indianapolis, David Osborne, and others to immerse myself in the subject. I also visited America Works, the innovative contractor that prepares and places welfare recipients in jobs. As a Republican mayor in a city dominated by Democrats, many of my philosophical underpinnings were not then accepted New York City political thinking. But privatizing services—basically, getting government out of the way of the private sector—was something I believed in, and, as with lowering taxes and strengthening law enforcement, I felt that the city would benefit from these policies regardless of their popularity at the time.

When I became mayor I set about implementing privatization plans. We began by asking each city agency to identify services that might be better performed by the private sector. We looked for assets we might be able to sell, as well as areas where city employees could become more productive through competition. Just a month after taking office we announced detailed privatization plans, including selling some of the city-owned gas stations that were used for fueling municipal vehicles. I also did not believe that the city belonged in the broadcasting business—we sold WNYC-TV for $207 million and WNYC radio for $20 million. The same sort of reasoning inspired my decision to divest the city of the United Nations Plaza Hotel, a sale which brought in $85 million plus annual property taxes.

With literally thousands of municipal functions, it is not hard to find good candidates for privatization. It is hard, however, to implement those plans in the face of determined political opposition. Nevertheless, New York City now has a broad array of privatized programs that affect nearly every aspect of city government. We privatized some, or all, of the custodial services in public schools, job-placement services, security guard services, vehicle-fleet maintenance, data-entry services, tax billing, medical labs, road resurfacing, delivery of office supplies, copying and mail room services, and many other city activities.

Practitioners and public policy analysts alike are fortunate that Steve Savas has captured our experience in this volume. Steve is a pioneer in privatization, beginning with his experiences as first deputy city administrator of New York in 1969. He was also involved in my administration's efforts from the start, and as my term approached its mandated limit, he decided to write a book about our work. The result is a book that examines and documents the entire privatization program in a city. Other big cities have privatized functions, but only New York and Indianapolis have gone this far. Although individual cases and summaries have been reported elsewhere, New York is the first city in which the entire range of efforts is examined and comprehensively documented.

I am pleased to see this important story take shape as a book that will find its way into the hands of government officials and students heading for government careers. I hope that as others see what we have done in New York they will create ways to innovate privatization solutions to public challenges in their own unique settings.

Preface

It has taken thirty-five years to come full circle. When I was first deputy city administrator of New York in 1969, my heretical recommendations for public-private competition and competitive contracting with the private sector were pushed aside. New York's municipal government remained an infertile medium for privatization, while other cities, states, and whole nations embraced the concept and benefited greatly. Finally, when Rudolph Giuliani became mayor in 1994, the city at last joined the movement that had passed it by. It was my good fortune that he sought my advice, and I worked with his senior adviser, Richard Schwartz, and mayoral assistant, Richard Rogers, in the early planning of the mayor's privatization program.

Properly executed, privatization and public-private partnerships offer great benefits to government: lower costs, avoided costs, increased revenue, better quality of public services, more responsive government, and direct savings to the public. Poorly executed, these opportunities will be squandered.

This book summarizes privatization efforts in nine large U.S. cities and reports in detail on the Giuliani administration's privatization program and the steps that led to it. It catalogs successes and failures, and it draws lessons that others can use. Chapter 1 defines privatization and explains its prominence in the "new public management." Chapter 2 explores privatization initiatives in cities across the United States. Readers will learn in chapter 3 about the evolution of privatization in New York since colonial times, and in chapter 4 about the groundwork for Mayor Giuliani's privatization program. Chapter 5 describes the extent of privatization and the pattern and results of the privatization efforts. Successful privatizations are the subject of chapter 6, whereas chapter 7 addresses their thwarted and failed counterparts. Chapter 8 concludes with lessons learned and identifies promising candidates for future privatization; it also reflects back to the first chapter on public management and urban policy. Chapter 9 is an absorbing case study of the obstacles that one department (the Department of Parks and Recreation) overcame to achieve outstanding success. Appendix A summarizes the results in a convenient table, and Appendix B offers detailed information about each of the eighty-two privatization initiatives.

Acknowledgments

Many people deserve my thanks for making this book possible. I presented the idea to Mayor Giuliani in 2000, his next-to-last year in office; he liked it and gave it his support. Deputy Mayor Anthony P. Coles mobilized cooperation, and the Mayor's Office of Operations, through a project headed by Tony Longo, undertook much of the agency data collection. Keith Kerman, a brilliant young official in the Department of Parks and Recreation, directed that department's privatization efforts under Commissioner Henry Stern and produced perhaps the greatest successes and surely the best documentation in the city. Larry Levy provided useful assistance. I also thank the scores of current and former city personnel and others who dug through their files and memories to answer my persistent questions and to quench my thirst for facts and figures. I retain responsibility for introducing any errors.

My colleagues, Professors Fred Lane and Lynne Weikart at the School of Public Affairs of Baruch College of the City University of New York, offered helpful suggestions at crucial points during the gestation of the manuscript. I thank the reviewers selected by CQ Press, and the editor, Charisse Kiino, who improved the book by encouraging me to expand coverage of privatization in other large cities. The book now has a larger potential audience, for it is the first, I believe, to pull together descriptive information on nine big-city privatization programs. Vanita Gangwal helped organize the mass of city data and was the best graduate assistant I ever had. My friend, Stanley Smith, introduced me to Rudy Giuliani when he was making his first run for the mayoralty in 1989. I remain in the debt of Lin Ostrom, who illuminated my first steps in this field, and my earliest coworkers, Barbara Stevens and Eileen Brettler Berenyi. Finally, I acknowledge with gratitude the support of the Achelis Foundation and its executive director, Joseph S. Dolan.

1 | Introduction

A new approach to managing cities emerged in the last two decades of the twentieth century in America. Whereas in the 1960s and 1970s mayors looked primarily to Washington to solve their problems, in the 1980s a new concept took hold, and mayors began to look elsewhere—inward—to tackle their troubles.

Nowhere was the old approach better illustrated than in Washington, D.C., itself, by Mayor Marion Barry—arguably one of the worst of the big-city mayors—when he blamed the federal government for crime in his city because it was not giving him enough money. Assuming the role of helpless victim, he exclaimed, "I'm not going to let murder be the gauge, since we're not responsible for murders, we can't stop the murders." [1] This typified the practice of denying any ability to solve local problems and seeking handouts from the federal government, pleading poverty and insisting that the problem was insufficient spending.

A draft report from the U.S. Department of Housing and Urban Development (HUD) in 1982 asserted that: "Bold mayors of self-reliant cities have been transformed into wily stalkers of federal funds." Opponents of this heretical idea leaked the draft to the *New York Times* on the first day of the annual gathering of the U.S. Conference of Mayors, the organization of big-city mayors, and the *Times* featured it on the front page of the Sunday edition that day.[2] Predictably, the report triggered an angry, if not horrified, reaction from the assembled mayors. Ironically, they had gathered for the precise reason of demanding more money. Years later Mayor Kenneth Gibson of

Newark, New Jersey, articulated the self-defeating and contradictory nature of the mayors' position: On the one hand mayors were going to Washington with hat in hand, rattling their tin cups, crying that their cities were hopeless morasses doomed to disaster, while the next day they were wooing corporate leaders to set up new factories in town, claiming that their cities were great places to live and to do business, with trained workforces, good school systems, fine amenities for executives, and wonderful cultural attractions. This schizophrenic strategy failed to achieve either objective.[3]

Although the provocative "stalker" sentence did not appear in the final version of President Reagan's 1982 *National Urban Policy Report* to the Congress, the policy thrust was clear.[4] (Full disclosure: I was the assistant secretary for policy development at HUD responsible for the report and that sentence.) Cities had become overly dependent on federal aid and were overlooking their natural strengths and advantages, namely the large pool of leaders and resources in the private sector—business, community, religious, civic, academic, and nonprofit organizations. Inspired local government leaders needed to tap these resources. The policy report stressed that cities historically arose and grew to assume dominant economic roles in their regions. As change is constant, cities continually have to call on local resources to help understand their new roles, promote them, and prosper in them. The report further stated that the diversity of cities and states meant that, properly unfettered, these areas could manage themselves more wisely and creatively than the federal government could. The report also called attention to privatization (defined as relying more on the private institutions of society and less on government to satisfy people's needs), public-private partnerships, and competition in municipal services as particularly important ways to improve services, improve the quality of life, and reduce costs in financially strapped cities.

Gradually these ideas gained currency and were adopted—or discovered anew—by a new breed of mayors.[5] Mayors began assuming responsibility for the condition of their cities. Mayor John Norquist of Milwaukee, a Democrat, was among the first, in 1989, and he withdrew from the U.S. Conference of Mayors because he considered it an organization devoted to begging—"tin-cup federalism," he called it. Norquist thought he could make better use of his time and achieve greater success by working with other local leaders to address the needs of his city. "You can't build a city on pity," he said.[6]

Mayor Stephen Goldsmith of Indianapolis pointed out in 1993 that the federal government had spent more than $2.5 trillion on America's cities in the thirty years since the days of the Great Society, enough to buy all the assets of the Fortune 500 companies and all the farmland in America. Bigger checks from the federal government are not the answer to our urban woes, he said. Only private enterprise, private capital, neighborhood empowerment, and a market-based economy can rejuvenate the cities.[7] Other mayors emerged with similar activist and solution-oriented approaches, strikingly different from their predecessors:

> Richard Daley in Chicago, the home of patronage, changed rules and allowed the private sector to participate in providing city services. . . . Edward Rendell in Philadelphia took a watershed action in urban governance when he battled his public employee unions to reduce the cost of government. . . . Cleveland's Michael White stood up to old-style politicians and unions when he demanded that the provision of public services be opened up to competition. . . . Baltimore's Kurt Schmoke, in a remarkable action, not only gained control of the public schools but also contracted with a private company to run some of them.[8]

Other mayors in this mold included Bret Schundler in Jersey City, Patrick McCrory and Richard Vinroot in Charlotte, Wellington Webb in Denver, Thomas Menino in Boston, Jerry Abramson and David Armstrong in Louisville, Richard Riordan in Los Angeles, Kurt Schmoke and Martin O'Malley in Baltimore, Dennis Archer in Detroit, and Anthony Williams in Washington, D.C.[9] Mayor Williams endorsed school choice through vouchers and charter schools to overcome the dreadful public school system in his city. Manuel Diaz in Miami said "We [new mayors] want to control our own destiny." [10]

The apotheosis of the new mayors was Rudolph W. Giuliani, who gained worldwide fame first as the mayor who proved that New York City was manageable after all and then for his superb handling of the terrorist attacks on September 11, 2001. Giuliani promoted a new urban agenda calling for more self-reliance, and instead of seeking more federal aid, he wanted relief from federal and state government constraints. He said, "The old agenda was based on looking to others to solve our problems—look to Albany, look to Washington, someone will come along to bail us out. The new urban agenda should declare that we can solve our own problems, without direction from state or federal authorities." [11] This was strikingly similar to the position set forth presciently in President Reagan's *National Urban Policy Report* thirteen years earlier.

Mayor Jerry Brown of Oakland, formerly governor of California, extols the benefits of local control and describes with pride the improvements made in his city without assistance from the federal or state government.[12] Ed Rendell, the Democratic mayor of Philadelphia, attributed part of his success to the fact that he "didn't go whining to Washington" or to Harrisburg (the state capital) to solve problems but worked on them at home. A spokesperson for the National League of Cities said of Rendell, "He's been very focused on the things that concern his city in particular. . . . He marshals his resources in his own city to get things done." Instead of blaming and deflecting and saying that the answer lay in more help from the federal and state governments, he said that the city had no right to ask anyone for anything until it got its own house in order.[13] And whereas Mayor David N. Dinkins of New York City and Mayor Raymond L. Flynn of Boston gleefully handed Bill Clinton a list of suggested urban initiatives the morning after his election victory, Rendell, an early Clinton supporter, refrained. Rendell was conspicuously absent when the U.S. Conference of Mayors gave the new president a $27 billion wish list. Rendell said, "Our problems [referring to America's cities] come from a quarter century of mismanagement." [14] His approach stood in sharp contrast to the hand-wringing style of Mayors Dinkins and Flynn, who spent many days in Washington pleading for funds and who marched down Pennsylvania Avenue to make their plight known to President George Bush.[15] Nowadays, in a sweeping reversal emblematic of the changing times, leading has replaced whining, and the same U.S. Conference of Mayors that was appalled by President Reagan's draft report gives awards to mayors for excellence in public-private partnerships.[16]

The New Public Management

Government leaders like these are changing the very nature of public administration. Academics call their approach, in the aggregate, "the new public management." It is the latest manifestation of the never-ending process of government reform, and it is taking place at all levels of government and in many countries. The term generally encompasses the following elements:

- Reverting to core functions.
- Restoring civil society.
- Adopting market principles.
- Decentralizing and devolving authority.
- Focusing on management.

- "Rightsizing" government.
- Institutionalizing e-government and other new technologies.[17]

Let us look at each of these in detail.

Reverting to Core Functions

Governments own and operate a bewildering variety of businesses. The New York City government owned two radio stations and a television station. The state of Michigan owned an insurance company. Government agencies in New York state own and operate golf courses and ski resorts and owned the World Trade Center, including a luxury hotel that was destroyed in the 2001 terrorist attack. The U.S. Naval Academy until recently owned and operated an 865-acre dairy farm. The federal government owned a railroad and helium plants before selling them in the 1980s and 1990s, respectively.[18]

Governments, already overloaded with responsibilities, often operate businesses that do not constitute core functions of government, and lose money besides. One should recall that the English word "govern" is from the Greek word for steering. In other words, the task of government is to steer, not to row.[19] Raising cows, running golf courses, and operating radio stations are examples of rowing, and government is not well suited for rowing. The same is true of trash collection and vehicle maintenance. These activities are best placed in the hands of the private sector, with government doing only the necessary steering.

A redesigned government would unburden itself of nonessential responsibilities and devote full attention to functions that are intrinsically governmental. Among such core functions are supplying capital for untested ventures such as the space program; establishing rules to reduce conflicts; planning and providing necessary public services and subsidizing them if the market cannot provide them; handling external costs, like pollution, that otherwise desirable activities impose on others; and regulating natural monopolies. Another burden to be cast off government shoulders is obsolete activities. For example, the federal government owns and operates the Uniformed Services University of Health Sciences, which graduates physicians for the military at a cost of $562,000 each, whereas the federal Health Professionals Scholarship program, with the same goal, costs only $111,000 per physician.[20] Massachusetts used to send state employees in their automobiles to deliver state lottery tickets to all the vending locations throughout the state, a process that took up to two weeks. Now they use express mail services to deliver the tickets in two days at a fraction of the cost. Although not exactly a technological breakthrough, this simple reengineering provided speedier service and saved millions of dollars by eliminating scores of light-duty patronage jobs.

Increasingly the private sector is reverting to core functions and moving away from the old pattern of vertical integration (for example, an automobile company being self-sufficient in everything from iron ore and coal mines to automobile showrooms). The idea is to focus on activities critical to the mission of the organization and contract out noncore activities to firms that, in turn, specialize precisely in those noncore areas. Naturally enough, what is noncore to one organization is core to another. "Do what you do best and outsource the rest," is the reigning philosophy.

Take the following examples. Corporations in the financial business now outsource their company cafeteria operations to firms that specialize in food service. A manufacturer may outsource its warehousing and delivery function to a parcel-delivery firm. Staff services such as processing payrolls and handling benefit claims are similarly outsourced. Nonprofit organizations, too, are adopting this approach. Universities, for example, often outsource their food, travel, and security services while retaining their core functions of teaching and research.

Because information technology and telecommunications, for example, are not core competencies for governments, many governments decided to concentrate on what they do well and outsource the high-tech business to firms with that core competence. This reversion to core functions is becoming increasingly common as many areas previously deemed "inherently governmental" are being reevaluated from this new perspective.

Restoring Civil Society

Inherent in the move toward core competencies is this fundamental question: What is the role of government? Throughout the world there is a growing realization that government is only one element of society, an indispensable and vitally important one to be sure, but nevertheless only one; the private sector also plays a vital role in a healthy society. This is most obvious in the post-socialist countries of Central and Eastern Europe struggling to create a civil society, a private-sector counterweight to the state.

A better balance is needed—a better allocation of societal responsibilities—between government and civil society. Civil society has been defined as a "vast network of networks, beginning with the individual and moving outward to encompass families, community organizations, and businesses—all invented by individuals coming together voluntarily."[21] These are the private institutions of society: the family, which is, after all, the original Department of Health and Human Services, Department of Housing, Department of Education, and Welfare Department; voluntary civil associations of all kinds—neighborhood groups, faith-based institutions, charities, civic organizations, unions, sports teams, and clubs, for example; and the marketplace, with private firms and market forces working under the minimum necessary degree of regulation.

The relatively unfettered marketplace increasingly is seen as having primary responsibility for economic progress, under the appropriate type and minimal necessary amount of government regulation. Nongovernmental organizations and the family, however, are seen as responsible for fulfilling social needs and addressing social problems, such as drugs, teen pregnancy, motherhood without marriage, and dropping out of school. Nongovernmental organizations are better than government bureaucracies at dealing with such problems. This calls for a different and more circumscribed—more focused—role for government, one that empowers citizens and communities to address their problems instead of treating them as clients permanently dependent on professional bureaucracies.

In the United States, in contrast to the challenge faced by the post-socialist countries, neighborhood and civic associations, faith-based institutions, charities, fraternal groups, and other such organizations can and do undertake many functions that government attempts to handle with limited success. These have been called "mediating institutions" as they serve to buffer the individual from large, impersonal government and market organizations.[22] They are the "little platoons" cited by de Tocqueville that create a sense of community, develop citizenship skills, and satisfy people's needs that neither the marketplace nor government can do as well.[23] Devolving power can help restore civil society.[24] Programs promoting faith-based and community institutions, charter schools, and vouchers for school choice exemplify this movement. In Louisville, Mayor Abramson relied on neighborhood organizations for economic revitalization of their communities.[25] Boston's Mayor Menino called on local communities as part of his program to revitalize commercial streets and neighborhoods. Mayor McCrory of Charlotte implemented a program where neighborhood strategic plans were developed with strong citizen involvement and neighborhood action teams.[26] The goal of a healthy society is well-functioning communities of citizens, not clients.

Adopting Market Principles

A market economy has proven over the centuries to be best for producing a high standard of living and a bountiful cornucopia of goods and services. Governments are increasingly adopting five important elements of market systems: competition, privatization, deregulation, user charges, and pricing strategies.

Competition. Past efforts to improve government services all failed to identify, let alone address, the underlying problem of government monopoly.[27] This is an important structural cause of government underperformance. This problem will not yield to managerial fads, preaching, indignation, scapegoating, or finger pointing. Competition is key to breaking up the *unnecessary* monopolies that we have established in the public sector. (Not all government monopolies are unnecessary.)

Adam Smith in his 1776 book, *The Wealth of Nations,* recognized the power of competition in achieving efficient use of resources. Generally speaking, the more providers in any market, the greater the competition, resulting in more efficient production of desired goods and services. It is curious, therefore, that monopolistic agencies still carry out so many government activities even when monopolies are not warranted. The situation is changing, however, as governments introduce competition through outsourcing conventional public services, awarding concessions for infrastructure, and auctioning assets—although sometimes not wisely or well. "Managed competition" and competitive sourcing encourage in-house employees to bid against private firms in order to retain their current work, a mandatory practice in Great Britain for local governments. Experience shows that after losing several such competitive bids, public agencies often improve their operations, increase their efficiency and effectiveness, and win subsequent competitions against their private rivals.[28] Numerous careful studies of government outsourcing in many countries show that average savings range up to 30 percent, depending on the function, for the same level and quality of service.[29]

Competition leads to choice because people are not restricted to a single service provider. This is an important issue in the United States today, as school choice becomes a potent rallying cry for parents dissatisfied with their children's education in conventional public schools. But Donahue and Nye warn about uncritical enthusiasm for market approaches, raising questions about accountability and the definition of success, among other issues.[30] At a broader level, it is obvious that well-functioning societies need both cooperation and competition; Rosenau attacks what she sees as worldwide zeal for competition and draws attention to the high cost and harm it causes in many domains of human activity. Her prescription, however, is unexpectedly modest: more constructive and less destructive competition, and more cooperation.[31]

Although competition can be lauded, it is not so easy to carry out. Procurement—in both the public and private sectors—is riddled with examples of favoritism, bias, corrupt practices, bribery, and extortion. Similar problems are found in selling government assets. Moreover, outsourcing that is intended to introduce competition for a public monopoly, for example, can degenerate into a private monopoly if the government agency fails to set limits on how much of the service can be supplied by one provider. It takes a determined effort to construct and carry out truly competitive processes.

Privatization. If government should revert to its core functions, stick to steering instead of rowing, and restrain its growth, how will people's many needs be satisfied? Who will do the rowing? The answer, of course, is the private sector. Broadly defined, privatization means relying more on the private institutions of society and less on government to satisfy people's needs, that is, changing to a smaller or less direct role for government.[32] As noted earlier, the private sector has three components relevant to this issue: the market, nongovernmental institutions, and the family. Broadly speaking, the private sector can provide private (individual) goods through the marketplace, merit (worthy) goods through voucher programs, and public (collective) goods through contracts for service.[33] Contracts can be with for-profit or nonprofit organizations.[34] Even something as "governmental" as the justice system is being privatized through alternative dispute resolution and privatized prisons.[35] As noted earlier, private firms also "contract out" when they outsource selected functions to more specialized private firms. Privatization is discussed later in more detail.

Deregulation. Governments tend to be populated by lawyers, many of whom seem to believe that whatever is wrong with society can be set right by passing new laws, issuing new regulations, and lengthening the lists of rules. Some other reasons for regulating have even less merit, namely, to give an advantage to a favored special interest.

Of course, civilized societies require regulations. Rights must be protected. Public safety must be assured. External costs must be internalized and compensated. For example, pollutants dumped into a river impose cleanup costs on downstream communities; proper regulation would cause those costs to be borne by the original polluters. Many regulations are two-edged swords, with both positive and negative effects on society. Often the cost of regulation exceeds the societal benefit. For example, requiring elaborate procedures to obtain a license to start a business may protect society from fraud and dissatisfaction, but it may also prevent an honest citizen from earning a decent living. To become a licensed cosmetologist in New York state, for instance, an applicant once had to submit verification from a doctor that he or she was free of communicable diseases. The governor's Office of Regulatory Reform challenged this policy and succeeded in getting it dropped for the State's 172,000 licensed "appearance-enhancement professionals," thereby saving New Yorkers about $8.6 million in doctors' fees and saving cosmetologists time by not having to visit doctors' offices.[36]

Welfare reform can be considered a form of deregulation. Congress changed federal laws to allow cities to put welfare recipients to work, which was previously illegal. Economic regulations are very different from safety regulations. For example, passenger vans in New York are properly regulated as to driver and vehicle safety and insurance, but, arguably, vans and taxicabs should be free of economic regulations concerning entry into and exit from the business.

User Charges. A basic principle of public finance is that the beneficiary should pay. Where a direct beneficiary of a public service can be identified and charged for service, a user fee should be imposed. This has the salutary effect of confronting the user with the cost of the service and thereby providing an incentive for using a limited resource wisely. Besides, when user charges are used instead of the general budget to fund an activity, unjustified cross-subsidization by nonusers is avoided. Mayor Donald L. Plusquellic of Akron, Ohio, was able to gain acceptance for a regional economic development plan by expanding the water and sewer system to willing suburban communities at the city's expense in exchange for user fees (and other revenue) from those suburbs.[37]

Pricing Strategies. Prices rather than edicts can be used to affect behavior. A good example is the use of tolls on congested transportation choke points such as bridges, tunnels, and limited access highways. Time-of-day pricing with higher tolls during rush hours and lower ones during off-peak periods causes commuters to revaluate their preferences and modify their driving patterns. Prices can also be a substitute for regulation. States are successfully controlling pollution by allowing the trading of pollution credits rather than imposing prohibitions. Industrial plants can decide whether to spend money to upgrade their pollution-control equipment or to purchase pollution credits from another firm that emits less than its permitted load of pollutants.

Decentralizing and Devolving Authority

Too often government is too highly centralized. Whereas many decisions are best made at the national level, many others are appropriate to the local level—the level closest to people's daily lives. International aid organizations recognize this and have recommended empowering lower levels of government, giving them responsibility, authority, and access to resources to address a wide range of issues that fall naturally in their domain. Some international aid programs focus on very local assistance, not aid to central governments, in part to reduce theft but mostly to achieve greater effectiveness.

In the United States, state, county, and municipal governments and even local, neighborhood-based community organizations are the appropriate levels for many government activities currently directed by higher levels of government. Relegating such functions to a distant, overcentralized government is a prescription for bad, unresponsive government. Mayor Schundler of Jersey City made a strong case for greater empowerment of local governments and offered illustrations ranging from garbage collection to school choice, school construction, and policing.[38]

The concept of decentralization applies just as well within government agencies. Decentralized institutions can be more flexible, innovative, and effective than centralized ones, and they can improve morale, deepen commitment, and raise productivity among workers.[39] Centralized personnel departments are sometimes notorious for the Byzantine processes they devise. The National Performance Review (NPR) discovered that layer upon layer of rules were piling up in government, resulting in "850 pages of federal personnel law, augmented by 1,300 pages of . . . regulations on how to implement those laws and another 10,000 pages of guidelines from the Federal Personnel Manual." NPR proposed drastic decentralization to eliminate red tape, devolve authority for recruiting and examining job applicants, simplify the rigid civil-service classification system, allow agencies to design their own performance management and reward systems, and reduce the time required to terminate unsatisfactory employees for cause.[40] Procurement and budgeting are other internal functions where decentralization can make sense.

Prominent leaders have adopted decentralization and devolution (giving authority to lower levels of government) in their policy making. As governor of Texas, George W. Bush decentralized the school system and devolved substantial authority to local school boards. Mayor McCrory of Charlotte gave a large voice to neighborhoods in policing and economic development. Mayor Armstrong of Louisville and Mayor Menino of Boston decentralized neighborhood revitalization. Mayor Wellington Webb gave substantial authority to nearby communities to better the regional economy of Denver. Mayor Bret Schundler of Jersey City argued persuasively that devolution of authority is needed to fight drug dealing and improve education. He further asserted that state usurpation of local discretion hinders cities in addressing their local problems.[41]

Focusing on Management

There is renewed emphasis on public management throughout the United States and by international bodies that promote good government. Leaders are devising strategies, formulating management agendas, setting goals, and managing for results.[42] Performance measurement is in and outputs, not inputs, are targeted for attention. In the past, government agencies typically reported inputs and workloads but not outputs or outcomes. Now it is no longer enough for a highways department to report the cost of road repairs and the number of hours spent on that activity; ideally the department should report on the condition of the road before and after the work, or the time and money saved by drivers due to improved road conditions. Inputs are recognized as valuable only insofar as they produce desired outputs and measurable results.[43]

It is almost always possible to measure government outputs and outcomes in a useful way although generally more difficult than for profit-oriented businesses.[44] More and more governments, particularly at the local level, are adopting proven methods of measuring performance and, increasingly, they are issuing formal reports to the public.[45] Business groups, civic associations, and chambers of commerce engage in such evaluations, and so do citizen groups concerned about particular issues such as parks or transportation. Enterprising journalists, too, investigate government performance. Measuring government performance is a desirable trend to be encouraged.

Moreover, citizens are also consumers of government services, and therefore government must, like all service providers, satisfy its customers (among its other tasks). The citizen-consumer-customer is king. Customer service is a major thrust of modern managers in government and is an essential component of innovative government.[46] This means getting things done right, quickly, courteously, and knowledgeably. Local governments conduct citizen surveys to measure satisfaction with their services.[47] Charlotte, North Carolina, conducts such surveys biannually, and San Diego employs surveys frequently with results shown by department in the city's annual report. The federal government has identified and set forth in detail customer service standards for its services.[48]

Measuring and reporting on government performance is not enough, however. In a democracy officials must satisfy public expectations or expect to be replaced. Government is responsible for results and elected officials are going to be held accountable; a more educated public demands it.

"Rightsizing" Government

The world has learned that governments are not omnipotent. On the contrary, often they are impotent, unable to achieve promised goals despite awesome powers and huge expenditures. Often a new government program, launched with fanfare and grand rhetoric, in retrospect turns out to be merely a costly and symbolic gesture that does no more than demonstrate politicians' heartfelt concern about a current issue of public interest. The end result is squandering the people's money.

Voters are casting a critical and skeptical eye on proposed government expansions. Governments are thoroughly exploring alternatives before embarking on any effort, however well intentioned, to enlarge their role.[49] These alternatives include streamlining and restructuring agencies, eliminating or consolidating agencies, and trimming overstaffed agencies.

Although these alternatives all reduce the size of government, the term "rightsizing" was coined to include efforts to downsize or upsize depending on need. After assessing services and establishing priorities, government leaders expand certain services and reduce others. For example, Mayor Goldsmith of Indianapolis drastically reduced the size of the public works department but expanded the police and fire departments and increased spending on infrastructure. Governor Tommy Thompson of Wisconsin downsized the state government by dramatically reducing the number of residents on welfare and placing them in jobs. Mayor Vinroot aggressively "rightsized" the city government of Charlotte, North Carolina. Mayor Plusquellic of Akron halted that city's annexation program and instead worked out a mutually beneficial sharing of taxes with adjacent towns based on economic expansion instead of government expansion.[50]

Institutionalizing E-Government and Other New Technologies

Many processes and procedures in government, unchanged for decades, are being reengineered to take advantage of technological advances in communications, computers, and the Internet, for example. Information kiosks (stand-alone computer terminals in public places where citizens can get government information, make requests, and pay fees, fines, and taxes) are springing up like mushrooms on the urban landscape. Citizens can engage in transactions with government agencies without leaving their homes, thanks to the Internet. Fees and fines can be paid automatically using a telephone and a credit card without the help of a clerk. Forms can be downloaded and filed without a trip to the municipal center. Modern, integrated systems are being designed so that government can serve its citizens better and at lower cost. This is the route to more efficient and effective government.

Mayor Giuliani and Governor Mike Leavitt initiated broad-based transformations through e-government in New York City and the state of Utah. They set a new standard for responsiveness and service to citizens and established models that others can follow. Governor Jim Geringer of Wyoming focused on telecommunications technology to connect schools, communities, and government offices in his large but sparsely populated state. A high priority of Governor Rick Perry of Texas was to connect students to the Internet as a means of developing the state's human infrastructure and preparing it for a high-tech economy. Governor Bill Owens of Colorado applied similar ideas on a broader scale to diversify Colorado's economy from one dependent on agriculture, mining, and tourism into one with a rich component of high-tech industry.[51]

Privatization and Public-Private Partnerships

Adopting market principles in government activities is an important feature of the new public management, and privatization is its principal element. There are numerous definitions of privatization, each one focusing on only one narrow aspect or managerial technique.

Defining Privatization

This section discusses ten definitions of privatization. (1) In countries with many state-owned enterprises, including many developing countries, post-socialist countries, and countries in Western Europe, privatization is the transfer of enterprise ownership—in whole or in part—from the state to private hands. This is also called denationalization and "destatization." (2) Although there is general agreement that the sale of government enterprises represents privatization, there is less unanimity about defining the sale of other government assets, such as land and buildings, as examples of privatization. Such divestments are viewed here as privatizations.

In the United States, which has relatively few state-owned enterprises, (3) the term "privatization" is commonly applied to the act of contracting for public services. (4) Others call this practice "outsourcing"; outsourcing is found within the private sector as well, for example, when one company contracts with another for a specific service or function, such as operating the company cafeteria or warehouse. Some consider contracting to be a form of decentralization, but this seems unhelpful and unnecessarily confusing. (5) Another term, "managed competition" refers to competition between public employees and private contractors. If a contractor wins, it is called privatization or contracting out. If the public employees win, it is obviously not privatization; sometimes it is called "contracting in." "Competitive sourcing" is a better term than "managed competition" for this practice. (6) To add to the jargon confusion, on Wall Street privatization can refer to the act of transforming a company from one whose shares are listed on a stock exchange and can be bought by members of the general public to one that is no longer listed or publicly traded because it has been bought by a private group. (7) When a government agency is forced to operate in a market environment, for example, raising funds in capital markets and selling its services to willing buyers, this is best called "marketization," not privatization. (8) The transformation of a public agency into an independent authority or government corporation, such as the U.S. Postal Service, is sometimes called privatization, but "commercialization" is a better word.

The term "public-private partnership" (9) is particularly malleable as a form of privatization. It is defined broadly as an arrangement in which a government and a private entity, for-profit or nonprofit, jointly perform or undertake a traditionally public activity. It is defined narrowly as a complex relationship—often involving at least one government unit and a consortium of private firms created to build large, capital-intensive, long-lived public infrastructure, such as a highway, airport, public building, or water system, or to undertake a major civic redevelopment project. Private capital and management of the design, construction, and long-term operation of the infrastructure are characteristic of such projects, along with eventual public ownership. Despite the term's ambiguity, "public-private partnership" can be politically useful because it avoids the inflammatory effect of "privatization" on those ideologically opposed.

The final word on privatization is a whimsical definition (10) that is simply too delicious to pass up: Janusz Lewandowski, post-communist Poland's first privatization minister ("minister of ownership transformation," to be exact) defined privatization in his country as "the sale of enterprises that no one owns, and whose value no one knows, to people who have no money."[52]

I attempt here to clarify the confusing definitional picture and offer a general definition that captures the broad essence of privatization and leads to implementation techniques. Fundamentally, privatization is much more than a financial or managerial action; it is a philosophical position concerning the roles and the relationships of society's private institutions and government. Society's principal private institutions are the market, voluntary nonprofit associations of all kinds (civil society), and the family. *Privatization is the act of reducing the role of government or increasing the role of the private institutions of society in satisfying people's needs, that is, producing goods and delivering services.*

Both the public and private sectors play important roles in privatization, and it is increasingly common to refer to "public-private partnerships," for reasons noted earlier. The fundamental, philosophical view of privatization brings forth strong ideological opposition and distracts from privatization as a pragmatic tool to improve government performance and societal functioning.

Privatization by contract is not new in the United States. Queen Isabella of Spain outsourced exploration of the western ocean to an Italian contractor in 1492. The British contracted for Hessian mercenaries to fight in the U.S. Revolutionary War. Contractors were cleaning the streets of New York by 1676. The fledgling United States contracted out mail service in the 1790s and continued to do so with the Pony Express in the nineteenth century. What is new—since the 1970s—is contracting with private firms in a deliberate effort to introduce competition and thereby reduce the cost of ongoing government activities.

Some opponents still regard privatization as a simplistic call to cut back government and regress to a Darwinian state where only the fittest survive and the poor and sick are left to cope as best they can. This is a serious misunderstanding of the concept. Privatization can be at least as compassionate as the welfare state; properly implemented, it offers even more for the less fortunate among us. Indeed, advocates of privatization do not deny the need for government, preferably an effective one; they are not anarchists. Government intervention in society and the economy in various forms and to varying degrees is necessary. The classical reasons are to supply risk capital when massive investments are needed in uncharted areas; to establish rules for an increasingly interactive, urbanized nation where people get in each other's way; to plan for and provide, directly or indirectly, services deemed necessary and to subsidize them if unaided market forces cannot satisfy society's need; to handle external costs that otherwise desirable activities impose on others; and to regulate natural monopolies.

The remainder of this chapter describes how to change from an arrangement that relies heavily on government to one that relies relatively more on the private sector. Drawing on earlier work, this section presents a simple classification taxonomy that encompasses three broad methods that result in privatizing government-run services and functions and government-owned enterprises and assets:

- *Delegation,* in which government retains responsibility and oversight but uses the private sector for service delivery.
- *Divestment,* in which government relinquishes responsibility.
- *Displacement,* in which the private sector grows and displaces a government activity.[53]

Each of these incorporates several specific approaches, which are discussed in the next sections (See table 1.1).

Delegation

Delegation calls for a positive act by government. Also known as partial privatization, delegation requires a continuing, active role for government, which retains responsibility for the function while delegating the actual production activity to the private sector. The "tools of governance" most suitable for delegation are contracts, public-private competition, franchises,

Table 1.1 Three Types of Privatization and Their Components

Type of privatization	*Components*
Delegation	Contract
	Public-private competition
	Franchise
	Public-private partnership
	Grant, loan, favored tax status, and so on
	Voucher
	Mandate
Divestment	Sale
	Free transfer
	Liquidation
Displacement	Default
	Withdrawal (load shedding)
	Voluntary action (voluntarism)
	Deregulation

Source: E. S. Savas, *Privatization and Public-Private Partnerships* (New York: Chatham House, 2000), table 5.2.

public-private partnerships, subsidies—by grants or vouchers, for example—and mandates.[54]

Contracts. Government can privatize an activity by contracting with a private organization, for-profit or nonprofit, to perform the work. Increasingly this is known as competitive sourcing, the term used in President George W. Bush's 2001 *Management Agenda.*[55] This is the most common form of privatization in the United States, used by federal, state, and local governments, and the most direct form of delegation. (The most common form of privatization elsewhere is divestment, because of more state-centered economies and the correspondingly larger number of state-owned enterprises.) Competitive contracting ("tendering") is compulsory for selected local government services in Britain.

But contracting is surprisingly complex and accordingly deserves more space here than other forms of delegation. To simplify Oliver Williamson's crucial analysis, functions can be carried out externally through markets or internally through vertically integrated hierarchical organizations (firms or governments).[56] Both methods incur costs. Markets incur transaction costs (see below); hierarchies incur costs due to the chain of goal-displacing principal-agent links (see below) between the top and bottom of the hierarchy and to limitations of human understanding and competence. The shortcomings of hierarchies and human limitations together lead to nonmarket failure.[57] Leaders have to gauge the costs of each approach to decide whether to use markets and explicit external contracts or their own hierarchy and implicit internal contracts.

Phillip Cooper points to the underlying structural problem:

> [T]he public manager operates at the intersection of a vertical, authority-based model and a horizontal, negotiation-driven one. The vertical model draws its authority, resources, and influences from the constitutional and political processes at the heart of governing. The horizontal model operates on negotiations between two or more presumptively equal participants who create individual relationships governing their behavior and decide which parties will handle certain discrete functions. The horizontal relationship is based on the concept of contract, which differs greatly from the vertical, authority-based approach and is in many respects in tension with it.[58]

Let us distinguish between the purchase of goods and the purchase of services. Local governments, for example, buy all sorts of goods: potatoes (for schools and hospitals), underwear (for prisoners), chalk, chairs, sand, buses, and thousands of other items. Procurement is fairly straightforward for such goods but much more complex for such other goods as computers and computer networks, an issue that Steven Kelman has studied at length.[59]

Purchase of services is more complicated. Direct services, support services, and services to third-party clients can all be bought and sold through contracts. Local governments purchase (outsource) direct services (services directly to the public) such as solid-waste collection, street repair, street cleaning, snow removal, and tree maintenance. It is relatively easy to monitor and measure contractor performance of such services. Charlotte saved almost $5 million annually by contracting out thirty-eight functions. The state of Wyoming contracted with private firms to own and operate the intranet system connecting all public schools in the state. The average U.S. city contracts out almost a quarter of its common municipal services to the private sector (see chapter 2).[60] The average U.S. state contracts out 14 percent of its activities,[61] including the operation of some prisons.

Government agencies at all levels contract for support services (services that government needs to help it perform direct services to the public) such as data processing, loan processing, architecture and civil engineering, training, audiovisual services, food services, reference checking and testing of job applicants, employee medical examinations, and vehicle maintenance.

Services purchased from organizations (often nonprofit) for delivery to third-party clients commonly include programs such as family counseling, employment training, senior-citizen day care, "meals on wheels," foster care, adoption programs, drug counseling, and shelters for the homeless and for victims of spousal abuse. Purchase of such personal services for third parties poses different problems than contracting for direct services because they are much harder to monitor and measure.[62]

Contracting presents the ever-present principal-agent problem: Is the agent (the contractor) pursuing the principal's (government's) goals or its own? Moreover, market imperfections may override government imperfections or vice versa. Transaction costs can be high enough to forestall contracting attempts—establishing the requirements, assuring the existence of a competitive market, designing the proposal or bidding process and the contract instrument itself, defining and choosing the best bid, overcoming political and public opposition and skepticism, dealing openly and fairly with affected employees, working with the contractor cooperatively and at arm's length simultaneously, monitoring the work, evaluating the results, and determining whether to renew or terminate the contract upon completion. Government has to be a smart buyer, meaning knowing what to buy, deciding from whom to buy it, and then determining what it has bought. This entails preparing careful specifications as to what is to be purchased, conducting a competitive procurement, and monitoring the contractor's performance.[63]

Many complex questions arise and have to be dealt with in the contract document:

- Which services are most suitable for outsourcing?
- Should contractor selection be sole source, by limited competition, or by open competition?

- Should the contractor be paid a fixed price, reimbursed for his or her costs, paid only for successful completion, or paid for making a best effort (as in high risk projects)?
- Should the contract call for providing the service on one occasion only, or on multiple occasions, or should it allow the government to purchase the service on numerous occasions to be specified later (an indefinite-quantity contract)?
- Should the contract offer incentives and allow modifications?
- How should claims and disputes be resolved?
- What are the criteria for evaluating bids?
- How much official discretion should be allowed?
- What will be the nature and degree of oversight? [64]

Contracting is likely to be better than direct, in-house provision under the following circumstances:

- The task to be contracted is precise and can be specified in advance.
- Performance can be easily measured and evaluated.
- There is ample competition among potential providers.
- The task is not central to the agency's mission.
- Demand for the service varies over time.
- Private providers can hire people with the needed skills more easily than government can.
- Private providers have greater economies of scale in delivering the service.[65]

Because of the complexity and challenges of public contract management, managers must be firmly committed to building capacity for effective contracting.

Public-Private Competition. The goal of contracting is competition, not necessarily contracting with a private firm. Increasingly therefore, governments are encouraging their own workers to compete for contracts with private contractors. This has come to be called "managed competition" and "competitive sourcing," and it has proven to be a powerful incentive for public agencies—under the threat of privatization—to improve their performance. "Competitive sourcing" is the more general term; it gained prominence in President George W. Bush's 2001 *Management Agenda* and was an important thrust of his government reform effort. The term "managed competition" is used primarily in local government; this process became the standard approach in Indianapolis and in San Diego County, for example, for many municipal services. This term is unsatisfactory, however, because all competitions have to be managed; therefore "public-private competition" is frequently—but not exclusively—used here.

Public-private competition requires a level playing field so the in-house group can compete fairly with outside private contractors, and vice versa. Martin identifies many of the principal design features of a fair system (See box 1.1).

Franchise. Franchising is another method of privatization. Under a franchise, government awards a private organization the right (often the exclusive right) to sell a service or a product to the public. The private firm usually pays the government a fee. There are two forms of franchising. One involves the use of the public domain—airwaves, air space, streets, underground space. For example, broadcasters, airlines, bus and taxi companies, and utilities (electricity, gas, water, telephone) use the public domain to conduct their commercial activities. This arrangement is usually called a concession. Infrastructure projects—water supply, wastewater treatment, highways, airports, and bridges—that are built, expanded, or upgraded through public-private partnerships are franchises, usually in the form of concessions. The second form is a lease, where a private lessee uses tangible, government-owned property such as land or a building to engage in a commercial enterprise.

There is no sharp distinction between a lease and a concession. Some differentiate the two in that capital investments under a lease are made by the owner (the government), while under a concession they are made by the concession holder (the franchisee). This is important in some privatizations, but the distinction has little significance with respect to infrastructure privatization.

Public-Private Partnership. Infrastructure projects are increasingly being built through public-private partnerships (PPPs). Unlike the general use of this term as mentioned above, PPP in this sense refers to an arrangement where government states its need for capital-intensive, long-lived infrastructure, and the desired facility is built using a complex combination of government and (mostly) private financing and then operated by a private entity under a long-term franchise, contract, or lease. The payments are usually spread over twenty to ninety-nine years and cover construction, operation, maintenance, and capital costs. Typical PPP projects are roads, bridges, airports, water systems, pipelines, and power plants. Prisons, stadiums, and municipal buildings have

Box 1.1 Designing a Level Playing Field for Public-Private Competition

Designing a level playing field to optimize public-private competition requires attention to process design, costs, and contract administration.

Process design issues

- Public and private sectors should submit their bids in parallel, not in sequence.
- The public agency should have access to consultant help.
- An independent body should evaluate public-sector proposals and bids.
- The government purchaser and the government provider should be separate entities.

Cost issues

- Government should not mandate private-sector wages or benefits.
- Government should not establish a minimum savings threshold.
- Using "avoidable cost" in the cost calculation favors the public sector; using "fully allocated cost" favors the private sector.
- Transaction costs should be either excluded or included symmetrically. That is, included for the public sector when current delivery is private and for the private sector when current delivery is public.
- Contract administration and monitoring costs should be either excluded or included symmetrically, like transaction costs.

Contract administration

- If a contract is awarded to the public agency, the terms should be documented in a memorandum of understanding.
- The performance of the public or private sector contractor should be monitored.
- The contract terms for the public or private contractor should include a penalty for failure to perform, and the penalty should be imposed whenever justified.

Source: Adapted from Lawrence Martin, "Determining a Level Playing Field for Public-Private Competition," paper presented at the Northeast Regional Conference of the American Society for Public Administration, New York, October 29, 1999.

also been developed through this method, as have urban economic development projects.[66] Mayor Webb used a public-private partnership in Denver to redevelop a former military base. This method has been used to build public schools on public property where there is also enough space for a private commercial development. The latter generates the income to allow the developer to pay for the former.

Grants and Other Subsidies. Delegation is also carried out by awarding grants, below-interest loans, favored tax treatment, and other kinds of subsidies. Instead of government itself carrying out an activity, it arranges for a private entity to do the work, and it provides financial support. In the United States grants are used for mass transit, low-income housing, maritime shipping, and innumerable other activities. Grants are distinguished from contracts in that grants usually involve only the most general requirements (run a bus service, build houses that rent at below-market prices, conduct research, promote the arts), whereas contracts are usually specified in great detail for a particular service (sweep the west side of certain north-south streets between 7 a.m. and 9 a.m. on Tuesdays and Fridays). Grants and loans can generally be thought of as one-time payments, often to initiate a new activity, while favorable tax treatment and other subsidies tend to be continuing and to cover preexisting as well as new services.

Voucher. Governments can also delegate by issuing vouchers to eligible recipients of formerly state-run services. Instead of subsidizing producers, as grants do, vouchers subsidize consumers. Vouchers are used in the United States for food, housing, education, job training, health care, drug treatment, treatment of developmental disabilities, child day care, cultural activities, and transportation. For some services, such as food and housing, eligible recipients can supplement food stamps or housing vouchers with their own funds when purchasing these goods and services in the marketplace.

The ideal conditions for a voucher system are as follows:[67]

- There are widespread differences in people's preferences for the service, and society accepts these differences as legitimate.
- There are many competing suppliers of the service, or start-up costs are low and additional suppliers can readily enter the market if the demand is there.
- Individuals are well informed about market conditions, including the cost and quality of the service and where it may be obtained.

- The user can easily determine the quality of the service, or else the state licenses and inspects the service producer.
- Individuals have incentives to shop aggressively for the service.
- The service is relatively inexpensive and purchased frequently, so the user learns by experience.

Food stamps and housing vouchers satisfy all these conditions; Medicare and Medicaid satisfy only the first one. School vouchers are difficult to classify in terms of these conditions, because they involve a range of policy and design alternatives.

- Should pupil eligibility be universal or based on family income?
- Should all schools be eligible to accept pupils with vouchers, or only nonreligious schools? What about for-profit schools?
- Should the value of the voucher be equal to, or less than, current per-pupil expenditures? Should it be related to family income or to gains in achievement?
- Should parents be given information about school rank and performance or get it themselves? Should advisement on school selection be available?
- What degree of regulation should be imposed on private schools? By what criteria should schools be dropped from participation?
- Should admissions be according to the school's criteria (subject to civil rights laws) or by lottery?
- Should transportation be provided, subsidized partially or fully (perhaps by a transportation voucher), or not subsidized at all?

Vouchers offer great promise but also great complexity, depending on the service being "voucherized."

Mandate. The fifth and final form of privatization by delegation is a government mandate requiring private agencies to provide a service at their expense. Unemployment insurance is a longstanding example of such a mandate in the United States; private employers provide it for their employees. Privatization connotes a direction of change and therefore mandates, like grants, vouchers, franchises, and contracts, can be considered forms of privatization only when they lead to a lesser, not a greater, role for government. Thus if the government-run Social Security (retirement) system in the United States were partially replaced by mandatory, individual retirement accounts, this would be privatization by mandate, a form of delegation—in this case, to private individuals. On the other hand, if market-based health care were replaced by mandatory, employer-provided health care, this would be the opposite of privatization, as it would involve a greater rather than a lesser role for government. A trend in the United States that many consider ominous is to create new social programs (for example, family leave, aid to the handicapped, job training) by imposing government mandates on private employers. The net economic effect is the same as if government had provided the service, but the public is forced to pay covertly through higher prices rather than openly through taxes.

Divestment

Divestment means shedding an enterprise, function, or asset. Like delegation, this requires a direct, positive act by government; but unlike delegation it is a one-time event. The enterprise or asset is either sold or given away as an ongoing business, or shut down. Where state-owned enterprises are abundant, "denationalization" is frequently used to mean divestment. The following sections provide details on three means of divestment: sale, free transfer, and liquidation.

Sale. Throughout the world, state-owned enterprises are being sold and thereby transferred to the tender mercies of the marketplace. There are four common ways to divest by sale. The first is to sell the enterprise (or asset) to a single buyer, as was done with the Vista Hotel in New York City, which had been owned by a government authority and was sold to a major hotel chain. The second is to issue and sell shares to the public, as was done with Conrail, the government-owned freight railroad in the United States, in 1987. The third way to divest is to sell the enterprise to the managers or, more broadly, to the employees, as was done with the National Freight Company, the state-owned British trucking company. And the fourth way is to sell the enterprise or asset to its users or its customers. For example, state-owned land may be sold to ranchers or loggers, and a rural electricity or water system may be sold to a cooperative of local users.[68]

Governments in the United States own more than $4 trillion in real estate assets, a tempting target for privatization.[69] It is commonplace for government to sell land, buildings, equipment, and other assets that are no longer needed, or to avoid future departmental expansions. Mayor Bret Schundler of Jersey City, New Jersey, pioneered a highly original divestment by securitizing and selling tax liens, an idea replicated in New York City by Mayor Giuliani (See chapter 6).[70] At the federal level the largest privatization in the United States since the Homestead Act took place when the Clinton administration began to sell government-owned uranium enrichment plants, helium plants, power-marketing agencies, and oil fields.

Free Transfer. Divestment does not require sale of an enterprise; it could be given away, for example, to employees, to users or customers, to the public at large, or to a qualified class of people.

New York City proposed to privatize its municipal hospitals by giving them away to newly created, local, nonprofit, community-based boards representing the residents (in other words, users) who rely heavily on that hospital. Proposals to privatize the nation's air-traffic-control system call for giving or selling the assets and responsibilities to a consortium of airport users.[71]

Liquidation. Finally, divestment can be carried out by shutting down and liquidating a poorly performing government enterprise. Government can sell the assets if no buyer can be found for the enterprise as a whole and if the prospects are bleak for ever making the enterprise profitable. This can be considered privatization because the assets are recycled into the marketplace and become available for better uses.

Displacement

Besides divestment and delegation, privatization can proceed by displacement, as shown in table 1.1. In contrast to the first two methods, which require positive acts by government, displacement is a more passive or indirect process that leads to government being displaced more or less gradually by the private sector—a withering away of the state, so to speak, as markets develop to satisfy unmet public demands. It has also been called privatization by attrition, or by stealth.[72] Often unrecognized as a form of privatization, displacement is both commonplace and a crucial process by which privatization often occurs with relatively little political battling.

Displacement occurs by several mechanisms, and it depends on local initiatives and entrepreneurship. It can be accelerated by imposing market-based user charges on hitherto "free" government goods and services—

making the cost of government provision clear and inviting private competitors—and by encouraging voluntary action. Generally speaking, it does not involve competition per se, but it does involve choice on the part of the entrepreneur or volunteer who initiates the alternative and on the part of the customer who patronizes the nongovernmental option. The next sections describe the four forms of displacement: default, withdrawal, voluntary action, and deregulation.

Default. When the public considers government production of goods or services to be inadequate, and the private sector recognizes and satisfies this unmet demand, this is displacement by default. This satisfies the definition of privatization—namely, relying more on the private sector and less on the state to satisfy people's needs. If the private service grows over time and the government-supplied goods or services continue to be neglected or the government role shrinks in relative terms, the private sector will play a larger and larger role. Simply put, customers desert or avoid the public service. A common example is the growth of private transportation where the public deems government-provided bus service unsatisfactory or inadequate. Gypsy cabs, commuter vans, minibus systems, and other informal, quasi-legal, or technically illegal transport services have emerged in numerous cities throughout the world. We are also seeing displacement by default in public education in large U.S. cities: Even parents of limited means have been withdrawing their children from the public schools in droves, enrolling them in proliferating private schools and schooling them at home.

Private police offer another example. The public's unsatisfied demand for conventional police protection and dissatisfaction with the level of public safety in the United States led to the growth of private guard and patrol services. Although the latter have not displaced the former, in the United States the growth has been primarily in the private sector: By 1990, private police comprised three-fourths of all police.[73]

Throughout the United States and elsewhere, private firms are satisfying infrastructure needs that government agencies alone cannot. Thus the private sector is financing, building, owning, and operating roads, bridges, water systems, and wastewater-treatment plants. The pressing need for such facilities can be considered examples of "default," but these are, in effect, franchises, and often involve some public support through complex public-private partnerships.

Withdrawal. Whereas default is unintended or inadvertent, government can engage in deliberate withdrawal, or "load shedding," by constricting the growth of a government agency or shrinking its size while the private sector expands into that field.[74] This has also been termed "privatization by extinction." [75] In the United States local governments often give funds to nonprofit organizations such as museums, zoos, opera houses, theaters, libraries, and social service agencies. Such institutions are in the anomalous position of paying no taxes but receiving city services, while businesses pay taxes but do not receive certain city services (for example, refuse collection). City governments could withdraw some or all of their support, reduce their subsidies, or otherwise encourage—for example, with matching grant programs—the cultural institutions to raise more funds from patrons and philanthropists.

Withdrawal often goes hand in hand with default. In Britain, private health care is reemerging as the system of socialized health care deteriorates in quality and availability and funds are cut.[76]

Load shedding, or withdrawal, can occur by accommodation, that is, informal cooperation between government and private-sector providers. This happens when the latter relieve the former of a function the public agency would rather not perform. For example, private companies provide security inside shelters for the homeless; it is agreed that regular police officers will respond expeditiously to calls for help from such private guards.[77] Some states grant campus police and other private security personnel the power of arrest and give them jurisdiction on public streets in the vicinity of their employer's property.

Government withdrawal from established services is not easy, for a new political consensus must be achieved to replace the one that brought about government entry in the first place. Nevertheless, discontent with government services suggests that such a consensus may emerge for specific services. This need not involve a bruising battle between opposing ideologies but rather appropriate encouragement of forces already at work. For example, a study of employees in a large U.S. insurance company showed that 28 percent of full-time employees over the age of thirty provided regular care for elderly relatives and friends; they devoted an average of 10.2 hours per week to such care, and 42 percent of the caregivers had daily contact with the elder.[78] To the extent that family care, rather than institutional care, for elders can be encouraged by government through changes in tax and zoning policies and in building codes (for example, allowing extensions to single-family houses to accommodate aging parents—"grandma flats"), the demand for more government provision of such care will be reduced.

Voluntary Action. Voluntary action by citizens and encouraged by government may lead to cost displacement. Examples are programs to "adopt" highways and parks for cleaning and to adopt libraries, zoos, and schools. Such adoption generally means making voluntary contributions to subsidize those activities and institutions. These go beyond ordinary and conventional contributions to charitable and other nonprofit organizations.

Another form of voluntary action occurs through a new, very local level of government in the United States. Ranging in size from a single building to a condominium, a neighborhood organization, a civic association, or a large community, this new level of government can be called a voluntary microcollective, a micropolis, or a common-interest community.[79] These provide an array of collective goods, including cleaning and maintaining local streets and parks, removing snow, collecting refuse, operating volunteer ambulance and fire services and block patrols, and providing plantings and attractive urban "street furniture" (signs, litter baskets, benches, bus shelters, street lights, and consolidated newspaper vending machines).[80] City services are often reduced in these areas as local governments step aside. Almost one-fifth of the U.S. population lives in communities governed by such associations.[81]

Besides improving the local quality of life, such organizations can forge a desperately needed sense of community and can restore and hone citizenship skills atrophied from disuse, skills without which a democracy cannot long survive. Voluntary associations purchase or directly produce the services they want, custom tailored to their specific local needs and preferences, thereby exercising direct influence over the quality of their surroundings. Complaints are growing, however, about the intrusiveness and dictatorial behavior of such bodies.[82]

These kinds of units can best be formed in established communities that have well-defined geographic boundaries, are relatively homogeneous in terms of income or ethnicity, and have shared values with respect to the services to be provided through this mechanism. Local leadership is necessary, as is an encouraging posture by the local government. Such encouragement can mean giving tax rebates to residents in areas that forgo city services. This poses a minor administrative problem for the local government, but many communities do it, including those in Houston and Kansas City, Missouri. In Kansas City local homeowner associations can opt out of municipal refuse-collection service and receive a proportional rebate on their property taxes, but they contract with private firms for a higher level of service than the city provides. Moreover, government can encourage the creation and assure the viability of such self-governing associations by granting them taxing authority as special assessment districts. New York has such legislation.[83] Dozens of business improvement districts ("BIDs") in New York City and elsewhere use this approach.

An important attribute of such microcollectives is that members may have an opportunity to contribute their labor instead of their money. For example, local residents can volunteer for anticrime block patrols or contribute money to cover the organization's expenses. In the days of a barter economy, people could pay their taxes in specie such as grain and livestock. In a market economy people must pay cash. Voluntary associations can restore to the taxpayer the choice of paying in kind—with labor. One might then think of "off the books" earnings in the underground economy as having their counterpart in "off the books" tax payments, that is, payments in kind for collective goods.

As the demand for certain collective goods exceeds the ability of government to supply them at a suitable price and quality, dissatisfied citizens subsidize, supplement, or supplant the municipal service. Displacement occurs through government default and withdrawal and as citizens desert municipal services and band together in voluntary action.

Deregulation. Government-owned enterprises and government activities often exist because they have monopoly status. Deregulation facilitates privatization if it enables the private sector to challenge a government monopoly and even displace it altogether. In the United States message delivery by facsimile and express mail services and parcel delivery by competing companies have grown rapidly by de facto deregulation, at the expense of the U.S. Postal Service. The Postal Service claims and vigorously defends its exclusive right to handle first-class mail and prohibits its competitors from depositing mail in recipients' mail boxes, but the regulations are under attack, and their repeal was advocated by President Reagan's Commission on Privatization.[84]

Day care is a good candidate for deregulation. Since time immemorial, parents have arranged for relatives, friends, and neighbors to care for their children, and parents have taken into consideration the character and qualities of individuals to whom they entrust their children and the surroundings in which their children are placed. In recent years, however, day care became the object of increasing government involvement and financing. The result has been an increasingly complex web of legal restrictions as to who can provide the service, the number and kind of personnel who must be in attendance, the nature and design of the facilities, and so forth. The statement of an incredulous and indignant day-care operator to a zoning board in Washington, D.C., is worth quoting: "You're telling us we cannot operate a day-care facility in a residentially zoned middle-class neighborhood with a large number of working mothers, but we can operate a center in a commercial zone between two topless bars?" [85] The bizarre result of all the restrictions, however well intended, was that most families and homes would not be certified by government as suitable for child care. In fact, the situation has been changing: Government has introduced vouchers for child care, and parents can use them for any provider of care.

In many countries, years of state regulatory intervention have produced economic stagnation due to bureaucratic obstacles for entrepreneurs. Hernando de Soto illustrates how much time is wasted in Peru following the labyrinthine official procedures to start a business or build a house: It takes 289 days to register an industrial enterprise and 26 months to license jitney operators, for example. The informal economy (black market) encourages far greater productivity than the official sector.[86] (Getting a jitney license is even more difficult in New York City.[87]). De Soto advocates deregulation, debureaucratization, and decentralization. One prominent journal opined that "[B]ad government is the biggest single reason for poverty in the third world, and less government is the most effective single remedy." [88]

Postsocialist countries revived their devastated economies by repealing laws that prohibited private ownership, thereby encouraging entrepreneurs and allowing market mechanisms to prevail. "Marketization" is another term for this process, which aims to achieve economic efficiency through exposure to market discipline. The end result of deregulation is the emergence of demand-driven, market-based arrangements to satisfy unmet needs.

The People's Republic of China offers the best example of privatization by displacement. The first step was the deregulation of agriculture in 1978. Farmers were able to exercise virtually all property rights customarily associated with ownership of specific parcels of land, provided they paid rent to the state in the form of contracted deliveries of grain. Agricultural production mushroomed, in sharp contrast to the famines that occurred under collective farming, when millions died. The resulting rural wealth, coupled with further de facto deregulation, led in turn to the creation of village and township enterprises that engaged in manufacturing that contributed immensely to China's economic boom. (Such capitalist enterprises were politically acceptable inasmuch as they appeared to conform to the prevailing socialist ideology.) Although some may question whether this can be called privatization, such enterprises are analogous to employee stock-ownership plans. In the 1990s this nominally communist country withheld support for state-owned enterprises, often by failing to pay the workers, thereby hastening the workers' departure from the inactive, moribund enterprises. This is withdrawal of sorts, but it aroused social unrest. At the same time the rulers were encouraging private enterprises instead of forbidding them, as in the past. Many displaced workers were getting jobs and starting businesses in the new, booming private sector. Finally, in 2004 China legalized private property rights, essentially ending the fifty-five-year communist reign and driving the final nail in the socialist coffin. The end point of economic deregulation in this former socialist state is market-based capitalism.

Pitfalls of Privatization

Criticisms of privatization are both pragmatic and theoretical (or ideological or philosophical). The pragmatic criticisms cluster about the kinds of failures that sometimes occur under privatization:

- The service to be purchased from contractors or assigned to franchisees is not specified fully; this inevitably leads to misunderstandings and disputes. Contractors will usually take full advantage of any loopholes.
- An asset to be divested is undervalued, and the public is therefore shortchanged.
- Procurement of a service or the sale of an asset is not conducted competitively. Conflicts of interest are a constant danger in the purchasing process of both public agencies and private companies, and bribery and extortion are not unknown. Vigilance and oversight are necessary. Sole-source procurement is not necessarily bad, but one resorts to it with caution and only after full justification.
- Contractors are not monitored and poor performance is not penalized. Agencies that fail to monitor the performance of a private provider abdicate their responsibility and leave an opening for an unscrupulous provider to cut corners and lower service quality. Such failure may result from an improper, cozy relationship between the monitor and the provider.
- Performance standards in a voucher system are not set and maintained; agents authorized to accept vouchers and provide services

(such as for schools or private housing) must satisfy certain conditions germane to the service.

- A competitive environment is not maintained after privatizing by delegation (for example, contracting and franchising). A competitive environment is necessary lest the incumbent provider gradually acquire and exploit a monopoly. Trading a public monopoly for a private one is not a prescription for better government.
- The effect on employees displaced by privatization should be minimized.

Privatization advocates counter these concerns by pointing out that while privatization can indeed be mismanaged, management of ordinary public services suffers from many of these same shortcomings; that is, poor management can be found whether government is managing public employees or the privatization process. Poor management is not inevitable, however, and it is easier to manage a privatized service than an in-house one, asserts Mayor Stephen Goldsmith of Indianapolis.[89] (When mismanagement occurs in the private sector, market forces tend to weed it out ruthlessly. This rarely happens in the public sector; indeed, public agencies that perform poorly are often given a larger budget to improve their performance.)

As for the concern about inadequate protection of current public employees, privatization proponents reply that many effective policies are commonly used both to protect workers and to balance the public interest with the workers' interest. Moreover this is a value judgment; many argue that public employees are not entitled to greater job security than the vast majority of taxpayers who work without the dual protection of public-employee unions and tenure under a civil service system.[90]

Privatization has also been challenged on more basic ideological and political grounds. By emphasizing and extolling the virtues of the private sector, privatization may undermine the foundation of public purpose and public service. Privatization tends to shift power to those who are more skilled in exercising market power; this is worrisome in a democracy as it may shift income and wealth and produce even larger, unhealthy differences between rich and poor. Private service providers often achieve efficiency and maximize profits by seeking out the least costly clients for social services or by employing lower-wage, part-time workers. For better or worse, wages tend to be more equal in the public sector, so privatization may skew income toward greater inequality. Also, while unions have lost ground in the private sector, they have made great gains organizing public employees, taking advantage of their monopoly power. Privatization tends to undermine these gains. At its extreme, privatization can become a political instrument when it is used to weaken public employee unions.

Paul Starr expresses the fundamental concerns of many privatization opponents:

> Privatization is . . . a signal about the competence and desirability of public provision. It reinforces the view that government cannot be expected to perform well. If, to many Americans, private means better, it is partly because of long-existing restrictions on the scope and quality of public provision. We commonly limit public services to a functional minimum and thereby guarantee that people will consider the private alternative a step up. The restricted quality of public provision is a self-reinforcing feature. Because the poor are the principal beneficiaries of many programs, the middle-class public opposes expenditures to produce as high a quality of service as they must pay for privately; and because the quality is held down, the poor as well as the middle class develop a contempt of the public sector and an eagerness to escape it. The movement toward privatization reflects and promotes this contempt, and therein lies part of its political danger.[91]

There are numerous examples of privatization gone awry. For the most part, privatization in Russia was thoroughly corrupt. Well-placed Communist Party leaders practiced self-privatization, essentially stealing government property that they managed: oil fields, refineries, mines, factories.

Mexico entered into a public-private partnership to build much-needed toll highways but did a poor job of predicting road usage. The government wanted modest tolls and promised to make up the difference if usage was below the expected level. The government had to pay millions of dollars annually when the toll collections it had predicted failed to materialize.

A contract for refuse collection in a U.S. city failed to state how many times a week garbage was to be collected. In New York City, a low bidder for park maintenance performed poorly and the contract was terminated after seven months (See chapter 9). Privatization advocates would argue that this was ultimately an example of successful privatization in that a poor contractor was readily replaced by a good one; this could not have happened with unsatisfactory city workers.

Summary

Bold mayors of major cities have been turning away from the earlier posture of helpless dependence on the federal government and turning more toward solving their own problems, relying on their inherent strengths and advantages—political leadership, their cities' economic and social dynamism, and vigorous business, community, religious, academic, and civic leaders. New York's Mayor Rudolph Giuliani illustrates many elements of this new philosophy, and I will explore his accomplishments in later chapters.

The rubric for this reformed approach is the New Public Management, which encompasses the concepts of reverting to core functions, restoring civil society, adopting market principles, decentralizing and devolving authority, focusing on management, "rightsizing" government, and institutionalizing e-government and other new technologies.

Privatization and public-private partnerships reflect market principles and together constitute a strategy for improving the management of our cities. Among the particular tools employed are contracts, public-private competition, franchises, vouchers, divestment, withdrawal, and voluntary action.

Opposition to privatization is based on numerous examples of poor management of the process as well as fundamental opposition to the concept on ideological grounds.

Notes

1. Fred Siegel, "The Death and Life of American Cities," *The Public Interest* 148 (summer 2002), 8.
2. John Herbers, "Administration Seeks to Cut Aid to Cities, Charging It Is Harmful," *New York Times,* June 20, 1982, 1.
3. Statement made to the author by former mayor Gibson.
4. U.S. Department of Housing and Urban Development, *The President's National Urban Policy Report* (Washington, D.C.: 1982).
5. Siegel, "Death and Life."
6. Charles Mahtesian, "Urban Theorist as Mayor," *Governing* 12, no. 7 (November 1998), 33–34; "A Genuine New Democrat," *Wall Street Journal,* March 21, 1996.
7. Steve Goldsmith, "Federal Handouts Won't Fix Urban Troubles," *Indianapolis Business Journal,* April 19, 1993.

8. Ibid.
9. Boston's revival is a perfect illustration of the policy articulated in President Reagan's urban policy report. See Edward L. Glaeser, "Reinventing Urban America: Lessons from Boston," *The Taubman Center Report,* John F. Kennedy School of Government, Harvard University, Cambridge, 2004, 2–3.
10. Manuel Diaz, "The Miami Renaissance: A Road Map for Urban Leadership," *Civic Bulletin* 37 (October 2004), Manhattan Institute, New York.
11. Alison Mitchell, "Giuliani Urges New Agenda for Cities: Self-Reliance," *New York Times,* January 12, 1995.
12. "Mayor Brown Receives Urban Innovator Award," *Cities on a Hill,* newsletter of the Center for Civic Innovation of the Manhattan Institute, summer 2001, 3.
13. Buzz Bissinger, *A Prayer for the City* (New York: Random House, 1997), 21.
14. Neil Barsky, "Bootstrapping Mayor Raises Hope of Revival in, Yes, Philadelphia," *Wall Street Journal,* February 22, 1993, A1.
15. Ellen Shubart, "A Philly Turnaround," *City & State,* August 16, 1993, 9.
16. "CCI Delivers Urban Innovator Award to Norm Coleman," *Cities on a Hill,* spring 2002, 2.
17. Paul J. Andrisani, Simon Hakim, and E. S. Savas, *The New Public Management: Lessons from Innovating Governors and Mayors* (Norwell, Mass.: Kluwer, 2002), chap. 1.
18. E. S. Savas, *Privatization and Public-Private Partnerships* (New York: Chatham House, 2000).
19. David Osborne and Ted Gaebler, *Reinventing Government* (New York: Addison-Wesley, 1992), 25.
20. Al Gore, *Report of the National Performance Review: Creating a Government That Works Better and Costs Less* (Washington, D.C.: U.S. Government Printing Office, 1993), 94–104.
21. George Melloan, "Pondering the 'Civil State' at the Prince of Wales," *Wall Street Journal,* March 9, 2004, A17.
22. Peter L. Berger and Richard John Neuhaus, *To Empower People: From State to Civil Society* (Washington, D.C.: AEI, 1996); Don E. Eberly, ed., *The Essential Civil Society Reader: The Classic Essays* (New York: Rowman and Littlefield, 2000).
23. Alexis de Tocqueville, *Democracy in America* (New York: Washington Square, 1964).

24. William D. Eggers and John O'Leary, *Revolution at the Roots: Making our Government Smaller, Better, and Closer to Home* (New York: Free Press, 1995), chap. 3.
25. Andrisani, Hakim, and Savas, *New Public Management.*
26. Ibid.
27. These efforts include better public administration, preservice education, in-service training, civil service reform, performance budgeting, planning-programming-budgeting systems, zero-based budgeting, computers, quantitative methods, reorganization, organizational development, sensitivity training, incentive systems, management by objectives, productivity programs, joint labor-management committees, total quality management, reengineering, and the like.
28. Savas, *Privatization and Public-Private Partnerships,* 196–199.
29. Ibid., chap. 6; Graeme A. Hodge, *Privatization: An International Review of Performance* (Boulder, Colo.: Westview, 2000), chap. 7; Jeffrey D. Greene, *Cities and Privatization: Prospects for the New Century* (Upper Saddle River, N.J.: Prentice Hall, 2002), chap. 2; Robert M. Stein, *Urban Alternatives: Public and Private Markets in the Provision of Local Services* (Pittsburgh: University of Pittsburgh Press, 1990), 187–188.
30. John D. Donahue, "Market-Based Governance and the Architecture of Accountability," in *Market-Based Governance,* ed. John D. Donahue and Joseph S. Nye Jr. (Washington, D.C.: Brookings, 2002), 1–25.
31. Pauline Vaillancourt Rosenau, *The Competition Paradigm* (New York: Rowman and Littlefield, 2003).
32. E. S. Savas, *Privatization: The Key to Better Government* (Chatham, N.J.: Chatham House, 1987), 3.
33. Ibid., chap. 4.
34. Steven Rathgeb Smith and Michael Lipsky, *Nonprofits for Hire: The Welfare State in the Age of Contracting* (Cambridge: Harvard University Press, 1993).
35. Charles H. Logan, *Private Prisons: Cons and Pros* (New York: Oxford University Press, 1990); Gary W. Bowman, Simon Hakim, and Paul Seidenstat, eds., *Privatizing the United States Justice System: Police, Adjudication, and Corrections Services from the Private Sector* (Jefferson, N.C.: McFarland, 1992); Bowman, Hakim, and Seidenstat, eds., *Privatizing Correctional Institutions* (New Brunswick, N.J.: Transaction Books, Rutgers University Press, 1993); Alexander Tabarrok, ed., *Changing the Guard:*

Private Prisons and the Control of Crime (Oakland, Calif.: Independent Institute, 2003).

36. Governor's Office of Regulatory Reform, New York, "Permits Team Success Stories," www.gorr.state.ny.us/gorr/success_permits.html. January 2, 2005.
37. Andrisani, Hakim, and Savas, *New Public Management.*
38. Bret Schundler, "Innovative Government in Jersey City," in Andrisani, Hakim, and Savas, *New Public Management,* chap. 17.
39. David Osborne and Ted Gaebler, *Reinventing Government* (New York: Addison-Wesley, 1992), chap. 9.
40. Gore, *Report of the National Performance Review,* 20–25.
41. Andrisani, Hakim, and Savas, *New Public Management.*
42. Don Kettl, *The Global Public Management Revolution* (Washington, D.C.: Brookings Institution Press, 2000); Thomas G. Kessler and Patricia Kelley, *The Business of Government: Strategy, Implementation, and Results* (Vienna, Va.: Management Concepts, 2000).
43. Osborne and Gaebler, *Reinventing Government,* chap. 5.
44. Harry P. Hatry, *Performance Measurement* (Washington, D.C.: Urban Institute, 1999); Elaine Morley, Scott P. Bryant, and Harry P. Hatry, *Comparative Performance Measurement* (Washington, D.C.: Urban Institute, 2001).
45. See, for example, the mayor's *Management Report of New York City,* which is issued annually by the Office of the Mayor.
46. Osborne and Gaebler, *Reinventing Government,* chap. 6.
47. Kenneth Webb and Harry P. Hatry, *Obtaining Citizen Feedback: The Application of Citizen Surveys to Local Government* (Washington, D.C.: Urban Institute, 1973).
48. Donald F. Kettl, *The Global Management Revolution* (Washington, D.C.: Brookings, 2000), 41–44; Bill Clinton and Al Gore, *National Performance Review: Putting Customers First '95—Standards for Serving the American People* (Washington, D.C.: U.S. Government Printing Office, 1995).
49. William D. Eggers and John O'Leary, *Revolution at the Roots: Making Our Government Smaller, Better, and Closer to Home* (New York: Free Press, 1995).
50. Andrisani, Hakim, and Savas, *New Public Management.*
51. Ibid.
52. Janusz Lewandowski, Tomasz Stankiewicz, and Jan Szomburg, "Transformation Model of Poland's Economy," *Proceedings of the International*

Conference on Privatization, Saskatoon, Saskatchewan, Canada, May 13–16, 1990, 410–421.

53. E. S. Savas, "A Taxonomy of Privatization Strategies," *Policy Studies Journal* 18, no. 2 (1990): 343–355.
54. Lester M. Salamon, ed., *The Tools of Government: A Guide to the New Governance* (New York: Oxford University Press, 2002).
55. Executive Office of the President, *The President's Management Agenda, FY 2002* (Washington, D.C.: Government Printing Office, 2001).
56. Oliver E. Williamson, *Markets and Hierarchies* (New York: Free Press, 1975), 8–9.
57. Charles Wolf, Jr., *Markets or Governments: Choosing between Imperfect Alternatives,* 2d ed. (Cambridge: MIT Press, 1993).
58. Phillip J. Cooper, *Governing by Contract: Challenges and Opportunities for Public Managers* (Washington, D.C.: CQ Press, 2003), xiv.
59. Steven Kelman, *Procurement and Public Management: The Fear of Discretion and the Quality of Government Performance* (Washington, D.C.: AEI, 1990).
60. R. Miranda and K. Andersen, "Alternative Service Delivery in Local Government, 1982–1992," in *Municipal Year Book 1994* (Washington, D.C.: International City-County Management Association), table 3/5.
61. Council of State Governments, *State Trends and Forecasts* 2, no. 2 (November 1993).
62. Ruth Hoogland DeHoog and Lester M. Salamon, "Purchase-of-Service Contracting," in Salamon, *The Tools of Government,* 319–339.
63. Donald F. Kettl, *Sharing Power: Public Governance and Private Markets* (Washington, D.C.: Brookings, 1993), chap. 8.
64. Steven J. Kelman, "Contracting," in Lester M. Salamon, ed., *The Tools of Government,* 282–318.
65. Ibid. See also John D. Donahue, *The Privatization Decision: Public Ends, Private Means* (New York: Basic Books, 1989), 81–100.
66. Savas, *Privatization and Public-Private Partnerships,* 237–258.
67. Gary Bridge, "Citizen Choice in Public Services: Voucher Systems," in *Alternatives for Delivering Public Services: Toward Improved Performance,* ed. E. S. Savas (Boulder, Colo.: Westview, 1977).
68. Cento Veljanovsky, *Selling the State: Privatisation in Britain* (London: Weidenfeld and Nicolson, 1987), 136–139.

69. Ron Lobel and Jay Brown, "Privatization Promises to Build Military Family Houses Better, Faster, Cheaper," *Council Insights,* National Council for Public-Private Partnerships, May 1998.
70. Andrisani, Hakim, and Savas, *New Public Management.*
71. E. S. Savas, "Is Air Traffic Out of Control?" *New York Newsday,* June 9, 1995; Robert W. Poole Jr., "Privatizing Air Traffic Control," Reason Foundation, Los Angeles, Calif., February 1995.
72. Paul Starr, "The Meaning of Privatization," in *Privatization and the Welfare State,* ed. Sheila B. Kamerman and Alfred J. Kahn (Princeton: Princeton University Press, 1989), 24; Fuat Andic, "The Case for Privatization: Some Methodological Issues," in *Privatization and Deregulation in Global Perspective,* ed. Dennis J. Gayle and Jonathan N. Goodrich (New York: Quorum Books, 1990), 35–47.
73. National Institute of Justice, *Private Security and Police in America,* Hallcrest Report II (Washington, D.C.: 1991).
74. E. S. Savas, *Privatizing the Public Sector: How to Shrink Government* (Chatham, N.J.: Chatham House, 1982), 118.
75. Roberto Salinas-Leon, "Between Mercantilism and Markets," in *The Privatization Process,* ed. Terry L. Anderson and Peter J. Hill (Lanham, Md.: Rowman and Littlefield, 1996), 192.
76. Sarah Lyall, "For Britain's Socialized Health Care, a Grim Prognosis," *New York Times,* January 30, 1997, A1.
77. Marcia Chaiken and Jan Chaiken, *Private Provision of Municipal and County Police Functions,* report prepared for the National Institute of Justice (Cambridge, Mass.: Abt Associates, 1986), 5–7.
78. Glenn Collins, "Many in Work Force Care for Elderly Kin," *New York Times,* January 6, 1986, B5.
79. Council of the City of New York, "Cities Within Cities: Business Improvement Districts and the Emergence of the Micropolis," staff report to the Finance Committee, November 8, 1995; Stephen Barton and Carol Silverman, eds., *Common Interest Communities: Private Governments and the Public Interest* (Berkeley, Calif.: Institute of Governmental Studies Press, 1994).
80. Heather MacDonald, "BIDs Really Work," *City Journal* 6, no. 2 (1996): 29–42.
81. Motoko Rich, "Homeowner Boards Blur Line of Just Who Rules the Roost," *New York Times,* July 27, 2003, 1.
82. Ibid.

83. NYC BIDs Association, *The BID Manual: Establishing and Operating a BID* (New York: 1995).
84. President's Commission on Privatization, *Privatization: Toward More Effective Government* (Champaign: University of Illinois Press, 1988).
85. Robert L. Woodson, "Day Care," in *This Way Up: The Local Official's Handbook for Privatization and Contracting Out,* ed. R. Q. Armington and William D. Ellis (Chicago: Regnery, 1984), 159.
86. Hernando de Soto, *The Other Path* (New York: Harper and Row, 1989).
87. "Let the Vans Roll," *Wall Street Journal,* July 14, 1997, A14.
88. "Growth Beats Poverty," *Economist,* May 26, 1990, 15.
89. Goldsmith, *The Twenty-First Century City,* 70.
90. Savas, *Privatization and Public-Private Partnerships,* 291–296.
91. Starr, "The Meaning of Privatization," 42–44.

2 | Municipal Privatization in the United States

The private sector has been providing municipal services, such as waste management, vehicle towing, and public utilities management, for decades. What is new since the 1970s is using privatization explicitly and aggressively to improve government performance. This chapter reviews the status of privatization in U.S. cities in general and then examines a few cities in particular that made privatization a priority.

Overview

The value of federal, state, and local government contracts to private firms has increased by 65 percent since 1996 and exceeded $400 billion in 2001, according to the Government Contracting Institute.[1] Competitive contracting is the most common form of municipal privatization and has been growing since the 1970s regardless of the political affiliation of elected officials. Contractors provide more than 200 different services to local governments.[2] The International City and County Management Association (ICMA) started studying the extent of municipal privatization in 1977. The first survey was carried out by phone; the ICMA then switched to a mail survey every five years beginning in 1982.[3] ICMA administers the survey to all cities in the United States with populations of 10,000 or more and all counties with populations of 25,000 or more. The first survey (by phone) achieved a response rate of nearly 100 percent; by 1997 the response rate to the mail survey had dropped to 32 percent, with 1,586 local governments responding out of 4,952 contacted. Between 1982 and 1992 private contracting increased by 121 percent in the 596 cities where comparable data were available.[4] Between 1988 and 1997 the fraction of city services provided exclusively or in part by municipal employees declined.[5] That is, additional cities had introduced alternative service arrangements that displaced public employees.

The Reach of Privatization

The average U.S. city had private contracts for 23 percent of its sixty-four common municipal services in 1997.[6] Another way to look at this is that the average common municipal service is contracted out by 27 percent of cities.[7] A different study found that the average large U.S. city (of the largest one hundred cities) contracted out 15 percent of its forty-seven common services.[8] In other words, small cities do relatively more outsourcing than large cities.

These figures require qualification, however. To begin with, the nature of the ICMA mail survey introduces uncertainty. The response rate is less than a third, compared to the near-100 percent response rate of the first phone survey. Cities that respond may be very different from cities that do not. Moreover, the city representative who completes the survey one year may not be the same person who completes it the next time. This calls into question analyses purporting to show changes over time. Interpretations of the survey questions will also differ greatly. To say that a contractor provides a particular service is not to say that the contractor does all of that work; public employees may still perform most of it, and the budget for the contract may be much less than the budget for the in-house operation. One respondent may interpret this public-private balance differently than another. Also, the list of services is very coarse. For example, the typical service consists of many subservices. Child welfare programs may include a contract to track down "dead-beat dads" to pay child support, but child welfare encompasses many other programs that agency employees may be carrying out directly. Uniformity of interpretation is not likely. A telephone survey—much more expensive than mail—reduces these interpretation problems because a discussion takes place between the questioner and the respondent.

The most thorough study (known to the author) to analyze the extent of privatization in a city avoids these problems.[9] Anaheim, California, with a population of 328,000 in the 2000 census, carried out a highly detailed analysis of its contract services. It listed its 189 separately budgeted functions and noted that 122 of them—or 65 percent—were provided in whole or in part by contract. Those 122 functions used a total of 341 specific contracts with a value of $132 million; this figure represented 30 percent of the total city budget excluding capital expenditures and debt service.

Nowhere else has such a comprehensive study been conducted—or even attempted. After New York City introduced Mayor Michael Bloomberg's 311 system in 2003, through which citizens can lodge complaints or request information about city services, an analysis of the calls showed that the city provided more than 7,000 discrete services from repairing potholes to picking up discarded refrigerators and issuing permits for bakers' ovens.[10] Perhaps some day the database will enable a researcher to analyze those 7,000 services and produce a report similar to the one from Anaheim.

The most frequently contracted services in the United States are contracted by at least one-third and up to three-quarters of all cities (See tables 2.1 and 2.2). Many private firms supply everyday services such as vehicle towing and solid waste management, and so it is no surprise that two of the ten most common municipal contracts are for these services. Management of public utilities—gas and electricity—are other popular candidates for contracting, presumably because they require expertise that is very different from that required in most municipal functions.

Table 2.1 Most Frequently Contracted Municipal Services

Service	*Cities*
Vehicle towing and storage	78%
Gas management and operations	56
Legal services	50
Commercial solid waste collection	50
Operation of day-care facilities	41
Disposal of hazardous materials	39
Management and operation of hospitals	38
Electricity management and operations	37
Residential solid waste collection	37
Solid waste disposal	34

Source: Adapted from Robin A. Johnson and Norman Walzer, eds., *Local Government Innovation* (Westport, Conn.: Quorum Books, 2000), 174.

Table 2.2 Most Frequently Contracted Municipal Services in Large Cities

Service	*Large cities*
Vehicle towing	80%
Solid waste collection	50
Building security	48
Street repair	40
Ambulance services	36
Printing services	35
Street lighting and signals	26
Drug and alcohol treatment centers	24
Employment and training	24
Legal services	24

Source: Robert Jay Dilger, Randolph R. Moffett, and Linda Struyk, "Privatization of Municipal Services in America's Largest Cities," *Public Administration Review* 57, no. 1 (1997): 21. Reprinted with permission of Blackwell Publishing.

When the survey is limited to large cities, the contracting pattern is somewhat different; although vehicle towing and waste collection are still in the top four, they are joined by building security and street repair. Officials in large cities noted that they were "most satisfied" with private provision of street lighting/signals, solid waste collection, printing services, and street repair; "satisfied" with ambulance services, vehicle towing, legal services, and building security; and "somewhat satisfied" with privatized employment and training services and drug/alcohol treatment centers.[11]

Why Cities Privatize

Why do cities privatize? A large-scale ICMA survey in 1992 asked local officials this question. The questionnaire targeted the chief administrative officer of every municipality with a population of more than 10,000 and every county with a population of more than 25,000 for a total of 4,935 governments; 1,504 responses were received, a rate of 30 percent.[12] The top two reasons that governments privatize are an internal effort to reduce costs (about 90 percent of the respondents) and external fiscal pressures (about 53 percent). In other words, governments privatize to save money (See table 2.3). An earlier survey identified infrastructure decay as another important reason; municipalities needed costly new or rehabilitated infrastructure and

Table 2.3 Why Local Governments Contract Services to the Private Sector

Reason	*Officials reporting this reason for considering privatization*
Internal attempts to cut costs	90%
External fiscal pressures	53
Unsolicited proposals from private sector	23
Political climate	23
State or federal mandates tied to intergovernmental financing	20
Concerns about liability	18
Citizen group pressure	8
Other	7

Source: Adapted from Rowan Miranda and Karlyn Andersen, "Alternative Service Delivery in Local Government, 1982–1992," in *Municipal Year Book 1994* (Washington, D.C.: International City-County Management Association), 26–35, fig. 3/1.

thus entered into public-private partnerships.[13] Yet other studies, probing the same question differently, revealed that new services were particularly good candidates for privatization because the city lacked in-house expertise, no current employees would be affected, and the service could be started up more rapidly.

Privatization did provide the expected cost savings. A 1988 ICMA survey found that 40 percent of cities reported savings of more than 20 percent and another 40 percent reported savings of 10–19 percent.[14] A survey of large cities reported average savings of 17 percent and found that contracting improved service delivery by an average of 26 percent.[15] A summary of nine major comprehensive studies, covering every contract entered into by the reporting jurisdictions over a period of years—7,168 contracts in all—showed average savings of 29.5 percent. These nine before-and-after studies included federal, state, county, and city governments in the United States, the United Kingdom, and Australia. The results were compiled by independent outside agencies, not the contracting agencies or jurisdictions themselves. Although before-and-after studies have well-known shortcomings, these results are nevertheless eye opening (See table 2.4).[16]

The best and most compelling studies were conducted by E. S. Savas and Barbara J. Stevens and by Stevens alone. These were multivariable econometric studies in cities selected randomly from those using contractors and those using in-house employees for the same service. One study, funded by the National Science

Foundation for $1 million after a competitive selection process in the 1970s, covered only residential solid waste collection. Trained researchers visited 102 cities and used a uniform cost-accounting system—activity-based costing—to determine costs regardless of the form of the local budget. To measure service effectiveness, researchers surveyed citizens in those cities. For the same level and quality of service, municipal service cost 29 percent to 37 percent more than contracting. A review of nine other studies, which were much less thorough, found generally similar results.[17]

Using the same method of random selection of in-house and contract cities, Stevens studied seven services in California with funding from the U.S. Department of Housing and Urban Development. She found the municipal service to be substantially more expensive by anywhere from 37 percent to 95 percent: street-tree maintenance, 37 percent; landscape mowing, 40 percent; refuse collection, 42 percent; street cleaning, 43 percent; traffic signal maintenance, 56 percent; janitorial services, 73 percent; and asphalt overlay for street construction, 95 percent. Service level and quality was found to be the same.[18]

These differences do not arise because the people who work for government are somehow inferior to the people who work for private firms; they are not. What accounts then for the large cost difference? Stevens found no statistically significant difference between municipal and contract work with respect to salaries, the cost of fringe benefits, or service quality. Instead, contractors provide less paid time off for their employees (fewer vacation days, limited sick leave, and less allowed absenteeism), use part-time and lower-skilled workers where possible, and are more likely to hold their managers responsible for equipment maintenance as well as worker activities. In addition, contractors are more likely to give their first-line managers the authority to hire and fire workers, are more likely to use incentive systems, are less labor intensive (that is, they make greater use of more productive capital equipment), have younger workforces with less seniority, and have relatively more workers and fewer supervisors. Stevens concluded that

> in the majority of public agencies, the concepts of clear, precise task definitions and job definitions, coupled with easily identifiable responsibility for job requirements, are not enforced as vigorously as in the majority of private enterprises. It is this difference that appears, in general, to be responsible for the very significant public sector–private sector cost differences.[19]

Table 2.4 Cost of Municipal Services before and after Contracting

[Source of study]	*Number of contracts*	*Cost before contracting ($ million)*	*Cost after contracting ($ million)*	*Savings*
Los Angeles County, 1979–1987				
[Los Angeles County auditor-controller]	651	$268	$182	32%
Los Angeles County, 1979–1989				
[Los Angeles County auditor-controller]	812	701	505	28
U.S. Department of Defense, 1980–1982				
[Office of Federal Procurement Policy, OMB]	235	1,128	778	31
U.S. Department of Defense, 1983–1984				
[Office of Federal Procurement Policy, OMB]	131	132	88	33
U.S. Department of Defense, 1978–1986				
[U.S. General Accounting Office]	1,661	2,270	1,657	27
U.S. Department of Defense, 1978–1994				
[Center for Naval Analyses]	2,138	4,768	3,290	31
Wandsworth Borough, London, 1978–1987				
[Centre for Policy Studies]	23	174	127	27
General Services Administration Public Buildings Service, fiscal 1992				
[U.S. General Accounting Office]	576	n.a.	n.a.	25
State of Western Australia, 1993–1994				
[University of Sydney]	891	324	259	20

Source: E. S. Savas, *Privatization and Public-Private Partnerships* (New York: Chatham House, 2000).

Privatization in Indianapolis

By the mid-1990s several large cities had made significant headway in privatization. Indianapolis was far and away the best known of these pioneering cities thanks to the highly visible leadership of its charismatic mayor.

Mayor Stephen Goldsmith of Indianapolis (the nation's twelfth largest city with 800,000 people) gained international recognition as a leader in privatizing municipal services, and many other mayors sought him as a guru. Although this was not a big-government city—of the fifty largest cities in the country, it had the fewest employees per thousand population—Goldsmith promised to reduce the city's workforce by 25 percent in four years, except for the police and fire departments.[20] He considered himself a "small government mayor" who believed that government spending was inherently less productive and produced fewer jobs than private investment and therefore should be minimized. He valued empowerment, the art of citizenship, the long-term viability of the city, and economic opportunity, and he believed in free markets—that opportunity was better than redistribution. "I believe government should operate to move the marketplace around to create value, not to do things itself." [21]

Goldsmith campaigned aggressively on a privatization platform. His aides joked that he thought the city could be run with a mayor, a police chief, and four purchasing agents. When he took office in 1992 he promised to increase efficiency and reduce the cost of local government by introducing competition from the private sector for many city/county services. (The city and county have a single, consolidated government.) His objective was to cut costs without cutting services and thereby to reduce or at least stabilize taxes. He followed through on a large scale despite bitter opposition from city employees and their labor union. In his second term he expanded reliance on the private sector in a different way, contracting with neighborhood groups and churches to provide local services and address social problems and to rekindle hope in the poorest areas. By the time he left office at the end of 1999, he was almost universally admired for his accomplishments and had been honored with numerous awards for leadership.

Goldsmith began his privatization effort by establishing an office to lead the competition drive, and he recruited nine prominent business leaders to serve as unpaid consultants to identify candidate services for competition. Within two months an army of eighty volunteers was analyzing city operations from this perspective.

Some basic principles guided the privatization/competition effort:

- The key is competition; privatization is just one possible outcome.
- Competition will be public and open to all qualified contestants.
- Cross-functional evaluation teams will evaluate competitive responses.
- As far as practical, current employees will be encouraged to compete.
- Accurate cost-accounting information is needed to compare proposals.
- When in doubt about possible savings, let the marketplace speak.
- Contracts have to state performance standards and provide economic incentives for good performance, and they should be managed effectively.

An additional, informal principle was the "yellow pages" test: If a service was available from three or more firms in the phone book, chances were that the city was not the low-cost provider.

The most tempting targets were public works and transportation, specifically street repairs, wastewater treatment, solid waste collection, and vehicle repairs (See table 2.5). These services met three criteria for successful privatization: They had been privatized in other cities, one could write relatively simple and unambiguous contract terms, and one could easily monitor and measure contractor performance. Goldsmith was keenly aware, however, that the local chapter of the American Federation of State, County, and Municipal Employees (AFSCME) worked hard to prevent his election and would vigorously oppose any privatization attempt. Public-employee unions were rather weak, however, because of Indiana state laws. There was no right to collective bargaining, and the mayor—with the approval of the City-County Council—could eliminate lines and positions at will. But the union could find support from the council, many of whose members had ties to city employees. Moreover 60 percent of the union members were African Americans in modestly paid jobs in a city that was only 25 percent nonwhite. A nasty and divisive emotional battle could erupt.[22]

Goldsmith also worried that an angry union could cause major disruptions by launching strikes or slowdowns in such highly visible public services as trash collection and snow plowing. He visited garages and other facilities to assure employees that he was not contemplating mass or sudden layoffs. Nevertheless, he soon switched direction and tempered his philosophical position; he adopted a policy of managed competition, which meant that the competition would not be restricted to private companies and that work

Table 2.5 Selected Privatizations in Indianapolis

Public Works	Public Safety
Abandoned vehicles	Bike patrol
Asbestos abatement	Jail expansion
Billing for trash collection	Photo finishing
Billing for sewer service	
Hazardous materials emergency response	Administration
Laboratory services	Copying
Mass burning (of solid waste)	Courier service
Recycling program	Facility security
Sewer maintenance	Graphic arts
Street sweeping	Light towing
Trash collection	Microfilming
Wastewater treatment	Window washing
Waste solvent management	
Street repairs	Parks
Vehicle repairs	Concessions
	Golf academy
Transportation	Golf courses
Airport operation	Janitorial services
DOT Laboratory	Landscaping
Paratransit	Pedal-boat rentals
Parking enforcement	Pool operation
Parking meter collection and counting	Portable toilets
Public transit	Tree nursery
Snow plowing	Tree removal
Street maintenance	Velodrome operations
Vehicle maintenance	
	Social services
Information technology	Welfare-to-work assistance
Computer and data-network services	

Source: Office of the Mayor, Indianapolis.

would not automatically be awarded to private firms as he originally intended. The city's own employees could compete against private firms, with the possible outcome being insourcing instead of outsourcing—contracting in instead of contracting out.[23] The basic principle of competition ("marketization," it began to be called) remained the lodestar as the city undertook several major initiatives.

Street Repairs

The city's geographic latitude meant that it was subject to many freeze-thaw cycles in the winter and therefore a proliferation of potholes in the spring. Crews of up to eight employees in two or three vehicles sallied forth to fill the cracks and holes in the city streets, overseen by an army of middle managers whose principal aptitude was delivering votes for the Republican Party. Street repair seemed an ideal target for outsourcing: Several private asphalt contractors had listings in the phonebook for paving driveways and parking lots. A good and prompt job of filling potholes would eliminate a highly visible nuisance and would be lauded by grateful drivers. Contracting the work could be done initially as a small-scale experiment. Within a few weeks of assuming office in January, Goldsmith asked for public and private bids to repair streets in a ten-block area in the spring.[24]

It is no small task, however, to write contract specifications for pothole repairs. What is a pothole? Or, in other words, how large a hole constitutes a pothole that should be repaired?

> A contractor cannot respond sensibly to a specification that calls for "the repair of all potholes that may occur on a given street" nor to a broader specification "to maintain a given street free of potholes," for in the latter case he cannot intelligently weigh the tradeoffs of repaving the entire street or repairing individual potholes. Finally, because it is technically difficult to identify particular potholes, letting a contract on a "per pothole" basis is inviting trouble.[25]

No wonder it seemed reasonable when big-city bosses in a bygone era created the job of "pothole inspector" and filled the positions with well-paid phantoms who never showed up for work.

The city soon realized that the ultimate measure was the cost of laying down a ton of asphalt. New York's experience is a lesson in what not to do. New York decided to measure the performance of its Highways Department and award bonuses on the basis of the number of tons of asphalt laid per worker per year. It soon learned how ingenious its workers could be when presented with such an incentive and how poor a measure this was. Tons of asphalt spiked dramatically in one year, but analysis revealed that three factors—if not the employees—were at work: Employees applied a much thicker overlay than was standard, they dumped asphalt in vacant lots, and they repaved all the streets near the asphalt plants. Trucks could pick up and deliver hot asphalt very quickly to nearby locations, so that not many trucks were needed in the fleet to generate a high rate of asphalt consumption.[26]

Indianapolis officials asked disarmingly simple questions: "How much does it cost to fix a pothole? How much does it cost to lay a ton of asphalt?" But it took months to get a reasonable answer, because city finances were traditionally reported not for discrete activities but as budgets of conventional departmental units. Budgets showed only line items such as labor, materials, and spare parts, without allocating them to individual activities such as street repaving or trash collection. There was no depreciation schedule for capital equipment such as buildings and trucks, vehicle maintenance costs appeared in another department's budget, and necessary overhead costs were allocated simplistically among departments.

Given the city's new emphasis on competition rather than privatization, the city asked the in-house unit to submit a bid. The union's enlightened regional leader, Stephen Fantauzzo—a former city manager—was surprisingly cooperative but said that the union employees and agency managers would need consulting help and training in accounting to prepare a bid. Consultants developed an activity-based cost accounting system, and determined the cost of repairing potholed streets: $407 per ton of asphalt. The city still had to make fair and valid cost comparisons, as comparing current city costs to contractors' bid prices was not a simple matter either: The city paid no property or sales taxes and used tax-free bonds to pay for capital purchases, for example. It had to devise a formula to level the playing field to attract bidders. Only then would the city be in a position to initiate competitive contracting.

At this point the unionized employees came forth with an unexpected proposal: They would decrease the cost of labor, equipment, and management to prove that they could do the job more cheaply than the private sector. Instead of six to eight members in the street-repair crews and two or sometimes three vehicles, they would do the job with four workers and a single, smaller vehicle. The union was forward thinking, reasoning that although fewer workers would be needed for street repair, Mayor Goldsmith's plans to invest in infrastructure would mean more workers overall.

The union proposal to reduce the cost of management posed a serious political problem for Goldsmith. The activity-based cost accounting system showed the true cost of the seriously overstaffed middle management ranks—the political hacks, as the union called them. The middle managers were long-standing Republican stalwarts hired as a reward for service to the party, and

Mayor Goldsmith himself was a Republican. As one truck driver said, "Most of them were precinct committee people or ward chairmen or someone's nephew. We were taking four guys out to do a job when we only needed three." [27] Fantauzzo said, "Get these guys off our backs. We're not going to lose bids because you're making us carry managers that we don't think we ought to be carrying." [28] In an extraordinary display of political bravery and executive integrity, Goldsmith swallowed hard and laid off half of the thirty-eight supervisors who managed the ninety truck drivers responsible for patching potholes.[29]

It is not every day that a conservative mayor in a Republican stronghold takes jobs away from the party faithful to preserve the jobs of union members who opposed him politically. The public employee unions, however grudgingly, had to respect this action by Goldsmith and did ultimately cooperate with him. Union rank-and-file members deemed Fantauzzo a hero. "It's one thing to have two or three people telling you what to do," he said. "It's another to have two or three people who you know are political hacks and don't know the first thing about what you do telling you what to do. Eliminating these guys, in and of itself, was something we'd been trying to do for a decade." [30]

As a result of these changes, the cost of repairing potholes was reduced by 25 percent, from $407 to $301 per ton of asphalt used. This turned out to be by far the lowest price when the private bids were opened. The total agency bid for the small test section of the city was $6,700; of seven private bids, the lowest was more than six times the city bid and they ranged as high as $450,000.

Three factors accounted for the high private bids. First, private firms were accustomed to paving entire areas like parking lots and driveways, not potholes. They interpreted the city's bid request as requiring full paving of those streets. Second, bidders were unfamiliar with the pattern of accident claims and included in their bids the cost of large insurance premiums to protect themselves against liability claims. Third, some bidders assumed that the in-house cost would be exorbitant and easily beaten, and they figured that the city wanted to give the work to private firms in any event, so they factored in very generous profit margins.

The city hesitated to keep the work in-house. What if the Transportation Department failed to meet their bid price and the true cost turned out to be much higher? There was no way the union and agency management could offer a price guarantee or post a bond. Failure would make the mayor look ridiculous after all his preaching about privatization and competition and after mobilizing private sector volunteers to canvass city operations from that perspective. Mitch Roob, the transportation director who had carried out the entire process to this point, recommended to Mayor Goldsmith that they take the risk if they ever wanted the union to cooperate with them again. The mayor agreed and selected the Transportation Department to do the work.[31]

Roob hired a private inspection company to monitor the work to guard against cost overruns. In fact, his agency spent more money checking the work than doing it. The job came in on time and on budget. The stage was now set in Indianapolis for an expanded and aggressive marketization drive.[32]

Wastewater

The city's single greatest success was privatizing its two wastewater treatment plants. These were large, modern, well-run, award-winning plants that consultants said would yield no more than five percent savings if privatized. Overcoming severe opposition from many quarters, Goldsmith persevered and contracted the operations after a well-run competition and spirited bidding. The in-house bid was $27 million, ten percent less than the $30 million the same management had said only weeks earlier was the irreducible, minimal budget. But the eventual winner—a joint venture consisting of an internationally known French firm, a U.S. engineering company, and the local private water company—guaranteed savings of an astonishing 40 percent.[33]

Savings amounted to $72 million over five years, which was more than the $65 million expected from the promised 40 percent savings, and privatizing the sewer collection system saved another $6 million.[34] Moreover the quality of effluent water from the plants improved from an average of 7 permit exceedences per year (that is, violations of state pollution-control standards) under city operation to an average of 2.6 per year. The number of work days lost due to accidents dropped by 91 percent, wages and benefits increased from 9 percent to 28 percent over comparable city levels, and the number of employee grievances declined from thirty-eight in the year before privatization to only two during the entire five years of the contract. In addition, 22.7 percent of the company's purchases were from minority- and women-owned firms.

Thanks to these efficiencies, sewer rates did not go up. Despite inflation, residents paid no more for sewer service in 1999 than they did fourteen years earlier in 1985.[35] The contractor needed only 196 of the original 321 workers to achieve these remarkable results. The other 125 had a choice of a severance package or another job in a city department when an opening became available through attrition; about half took advantage of each option.[36]

Mayor Goldsmith learned two main lessons from this experience. First, daily communication with stakeholders, the Council, and the general public was essential to moving the process along. Second, markets, not consultants, were the only reliable guide to likely savings.[37]

Fleet Management

Indianapolis Fleet Services (IFS), the department that managed and maintained the city's fleet of 2,900 vehicles, was another attractive privatization target. Years earlier vehicle maintenance had been decentralized and each department had acquired its own facility. When this proved inefficient, fleet management was gradually centralized in IFS to cut costs, but by the time Goldsmith became mayor the unit was known for a bloated middle management, reportedly with one supervisor for every two workers. Department heads complained that they could get faster, cheaper, and better service in local auto repair shops. A new $7.5 million maintenance garage was under construction, and if the mayor had been able to halt the project IFS would have been quickly privatized. Contractual obligations made cancellation difficult, however, and union opposition was intense, so the city embarked in a new direction instead.[38] The agency was given two years to improve its operations before having to compete with the private sector.[39]

The IFS director, John McCorkhill, made a remarkable turnaround in that time, more evidence that the threat of competition concentrates the mind wonderfully, much like the imminent prospect of being hanged in the morning. Middle managers were cut by more than half and the total employee count dropped from 113 to 82, or 27 percent, with attrition but no layoffs among the unionized employees. The agency instituted a stringent and meticulous activity-based costing system for all work, and IFS developed a system to track time and charges for work on each agency's vehicles; agencies were charged realistically for the work. Union base pay increased only two percent in the first year of a new labor contract, and after that the only increase was a novel bonus system. Savings above the accurately projected budget would be split, 75 percent to the city treasury and 25 percent to management and labor. (In 1996 Mayor Goldsmith handed out $75,000 in checks to the employees.) Another management innovation in IFS was a system for reporting vehicle abuse and vandalism. Traditional union reluctance to inform on members in other departments was overcome by the incentives of the bonus system.[40] Overall, costs were cut by $3.9 million dollars.[41]

By the end of 1994 IFS was ready to compete against private contractors for the right to continue doing its accustomed work, and the city and the union had developed a trusting relationship.[42] The city prepared the request for proposal (RFP) in an exemplary process. A consultant wrote the document, and the team overseeing the writing included two union members; an administrator; a representative each from the legal department, the purchasing department, and a customer agency (Department of Public Works); and Deputy Mayor Skip Stitt representing the administration. The RFP was sent to thirty-three firms in November 1994 with responses due in January. The selection was to be in February, and the contract would commence in May 1995.[43]

Four bids were submitted, and IFS won the contract with the lowest bid, $16.3 million for three years. Two of the other bids were very close behind: $16.4 million and $16.5 million, and the last was $20.2 million. The agency performed well and employees started earning incentive payments—30 percent of whatever savings they achieved. The average bonus for city mechanics was $934 in 1995. The fraction of vehicles repaired within eight hours increased from 70 percent in 1992 to 82 percent in 1996. The number of complaints from the agency's customers, the other city departments, dropped from 149 to 5.[44] By the end of the contract IFS had saved the city an estimated $8.4 million since the beginning of the Goldsmith administration.[45] Competition and incentives energized the employees, and they were proud of their success.

Solid Waste Collection

When the city and county were amalgamated in the 1970s, the resultant local government inherited a variety of direct, contract, and individual household arrangements for collecting garbage and trash throughout an area that previously had many separate and independent jurisdictions.[46] Twenty small "mom and pop" private haulers served the area. Mayor Goldsmith consolidated the twenty-five small districts outside the city's core into eleven districts and introduced competitive bidding. The city's core was reserved, as in the past, for the city's public works crews, who could remove snow in the winter and respond to other emergencies; however, the city agency could and did compete for contracts in the outer areas. No bidder would be awarded more than three districts, a constraint intended to assure continued competition and to protect small local haulers from the large national waste-management firms.[47]

The result of the bidding was that four private firms won eight districts, and the city's Solid Waste Division won three. Ironically, the city agency was the low bidder in four districts but was also bound by the three-district limit. It succeeded, however, only because it reduced its costs significantly: The unionized employees decided to increase from 800 to 1,200 the number of homes that a four-person crew would serve daily, an immediate fifty-percent jump in labor productivity.[48] Overall, competition reduced waste-collection costs by 20 percent and saved the city $15 million over three years.[49]

Airport Management

The Indianapolis Airport Authority (IAA) managed the city's airport. The IAA was an independent municipal corporation governed by a board of seven members—five of whom were appointed by the mayor. Airlines used the airport under contracts with the IAA. Whatever airport operating expenses were not covered by parking, concessions, and other nonairline earnings was charged to the airlines. This agreement protected taxpayers but had no incentives for the IAA to operate the airport efficiently, because excess costs were simply passed on to the airlines. The airport's cost per emplaned passenger was rising fast, up 38 percent over the preceding ten years, while concession revenues were flat. This arrangement had to change if the airport was to become a major distribution hub in North America, a strategic goal of the city.[50]

The board considered and rejected the idea of selling the airport, deciding instead to contract out management of airport operations. Many of the airlines were concerned, however, that any savings would be drained from the airport and used for other municipal purposes; the city had to reassure the airlines that they would be the principal beneficiaries of any savings from outsourcing. Taxpayers would benefit from better airline service and additional economic development at the airport.

A request for the qualifications (RFQ) of potential bidders was issued and responses came from some of the world's most qualified airport operators. Five prospective operators, including the existing airport management team, were selected and asked to submit proposals that included four topics: ideas for better service at the same or lower cost, ideas for attracting new economic development at the airport, long-term plans for strategic positioning of the airport for the next century, and plans to increase the expertise and diversity of the airport staff.

Excellent responses came in from all the bidders, including the current management staff, but the latter could not match the resources and creativity of the private firms, nor could they offer guaranteed savings like the private firms could. Final negotiations resulted in a ten-year contract with BAA USA, the U.S. subsidiary of a British firm that, fittingly, had been state owned and was privatized by Prime Minister Margaret Thatcher. The contract terms called for payment based on performance alone. BAA was selected because of its corporate resources, long-term approach, commitment to customer service, and successful record in similar airports.

BAA identified $100 million in savings and increased nonairline revenue over the ten years of the contract and guaranteed minimum savings of $3.2 million each year; the company would be paid only after it achieved those savings. BAA and IAA would share all savings beyond the contract price: IAA would receive 60 percent in the first year, 65 percent in the second year, and 70 percent thereafter. BAA hired all the airport employees at comparable wages and benefits; the savings came from improved operations, aggressive pursuit of new retail shops, and better services for airport customers, not from layoffs and wage cuts. BAA also agreed to contract extensively with minority- and women-owned businesses.

BAA more than doubled the revenue from parking and concession fees per passenger from $2.08 in 1994 to $4.26 in 1999. After little more than a year of operation, BAA had reduced the cost per emplaned passenger by 42 percent to $3.87 per passenger. (This is not a trivial amount for airlines: American Airlines earned only $3.70 per passenger in its best year, 1988.[51]) Therefore BAA reduced landing fees by 70 percent, saving airlines $7 million in the first fifteen months of operation. The lower landing fees were expected to make the airport a magnet for more business activity. Cumulative savings totaled $19 million in the first three years of the contract.[52]

Golf Courses

Municipal golf courses are popular but often neglected amenities. Indianapolis turned over management of eleven of its run-down golf courses to eleven different professional operators. They maintain and operate the courses, buy supplies and equipment, hire the personnel, operate the snack bar and pro shop, and handle golf-cart rentals. The operators competed to attract players by installing ball washers, yardage signs, flagpoles, tee markers, trashcans, water fountains, and new golf carts.[53] Golfers played more rounds on the improved courses despite higher fees. Revenues increased by 150 percent and the city, which receives a percentage of course revenues, earned more than a million dollars annually, doubling its previous income.[54] The city no longer pays for capital improvements, which are now funded from the contractors' course revenues. [55]

Criticisms of the Contracting Program

Mayor Goldsmith used contracting to revolutionize the aforementioned services. Although some successes were indisputable, critics of the contracting program were outspoken and pointed to several issues.[56]

- Two contractors failed to maintain the city parks.
- New managers of the golf courses hired subcontractors for construction work without adhering to state bidding laws; the violation was inadvertent, and a criminal investigation resulted in no charges, but a whistle-blower complained of harassment and demotion and filed a lawsuit that the city settled out of court.
- The city, which had been spending $200,000 a year to get rid of abandoned cars in the streets, arranged for a contractor to do it, and the contractor *paid the city* $200,000 a year. However, an audit showed that $6,400 was missing, and the company dismissed the manager and another employee. Another contractor took over the program with no further problems.
- Vendors doing business with the city made campaign contributions to Goldsmith; but this is symmetrical with contributions routinely made by public-employee unions to incumbent officials running for reelection with the expectation that it will gain them favorable treatment.
- The savings were overstated.[57] If the city had saved as much money as the mayor claimed, why were taxes no lower and the budget no smaller? The explanation, as Goldsmith had announced, is that the savings were invested in rebuilding infrastructure and increasing police protection.[58] Deputy Mayor Skip Stitt adds that the proof of the savings is that the city cut its operating budget seven years in a row and cut property taxes four times.[59]

Naval Air Warfare Center

Mayor Goldsmith carried out a particularly innovative and entrepreneurial privatization, one that did not involve contracting, as in the cases discussed above. Indianapolis was the home of the Naval Air Warfare Center (NAWC), a military facility that designed and produced advanced electronic equipment for aircraft, ships, satellites, and other vessels. It was also one of the largest local employers with 2,400 workers who earned a high average salary. Anticipating that the federal government might close the center as part of a nationwide base-closing effort, Goldsmith mounted an unusual campaign to avoid such a serious economic blow. The city proposed several different options to the Pentagon to no avail; the center would not remain open as a government military base.[60]

Instead of organizing a conventional lobbying effort to keep the base open, the mayor proposed a totally different tack: privatization. NAWC would be closed as a base and its employees would no longer be on the government payroll. The city would take ownership of the site and all its equipment and assume responsibility for operating and maintenance costs. One or more private companies would come in and provide products and services to the military under a sole-source agreement, but within five years they would have to compete for contracts. Under this strategy, the risk of failure would be borne by the city, not the Navy. Moreover the Pentagon would avoid the estimated $180 million cost of closing the base.

Although the congressional Base Realignment and Closure Commission did not accept the plan, it specifically identified privatization as an option the Navy could pursue. In President Clinton's letter submitting the entire closure list to Congress, Clinton supported the city's plan and encouraged the Navy to look at it closely.

The city formed a broadly representative Reuse Planning Authority to manage the privatization and base closure, and it obtained additional senior management support from local companies to prepare the request for proposal. But the first step was to determine the true cost to the Navy of closing the base outright. The major cost was not the monetary real estate and personnel cost but the cost of losing the expertise of the NAWC. Only 26 percent of NAWC employees would move elsewhere to stay with the Navy; the rest preferred local jobs in the private sector. The loss of experienced technical specialists combined with the president's approval for the city's plan, the cost of closure, and the city's enthusiastic support of privatization tipped the balance in favor of the city's plan.

The city's privatization plan set broad goals for the different stakeholders. For the city, the plan promised economic development, growth in technology, a new taxpayer, and a long-term commitment from the private buyer. For the buyer, the plan promised long-term growth; for employees, new job opportunities; and for the Navy, cost savings and continued access to high-quality technical capability.

Seven firms submitted excellent proposals, and the city selected Hughes Technical Services Company, a subsidiary of Hughes Electronics. The company agreed to keep all existing employees and to pay them the same or higher salaries and benefits and to increase local employment by at least 3,000 jobs within six years. Whereas the Navy paid no property taxes to the city, Hughes would pay some $3 million annually. Moreover Hughes promised to invest more than $200 million in employee training, applied research, and capital improvements.

Privatization was expected to save the federal government an estimated $1 billion over ten years. The Navy leased the property, facilities, and equipment to the city, which in turn leased it to Hughes; both leases were for ten years for a dollar a year, and Hughes would gain title. Mayor Goldsmith summarized the end result:

> Under privatization, each party . . . comes out a winner. The Navy will reduce personnel, save considerable amounts of money, and close a base while retaining access to world-class electronics expertise. NAWC's employees will keep or increase their pay and benefits and have greater job opportunities . . . Hughes will take over a successful operation that has enormous potential in a growing market and that is staffed with highly experienced workers. The city will preserve jobs and create new ones, put a new entity on the property tax rolls, and further its edge in the field of advanced electronics. All this occurred because the artificial barrier between public and private was removed—replaced by innovative and profitable solutions.[61]

Faith-Based Institutions

Goldsmith hoped his legacy would be more than introducing competition and holding the line on taxes and spending. His goal was to revitalize downtown and bring optimism and renewed hope to inner-city neighborhoods. Earlier in his career, as county prosecutor, Goldsmith experimented with alternatives to prison and with ministries that worked with juvenile offenders. He pioneered in calling for faith-based organizations to address social problems at the neighborhood level, problems that government is ill equipped to solve. Both Vice President Al Gore and, later, President George W. Bush endorsed this approach.[62]

As mayor, Goldsmith recognized that a revitalized civil society requires a healthy community with rekindled hope. He created the Front Porch Alliance, a network of hundreds of partnerships that serves as a "civic switchboard" matching churches and neighborhood groups with government resources and expertise. This is not merely a matter of delivering social services; Goldsmith said, "the grander purpose is to create a human infrastructure in the neighborhoods." [63]

Summary of Results

During the Goldsmith administration, Indianapolis opened eighty-six services to competitive bidding. By drastically cutting costs, city employees won thirty-seven, or 43 percent, of these bids. "We got real efficient real quick," said a worker in the street program, explaining that if his crew were to lose many bids, pink slips were sure to follow.[64] Overall the competitive bidding program had an enormous impact: It cut the number of city employees by a third, reduced the cost of local government by almost a quarter, and led to projected savings totaling $450 million through the end of the contracts currently in effect.[65] The savings paid for one hundred more police officers to reduce crime and contributed to a $530 million fund to rebuild the city's crumbling infrastructure—its neglected streets, sewers, bridges, and other city property. No union members lost jobs; they were hired by contractors, placed in vacant city positions, or retired. Civilian agencies whose work was contracted out lost workers, but the enlarged police and fire departments now employed half the city's workforce.

Mayor Goldsmith demonstrated convincingly that it is competition, not privatization per se, that accounted for his success.

> Competitive bidding programs should provide incentives for city agencies to trim bureaucratic bloat, eliminate waste, increase productivity, and focus on outcomes. When union workers are given the freedom to put their own ideas into action, they can be as innovative, effective, and cost-conscious as their private-sector counterparts. The problem is that union workers have been trapped in a system that punishes initiative, ignores efficiency, and rewards big spenders.[66]

Privatization in Phoenix

The Phoenix economy was suffering. It was the 1970s, and the city was facing inflation, a high growth rate, and limitations on revenues and expenditures.[67] Private contractors promised cost savings if the city were to privatize selected services, but city officials chose a different approach, one recommended by the author to city officials:[68] introducing competition and comparing the cost of municipal service with the cost of a private contract for that service, then awarding the contract to the least-cost provider. Today the city of Phoenix has the following policy: "Operations will be performed at the most economical cost while maintaining desired service levels. The City will periodically call for bids from private industry for purposes of evaluation." [69]

Background

Phoenix has a history of change and willingness to experiment; its rapid growth has necessitated revisions in functions and charter. The city has a council-manager form of government, which many public administration experts consider particularly efficient.

Ron Jensen, the Phoenix public works director and architect of the city's system of public-private competition, was fully aware of the barriers to privatization.

> Older eastern cities have saddled themselves . . . with binding union contracts that prohibit or restrict the city's ability to contract with private firms. These contracts, while intended to protect workers, have severely damaged the reputation of local government, and have created a negative stereotype of lazy and inefficient workers standing behind a shield of contract protection. . . . [but] department managers do more to oppose and block privatization efforts than unions . . . [because] the compensation package of most government agency managers in civil service environments is based on three primary factors: (1) number of employees in the department, (2) size of budget, and (3) span of control.[70]

All three components would suffer if many operations were contracted out.

By focusing on taxpayers as the principal beneficiaries of competition, Jensen says, "it is not hard to make private companies and public employees winners as well." Identifying all the participants (stakeholders), and involving them in the process with the potential for winning in the future, he believes, will keep all parties involved and committed.[71] Flanagan and Perkins also emphasize public benefits that make this work. They write that the "greatest benefit of the competitive process is the ability to positively influence expectations about government and gain public support," something Phoenix has done.[72]

The city adopted a policy on employee layoffs that minimized hostility and intransigence. The winning firm was required to offer jobs to the affected workers and to match the city's health benefit package for such workers. In anticipation of future competitions, the city prudently filled any openings with temporary employees who had no claim to permanent positions. The city's rapid growth meant that displaced employees could generally be assigned to productive jobs elsewhere in city government. Older workers tended to stay even in lower paying positions to maintain their pension benefits.

The contracts were for a fixed price, not "cost plus rate of return." For refuse collection the price was quoted per household and for bus service it was quoted per route mile. A winning private contractor has to post a performance bond, although the city does not. Contracts varied in length from one to six years, many with optional renewal clauses depending on the service. Services that require large outlays for capital equipment pose a special problem; Phoenix addresses it by informing bidders of the amount and price of its equipment that is available for sale if a private contractor wins. The contractor can then factor that into his bid price. The city auditor evaluates service levels, for example, by examining responsiveness, customer complaints, and property damage, and conducting customer satisfaction surveys. Financial penalties are imposed for poor service in some cases. For example, a contract requires 99.5 percent accuracy for data entry, and accuracy of only 98.5 percent leads to a one percent deduction from the bill, a 96.5 percent accuracy rate leads to a six percent deduction, and so on.

Between 1979 and 1994 Phoenix awarded fifty-six contracts in fourteen municipal services by this process, with thirty-four contracts (61 percent) going to private contractors (mostly for public works) and twenty-two (39 percent) remaining with city agencies (See table 2.6).[73] From the start of the competition program in 1979 through June 30, 2003, the savings totaled $41.8 million and averaged 24 percent (See table 2.7).[74] Phoenix institutionalized competition and it became a fixture of the municipal landscape (See table 2.8). Public and private sectors contested vigorously, and no sector dominated for long.

Table 2.6 Public-Private Competition in Phoenix, 1979–1994

Service	*Contracts won by private firms*	*Contracts won by city agencies*
Ambulance service	0	1
Ambulance billing	1	0
Data entry	0	1
Fuel distribution	0	1
Instrument maintenance	0	1
Landfill operation	1	0
Landscape maintenance	23	7
Public defender	1	0
Refuse collection	7	5
Senior-housing management	0	1
Street repair	0	2
Street sweeping	0	2
Water billing	1	0
Water meter repair	0	1
TOTAL	34	22

Source: Robert Franciosi, *Garbage In, Garbage Out: An Examination of Private/Public Competition by the City of Phoenix* (Phoenix: Goldwater Institute, 1998), 5.

Let us look in depth at three important areas: refuse collection, emergency ambulance service, and bus service.

Refuse Collection

Public Works Director Ron Jensen initiated managed competition in refuse collection in 1979. He divided the city into three sectors and put each sector out to bid on a rotating schedule. Private firms bid against the in-house unit; the total number of bidders ranged from three to six in each competition. The contract specified a fixed rate per house per month and penalties for missed collections, spillage, deviation from established routes, and other failures. Private firms can serve no more than one of the three sectors; this has the effect of institutionalizing and perpetuating public-private competition and preventing complacency and collusion.

Table 2.7 **Actual Cost Savings and Cost Avoidance from Public-Private Competition in Phoenix, 1979–2003**

Department	*Service*	*Savings*
Aviation	Airport landscaping	$1,000
	Nursery and plant maintenance	14,400
Fire	Emergency transportation	2,898,000
	Billing and collection services	560,600
Housing	Low-income housing maintenance	23,000
	Senior housing management	116,000
Neighborhood Services	Lot maintenance	13,600
Parks, Recreation, and Library	Median maintenance	470,000
	Landscape maintenance	145,800
Public Works	Refuse collection	23,768,400
	Landfill operation	7,711,000
	Solid waste transfer hauling	4,486,700
Street Transportation	Street sweeping	36,000
	Street repair	109,000
	Landscape maintenance	653,800
Water Services	Water meter repair	176,000
	Wastewater instrument calibration	161,500
	Painting manholes with insecticide	468,000
TOTAL		41,812,800

Source: City Auditor Department, Phoenix, "Public/Private Competitive Proposal Process," Phoenix, n.d.

By demanding both high quality service and efficient service delivery, Phoenix forced its solid waste agency to reorganize, adopt more efficient practices, and compete with private companies for residential solid waste collection. After private firms won several contracts, the city agency improved its performance and by the late 1980s won back the districts it had lost. (Subsequently, however, private firms started winning again.) Over twenty-one years the real, inflation-adjusted cost of citywide garbage collection declined by 60 percent (See figure 2.1). This saved the city $23.8 million, arguably pleasing taxpayers and city employees alike.[75]

Table 2.8 Chronological List of Competitions in Phoenix, 1979–1991

Date	*Service*	*Area*	*Winner*
January 1979	Street sweeping		Public
October 1979	Contained collection, northeast		Private
April 1980	Uncontained collection	Area 1	Private
		Area 2	Private
		Area 3	Public
		Area 4	Private
		Area 5	Public
May 1980	Commercial bin refuse		Private
Janary 1981	Water billing		Private
	Median maintenance	Area 1	Public
		Area 2	Private
		Area 3	Private
		Area 4	Private
		Area 5	Private
		Area 6	Private
		Area 7	Public
June 1981	Grounds maintenance	Wash. Manor	Public
July 1981	Street repair, concrete		Public
	Street repair, asphalt		Public
February 1982	Street sweeping		Public
April 1982	Landfill operation		Private
	Median maintenance	Area 1	Private
		Area 2	Private
		Area 3	Private
		Area 4	Private
		Area 5	Private
		Area 6	Private
		Area 7	Private
July 1982	Water meter repair		Private
May 1983	Median maintenance	Area 1	Public
		Area 2	Private
		Area 3	Public
		Area 4	Public
		Area 5	Private
June 1983	Contained and uncontained collection, southwest		Private
March 1984	Fuel distribution		Public
August 1984	Contained and uncontained collection, north		Public
February 1985	Ambulance service		Public
	Median maintenance	Northwest	Private
		Northeast	Private
		East	Private
		South	Private
		West	Private
February 1987	Contained and uncontained collection, southeast		Public
December 1987	Landscape maintenance		Private
February 1988	Contained and uncontained collection, southwest	Public	
March 1990	Landscape maintenance		Private
April 1991	Management information system data entry	Public	
October 1991	Plant maintenance		Private

Source: Suzanne Denise Miller, "Public-Private Competition: The Case of Phoenix" (Ph.D. diss., University of Chicago, 1996), table 2.1. Reprinted with permission.

Note: "Area" refers to the city's designation for geographic service districts.

Figure 2.1 Cost of Lowest Bid for Refuse Collection in Phoenix, 1979–2000

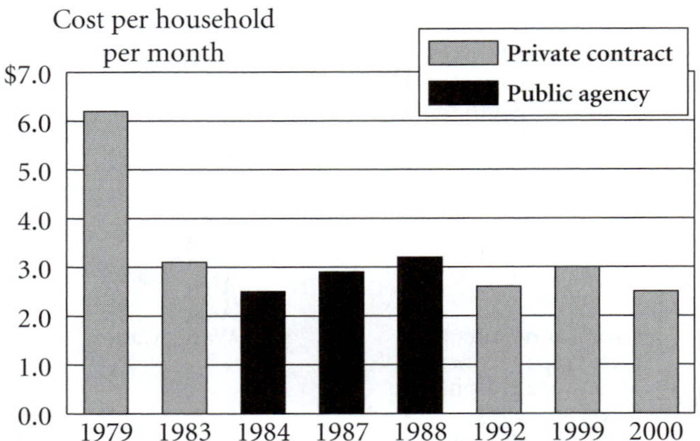

Source: City Auditor Department, "Public/Private Competitive Process Overview," Phoenix, n.d.

Moreover, citizen surveys by an independent research firm validated the impression that service levels had improved. Customer satisfaction increased steadily from 7.6 to 7.9 (on a scale of 1 to 10) in four years (See figure 2.2).[76]

According to Jensen, people in the private sector believe that managed competition gives government an unfair advantage; they say municipal overhead costs are not properly allocated to the cost of the service. Public agencies that are inefficient also oppose managed competition, but for the opposite reason: They fear they cannot win the competition and prefer to maintain the status quo. Private firms would hesitate to compete with a well-run agency using good business practices. Most public agencies, however, do not fit this mold of good service delivery and therefore oppose both managed competition and privatization.[77]

But, Robert Franciosi asserts, the bid terms and the bid process have counterproductive features that limit the amount of competition, increase the cost for private bidders, and favor the in-house bidder, thereby leading to higher costs for Phoenix taxpayers. He questions the need to restrict contractors to less than half the work and says that seven-year contracts for each of the three districts leads to infrequent competitions; they should be conducted more frequently. Franciosi also believes that department overhead should be included in the calculation of the city's cost and notes correctly that contractors

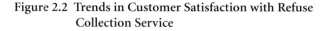

Figure 2.2 Trends in Customer Satisfaction with Refuse Collection Service

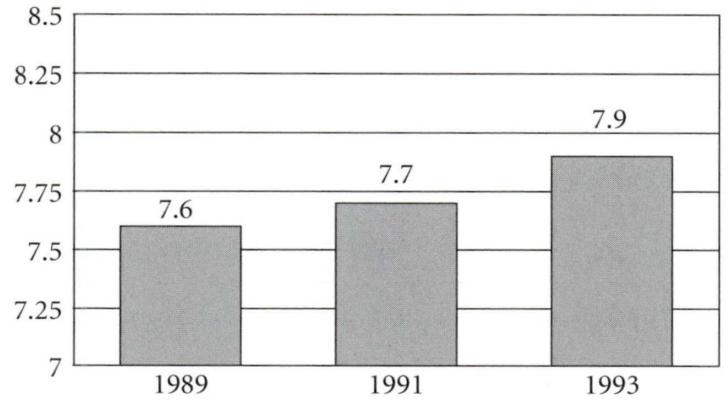

Source: Jim Flanagan and Susan Perkins, "Public-Private Competition in the City of Phoenix," *Government Finance Review,* June 1995, 7–12. Reprinted with permission of the publisher.

have to provide surety bonds but the public agency does not; hence, there is no corresponding accounting for the risk (to taxpayers) of cost overruns by the city agency.[78]

Emergency Ambulance Service

About 80 percent of all calls to the Phoenix Fire Department are for emergency medical assistance and transportation. In 1984 private firms sought and won the opportunity to provide ambulance service. Performance improved dramatically for four years. In 1988 the city won the competitive bid, and it was able to maintain the response time below ten minutes for at least 90 percent of the calls (See figure 2.3).[79] Customer satisfaction increased from 8.0 to 8.3 on a scale of 1 to 10 between 1989 and 1993 (See figure 2.4).[80] In 2004 about 98 percent of those surveyed were "very satisfied" with the emergency response services, while the remaining 2 percent were "satisfied." [81]

Although the citizen-survey data for refuse collection and for emergency ambulance service seem encouraging, they are not very useful. The survey authors give no information about the survey, so we know neither the questions asked nor the number of respondents. It is also unclear how

Figure 2.3 Emergency Ambulance Response Times, 1984–2000

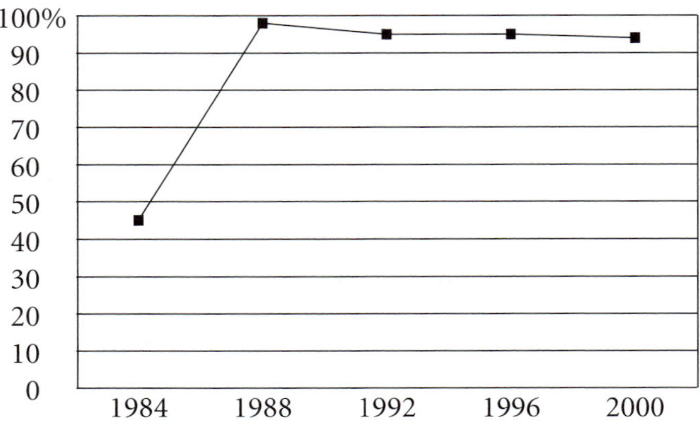

Source: City Auditor Department, "Public/Private Competitive Process Overview," Phoenix, n.d.

Figure 2.4 Customer Satisfaction with Emergency Ambulance and Paramedic Service, 1989–1993

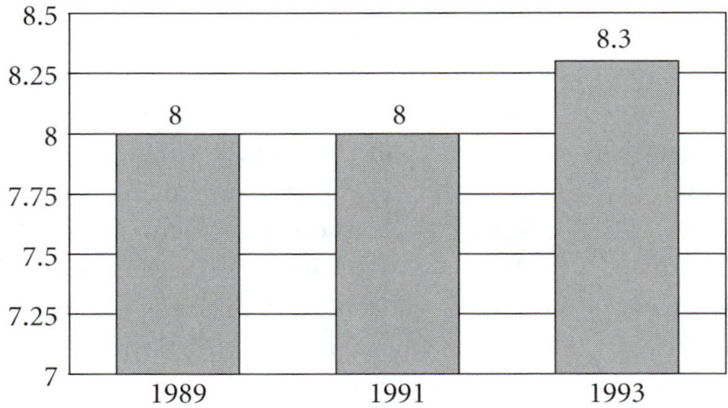

Source: Jim Flanagan and Susan Perkins, "Public-Private Competition in the City of Phoenix," *Government Finance Review,* June 1995, 7–12. Reprinted with permission of the publisher.

survey respondents were chosen. The absence of these factors makes this information less compelling. Despite these concerns, the apparent increase in customer satisfaction after privatization is notable.

Bus Service

Phoenix contracts with a national bus company to operate daily service on ten routes totaling about 4,700 route miles. This is a fixed-price contract; that is, Phoenix pays a fixed price per mile of service, and the contractor reaps gains from any increased efficiency and bears the cost of any overruns. In addition, Phoenix contracts with another private company for bus support services: radio communications, lost and found operations, vehicle fueling, fare-box data processing, security, and scheduling.

Contract specifications for bus operations cover cleaning and maintaining the buses, driver and mechanic training, and minimum employee benefits. Service standards specify how often buses must be dusted, mopped, fueled, and have fluid levels checked. The city mandates the ratio of mechanics to buses. The contractor must not miss any trips. In addition, the contractor must adhere to all relevant mandates for federally subsidized transit. The contractor therefore is required to comply with Buy America provisions, cargo preference requirements, energy efficiency, environmental standards, and burdensome labor regulations. For example, employees who are laid off are entitled to be paid a monthly allowance—equal to their average monthly pay—for up to six years.[82]

The contract is not performance based, however, as it does not explicitly refer to performance measurements, and it lacks both incentives for good performance and penalties for failure to satisfy performance specifications. This is in marked contrast to the specifications for refuse collection. Both services involve large vehicles driving on city streets along fixed routes, but while the refuse contracts impose financial penalties for nonperformance, the bus contract has none; it merely lists toothless mandates. At the very least, Franciosi asserts, accident rates and on-time performance should be monitored and subject to rewards and penalties.[83]

National Recognition

Phoenix received numerous awards for managerial excellence, in part because of its managed competition process. It received the Carl Bertelsmann Prize in

1993 for being one of the two best-run cities in the world. The city received straight "A"s on *Financial World* magazine's "State of the Cities" study in March 1995. Phoenix was ranked first—out of America's forty-four largest cities—in overall city efficiency for 1995–1998 on the Reason Public Policy Institute's "Competitive Cities Report Card." Finally, in 2000 *Governing* magazine named Phoenix the best city in its "Grading the Cities" report.[84]

Privatization in Other Cities

Several other cities also undertook major privatization efforts. The high points of their activities are reviewed here.[85]

Philadelphia

Newly elected Philadelphia mayor Edward G. Rendell took office in 1992 facing problems that seemed insurmountable. The city was on the brink of collapse. His predecessors had raised taxes nineteen times in the preceding eleven years, saddling residents and businesses with the highest tax burden on the East Coast. This accelerated the exodus of jobs as employers and residents fled Philadelphia. The city was nearly insolvent—the budget deficit was $250 million, 10 percent of the budget. As for city bonds, investors required an effective interest of 27 percent before they would lend money to the city. Eighteen months later the city posted its first budget surplus in seven years, and Standard & Poor raised its rating of the city's bonds from CCC to B, still below investment grade, however.

Taking Control. Mayor Rendell took two major steps to gain control over the runaway budget: He cut labor costs and privatized services. City employees were getting fifty-two days off in a year, which effectively translated into a four-day work week. Employees had twenty days off for sick leave, fourteen paid holidays including Flag Day, ten vacation days (up to twenty for longevity of service), five days to attend funerals, and three days for personal leave. The city funded the health plans but the money was given to and controlled by the unions. Moreover employees had free legal services at a cost of $5 million per year. The mayor was determined to slash these costs, but the unions vigorously opposed his plans and went on strike.

The strike withered under the general public outrage (the mayor aggressively publicized the cushy labor arrangements) and lasted only sixteen hours. The unions caved in, and the mayor won $98.6 million in concessions, or $374 million in four years. Workers did not take any cut in pay, but wages were frozen for two years, medical benefits were cut 25 percent, and overtime was cut. Paid holidays were reduced from fourteen to ten and sick leave was cut to fifteen days for new employees. The city made smaller contributions to the pension program, but it still remained among the most generous in the region. The unions gave up restrictive work rules that the city had ceded thirty years earlier.

Privatizing. Another vital concession allowed the mayor to bid out any city service if he could prove it would save money. This was the opening for an aggressive privatization program, an explicit element of Rendell's victorious election campaign. In the first five years of his administration, 1992 through 1996, the city subjected forty-five services to competition; private contractors won forty-one of them and the other four were retained in-house by the city's workforce. Annual savings were estimated at $42 million and cumulative savings were estimated to be $140 million. (See table 2.9, which lists only the first sixteen privatizations; savings averaged 37 percent.) Moreover service levels were equal or better.[86] Although this was only a small fraction of the city's $2.5 billion annual budget, it paid for hundreds of additional police officers. The city eliminated 1,600 jobs by contracting (about one-third of the positions were vacant at the time), thereby reducing the head count to 27,000, the lowest in decades. Attrition accounted for much of the reduction. Employees who did not want to bid against contractors nor work for winning bidders either retired or were offered other municipal jobs where vacancies had been allowed to accumulate. Only fifteen employees were actually laid off, and all were subsequently offered a chance to return to city service.

The contracted services ranged from a municipal nursing home to the city's print shop and prison food services. The privatization process gave a competitive jolt to the city bureaucracy. City workers won several competitive contracts, but they had to cut staffing and accept changes in work rules to accomplish that. Sludge processing is an example. The Water Department adopted an aggressive strategy to avoid privatization. It invested in more efficient equipment, streamlined work processes and work rules (after negotiating with the union), contracted out some functions that were not being performed cost-effectively (such as long-distance hauling of sludge to landfills), reduced staff, and adopted strengthened cost-accounting and performance-measurement systems. As a result of managed competition, the cost of

Table 2.9 Selected Privatizations in Philadelphia

Service or facility	*Annual in-house cost*	*Competitive contract cost*	*Estimated annual savings*	*Savings*	*Number of positions eliminated*
Emergency sludge removal	$2,328,000	$1,050,000	$1,278,000	55%	3
Vine Street maintenance	265,227	116,000	149,227	39	11
Monthly water billing	387,167	239,541	147,626	38	8
Park Equestrian Center	174,171	0	174,171	100	3
City Hall custodial	1,684,000	1,340,000	344,000	20	45
Art Museum security	3,600,000	2,200,000	1,400,000	39	115
Art Museum custodial	1,575,512	1,096,794	478,718	30	117
Waste transfer stations	4,800,000	2,317,000	2,483,000	52	26
City warehouse	3,981,847	2,828,994	1,152,853	30	86
Park turf maintenance	421,260	96,390	324,870	77	15
City print shop	1,399,960	851,176	548,784	39	13
Riverview medical services	689,681	454,272	235,409	34	49
Disability management	15,200,000	12,800,000	2,400,000	16	12
History museum building	289,676	(60,000)	349,676	121	46
Prison food service	9,287,574	5,835,974	3,451,600	37	30
Nursing home	8,570,000	3,000,000	5,570,000	65	350
TOTAL	54,654,075	34,166,142	20,487,934	37	929

Source: Office of the Mayor, "Calculation of Competitive Contracting Savings," Philadelphia, October 28, 1993.

$31.6 million in 1993 was reduced by almost half to $16.9 million in 1997. This more than doubled the annual savings projected from privatization.

Two principal benefits of outsourcing are that it takes advantage of the skills and economies of scale of outside specialists, and it frees city managers to focus on their core responsibilities. Philadelphia realized both benefits when it contracted management of its warehouse and distribution function. Whereas an order of pencils used to take a week to be delivered, for example, now it takes twenty-four hours. The city no longer carries excessive inventories of obsolete products, nor does it maintain or operate its warehouse. Savings are $1.2 million a year.[87]

Another example of taking advantage of contractors' capabilities is in processing city employee claims for injuries. Mayor Rendell said,

> Philadelphia was notorious for the mismanagement of its disability and workers' compensation claims. Historically the city failed to deliver professional safety and injury prevention programs, effective treatment, or responsive medical case management to its own employees hurt on the job. At the same time, poor system management enabled a handful of abusers to exploit system loopholes and drive the city's costs through the roof.[88]

The city contracted with one of the best firms in the business, which coordinates a network of professional facilities, physicians, and nurses to manage employee cases. As a result, total incurred liabilities decreased by more than $100 million, and the number of paid workdays lost dropped from 80,000 to 30,000 in five years.[89]

The icing on the cake was hiring a contractor to clean up and maintain the grimy and foul-smelling City Hall. Unionized workers in an eighty-year-old, family-run business clean its 750 rooms, wash its 1,400 windows, and scrub the inside floors and outside courtyard, saving approximately $477,000 per year. An added bonus for Philadelphians: Rendell's successful privatization program apparently influenced the regional transportation body, SEPTA, to privatize some of its bus routes.

Chicago

When Mayor Richard Daley took office in Chicago in 1989, he wanted to provide the city with more and better services at no additional cost to taxpayers. Daley is the son and namesake of the famous Boss Daley, whose well-oiled political machine ran on municipal patronage. It is striking, therefore, that privatization was an important element of his strategy, and his efforts saved the city money and generated additional revenue. The National Center for Policy Analysis reported that Mayor Daley had privatized more than forty government functions in Chicago and that "services now performed by private contractors have saved Chicago taxpayers $20 million." [90]

Towing Automobiles. Towing abandoned automobiles was an early example. When the Department of Streets and Sanitation did the towing, it cost the city roughly $25 per vehicle. Mayor Daley contracted with a private company to take over the work. The firm sold the junked vehicles for scrap or salvage and paid the city $25 for each car. The arrangement saved the city about $7.5 million a year and generated about $3 million annually. This privatization was a triple winner for Mayor Daley in his first year in office: It reduced costs, raised revenue, and eliminated a constant source of citizen complaints by removing 300,000 junked cars from city streets. In a 1997 speech on city management, Mayor Daley commented on the significance of this early act: "The privatization of towing . . . was an important model program. This program showed us that privatization could not only improve customer service, it could actually raise revenue for the city." [91]

Airport Parking. A great success of the Daley administration was the privatization of the parking service at O'Hare Airport, one of the busiest airports in the country. With 18,000 parking spaces and 145 employees, this was a $42 million per year moneymaker in 1993. But Mayor Daley wanted to turn over the responsibilities to a private company to "bolster city revenues, reduce delays, and provide motorists with new services that will range from car repair to valet parking." The Mayor also felt that privatization of the airport's parking services was a good idea because "Government knows nothing about garages. You should get a company that has that day-to-day responsibility of how to manage a garage." [92]

In October 1993 the Standard Parking Corporation, a Chicago-based firm, signed a five-year, $58 million contract with the city and took over the operation of O'Hare's parking services. Standard, which had served the city during most of the 1980s as a parking consultant, was awarded the contract over four other companies. The company would bill the city for operating costs and receive a management fee of $250,000 per year from the city. The estimated operational savings were $3 million annually. Some of the amenities put in place by Standard included monthly debit cards for frequent parkers to reduce cash handling and to speed exits, car repairs performed by Midas International, and beefed-up security.[93]

Interestingly, this represented a *reprivatization* of parking at O'Hare, as the city had taken control from a private parking firm in 1978 after a scandal in which the firm had been awarded the job only because of its political connections. Under the current contract, the city audits Standard periodically to prevent similar scandals.

Whereas the expected savings and new services benefited the city and the customers, the affected city employees were understandably disgruntled. Approximately 130 of them lost their jobs, and those who remained with Standard took a $3 per hour pay cut, reducing their hourly rate to $7.50.

Privatization of parking at O'Hare was a financial success. The *Chicago Sun-Times*, reporting on the subsequent Midway Airport privatization, stated that revenue at O'Hare had increased by almost $20 million in two years. In 1993 there were 3.9 million paid exits that generated $46.7 million in gross revenues compared to 4.3 million paid exits and gross revenue of $65.3 million in 1995, two years after privatization.[94] Impressed by those results, ten years later Mayor Daley began exploring public-private partnerships for his long-sought airport expansions, which were expected to cost $6.6 billion.

Soldier Field. In 1993 Mayor Daley sought to privatize another Chicago landmark—Soldier Field, the stadium built in 1924 as a memorial to the men and women of the armed services and now the home of the Chicago Bears. Mayor Daley and the Parks Department superintendent at the time, Forrest Claypool, favored privatization because the stadium was being used less than twenty days per year and Claypool "[hoped] to free funds for his highest priority: recreation and park activities." [95] The facility was turned over to a joint venture led by Spectacor, a national stadium management firm that also manages the stadium housing the Philadelphia Flyers and 76ers. The company started using Soldier Field for rock concerts and soccer games in addition to football games.[96] As a result, Soldier Field went from losing $1 million in 1993 to netting $2.9 million in 1996. The $2.9 million was the city's cut from the $10.9 million in total gross revenues earned by Spectacor events.

Parks. The Parks Department also considered additional privatizations. Major lakefront park facilities and functions—including Soldier Field—were privatized and three years later, in 1997, the Chicago Park District reported that private management helped produce $14 million in new revenues as well as decreased operating costs:

- Eight harbors showed a $1.2 million increase in net income since contracting with a California-based marina operator in 1995.
- Three underground parking lots in Grant Park showed a net income increase of 107 percent from $4.3 million in 1993 to $8.9 million in 1996.
- Net income from the McCormick Place underground parking lot went from $1.5 million in 1993 to $2.3 million in 1996.
- Privatized golf courses—still owned by the city but managed by Kemper Golf Course Management—posted a $279,000 increase in net income in 1996.[97]

The money saved and revenues earned by privatizing some functions of the Parks Department went into renovations and additions, such as $18.5 million for park acquisition and expansion, more than double the 1995 allocation of $8.8 million; expanding Senka Park by twelve acres and creating a new twelve-acre park in Chinatown; planting 7,000 new trees; renovating 175 ball fields; spending $10 million for new lighting; and spending on wrought-iron fencing and resurfacing projects.

More privatizations were being considered by the Parks Department: "[P]rivate industry may take over trash removal, major landscaping, road repairs, and median maintenance for Lake Shore Drive," as well as "window washing, maintenance of heating and cooling systems, technical services at Petrillo Band Shell in Grant Park and management of surface parking lots owned by the Park District." [98]

Chicago Public Schools (CPS). CPS, the city's education agency, outsourced both custodial and food services but did neither very well. Four private firms supplied 2,047 custodians to supplement the 719 custodians who worked for CPS. Large savings were achievable because the CPS custodians were only 26 percent of all custodians, but they accounted for 30 percent of the total cost. The private custodians were deployed in a curious pattern, however: 45 percent of the 624 schools were staffed only by private custodians, 9 percent only by public employees, and 46 percent by both public and private employees. In retrospect the results were predictable:

The schools with mixed staffs were the dirtiest because there was no accountability, and each group of workers blamed the other for failing to do the work.

CPS also contracted its food services, but only the management function; virtually all lower-level employees remained as CPS employees. The latter's sullen opposition to the private managers led to poor results, and the anticipated savings were not realized. This same misguided approach proved unsatisfactory in Atlanta's public schools (see below).

Public-Private Partnership for Transportation. Chicago is the nation's transportation hub and the world's third busiest intermodal hub (a transfer point between transportation modes, such as road, rail, and air), surpassed only by Hong Kong and Singapore. Mayor Daley created a partnership with the Chicago Department of Transportation, the Illinois Department of Transportation, the Association of American Railroads, and six railroads to identify critically needed improvements to the region's rail and highway transportation infrastructure. The ambitious objectives are to improve passenger rail service, reduce motorist delays, ease traffic congestion, increase safety, and provide economic, environmental, and energy benefits for the region.[99]

Other Privatized Services. Additional examples of privatized government services under Mayor Daley include copying police files, providing security at public libraries, removing graffiti, removing dead trees, providing custodial services, designing traffic signals, providing legal services, and the following:

- Contracts for drug and alcohol addiction treatment, with 200 more clients being helped at three sites instead of one for $700,000 less per year.
- Drug testing of employees of the Chicago Transit Authority.
- Dial-a-ride services for the Chicago Transit Authority.
- Purchase and distribution of office supplies by a private company, saving about $7.5 million per year.
- Water billing and collections, contracted to a private firm, saved money while increasing revenue. Moreover, the firm discovered and corrected a serious error: Chicago was losing $300,000 per year because it was still paying water bills for abandoned buildings.

Charlotte

The city of Charlotte, North Carolina, population 550,000, is one of the most successful—and little-recognized—cities in the United States in terms of its management reforms. It offers a model that can be profitably emulated by other cities large and small.

The city benefited by having two outstanding mayors, Richard Vinroot and Patrick L. McCrory, who were elected consecutively to six two-year terms from 1991 through 2003. They maintained a common focus and followed a constant path to make the city a paragon of municipal management. Their focus was a "recipe for downsizing" that had four stages:

1. A review of services and a determination of what was essential.
2. A review of the structure of city government and how it should be streamlined.
3. An evaluation of the cost of labor, the predominant expense of a public enterprise.
4. A study of privatization and its possibilities for providing a more competitive system of service delivery.[100]

In other words, privatization was the end point of a methodical process rather than the starting point as in Indianapolis and Philadelphia.

The review of services resulted in ranking the forty-one departments based on their cost-effectiveness, deficiencies, and importance—the latter as determined by citizen and employee surveys. The next stage was a major restructuring of the departments as recommended by a task force that included business executives and citizens from public, private, and academic circles. The forty-one departments were reorganized into nine "key business enterprises" (KBEs) and four "support" businesses. Departments were consolidated and many department heads were eliminated. The city initiated an early retirement program, retrained and moved employees from low-priority to high-priority KBEs, and terminated other employees. These actions reduced the workforce by 10 percent, from 4,100 to 3,700 employees.

Another task force with a similar composition reviewed the city's compensation and benefit programs and compared them to the marketplace—public and private. It recommended major changes with "broad banding" of civil service titles (that is, combining related titles to give management more flexibility in making job assignments); eliminating automatic, tenure-based, "step" pay increases within the broad bands and replacing them with performance-based pay; and sharing the cost of health-care plans with employees. These changes were put into effect and produced savings of $7 million in the first year.[101]

The Mayor's privatization task force proceeded to study privatization by establishing the criteria to evaluate which services or facilities to privatize, developing the list of privatization candidates, and presenting a timetable for action. The task force produced a list of sixteen service categories for contracting and fourteen assets or asset categories for divestment (See table 2.10). It concluded that 1,900 of the city's 4,772 city workers had jobs that could be performed by the private sector. The task force estimate of ultimate savings from implementing all the contracting recommendations was $13–$15 million annually, and the estimate of potential revenue from selling the assets was more than $1.9 billion.

Subsequently the mayor and the City Council appointed a citizens' advisory group, the Privatization/Competition Advisory Committee. The committee developed detailed guidelines for services contracting and for asset sales and other asset management approaches.[102] These were adopted by the city and used in its privatization program. The guidelines paid close attention to monitoring the performance of private contractors or city agencies that were awarded contracts under managed competitions.

In the first three years of the program, 1994–1996, the city conducted thirty-four competitions. Of these, twenty-four contracts were awarded to the city agency and ten to private contractors. By 2000 the city had achieved annual savings of $4.8 million by contracting out thirty-eight activities whose annual cost was $23.5 million; that is, the city realized savings of 20 percent. Of the thirty-eight functions contracted out, city agencies did not compete in thirty-two cases, city agencies competed and lost in five cases, and one case was a new activity, which was outsourced without competition by a city agency.

Each KBE developed a five-year plan for the services in its area that were also provided in the private sector. The plan had a timetable for subjecting each service to competition, a strategy for making its business more competitive, the reasons why a service would be retained in-house without competing, and the reasons to contract with a private firm without allowing its own unit to compete. Even the police and fire departments, often reflexively considered off-limits to privatization, identified particular functions that could

Table 2.10 Activities and Assets Recommended for Privatization in Charlotte

Services recommended for contracting	*Assets recommended for divestment*
Animal control	Airport and adjacent land
Building maintenance	Charlotte Housing Authority properties
Communication and Information services	Community development properties
Transportation Department construction and maintenance	Fire stations
Engineering	National Football League stadium land
Equipment services	Auditorium, coliseum, Independence Arena, old convention center
Finance	Parks not transferred to the county
Grounds maintenance	Vacant land
Meter maintenance and reading	Cemeteries
Police and fire communications	Wastewater treatment plants and facilities
Police records	Discovery Place
Sanitation	Government operational facilities
Special services	Government-owned land with private structures
Special transportation	Performing arts center
Wastewater and sewer construction and maintenance	
Water pumping and treatment	

Source: Richard Vinroot, "A Recipe for Downsizing Government: The Charlotte Story," in *The New Public Management: Lessons from Innovating Governors and Mayors,* ed. Paul J. Andrisani, Simon Hakim, and E. S. Savas (Boston: Kluwer Academic Publishers, 2002), 166. Reprinted with kind permission of Springer Science and Business Media.

be put up for competitive bidding. The resulting five-year competition plan for fiscal 2001–2005 listed sixty-five city services with an annual cost of $71 million and 825 employees to be opened up to competition.

With respect to asset divestment, the city examined its 1,100 city-owned properties following the committee guidelines. The city identified 162 surplus and marketable properties and sold 125 of them for a total of $15 million between 1995 and 1999.[103]

The city's emphasis on competition changed the day-to-day behavior of city workers. They constantly looked for ways to reduce costs and improve services, and by applying lessons learned from the private contractors they achieved savings of $2.4 million in other services that had not been formally subjected to competition.[104]

The most significant contribution from Charlotte is the policy statement and goal for service contracting that the Privatization/Competition Advisory Committee developed and the City Council adopted. Mayor McCrory summed it up as follows: "The city will seek the best service at the lowest cost either through city forces or the private sector. A competitive procurement process will determine who the service provider will be." [105]

Milwaukee

In Milwaukee Mayor John Norquist reacted to perennial complaints from city agencies about the city's computer services. Information systems were delivered late and over budget. Department heads were at the mercy of the city's computer managers, who decided what development projects to fund and when to carry them out. Norquist did not merely contract out the service. He gave every city agency a budget for computer services and let each one choose anybody it wanted to do the work, the city's computer agency or outside vendors. For the first few years most agencies used outside providers, but the in-house unit improved its performance under the threat of bureaucratic extinction and started winning back customers.

Milwaukee also signed a ten-year contract in 1998 with the New Jersey–based United Water Services for the operation and maintenance of its two large wastewater treatment plants (300 million gallons per day each), its regional sewage collection pipes and storage system, and its biosolids (sludge) plant that produces fertilizer. It is the largest wastewater treatment system under private management in the United States, serving 1.2 million residents. According to a two-year study, the agreement is expected to save local ratepayers more than $160 million, a cost savings of 30 percent compared with public operation; user fees have already been reduced by 16.5 percent. The fees are expected to be unchanged for the first four years and to increase only at the rate of inflation thereafter. The agency received the 1998 annual award of the National Council for Public-Private Partnerships as one of the country's best projects.

The winning contractor, one of four bidders, agreed that no current employees would be laid off during the term of the contract, and that compensation and benefits would equal or exceed the current package. This agreement may seem incompatible with such large savings at first glance, but it is both rational and commonplace: Normal attrition over the period will create openings that will not be filled, as private firms can usually operate such facilities with about half the size of the usual municipal workforce. That is also why private operators give more training to their employees and can pay higher wages. Other savings are generally achieved through more efficient use of chemicals and electricity, better maintenance, and more automation. In addition to the cost savings, an independent audit conducted for Milwaukee by a Seattle district sewage manager in 2003 concluded that "[t]he treatment performance levels place the system in the top rank of systems in the nation." [106]

Workplace accidents decreased by 60 percent in the first year of the contract, and grievances declined by a third. Employees became eligible for bonuses and training opportunities at the contractor's other operations throughout the country.

An unusual feature of this contract is the pension arrangement. Approved by the Internal Revenue Service and the U.S. Department of Labor, the employees remain part of Milwaukee's public employee pension fund, with the contractor making contributions to the city.

Atlanta

In 1993 Atlanta mayor Bill Campbell signed an agreement with municipal workers that—regardless of the cost to taxpayers—he would not contract or subcontract work done by present employees, except in the case of a financial emergency.[107] But in 1998 the Atlanta Board of Education, which was independent of the mayor, requested proposals to outsource the school system's $22.3 million, 60,000-student cafeteria services. The board did not want to repeat the $2 million subsidies made to the program in 1993 and 1997.[108] The board also sought a proposal from the cafeteria workers, asking them to design a plan for running the services.

The possibility of any privatization met with fierce opposition. Several weeks before proposals were due, cafeteria workers and clergy members picketed the Board of Education's meeting, and Rev. Timothy McDonald threatened to disrupt school business if necessary. The protesters felt that if services were handed over to a private company, the "lunch ladies . . . [who] play surrogate mother, teacher, and police officer to the children" would be out of work.[109] Another concern was that the quantity of food served and the number of children eating hot breakfasts and lunches would decline.

The privatization went through but with crippling modifications. The vote by the Board of Education called for the negotiation of only a one-year management contract with a private company, Aramark, which beat offers from the current managers and another company. Moreover, under the contract the cooks and "lunch ladies" would keep their jobs, although mid- and upper-level employees were given no such guarantees. Nevertheless, this meant that Aramark was denied full management control.

The Philadelphia-based food service company took over the Atlanta Public School (APS) food system in October 1999 in a joint venture with Gourmet Services, a local, minority-owned food service company. The contract reduced food costs by more than $1 million a year. Seven months later, in May 2000, APS renewed the contract with Aramark-Gourmet Foods despite numerous shortcomings in the contractor's performance. APS wanted to give the contractor more time, and the contractor, admitting to start-up problems, corrected some of the problems by revising the menus, marketing the food program more aggressively to students, and giving more training to workers.[110]

The fundamental problem was that the city signed a meal-rate contract but administered it as a management-fee contract. The meal-rate contract is used when the school system wants to outsource its entire food service; payment then consists of a fee for each meal served. On the other hand, in a management-fee contract APS would buy only the management function and would purchase the food and retain and manage the public employees. Because of the violent opposition to the meal-rate contract as originally negotiated, APS backed down, kept all its employees on the payroll, and supervised them with its own personnel. (The employees, some of them representing the third generation of their families working in APS cafeterias and with children in the schools, considered their jobs permanent family property.) The APS manager of the contract further compounded the problem. She opposed and resented the contract and felt that she had been demoted; she refused to exercise her new monitoring duties and undermined the arrangement. By the time she was reassigned, the damage had been done. This perverse arrangement persisted until 2003, and it is no wonder that the expected savings did not materialize. In essence, APS was not fully committed to this program; political will is essential for successful privatization.

Wastewater Treatment. Mayor Campbell soon lost his initial antipathy toward privatization when he was confronted with state mandates that required

Atlanta to expand and upgrade its three main wastewater treatment plants. This meant almost $1 billion for immediate capital improvements that translated into an 81 percent increase in water rates, an unacceptably huge jump. Therefore the mayor reluctantly announced in 1997 that the city would explore privatization as a last alternative. A private firm would maintain and operate the plants under a long-term contract and provide the capital to undertake the massive upgrade. The city proceeded prudently and engaged the best technical, financial, and legal support at a cost of $2 million. After a two-year battle with opponents, the city entered into a twenty-year public-private partnership with United Water Services (UWS) at an annual cost of $23.3 million, some $2 million less than the next lowest bidder. The city expected to save about $400 million over the twenty years. UWS agreed to a no-layoff policy for the 535 affected employees and took over operations in 1999.[111] This was hailed as the largest water privatization deal in the country.

Only four years later, however, a new mayor, Shirley Franklin, ended the partnership. The city complained of insufficient maintenance, poor bill collection, tardy meter installations, and UWS's request for more money. The contractor said that its operating costs had soared because of misinformation from the city: The number of water meter failures was ten times the reported number, 11,108 in a year instead of 1,171; there were 270 water main breaks in a year instead of 101; 1,633 hydrants needed repair in a year instead of 734. The system was in far worse shape than the city had let on. In retrospect the contactor can be faulted for not investigating the condition of the system more thoroughly and directly instead of accepting the city's assertions.[112]

The fact remains, however, that dissolving the partnership raised the city's annual cost to $40 million instead of the $22 million it was paying the contractor.[113] It remains to be seen if putting the system back under city management, at almost twice the price, will improve performance—which was poor before privatization. The city may have to triple its sewage bills to cover this increased cost and to pay for a $3 billion upgrade mandated by the Environmental Protection Agency.[114] Perhaps because of this looming cost crisis, proposals have surfaced to privatize Atlanta's giant Hartsfield International Airport.[115]

Much less contentious than the school and water privatizations were the privatizations of golf courses, tennis courts, and recycling, and the contract with Professional Probation Services to collect delinquent traffic court fines and to monitor community service and rehabilitation programs of offenders on probation.[116]

Washington, D.C.

Washington, D.C., pioneered a high-tech approach to red-light running, the cause of numerous traffic fatalities that put the city among the top twenty in the country in this category. Under Mayor Anthony Williams, the Metropolitan Police Department partnered with Lockheed Martin IMS to implement a red light photo enforcement program. Cameras connected to the traffic lights and vehicle sensors photograph a vehicle and its license plate in the act of driving through a red light. IMS handles all aspects of the program: installation, image processing, identifying vehicle owners, issuing notices, and collecting fines.[117] New York later adopted this program (see below).

Mayor Williams' Washington also became the first city in the nation to privatize its parking meter operations. Due to vandalism, half the city's forty-year-old, on-street meters became inoperable in 1996–1997, reducing revenue by 80 percent from $1 million a year to $200,000 and leaving thousands of headless meters as eyesores in the nation's capital. Lockheed Martin IMS, the city's private partner, installed newly designed, advanced meters that were more convenient for users and nearly impregnable; at any given time, 99 percent were operable. The contractor is responsible for all operations and maintenance under the city's policy control and gives the city a revenue guarantee.[118]

Mayor Williams' shining moment was his fight for school vouchers, a heresy among Democrats and anathema to the teachers' unions. The performance of the schools in Washington, D.C., was very poor despite very high spending per child. The U.S. Congress voted funds for a program that enables 1,700 poor children to attend private schools; President George W. Bush signed the bill in 2004.

Summary

Competitive contracting is the most common form of municipal privatization and has been growing since the 1970s regardless of the political affiliation of elected officials. Between 1982 and 1992 contracting increased by 121 percent in the 596 cities where comparable data were available. The average common municipal service is contracted out by 27 percent of cities.

Cities privatize first to save money and second to improve services. A summary of nine major, comprehensive studies covering every contract entered into by the reporting jurisdictions—7,168 contracts in all—showed average savings of 29.5 percent. These studies included federal, state, county, and city governments in the United States, the United Kingdom, and Australia. Cross-sectional studies corroborate these findings, as do many other studies, although every privatization is site specific.

Mayor Stephen Goldsmith gained national and international attention for his successful efforts in Indianapolis. He used public-private competition to bring about large improvements in street repairs, wastewater treatment, fleet management, solid-waste collection, airport management, golf courses, and a federal facility that designed and produced military electronics. All in all he put eighty-six services out to bid, of which city employees won 43 percent—but only by drastically improving their productivity. The number of employees declined by a third but no union members lost jobs, and the city projected cumulative savings of $450 million.

Phoenix is another major success story, with cost savings of 24 percent in fifty-six vigorously contested public-private competitions, of which the city agencies won twenty-two (39 percent). Philadelphia, Chicago, Charlotte, Milwaukee, Atlanta, and Washington, D.C., also undertook major privatizations. Some projects encountered problems because they were not designed or managed well. In particular, both Chicago and Atlanta outsourced the food service in their public schools but, by contracting only for management of the service while retaining their entire operating staffs, they failed to achieve the expected savings.

Privatization efforts are misguided if applied to unpromising candidates and can fail when competition is absent, elementary safeguards are ignored, and necessary political will is lacking.

Notes

1. Government Contracting Institute, www.ucg.com/govt.
2. E. S. Savas, *Privatization: The Key to Better Government* (Chatham, N.J.: Chatham House Publishers, 1987).
3. As the recipient of a $1 million grant (competitively awarded) from the National Science Foundation to study alternative service delivery, the author subcontracted with ICMA and worked with them to design and conduct a telephone survey of solid waste services in 1,378 cities. The survey resulted ultimately in responses from all but one city. See E. S. Savas, "Policy Analysis for Local Government: Public vs. Private Refuse Collection," *Policy Analysis* 3, no. 1 (winter 1977): 49–74.

4. Jeffrey D. Greene, "How Much Privatization?" *Policy Studies Journal* 24, no. 4 (1996): 632–640.
5. Robin A. Johnson and Norman Walzer, "Privatization and Managed Competition: Management Fad or Long-Term Systematic Change for Cities?" in *Local Government Innovation,* ed. Johnson and Walzer (Westport, Conn.: Quorum Books, 2000), 172.
6. Rowan Miranda and Karlyn Andersen, "Alternative Service Delivery in Local Government, 1982–1992," in *Municipal Year Book 1994* (Washington, D.C.: International City-County Management Association), 26–35.
7. Jeffrey D. Greene, *Cities and Privatization: Prospects for the New Century* (Upper Saddle River, N.J.: Prentice Hall, 2002), 159–162, appendix B.
8. Different studies count municipal services differently; in this instance the first study counted sixty-four common municipal services, whereas the second study counted forty-seven. Robert Jay Dilger, Randolph R. Moffett, and Linda Struyk, "Privatization of Municipal Services in America's Largest Cities," *Public Administration Review* 57, no. 1 (1997): 21–26.
9. Letter from City Manager Dave Morgan to the mayor and City Council of Anaheim, Calif., December 24, 2002.
10. Winnie Hu, "New Yorkers Love to Complain, and Hot Line Takes Advantage," *New York Times,* December 1, 2003, A1.
11. Dilger, Moffett, and Struyk, "Privatization of Municipal Services."
12. Miranda and Andersen, "Alternative Service Delivery."
13. Touche Ross, *Privatization in America* (Washington, D.C.: Touche Ross, 1987).
14. International City Management Association, *Service Delivery in the 1990s: Alternative Approaches for Local Government* (Washington, D.C.: 1989).
15. Dilger, Moffett, and Struyk, "Privatization of Municipal Services."
16. E. S. Savas, *Privatization and Public-Private Partnerships* (New York: Chatham House, 2000), 149–153.
17. E. S. Savas, "Public and Private Refuse Collection: A Critical Look at the Evidence," *Journal of Urban Analysis* 6 (1979): 1–13.
18. Barbara J. Stevens, *Delivering Municipal Services Efficiently: A Comparison of Municipal and Private Service Delivery* (Washington, D.C.: U.S. Department of Housing and Urban Development, 1984), 544.
19. Barbara J. Stevens, "Comparing Public- and Private-Sector Productive Efficiency: An Analysis of Eight Activities," *National Productivity Review* 3, no. 4 (August 1984): 405.

20. "The Top Fifty Cities," *City and State,* November 19, 1990.
21. John F. Kennedy School of Government, "Organizing Competition in Indianapolis: Mayor Stephen Goldsmith and the Quest for Lower Costs," case C18-95-1269.0 (case A), 1995, 2–3.
22. Ibid., 6.
23. Ibid., 4.
24. The basis for much of this material is John F. Kennedy School of Government, "Organizing Competition in Indianapolis: Mayor Stephen Goldsmith and the Quest for Lower Costs," cases C18-95-1270.0 (case B) and C18-95-1270.1 (sequel), 1995.
25. Savas, *Privatization: The Key to Better Government,* 268.
26. The author's personal knowledge when he was first deputy city administrator of New York.
27. Jon Jeter, "A Winning Combination in Indianapolis," *Washington Post,* September 21, 1997, A3.
28. John F. Kennedy School of Government, "Organizing Competition in Indianapolis," case C18-95-1270.0, 4.
29. Ibid.
30. John F. Kennedy School of Government, "Organizing Competition in Indianapolis," case C18-95-1270.0 (case B).
31. John F. Kennedy School of Government, "Organizing Competition in Indianapolis," case C18-95-1270.1 (sequel).
32. Ibid.
33. Stephen Goldsmith, *The Twenty-First Century City: Resurrecting Urban America* (Washington, D.C.: Regnery, 1997), 199–211.
34. City of Indianapolis, "Goldsmith Announces Savings from Wastewater Privatization," press release, August 5, 1999.
35. White River Environmental Partnership, *City of Indianapolis Contract Operations of the AWT Facilities and Collection System, 5th Year Summary of Activities,* (Indianapolis: 1999).
36. Goldsmith, *Twenty-First Century City.*
37. Ibid.
38. Elliott D. Sclar, *You Don't Always Get What You Pay For: The Economics of Privatization* (Ithaca: Cornell University Press, 2000), 136–138.
39. John F. Kennedy School of Government, "Preparing a Public Sector Bid: Indianapolis Fleet Services Meets Private Competition," case C08-96-1323.0, 1996.
40. Ibid.

41. "Indianapolis Employees Win Fleet Maintenance Contract," *Public Works,* June 1996, 58.
42. Sclar, *You Don't Always Get What You Pay For,* 143–144.
43. Ibid., 239.
44. Jeter, "Winning Combination."
45. Ibid., 240.
46. E. S. Savas, "The Institutional Structure of Local Government Services: A Conceptual Model," *Public Administration Review* 38 (October/November 1978): 412–419.
47. John F. Kennedy School of Government, "Organizing Competition in Indianapolis," case C18-95-1270.1 (sequel).
48. Ibid.
49. Michael Yoder, "Competition in the Provision of Municipal Services," report prepared for the city of Indianapolis, July 1995.
50. The information in this section comes primarily from Goldsmith, *Twenty-First Century City.*
51. "Goldsmith Declares for Indiana Governor," *Public Works Financing,* June 1996, 16; "Cities Survey," *Economist,* July 29, 1995, 17.
52. Dennis Rosebrough, "Indianapolis International Airport: A Success Story," in *To Market, To Market: Reinventing Indianapolis,* ed. Ingrid Ritchie and Sheila Suess Kennedy (Lanham, Md.: University Press of America, 2001), 404.
53. "Goldsmith Declares for Governor," *Public Works Financing.*
54. Jack Miller, "Privatizing the City's Golf Courses," in *To Market, To Market,* 404.
55. Yoder, "Competition."
56. Ritchie and Kennedy, *To Market, To Market.*
57. Daniel Mullins and C. Kurt Zorn, "Privatization in Indianapolis: A Closer Look at Savings and the Wastewater Treatment Facility," *In-Roads* 1, no. 3 (1996): 9–21.
58. "Goldsmith's Glitter," *Economist,* August 31, 1996, 26; John Straus, "A Lasting Legacy," *Indianapolis Star,* December 26, 1999, 1.
59. Neal Thompson and Gady A. Epstein, "City Budget Savings Claimed in Midwest," *Baltimore Sun,* April 19, 2001.
60. Adapted from Goldsmith, *Twenty-First Century City,* 221–229.
61. Ibid., 238–239.
62. Russ Pulliam, "Goldsmith Legacy as a Pioneer," *Indianapolis Star,* December 26, 1999.
63. Straus, "A Lasting Legacy."

64. William M. Stern, "We Got Real Efficient Real Quick," *Forbes,* June 10, 1994, 43.
65. Jeter, "Winning Combination."
66. William D. Eggers and Stephen Goldsmith, "This Works: Managing City Finances," *Civic Bulletin No. 31,* New York: Manhattan Institute, 2003.
67. Jim Flanagan and Susan Perkins, "Public-Private Competition in the City of Phoenix," *Government Finance Review,* June 1995, 7–12.
68. E. S. Savas, "An Empirical Study of Competition in Municipal Service Delivery," *Public Administration Review* 37, no. 6 (November/December 1977): 717–724.
69. Suzanne Denise Miller, "Public-Private Competition: The Case of Phoenix" (Ph.D. diss., University of Chicago, 1996), 13.
70. Ronald W. Jensen, "A Wave of Privatization Efforts," in *Restructuring State and Local Services: Ideas, Proposals, and Experiments,* ed. Arnold H. Raphaelson (Westport, Conn.: Praeger Publishers, 1998), 65–72.
71. Jensen, "Wave of Privatization."
72. Flanagan and Perkins, "Public-Private Competition."
73. Ibid.
74. City of Phoenix, "Public/Private Competitive Process Overview," undated report by the City Auditor Department; Miller, "Public-Private Competition," 14.
75. Ibid.
76. Flanagan and Perkins, "Public-Private Competition."
77. Ron Jensen, "A New Approach to Managed Competition," *Privatization Watch* 304 (April 2002): 2.
78. Robert J. Franciosi, *Garbage In, Garbage Out: An Examination of Private/Public Competition by the City of Phoenix* (Phoenix: Goldwater Institute, 1998), 6.
79. City of Phoenix, "Public/Private Competitive Process Overview."
80. Flanagan and Perkins, "Public-Private Competition."
81. City of Phoenix, "Fire," City Manager's Executive Report, June 2004.
82. Robert J. Franciosi, *Carrots and Measuring Sticks: A Survey of State of the Art Contracting in Arizona* (Phoenix: Goldwater Institute, 2000), 16–18.
83. Franciosi, *Carrots and Measuring Sticks.*
84. Reason Public Policy Institute, "How Does Your City Stack Up? First-Ever Study Measures How Well Government Services Are Delivered in Nation's Largest Cities," Los Angeles, Calif., April 23, 2001, http://phoenix.gov/BUDGET/01budexc.html, August 28, 2004.

85. The information reported here was obtained from various academic, professional, and journalistic sources; it was not verified independently and apparently no critical evaluations were conducted.
86. Edward G. Rendell, "Competitive Contracting: The Philadelphia Story," in *Making Government Work: Lessons from America's Governors and Mayors,* ed. Paul J. Andrisani, Simon Hakim, and Eva Leeds (Lanham, Md.: Rowman and Littlefield, 2000), 223–231.
87. Ibid.
88. Ibid., 229.
89. Ibid.
90. National Center for Policy Analysis, "Idea House, Privatization in Chicago," www.ncpa.org/pd/private/privb3.html, July 31, 2003.
91. Richard Daley, address to the Financial Resource and Advisory Committee, September 22, 1997, www.cityofchicago.org/Mayor2/speeches/AddressToFRAC.html, July 24, 2003.
92. Ibid.
93. Fran Spielman. "New O'Hare Parking Firm Plans Service Improvement," *Chicago Sun-Times,* October 9, 1993, 10.
94. Fran Spielman, "Midway Airport Parking Going Private," *Chicago Sun-Times,* October 8, 1996, 2.
95. Adrienne Drell, "Soldier Field May Get Private Operator," *Chicago Sun-Times,* November 1, 1993, 1.
96. Adrienne Drell, "Park District Privatization Pays Off," *Chicago Sun-Times,* September 2, 1996, 6.
97. Adrienne Dell, "Lakefront Privatization a $12 Million Boon for Parks," *Chicago Sun-Times,* March 12, 1997, 3.
98. Adrienne Drell, "Park Budget Would Privatize More Jobs," *Chicago Sun-Times,* November 3, 1993, 17.
99. National Council for Public-Private Partnerships, *Case Studies from across the United States* (Washington, D.C.: 2003), 37.
100. Richard Vinroot, "A Recipe for Downsizing Government: The Charlotte Story," in *The New Public Management: Lessons from Innovating Governors and Mayors,* ed. Paul J. Andrisani, Simon Hakim, and E. S. Savas (Boston: Kluwer Academic Publishers, 2002), 157–166.
101. Ibid.
102. Jack Sommer, "Reprivatizing Charlotte Municipal Constitutional Economics," paper presented at the Southern Economic Association Conference, Atlanta, Ga., November 21–23, 1997.

103. Patrick McCrory, "Managed Competition in Charlotte," in Andrisani, Hakim, and Leeds, *Making Government Work,* 192.
104. McCrory, "Managed Competition," 185–209.
105. McCrory, "Managed Competition."
106. Ted Balaker, "Milwaukee Water Contractor Scores Well on Audit," *Privatization Watch* 28, no. 2 (2004): 4.
107. John Sherman, "Mayor's Deal May Have Cost Taxpayers Millions," *Atlanta Business Chronicle,* October 27, 2000.
108. "Privatization Bidding Starts," *Atlanta Journal and Constitution,* December 31, 1998, 6JD.
109. "Minister Vows to Stop Cafeteria Contract," *Atlanta Journal and Constitution,* March 11, 1999, 8JD
110. Rochelle Carter, "Board Retains Cafeteria Caterers," *Atlanta Journal and Constitution,* May 11, 2000, 4JD.
111. Bill Campbell, "A Bold, Innovative Approach to Privatization: Lessons Learned from Atlanta," in Johnson and Walzer, *Local Government Innovation,* 237–252.
112. Geoffrey Segal, "Issue Analysis: The Atlanta Water Privatization; What Can We Learn?" Georgia Public Policy Foundation, Atlanta, January 24, 2003; Segal, "Water Privatization: Learning from Atlanta," *Privatization Watch* 28, no. 2 (2004): 2–14.
113. Douglas Gehl, "As Cities Move to Privatize Water, Atlanta Steps Back," *New York Times,* February 10, 2003, A14.
114. Robert W. Poole Jr., "Airport Privatization," *Privatization Watch* 2, no. 2 (2004): 9.
115. Ibid.
116. Atlanta contracted with a joint venture, Browning-Ferris Industries and DreamSan, that charges residents $30 a year to collect their recyclable materials. Atlanta gets a cut of the $30, which adds up to a yearly profit of about $100,000 that goes to education and public information.
117. National Council for Public-Private Partnerships, *Case Studies,* 15.
118. Ibid., 16.

3 | Evolution of Privatization in New York

Privatization evolved slowly in New York City, but it had deep roots. In colonial times private parties provided what are today called municipal services and infrastructure. The first water supply system in New York was developed by the ancestor of Chase Bank; in fact, the current logo of the bank, an octagon, represents a cross-section of the original wooden water main. Thomas Edison's company installed the first electric power system, and its successor still provides electricity. This chapter summarizes the history of some highly visible city services and then moves ahead to recent times to discuss the pre-Giuliani period and the emerging groundwork for privatization.

Private Provision of Municipal Services in Early New York

In early New York the private sector provided most of the municipal services. The government assumed many of these services during the Great Depression and after World War II, when the command-and-control mindset carried over to civil affairs. This section reviews the evolution of fire protection, solid waste management, and local transportation.

Fire Protection

Fire protection in New York was a public-private partnership from the outset. Private volunteers did the work but the city government provided the fire equipment. In 1648 the Dutch colonial government of New Amsterdam appointed four eminent citizens—unpaid, part-time volunteers—as fire wardens, an office that was to survive more than 200 years. Their initial job was to visit every home and inspect chimneys for fire hazards. (In 1697 the fire wardens became the first persons to be remunerated for specific fire duties, retaining half the fines paid by property owners for violating the fire laws.) The city government paid for firefighting equipment; it imposed a one-time charge on homeowners so the city could purchase water buckets. The city issued what today would be called a request for proposal to make the leather buckets, and it contracted with two shoemakers who had bid for the work. Homeowners were required to keep three full buckets of water on their doorsteps after sundown to be used to fight fires in the neighborhood.[1]

This system worked for a time, but as more and more houses burned down people demanded better. In 1658 the government hired eight watchmen, each armed with a musket, pistol, sword, and a huge rattle. Called "prowlers," they patrolled the streets at night and were the first police department. Fire protection was added to their duties, and they—not the fire wardens—became the nucleus of the civic firefighting force. They had custody of the leather buckets and the hooks and small ladders for fighting fires. When a prowler discovered a fire he would sound the alarm with his rattle. Awakened citizens would grab their buckets and everyone would help fight the blaze.

This system, too, proved inadequate, and a volunteer fire department was formally organized in 1737. (Paid employees did not replace the volunteers until 1865.) Thirty "strong, able, discreet, honest and sober" men were appointed for "the care, management, working, and using of the fire engines and other tools and instruments for the extinguishing of fires" and "ready at a call by night and by day." [2] The volunteers were subject to rules and regulations and had to pay penalties for breaking them. The volunteers' typical occupations were blacksmith, carpenter, cooper (barrel maker), baker, bricklayer, cordwainer (shoemaker), gunsmith, cartman, and rope maker. An incentive to volunteer was exemption from some public duties, such as serving on juries and in the militia. At about the same time it became compulsory for citizens to help at fires, a practice that continues to this day in fighting forest fires in the West.

The overseer of fire engines was in effect the director of fire protection. He took charge of the volunteer force at fires and received ten pounds a year to "take Care of the fire Engines . . . to keep them Clean and in good Repair upon his own Cost and Charges. . . ." [3] The fire engines were pumps on wheels that were dragged to the fire by the firefighters and pumped manually to spray water.

Benjamin Franklin founded the colonies' first fire insurance company in 1752, in Philadelphia, and New York's first was formed in 1787 after independence. The great fire of 1835 drove twenty-three of the city's twenty-six fire insurance firms into bankruptcy.[4] Allied with the volunteer firefighters, private fire insurance firms provided fire protection during much of the nineteenth century. They affixed identifying plaques to the outside walls of their subscribers' buildings and protected those buildings while fighting rival units in their spare time. Whereas pillars of the community once staffed the volunteer fire companies, by the middle of the nineteenth century the companies had become little more than gangs of ruffians protected by Tammany Hall, the corrupt political machine that controlled the city government. Corrupt politicians took over financial control of the fire department and stole money by making large, padded expenditures—with corrupt kickbacks—for fire equipment and services and elaborate firehouses.

The fire insurance companies complained about large fire losses in the city, a consequence of the deteriorating performance of the volunteer fire companies. And the police complained about riots and fights between volunteer fire companies. Republicans complained about the blatant corruption of the Democrats in Tammany Hall. In 1865 this confluence of forces caused the Republican-dominated state government to emulate Boston, Baltimore, St. Louis, and Cincinnati by creating a professional fire department staffed by paid city employees to replace the volunteer department.

Solid Waste Management

By 1676, a full century before the Revolutionary War, private contractors were cleaning the streets of New York. Their equipment: pigs. Most waste in the streets was edible garbage, and pigs were the tool of choice to clean it up. (Pigs and goats perform this function in some developing countries to this day.) The contractors carried out a work stoppage that year, complaining that their fees were too low. To the author's knowledge, this was the city's earliest example of both privatization and a strike in a municipal service.

Pigs gave way to "solid waste management" by the nineteenth century. A public official, the superintendent of scavengers, was appointed in 1803 to oversee the cleaning of public streets and grounds. (Refuse collection was still secondary to street cleaning.) For the next seventy-eight years the city tried several schemes, including contracting for street cleaning and refuse collection. Horse-drawn transportation, however, left the city streets foul and fetid, and in 1881 the Department of Street Cleaning—a forerunner of the Department of Sanitation—was established as a separate entity within the city government.[5]

When the five boroughs were consolidated into Greater New York in 1898, street cleaning, refuse collection, and refuse disposal became the responsibility of the Department of Street Cleaning. In Manhattan and the Bronx, city personnel using hired, privately owned wagons performed these functions. In Brooklyn all collection and disposal was by contract. Queens and Richmond, being largely undeveloped, used hired men and wagons when necessary.

In 1902 Queens and Richmond placed their collection and disposal activities under the jurisdiction of the respective borough president's office, whereas city personnel took over Brooklyn's activities. In the same year the city stopped collecting waste from large manufacturing and commercial properties in Manhattan, Brooklyn, and the Bronx because of the shortage of city facilities and resources to handle the growing volume of waste. In 1916 the Department of Street Cleaning stopped collecting waste from all commercial buildings in Manhattan, Brooklyn, and the Bronx; municipal service was provided for residential buildings and for business establishments in such buildings in these boroughs. Queens and Richmond, however, served all residences and businesses, doing so with contracts to private carters.

The present Department of Sanitation (DOS) was created in 1929 by combining the functions of the Department of Street Cleaning in Manhattan, Brooklyn, and the Bronx and taking over contract carting in Queens and Richmond. The policy of free sanitation service for all business establishments in Queens and Richmond, despite its patent unfairness, remained until 1948, when the city established a uniform code to exclude all DOS services from exclusively business properties.

Eight years later, in 1956, DOS stopped collecting refuse from business establishments in residential buildings (primarily retail stores). This affected 52,000 establishments that had to turn to private carters, enlarging the carters' customer volume from 70,000 to 122,000. At the same time, Local Law 29 established the city's regulatory authority over the private carting industry for removal of trade waste (waste from commercial activities).

For years, however, the carting industry was tied to local racketeers and ridden with collusive, anticompetitive arrangements and extortionary practices. Mayor Giuliani finally cleaned it up in the late 1990s. Today the newly cleansed industry, composed primarily of national firms, has enlarged its role, as discussed in later chapters.

Local Transportation

In early America transportation was a private activity, like most communal services. The first ferry in the city began operating to Brooklyn in 1642. By the 1820s New York state had more than 200 private road companies, which together owned 4,000 miles of toll highways.[6] There were also innumerable private bridges and ferries. Land transportation was by privately owned, horse-drawn carriages, and there was no government involvement, although streets were maintained at public expense. Public money was also used to build the Erie Canal and to develop New York harbor—farsighted investments in transportation infrastructure that firmly established New York as the nation's commercial capital.[7]

Virtually everyone walked to work, but the distances got longer as the city grew. Seeing a need, an entrepreneur introduced the "omnibus" ("for everyone") in New York in 1827. Resembling a stagecoach, it was a twelve-passenger, horse-drawn vehicle that picked up and deposited passengers along a fixed route for a fare of 12.5 cents.[8] This was America's first fixed-route urban transportation service, in contrast to the for-hire hack, and represented the founding of the U.S. transit industry.[9]

"Urban mass transit" made its world debut in New York City five years later, in 1832, when the New York and Harlem Railroad Company introduced the horsecar, a thirty-passenger wheeled vehicle that rode on rails along Fourth (now Park) Avenue, pulled by a team of horses whose driver was called a teamster. The city's Common Council approved installation of the rails, which allowed the horses to achieve speeds considered breathtaking at the time. An extensive network of street railways was soon developed. Sociologists would later note that mass transit made class segregation possible as servants no longer had to live near their masters. Later, it became a great equalizer, as all classes and races used it. (In recent years, however, the wealthy have been abandoning mass transit, thus leading to segregation by income.)

The next major transit advance in New York was the world's first elevated rapid transit line (rapid because it was separated from other traffic, unlike the street railway), established in 1868 by the privately owned West Side and Yonkers Patent Railway, which was soon taken over by the Manhattan Elevated Railroad Company. Initially, propulsion was by cable from stationary steam engines, but soon this system was replaced by steam locomotives, which could not be used for street railways because they frightened the horses and endangered other users of the streets. The fare was five cents in the morning and evening, ten cents at other times. Thus began the nickel fare, which was to last far into the next century.

Discovery of electricity and its development into a clean and easily managed power source revolutionized transportation. By 1903 New York's elevated lines had been fully electrified. They totaled 189 miles and were all privately financed, built, owned, and operated. In the meantime, the electric streetcar was developed and by the 1890s had all but eliminated horsecars. Street railway companies boomed and rapidly extended their lines, which shaped the entire nation's urban and suburban districts, reaching their peak mileage in 1917.[10] Profits from real-estate development at the outer ends of lines contributed significantly to the financial success of the street railway companies. In time, electric trolley buses and buses with gasoline or diesel engines replaced almost all the streetcars. New, private companies usually introduced these buses, although some existing companies were able to adopt the new technology.

The city's formal involvement with rapid transit began in 1875, when the state legislature authorized the mayor to appoint temporary, special-purpose, rapid-transit commissions. These were empowered to define elevated transit routes, obtain the consent of owners of abutting property for construction of the lines, and arrange for the sale of franchises to private corporations that would build, own, and operate the lines in exchange for retaining the nickel fare and making annual payments to the city. Although these temporary commissions were to promote rapid transit, they were not authorized to provide transit services directly, to monitor the performance of private operators, nor even to maintain a permanent professional staff capable of evaluating service and planning improvements.[11]

In 1894, after a decade of vigorous debate in which the *New York Times*, among many others, opposed municipal expenditures for rapid transit, the government passed legislation that for the first time allowed municipal investment in, but not operation of, rapid transit. A new Rapid Transit Commission, by now a permanent body, was dominated by the Chamber of Commerce, whose members were assigned six of the eight seats. The limits on the legislation revealed city residents' philosophical opposition to local government going into business, not to mention their distrust of local government after the Boss Tweed era and lack of confidence in the government's operational skills. But the widely perceived need for an underground rapid rail system and the private sector's unwillingness to bear the entire financial risk of building a subway were enough to justify a larger role for government in transportation.[12]

In 1900 the city awarded a contract for the construction and operation of its first subway. In essence, the contractor got a low-interest, long-term loan from the city to build the subway; the contractor would provide all the necessary equipment and operate the subway on a fifty-year franchise, paying off the loan with interest while maintaining the sacrosanct nickel fare. Thus was founded the Interborough Rapid Transit Company (IRT), which began service in 1904 to great acclaim.[13]

New lines followed quickly, but by the mid-1920s the situation had changed drastically. The Brooklyn Rapid Transit Company had gone bankrupt after a serious accident on its subway line and was reorganized as the Brooklyn-Manhattan Transit Company (BMT), in which four-fifths of the employees owned stock. Extending new subway lines proved very costly to the city, which reneged on certain agreements, and the private companies could not make ends meet as long as fares were kept at five cents. Political agitation started for the city to take over and operate the private subways. A report endorsed by Mayor John Hylan in 1925 sounds amusingly ingenuous today:

> There can be no question but that under municipal operation the income from our subways will not only provide for all operating and maintenance expenses, depreciation, and interest on investment, but furnish substantial sums for the construction of future subways.[14]

The city built the Eighth Avenue subway in 1930 but received no satisfactory bid for private operation under its conditions, which included a nickel fare; therefore, for the first time the city entered into the business of operating a subway, the Independent System (IND). Soon after, in 1940, the city took over the BMT and the IRT when these could no longer operate under the city's financial constraints, namely, the five-cent fare. Thus the city became the owner and operator of all subway and elevated lines.

In the 1940s the city began taking over private ferries and bus lines as well; many of the buses had replaced earlier streetcar lines. Only a handful of privately operated local bus lines remained in the city, mostly survivors of the fifty or so that existed in the 1920s and 1930s, and they were kept in business only by public subsidies. By 2005 the city's responsibility for subway and bus operations, including those remaining local bus routes, had been turned over entirely to a state entity, the Metropolitan Transportation Authority (MTA).

The mass transit system that was essentially private as recently as 1930 is now entirely publicly owned and operated. This inversion of historical roles is remarkable. The impassioned resistance to government involvement in the transportation business (because it was considered a commercial activity) that characterized the decade-long debate in the late nineteenth century gradually gave way to a new public philosophy at the opposite extreme. Modern rhetoric might describe this still-reigning philosophy as distrust of the private sector, disdain for market mechanisms, contempt for the profit motive, trust in the efficacy of centralized control, belief that "government can do it cheaper because it doesn't make a profit," and the attitude that transportation is a public utility that everyone has a right to use at public expense. As this transformation proceeded, it gained adherents from the swelling ranks of new beneficiaries, and the result was growing political support for further movement toward public ownership.

A much different explanation, slanted in the opposite direction but arriving at the same conclusion, is that greater public intervention became necessary because the private sector was greedy and unreliable, could not or would not raise enough private capital, schemed to eliminate streetcars and dominate the bus industry, and produced uncoordinated subway and surface lines. Moreover, the economic health of the city required comprehensive public planning, support, and control of transportation, which could best be achieved by essentially full ownership and operation of all but for-hire transportation, and even that demanded total regulatory control.

But government intervention does not always achieve its avowed objectives, just as free markets do not always work. For example, it is ironic that government policy denied private operators any fare increases and kept the fare at a nickel for eighty years, a policy that drove private firms out of business. Then, under fifty-five years of public ownership, from 1948 to 2003, government raised the fare thirteen times, an average of once every four or five years, and multiplied it fortyfold from a nickel to two dollars. The fare increased more than fivefold in constant dollars; had it merely kept pace with inflation, it would be 38 cents instead of $2.00. (And new increases are threatened as this is written. Subsidies that could have been used to improve transit service were used instead to pay for increased labor costs: The MTA proved unable to withstand pressure from its employees, who, in effect, exercised the monopoly power of the public transit system.)

The Private Sector Responds: Ground Transportation. Innovative private responses to public transit needs continue, sometimes despite government interference. New York City today has a host of other private transportation services, many of them representing grassroots entrepreneurship.[15] These services evolved in recent times to satisfy unmet market needs; many were stimulated by the artificial, government-imposed limit on the number of conventional yellow cabs. Neighborhood taxi services, livery car services, gypsy cabs, "black cabs," and limousines all provide for-hire service. Private commuter services also evolved to satisfy other transportation needs that the city's mass transit system could not meet. Long-haul express services using buses, vans, or sometimes shared taxis bring passengers to subway stations, as do local shuttle services using vans and other vehicles. Members of minority groups own and operate many of these services, which often serve minority neighborhoods. Indeed, this has been a route into the middle class for some immigrant and minority entrepreneurs, and for most it represents an adequate living off the welfare rolls. Businesspeople whose names and scale of operations bear no resemblance to those of Jay Gould and August Belmont—New York's early transportation titans—nevertheless followed in their footsteps a century later.

The Private Sector Responds: Ferry Services. The first ferry was a rowboat, operating as a private service between Manhattan and Brooklyn in 1642. By 1904, 147 ferryboats were plying the harbor carrying 200 million passengers a year. By 1910, 125 private ferry services were functioning in the city; most belonged to railroads and provided "integrated, intermodal transportation" in today's jargon.[16] By 1975, however, with government-subsidized trains and cars dominating transportation (the cars traveling on tax-paid streets and roads), the private ferry services had disappeared and the number of boats had dwindled to nine, most of them in the city government's Staten Island fleet.

Private entrepreneurs saw the now-empty waterways as an opportunity—"a 50-lane, underutilized superhighway," in the words of one businessman.[17] Consequently in the 1980s seven firms sprang up, operating thirteen ferry routes—some with "park and sail" facilities.[18] By mid-2002, in part responding to the destruction of the World Trade Center's cross-Hudson transit hub on September 11, 2001, twenty-two ferry routes were operating on New York's various waterways, and ferries made 2,000 trips every weekday across the Hudson River alone.[19] Private firms carry about 60,000 passengers per day, about equal to the number carried by the public Staten Island

Ferry.[20] In addition, a private water taxi service started up connecting points along the shoreline of lower Manhattan, and more private ferry services are planned. (By 2005, however, the largest private ferry service was facing financial problems and seeking government subsidies.)

The Contributions of Private Entrepreneurs. History shows that the private sector made all the mass transit innovations in New York: omnibus, horsecar, elevated, electric streetcar, subway, trolley bus, bus, and ferry. Private companies played a major role in public transportation ("public" in the sense of serving the public, not ownership) in the past, and it continues to play a role today, albeit a modest one. Considering the profound problems that affect transportation in New York today (high public costs and inadequate service in many areas), and with transportation predominantly in the hands of public agencies, there is an opportunity to reassess the situation, allow and encourage greater mobilization of private resources, and strike a better allocation of responsibilities between the public and private sectors.

Privatization before Giuliani

Until the start of the Giuliani administration, New York City was an inhospitable place for privatization. A strong prolabor and antibusiness environment developed under Mayor Fiorello LaGuardia during the Great Depression and in many ways prevails to this day, paradoxical though this may seem in the world's business capital.[21] Moreover some feel that city government is a jobs program and that it must serve as the employer of last resort. In this, the ideological home of assorted liberals and leftists for decades, the concept of relying on the private sector for anything as important as public services was simply unimaginable.

Actually the concept of privatization was explicitly recommended as a tool to improve municipal performance as early as 1969 during the administration of Mayor John V. Lindsay (1966–1973).[22] Mayor Lindsay established a commission to consider the proposal for side-by-side experiments pitting municipal agencies against private contractors, but he changed political parties in 1971 and quietly abandoned the study as he sought labor union support during his run for the Democratic presidential nomination in 1972. For his successor, Mayor Abraham D. Beame (1974–1977), a former career civil servant, such an alien idea was beyond the pale, and in any event he was struggling to keep the city afloat during a fiscal crisis. Mayor Edward I. Koch

(1978–1989) paid no attention to the emerging nationwide privatization movement, and Mayor David N. Dinkins (1990–1993) was averse to the idea. At a Carnegie Council conference on privatization, Mayor Dinkins opened his address to the international audience with the sentence, "Privatization is no panacea."[23] Nevertheless several stepping-stones toward privatization were put in place during his administration as a result of the new city charter, as noted below, and his staff did explore some possible privatizations.

Contracting: A Brief Background

Government contracting with private firms is not a brand new idea in New York. After all, city employees did not build New York's schools and streets; contractors did. City employees did not manufacture pencils and light bulbs; private firms did. City workers did not grow fruits and vegetables and raise livestock to supply food for municipal hospitals, schools, and jails; private suppliers did. Moreover contracting was ongoing and routine for many commonplace city functions, such as custodial and clerical work, data entry, and guard services. Maintenance of streetlights was always contracted out, originally to Con Edison. When welfare programs and social services burgeoned in Lyndon Johnson's Great Society, contracting with nonprofits rapidly introduced new programs because no city agencies were doing this work. What was new under privatization in New York City, however, was the idea of introducing competitive contracting as an antidote to municipal monopolies to improve public service delivery and government performance.

The city's contracting process has evolved since the charter of 1898 established the city of "Greater New York." The Charter Review Commission devoted considerable attention to this issue in the late 1980s when the city was spending about $5 billion per year, a quarter of the city's budget, on roughly 100,000 contracts for goods and services. Contracting had been a perennial problem, and a series of reports from different sources catalogued the city's deficiencies. In 1986 the State-City Commission on Integrity in Government

> urged a "thorough overhaul of contract and procurement procedures" that it characterized as "highly fragmented, complex and opaque." A 1986 report by State Comptroller Edward V. Regan found a disturbing lack of record-keeping and written guidelines by the city agencies responsible for administering contracts. And a 1987 city-commissioned report by the Institute of Public Administration,

a nonprofit consulting firm, identified the city's contracting policies and practices as a major cause of hidden costs, deficient quality and delays in the city's purchase of goods and services.[24]

The state-city commission described contracting as a "black hole" of conflicting and inconsistent rules, inadequate record keeping and red tape that sometimes left the city itself uncertain about just how much it was spending and for what. . . . [M]ost agencies could not even say how many contracts they had awarded in a given year that drew fewer than three bids, which is considered the minimum necessary for healthy competition.[25]

Contracting under the New City Charter

The new city charter of 1989 established a Procurement Policy Board to set forth basic and uniform rules and procedures for contracting by all city agencies. The board issued its initial rules in 1990 after a series of hearings.[26] The charter also created the Mayor's Office of Contracts whose director served as the city's chief procurement officer, a new position. Mayor Dinkins deserves credit for appointing Michael Rogers, a professional public manager, to that post. Rogers promptly set about upgrading the city's contracting capability by recruiting a chief contracting officer—a position called for in the charter—for each agency and providing professional training programs for them and their deputy contracting officers. The first annual procurement conference was held in 1992, and 800 city procurement personnel attended.[27] The Dinkins administration created the Procurement Training Institute, which provided training for nearly 1,000 employees, of which 300 received certification. The focus of all these efforts was not privatization but simply better contracting for all the usual and conventionally purchased goods and services; the city had thousands of such contracts in effect at any one time and spent more than $1 billion annually on those contracts.

The charter gave additional attention to contracting. The city's annual budget document conventionally had been divided into three sections, the revenue budget, the expense budget, and the operations budget. A fourth section was added under the 1989 charter, the contract budget, which became operational in 1991. For the first time the city and the public could see how much money was budgeted for contracts and the general purpose of those expenditures. The costs of the contracts continue to be included in the expense budget. The costs were $6 billion for 20,465 contracts in fiscal 2002, or 15 percent of the city's $39.7 billion expense budget. In 1991 contracts comprised 10.7 percent of the budget.

To overcome a persistent problem that turned off interested bidders, the new charter required the Procurement Policy Board to set deadlines for agencies to pay contractors and to pay interest for late payments, and it required the board to issue reports on late payments. Late payments were identified as a problem in 1970:

> [L]ook at the elaborate, time-consuming, and costly bureaucratic system . . . designed . . . to assure that the city gets fair value in its purchases. The procedures were constructed to protect against graft and corruption in contracting for supplies, equipment, and services. However, the consequence for the city is an inordinately long delay in securing bids and paying bills; the result of these delays is that many potential vendors refuse to sell to the city, and that those who do . . . have to charge higher prices to make up for the additional expense of dealing with it.[28]

A related requirement of the new charter and the contract budget was cost comparisons for certain contracts. Therefore in 1990 the Dinkins administration prepared and issued the twenty-four-page "Contracting-In Cost Comparison Manual: A Guide to Determining Cost-Effectiveness." It provided a standard, detailed method for carrying out comparisons between in-house costs and contractors' bid prices to determine whether contracts are cost effective. The Giuliani administration later refined the manual and reissued it in 1995 as the fifty-one-page "OMB Cost Manual: A Guide to Determining the Cost of City Services."

The 1989 charter also requires the city comptroller, as the city's fiscal watchdog, to issue regular reports on contracting. The report for fiscal 1990, for example, before the new contracting rules were implemented, noted that 46 percent of the 11,007 contracts registered with the comptroller (not all contracts are registered), with a value of approximately $2.6 billion, were awarded without competition.[29] The report called for greater competition. A year later the fraction had dropped to 38 percent. Journalists, too, decried the absence of competition and identified instances of poor performance by lone bidders who were awarded contracts. More competitive contracting, it was reported, could save tens to hundreds of millions of dollars.[30]

Despite the new charter's emphasis on contracting and the Dinkins administration's credible efforts to implement the changes, improvements were slow in coming. As the administration drew to a close at the end of 1993, the executive director of the Procurement Policy Board released a lengthy report accusing the administration and the comptroller of failing to implement critical reforms in contracting.[31] The city's chief procurement officer rebutted this report vigorously in a City Council hearing a few weeks later, revealing significant differences of opinion between the Procurement Policy Board and the Mayor's Office of Contracts on their respective roles.[32]

Contracting in the Dinkins Administration

Aside from implementing the procedures called for in the city charter, the Dinkins administration—or, to be precise, some staff members—was interested in privatization by competitive contracting. The continuing stream of favorable articles in the mass media and in the public administration literature impelled the city's Office of Management and Budget to study the contracting of city services. The office looked at sixty different contracts in effect in twenty different departments for printing and mailing, temporary help, office cleaning, custodial services, food services, warehousing, training, data entry, microfilming, message delivery, security guards, and court reporting. They compared the contract cost with the cost of the work done in-house by municipal employees. Their report, completed in late 1990 but never published, showed that the total in-house cost would have been $56.29 million compared to the contract cost of $27.21 million. That is, contracting resulted in stunning savings of 52 percent. To put it another way, the city agencies cost more than twice as much as the contractors. In only one of the sixty cases was the contractor more expensive than the city agency. The Office of Management and Budget career civil servant who directed the study said that dissemination of these results and further action on this finding "was ruled out by the political folks." [33] The basic reason for Mayor Dinkins' lack of interest in privatization was his long-standing support from the municipal unions and therefore his understandable reluctance to antagonize those loyal backers. The fact that his budget director, Carol O'Cleireacain, had previously served as chief economist for the city's largest municipal union no doubt contributed to the de facto antiprivatization policy.

Inaction was also the reaction to a comprehensive 219-page study prepared jointly by City University of New York, Columbia University, and New York University faculty members that recommended a larger role for the private sector in New York's public transportation system. The report proposed prudent measures to contract competitively for some services and to legitimize and incorporate regulated van services into the city's surface transportation network. It estimated savings that would grow gradually to $600 million annually (1990 dollars) for the city and the Transit Authority, which would more than eliminate the city subsidy payments to the Transit Authority.[34]

To Mayor Dinkins' credit, he did try to privatize some services. The most ambitious contracting effort was an award of $150 million to Lockheed Information Management Services to handle parking violations, but this collapsed after an investigation found that officials had shown favoritism in selecting the company. Also, the Dinkins administration introduced legislation that would give builders of small residential buildings the option of hiring their own inspectors instead of relying on the Buildings Department, but municipal unions considered this a form of privatization, attacked the idea, and blocked the legislation.[35] The administration was successful, however, in turning over management of 330 centers for the elderly to local nonprofit organizations and turning over the inspection of boilers in commercial buildings to private firms. The city also privatized many residential buildings that it had previously taken over for failure to pay real estate taxes. Mayor Dinkins was also very supportive of Business Improvement Districts (BIDs), the private local entities that levied extra taxes on themselves to improve their local commercial neighborhoods. None of these actions affected a significant number of municipal employees.

Parks Commissioner Betsy Gotbaum created a BID–like organization that falls under the rubric of privatization, the City Parks Foundation. This private organization provided financial support for the parks. Gotbaum also carried out an interesting experiment in the Parks Department in 1992, comparing the performance of city and contractor crews in removing dead trees in the street medians. The city crews agreed to operate with fewer personnel and to schedule their own work instead of having it scheduled from above. In fact, during the two-month trial they outperformed the contractor in cost per tree removed.[36] When, however, the city tried to set that productivity level as a new work standard, the union reply was, in effect, "Oh, no. If you want us to work that way all the time you have to pay us a lot more." After this trial period, the crews returned to their normal work pace, and the city decided to continue using contractors for much of this work; it was cheaper.

In recognition of the broad acceptance of privatization throughout the United States, First Deputy Mayor Norman Steisel authorized the formation of the Alternative Service Delivery Working Group, which reported to the Office of Contracts and included the Office of Management and Budget, the Office of

Operations, and the Office of Labor Relations. The working group was to produce a "white paper," but their charge stated emphatically (emphasis in the original), **"the purpose of this paper is not to endorse privatization."** Four months before Dinkins left office, the working group completed a draft that discussed how to identify services to be considered for competition, how to compare costs, and what factors affect employees. The paper, "Options for Public/Private Competition," listed sixteen steps for performing a public-private competitive process.[37] It is difficult to avoid the conclusion that Dinkins delayed this working group effort to the very end of his term when it could not harm him politically, yet might help him get reelected by displaying his interest in improving government performance, with no commitment to do anything about it.

It was in this environment that the city's premier organizations of business leaders, the New York City Partnership and the New York Chamber of Commerce and Industry, collaborated in mid-1993 to produce the report, "Putting the Public First: Making New York Work through Privatization and Competition." [38] It pointed to savings of $16 billion over the next ten years if the city adopted its recommendations. But the report fell on deaf ears. A few months later, however, the November election set the stage for a new leader to take over, one attuned philosophically to these ideas.

Summary

Private entrepreneurs supplied municipal services in early New York. They provided water, fire protection, garbage collection, street cleaning, ferry service, electricity, and street transportation. As industrialization progressed, however, and city life became more crowded and complex, the role of government expanded until the municipality became the monopoly supplier of most services.

In the business capital of the world, a prolabor and antibusiness climate developed that prevails to this day. Although contracting for virtually all goods and some services (for example, construction) had long been commonplace, this was not privatization in the ordinary sense. The city was indifferent, if not hostile, to privatization until Mayor Giuliani came along.

Procurement—purchasing and contracting—was a cumbersome process and a constant problem for the city. A new city charter in 1989 revamped the process, and Mayor David Dinkins instituted changes to meet the charter's requirements and created a professional infrastructure for procurement. He undertook several relatively minor privatization initiatives but was basically averse to privatization. He served only one term, but his improved procurement procedures—although incomplete—set the stage for Mayor Giuliani to initiate an aggressive privatization program.

Notes

1. This section is from Lowell M. Limpus, *History of the New York Fire Department* (New York: E.P. Dutton, 1940).
2. Ibid., 17.
3. Ibid., 28–30.
4. Cynthia Crossen, "New York City Rebuilt with More Splendor—It Happened Before," *Wall Street Journal,* September 4, 2002, B1.
5. This section is from Office of the Mayor, "Refuse Collection: Department of Sanitation vs. Private Carting," New York City, November 1970.
6. C. Joseph Pusateri, *A History of American Business,* 2d ed. (Arlington Heights, Ill.: Harlan Davidson, 1988), 116.
7. David C. Hammack, *Power and Society: Greater New York at the Turn of the Century* (New York: Russell Sage Foundation, 1982), 230.
8. John A. Miller, *Fares, Please! A Popular History of Trolleys, Horse Cars, Street Cars, Buses, Elevateds, Subways* (New York: Dover, 1941).
9. Brian J. Cudahy, *A Century of Service* (Washington, D.C.: American Public Transit Association, 1982).
10. Boris S. Pushkarev, *Urban Rail in America* (Bloomington: Indiana University Press, 1982).
11. Hammack, *Power and Society,* 235–236.
12. Ibid., 234–251.
13. Benson Bobrick, *Labyrinths of Iron: A History of the World's Subways* (New York: Newsweek Books, 1981), 223–264.
14. Harry Gordon, "Subway Nickels: New York City's Transit Problem," survey submitted to Mayor John F. Hylan and to the Board of Estimate and Apportionment, January 29, 1925.
15. Sigurd Grava, "New Transportation Modes: Forward to the Good Old Days," *Urban Resources* 4, no. 1 (fall 1986): NY1-NY3.
16. For an account of ferry service, see Sigurd Grava, "Water Mode to the Rescue: Past and Future Ferry Service in New York City," *Transportation Quarterly* 40, no. 3 (July 1986): 333–356. The earliest ferry in New York was a private service between Manhattan and Brooklyn in 1642. In 1807

Robert Fulton invented the steamboat and within seven years steamboats were plying the waterways throughout New York in regular ferry service. The first tunnel under the Hudson River was built by the Pennsylvania Railroad in 1910.

17. Arthur Imperatore, founder of NY Waterways, Inc., circa 1985.
18. Department of Transportation, Bureau of Transit Operations, "Private Ferry Operations, 1989 Second Quarter Summary," New York City, July 1989.
19. Lydia Polgreen, "Batten Down the Hatches! Commuters Ahoy!" *New York Times,* August 12, 2002, B1.
20. Roberta Weisbrod, "Ferries Since 9/11 and into the Future," *New York Transportation Journal* 6, no. 1 (fall 2002): 6.
21. Fred Siegel, "The LaGuardia Myth," *The Public Interest* 154 (winter 2004): 119–123.
22. The author, as first deputy city administrator of New York, proposed in 1969 that competition be introduced for common municipal services, starting with residential refuse collection. The formal city report from the Office of the Mayor is "Refuse Collection: Department of Sanitation vs. Private Carting," November 1970. See also Richard Phalon, "City May Use Private Refuse Haulers," *New York Times,* April 6, 1971.
23. The author was present during this address.
24. Institute of Public Administration, *The Charter Review* 1, no. 4 (spring 1988): 1–5.
25. Todd S. Purdum, "New York City Tells All Agencies to Use Same Procedure for Contracts," *New York Times,* August 2, 1990, B4.
26. For a subsequent publication, see City of New York, "Procurement Policy Board Rules," September 2000.
27. City Club of New York, "Contract Watch," June 1992.
28. E. S. Savas, "Cybernetics in City Hall," *Science,* 168, no. 3935 (May 29, 1970): 1066–1071.
29. Comptroller of New York City, "New York City Contracts over $10,000 Registered in Fiscal Year 1990," annual summary report, June 1991.
30. Dean Baquet with Martin Gottlieb, "Without Competing Bids, New York Pays the Price," *New York Times,* February 19, 1991, 1.
31. Connie Cushman, "Fall Report to the Board," Procurement Policy Board, October 22, 1993; Barbara Ross, "Report Hits Dave, Liz on Contracting," *Daily News,* October 26, 1993, 24.
32. Michael C. Rogers, "Testimony Before the City Council Committee on Contracts," New York City, December 7, 1993.

33. Personal communication with the author, 2001.
34. E. S. Savas, Sigurd Grava, and Roy Sparrow, *The Private Sector in Public Transportation in New York City: A Policy Perspective* (New York: Institute for Transportation Systems, City University of New York, 1991).
35. Peter Grant, "Unions Block Dinkins' Privatization Move," *Crain's New York Business*, June 28, 1993.
36. Michael Janofsky, "Parks Workers' Test Fights Stereotype of Public Jobs," *New York Times*, November 16, 1992.
37. Mayor's Office of Contracts, "Options for Public/Private Competition," draft white paper, New York City, September 14, 1993.
38. New York City Partnership and the New York Chamber of Commerce and Industry, "Putting the Public First: Making New York Work through Privatization and Competition," June 1993.

4 | Privatization in the Giuliani Administration

Rudolph W. Giuliani (1994–2001), New York's 107th mayor, was elected as a Republican and therefore lacked the backing of local labor unions or Democrats. He was the first mayor of New York to embrace privatization. He advocated the idea as early as his losing 1989 mayoral campaign against David Dinkins. Giuliani ran again against incumbent Mayor Dinkins in 1993 and continued to endorse privatization as a tool to maintain city services while increasing productivity and reducing costs. During the campaign he learned from the experts on privatization and considered the opportunities where privatization—or rather, competition—could best be applied in New York City.[1] (As a candidate Giuliani visited America Works, a for-profit company that develops jobs for welfare recipients. This eye-opening experience helped shape his welfare reform program.[2]) This time he won the mayoral race and was able to put the ideas into practice.

Planting the Seeds of Privatization

As part of Giuliani's transition into office, his team prepared the "Privatization Advisory Report" on the potential for privatization in New York City.[3] The report listed thirty-two promising targets for privatization in seven categories (See table 4.1). The report also addressed the labor-relations strategy for implementing privatization. It recommended consulting with unions, conducting cost-benefit analyses of proposed projects, encouraging public employees to compete with the private sector for contracts, implementing

Table 4.1 Privatizations Recommended in the Transition Report for Mayor-Elect Giuliani

Recommended Service	*Eventually proposed by the administration?*	*Eventually realized by the administration?*
Solid waste management		
Collection of solid waste and recyclables	No	No
Solid waste disposal at Fresh Kills landfill	No	No
Solid waste disposal out of town	Yes	Yes
Processing of recyclables	Yes	Yes
Street sweeping	No	No
Southwest Brooklyn incinerator	No	No
Water supply and wastewater treatment		
Water and wastewater services	Yes	No
Wastewater treatment and sludge disposal	Yes	No
Bus and ferry transportation		
Franchised private bus services	No	No
Transit Authority bus operations	No	No
Staten Island, Hart Island, and City Island ferry operations	No	No
Other transportation		
Parking meter maintenance and collection	Yes	Yes
Parking lot long-term leasing for operation and maintenance	Yes	Yes
Pothole repairs	No	No
Traffic sign installation and maintenance	Yes	Yes
Bridge preventive maintenance	No	No
Cleaning and maintenance of city gateway roads	Yes	Yes
Healthcare/health and hospitals corporation/emergency medical services		
Municipal hospitals, for sale or spinoff as independent hospitals	Yes	No
Municipal hospitals, services such as laundry, pharmacy, food, physical therapy	Yes	Yes
Ambulance transport of noncritical patients	No	No
Emergency medical service (EMS)	No	No
Food services	No	No

(table continues)

Table 4.1 (continued)

Recommended Service	*Eventually proposed by the administration?*	*Eventually realized by the administration?*
Maintenance services and general services		
Maintenance and repair services and energy management of city buildings	No	No
Hydrant and hydrant piping—repair, maintenance, and replacement	No	No
Heating plant operation and maintenance	Yes	Yes
Tree pruning and removals	Yes	Yes
Capital asset sales		
Off-Track Betting Corporation	Yes	No
WNYC-TV and radio stations	Yes	Yes
Property tax receivables	Yes	Yes
In rem housing[a]	Yes	Yes
Bridge operation and maintenance	No	No
Kennedy and LaGuardia Airports	Yes	No

Source: The Privatization Advisory Report for the Honorable Rudolph W. Giuliani, Mayor-Elect of the City of New York, December 22, 1993.

[a] *In rem* properties are those that have been foreclosed for nonpayment of property taxes.

gain-sharing agreements, and requiring winning contractors to give displaced public employees access to jobs.[4]

The "soft infrastructure" for privatization seemed to be in place as Mayor Giuliani took office: the Procurement Policy Board, the Mayor's Office of Contracts, clear and uniform contracting procedures, the city chief procurement officer, chief contracting officers in each agency, the contract budget, the cost-comparison method, and the comptroller's strengthened contract oversight role. The transition report, however, called attention to the still incomplete reform of procurement and contract management. It stated,

> there are almost 300 pages of procurement rules for city agencies augmented by a similar amount of Rule Implementation Memoranda from the Mayor's Office of Contracts. These official rules appear to be supplemented by a hodgepodge of agency practices. The

system is focused (not always successfully) on corruption avoidance, and requires approvals by at least fourteen agencies to conclude a typical procurement action. For example, it can take 180 separate steps and 446.5 days to hire a consultant. The Mayor's Office of Contracts intends to streamline and automate the process, but this project has already been underway several years and the first phase of implementation is not scheduled until December 1995. The Comptroller's Office has tended to slow down the process further in its search for corrupt vendors, rather than relying on post-contract audits of smaller contracts to detect problems.[5]

The Beginning

Shortly after taking office on January 1, 1994, Mayor Giuliani invited Mayor Stephen Goldsmith of Indianapolis to meet with him and his commissioners; Goldsmith was well known for his city's successful privatizations (See chapter 2). Giuliani also had a similar meeting with David Osborne, coauthor of the book *Reinventing Government.* Through these meetings and in Giuliani's regular cabinet meetings, the mayor made it abundantly clear to his appointees that he favored reinventing government and wanted action on privatization. In the meantime, business leaders reiterated their call for privatized services.[6]

Giuliani put his senior advisor, Richard J. Schwartz, in charge of the privatization program. Schwartz had an ABD, "all but his doctorate," in public administration when he began working in the Giuliani campaign and was very familiar with the concept of privatization. Schwartz met with individual commissioners and discussed services that were promising candidates for privatization. Only a month after the inauguration, on February 2, 1994, Mayor Giuliani announced broad changes to reduce the city budget by $500 million; privatization figured prominently in his plans. A memorandum at that time asked each commissioner to develop more detailed plans for several privatization or public-private (managed) competition projects.

Looking back, Mayor Giuliani described the start of his program:

> We began . . . by asking each city agency to think "outside the box" and identify services that they were no longer equipped to perform well: where we could benefit from a public asset sale, where the private sector had better expertise for delivering a service, where we needed to reengineer services, or where in-house employees could become more productive through a competitive forum.[7]

City Council Opposition

Once upon a time, the City Council was ineffective and generally powerless. In 1965 council member Henry Stern, later to be parks commissioner under Mayors Koch and Giuliani, offered a withering and now classic assessment: "The City Council is less than a rubber stamp. A rubber stamp at least leaves an impression." [8]

Since then, however, under a revised city charter, the council has become a more powerful and more equal branch of municipal government. Indeed, it immediately opposed the mayor's privatization plans. In Giuliani's first month in office, the council introduced a bill to establish a high hurdle for privatization—an insuperable obstacle, some would say. It was merely the latest manifestation of a bill first introduced in 1992 during the Dinkins administration that would have forbidden the mayor from contracting for city services unless cost savings were at least 20 percent and the fringe-benefit savings at least 30 percent. Moreover the mayoral agencies would have to overcome numerous bureaucratic obstacles and retrain any displaced employees. To Mayor Dinkins' credit, he blocked this bill in his last month in office, as it represented legislative usurpation of executive authority.

The council held hearings on the bill and, after the administration forcefully challenged it, amended it substantially and eliminated some of the more objectionable features. Those testifying in support of the mayor's position included the Citizens Union; the Citizens Budget Commission; the General Contractors Association; the New York City Partnership/New York Chamber of Commerce and Industry; Ronald Lauder, a former rival of Giuliani's for the Republican nomination for mayor in 1989; Professor Peter Salins of Hunter College; the author; the Human Services Council; and the UJA-Federation. (The last two represent many small, voluntary human-service organizations.)

Supporters of the bill included several public-employee unions (District Council 37, the Civil Service Technical Guild, the Communications Workers of America, and the Emergency Medical Technicians and Paramedics Local), the New York Public Interest Research Group, Columbia University professor Elliott Sclar, and City Project.

The City Council passed the bill overwhelmingly (forty-three to eight), the mayor vetoed it, and the council overrode his veto (forty-three to seven) to enact the bill into law in 1994. This was only the third time in twenty-five years that the council had overridden a mayoral veto. Local Law 35 applies to any contract valued at more than $100,000 that displaces any city employee. It requires a cost-benefit analysis for the comptroller, employee-displacement estimates for the council and union representatives, extensive documentation to the council, and a cumbersome, time-consuming set of ten administrative steps: one certification, one hearing, two determinations, three submissions, and three separate cost-benefit analyses.[9] The phrase, "displacing any city employee," means any action that results in a reduction in the number of positions, even if it means no layoffs. The unions want to maintain budgeted positions, even vacant ones, because they remain available to be filled by dues-paying members under a new mayor.

This law attempts to thwart contracting by erecting bureaucratic barriers, creating unnecessary and costly delays, and burdening small would-be contractors. By requiring data on the compensation of a contractor's personnel, the law deters would-be bidders. On the positive side, the law encourages good management by requiring cost comparisons, justification for the decision to contract, and notification of expected effects on employees; but this is redundant—Procurement Policy Board rules and union agreements already mandate these practices. The law does not allow the council to prevent any mayoral privatization initiative; a contract can be awarded within thirty days after the documentation has been submitted to the council whether or not the council holds a hearing.

Local Law 35 was not nearly as bad a piece of legislation as the notorious Pacheco Law in Massachusetts, enacted in 1993 and named after its prime sponsor in the state senate.[10] This is the most restrictive state privatization law in the nation and appears to have been the model that inspired the New York City Council a few months later. It includes the following provisions:

- Comparing the cost and quality of service in a private bid not to the existing cost and quality of the service provided by state employees but to what would be achieved were the public employees to work "in the most cost-efficient manner."
- Adding lost tax revenue to the contractor's bid if any of the work is to be performed outside Massachusetts. No adjustment is made to the in-house cost to reflect tax revenues that would be realized if the work were performed by a business subject to state taxes.
- Regulating wages and benefits provided by the private contractor.

- Forwarding a proposal that manages to scale these hurdles to the state auditor, who may reject it for any of several reasons, including that the contract is not "in the public interest."

The net effect of this antiprivatization legislation was dramatic: In the two years before passage, 1991–1993, Massachusetts saved an estimated $273 million by opening thirty-six services to competition from private firms. In the nine years after adoption, 1993–2002, the state administration proposed only eight privatizations and gained approval for a mere six.

Preparing for Privatization

Sensible privatization requires comparing contract prices to the city's in-house costs. The problem is that many in-house costs are simply unknown. This remarkable assertion means merely that conventional agency budgets—which analysts automatically consult to look up costs—are not cost-accounting documents nor are they intended to be. Rather, they indicate personnel and other categories of expenses for organizational units, not for the services the units perform. To determine the cost of an activity, such as cleaning streets or operating emergency ambulances, one must painstakingly assemble costs based on actual personnel tasks and time spent on that activity, plus allocated capital costs, indirect costs, overhead, and the costs of supplies, equipment, vehicle usage, and so on. Recognizing the need for this basic "soft infrastructure for privatization," the city hired consultants to develop an activity-based costing system, "ABC," that would provide the information needed to make valid cost comparisons. This system was incorporated into the new city Office of Management and Budget cost manual mentioned in chapter 3 and was used in subsequent analyses in accordance with Local Law 35.

In November 1994 Peter J. Powers, deputy mayor for operations, issued "Guidelines for Public/Private Competition." Prominently featured on the cover was a fitting quotation by Thomas Jefferson: "It is better for the public to procure at the common market whatever the market can supply: Because it is by competition kept up in quality, and reduced to its minimum price." The guidelines were developed by the Competition Coordinating Committee, comprising representatives from the Office of the Deputy Mayor, the Office of the Senior Advisor, the Office of Operations, the Office of Management and Budget, the Mayor's Office of Contracts, the Office of Labor Relations, the Law

Department, and the Department of Personnel. Among other purposes, the document was intended to guide agencies in differentiating between five alternative delivery methods:

1. Managed competition: Through the request for proposal and bidding process, city agencies compete with private firms for service delivery.
2. Contracting out: The city hires a private firm to deliver a service without city agencies participating in the formal request for proposal and bidding process. Under Local Law 35 and the Municipal Coalition Agreement, however, the union has the right to submit a counterproposal.
3. Contracting in: City workers now deliver a service previously delivered by the private sector.
4. Public-private comparison: Both sectors deliver a service simultaneously in different areas or to different customers. Results are evaluated under the same criteria and used to identify the best means of future service delivery.
5. Privatization: The city sells assets or otherwise relinquishes direct control over delivering a service to a private for-profit or nonprofit entity.

The document would also guide agencies in selecting and implementing appropriate projects, and it incorporated instructions for complying with Local Law 35 (See box 4.1).[11] The guidelines made use of material from "Options for Public/Private Competition," produced at the end of the Dinkins administration. Later, the Competition Coordinating Committee issued a generic milestone chart to indicate how rapidly the steps could be pursued, but the whole process still required about fifteen months.

The cost manual, the guidelines, and the milestone chart could be improved in five areas. First, if such buildings as offices or garages are used in the delivery of a service, the equivalent rent should be included as a cost element. Second, the cost of unfunded pension benefits should be added to the cost of fringe benefits, because ultimately the city will have to pay it. Third, city taxes paid by a private contractor because of the contract should be considered a rebate to the city and should be subtracted from the price of his bid. Fourth, the cumbersome process imposed by Local Law 35 should be abbreviated and accelerated, because as it stands now a bidder could submit a proposal and then wait up to six months to find out if he or she has won; this also acts as a deterrent. Fifth, the city needs a policy to handle the situation in which its own agency submits a bid and is awarded the work but fails

Box 4.1 Guidelines for Public-Private Competition

Phase A. Preliminary Assessment

1. Identify service to be reviewed for alternative service delivery.
2. Review current scope of service, develop current cost estimate, and estimate total cost of contracting out.
3. Determine how other governments perform this service and their costs.
4. Review all cost and market analyses. Determine best method for service delivery.
5. Draft new scope of services and expected output.
6. If the decision is to pursue managed competition, contracting out, or public/private comparison, submit proposal to the Competition Coordinating Committee (CCC).
7. If Local Law 35 applies, submit to the comptroller the scope of work, the preliminary cost-benefit analysis, and all supporting documentation.
8. Prepare presolicitation review to define market, estimate contract cost, and determine method of procurement. Submit review with in-house cost estimate to Mayor's Office of Contracts and CCC for review and approval.
9. If the labor agreement applies, contact the Office of Labor Relations (OLR) in writing with details and follow their guidelines and timetable.
10. Examine any plans to reduce current operating costs; estimate revised costs.

Phase B. Methods of Procurement Source Selection

1. Draft specifications and request for proposal (RFP) or invitation to bid (ITB). Set performance standards, monitoring criteria, and criteria for evaluating bids; appoint evaluation committee.
2. Obtain approval of specifications from CCC and Office of Management and Budget.

Box 4.1 continues

Box 4.1 (continued)

3. Solicit competitive sealed bids or proposals.
4. Provide union with a copy of bid or RFP document.
5. Receive bids or proposals.
6. If Local Law 35 applies, immediately submit documentation to City Council through Office of Legislative Affairs and to union through OLR.
7. If applicable, evaluate union counterproposal.
8. Prior to award of contract, complete final cost-benefit analysis comparing winning vendor with in-house work. Submit analysis to comptroller, City Council, and union.
9. After Council hearing or at end of thirty-day waiting period, prepare recommendation for award (RFA) to selected bidder or to in-house unit or to union's counterproposal.
10. If selected bidder is a private firm and agency does not accept union proposal, agency submits RFA to CCC. Latter reviews and if it approves, agency registers the contract.
11. If agency selects union counterproposal, OLR will prepare memorandum of understanding after CCC signs off.
12. Execute contract, monitor performance, complete contract, and evaluate performance.

Source: Based on City of New York, "Guidelines for Public/Private Competition," September 1994.

to perform satisfactorily. For example, the city should increase the price of the in-house bid by the amount of the premium that would be paid by a private firm for a performance bond and, upon failure of the city agency, the city should contract immediately with the lowest qualified private bidder (if that firm is still interested).

Early Initiatives

By June 1994 several agencies had produced detailed plans in response to the mayor's orders. An initial list developed in September showed twenty-six privatization candidates (See table 4.2). Contracts were also contemplated for

Table 4.2 Initial List of Planned Privatizations

Department	*Project*
Transportation	Maintenance of life-protecting traffic signs (one way, stop, yield, do not enter)
	Street repaving
	Cleaning of arterial highways
	Parking meter inspection, repair, and collections
	Bridge repair
	Pothole repair
General Services	Vehicle maintenance
	Building services
	Fuel tank closure[a]
Parks and Recreation	Maintenance of local parks
	Building maintenance
Fire	Vehicle maintenance
	Building maintenance
	Medicaid compensation billing
	Computer services
	Office reproduction services
Corrections	Vehicle maintenance
	Switchboard maintenance
Health	Laboratory testing
Board of Education	Custodial services
	Fleet maintenance
Environmental Protection	Wastewater treatment in upstate watershed
	Wastewater treatment in local sewage plants
	Arterial catch basin cleaning
	Programmatic catch basin cleaning
	Facility maintenance

Source: Memorandum from the Office of the Mayor, New York City, September 12, 1994.

[a] Fuel tanks were to be closed in different departments, with credit cards to be used for purchasing fuel for city vehicles. This is privatization by load shedding.

operating the city's airports and two of the city's hospitals and for managing 2,500 city-owned residential buildings. In addition, the city was considering divestment for its radio and TV stations, the Off-Track Betting Corporation, the United Nations Plaza Hotel, thirteen city-owned parking garages, and 500 gas stations for city vehicles. Surprisingly, the City Council proposed selling three of the city's fourteen wastewater treatment plants. Why this sudden reversal of the council's antiprivatization stance? It saw an unexpected opportunity to obtain up to $750 million that it could spend.

Privatization proceeded quickly and without fanfare. By the end of Giuliani's first year in office the city had entered into numerous contracts: for street repaving in Queens (to be compared to city crews working in a similar area), for operating four homeless shelters, for cleaning and maintaining forty-seven parks and playgrounds in Queens (the in-house cost would have been 31 percent higher), and for maintaining Parks Department buildings in Manhattan. The Fire Department was analyzing bids to maintain and repair its 260 buildings, most of them firehouses. The Department of General Services was studying bids to maintain its headquarters building and was also planning to contract out maintenance of the city's large vehicle fleet, operation of its bookstore, warehousing, and management of leases for city offices. Not as advanced were plans to turn over operation of two of the city's eleven municipal hospitals and to contract for maintenance of traffic signs, for custodial services in public schools, and for operating the nine wastewater treatment plants in the city's upstate watershed areas. Most of these contracts were signed before the burdensome procedures of Local Law 35 went into effect.[12]

Steady pressure on agencies from City Hall continued. Richard Schwartz would tell an agency to develop privatization plans, then another mayoral assistant, Richard Roberts, and the author (as a consultant paid from a foundation grant to the mayor's office) would visit with the commissioner and his or her top staff to discuss their plans and to explore additional ideas. Later, Schwartz would meet with the commissioner in his City Hall office for a final commitment and timetable.

In the meantime, staff in the Mayor's Office produced a list of other recommended privatizations and estimated the annual cost savings (See table 4.3). They include ferry services and terminals, express bus routes, street resurfacing, vouchers for day care, and the sale of city-owned garages, office buildings, golf courses, and advertising space on city-owned properties. The potential savings totaled $75 million to $130 million.

Table 4.3 Additional Privatization Recommendations

Recommended privatization	*Potential savings*
Privatize the Whitehall and St. George Ferry Terminals and the Staten Island Ferry. Establish sale/leaseback or private management contract that would bring in professional management to maximize the revenue potential for the terminals and ferries. This would allow the city to reduce the subsidy.	$20–25 million
Privatize the express bus routes. Franchise out all routes and eliminate all city subsidies for private express bus services.	$10–15 million
Convert city-funded day care to an all-voucher system. Eliminate contracts and leases and instead provide vouchers directly to parents. Contract out the administration of the vouchers to a nonprofit agency.	$10–20 million
Sell three or four city vehicle maintenance garages. Contract out vehicle maintenance.	$5–10 million
Contract out all street resurfacing. Competitively bid all resurfacing work.	$10–20 million (capital savings)
Sell one or two city-owned office buildings. Consolidate offices or contract out existing functions.	$5–10 million
Sell a city-owned golf course or driving range. State approval is required to "de-map" park land.	$10–20 million
Sell advertising on city-owned properties. Garbage and other city-owned trucks, tops of public buildings, sidewalks surfaces, city bulk mailings, and so on.	$5–10 million

Source: Compiled by the author.

The New Environment

The city had entered a new era. Mayor Giuliani, the first Republican mayor since Mayor John V. Lindsay took office in 1966, was committed to shrinking government and cutting spending while maintaining services by using privatization to improve productivity. He did all of these despite strong opposition from public employee unions and their supporters on the City Council. Giuliani's actions were seen as the first steps toward restructuring government and saving millions of dollars by institutionalizing competition between public agencies and private firms.[13] The *New York Times* acclaimed the moves, and other cities sought Mayor Giuliani's advice.[14] Although Chicago, Indianapolis, Philadelphia, Phoenix, and other cities had already taken similar actions, prior administrations in New York held the parochial belief that New York could learn little from other cities because it was so different.

Mayor Giuliani's profound impact in changing the political environment showed itself in the mayoral campaign of Ruth Messinger, the Manhattan borough president, who was the Democratic candidate for mayor against Giuliani in 1997. She was a well-known liberal and supporter of municipal unions, considered by former mayor Edward Koch to be part of the "loony left." It was therefore a stunning change in her long-standing ideological position when she announced that city departments should compete with private companies for the right to pick up garbage and repair traffic signals, even if it resulted in the elimination of municipal jobs.[15]

Labor Relations

One of Giuliani's first actions as mayor was to reduce the size of the city's workforce. There were no layoffs, but the combination of a hiring freeze, normal attrition, and incentives for early retirement resulted in a decline of 18,000 employees (8 percent) in the first eighteen months of the administration.[16] The vacated lines were eliminated from the agency budgets and could not be readily refilled. Soon, some city agencies were understaffed and could not keep up with the workload.

Then two things happened. First, the city contracted for some services that neither it nor the private sector had been performing, such as cleaning the windows of public office buildings. Second, the federal government passed welfare reform legislation. The mayor eagerly embraced this reform and launched the Work Experience Program (WEP). This required welfare recipients to work enough hours each week to earn their benefits calculated at the minimum wage. They were assigned to jobs in various agencies, particularly the Parks Department. As with new contractors, they did not displace any city workers because the agencies were depleted; they filled the gap and performed work that was not being done at all. This circumstance muted union opposition.

In fact, unlike Mayor Rendell and his contentious relationship with unions in Philadelphia, Giuliani and the New York unions were not enemies. Giuliani talked tough about the unions, but he displayed a willingness to negotiate to achieve the concessions he wanted even as he continued to cajole and threaten.[17] The fiscal constraints left little room for the unions to maneuver; they understood that the mayor had to reduce the budget for the city to survive, and that he had an ultimate threat: layoffs. The city provided a severance package that induced 6,100 workers to leave the city payroll and left the city free to reassign workers to fill vacant positions. Reluctantly, the unions also agreed to a reduction in the city's share of pension payments and to increased productivity in solid-waste collection—a service that had been targeted for privatization by the mayor's transition committee. Critics pointed out, however, that overtime pay in that department had gone up and essentially consumed the vaunted "productivity savings."[18] Indeed, of the $600 million sought by the city in productivity savings in 1996, all the announced savings came from cutbacks in health care for retirees, reductions in health insurance rates negotiated by the city with its insurers, and deferred pension payments.[19]

The municipal unions were more successful in creating another obstacle to privatization, the "living wage" law. This mandates a minimum wage, higher than the federal minimum wage, which must be paid by all companies with municipal contracts. A coalition of ninety-seven labor unions made such legislation its highest priority in 1996. Initially the bill applied only to contractors in security, cleaning, food services, and temporary office work. The mayor vetoed the bill because it would require some contractors to pay their workers more than twice the minimum wage and would raise the city's costs by $500–$750 million a year. This would force further budget and service cuts. The council, on the other hand, claimed that the law applied only to 3,500 workers and would cost the city only $16 million more per year; it easily overrode his veto.[20]

Another tactic of the city government's largest municipal employee union, District Council 37, was to organize contractors' employees. In 1999 the union won an election to represent 108 computer employees of a consulting company that had a contract with the Administration for Children's Services. This followed a ruling by the National Labor Relations Board that the workers, although nominally temporary employees, had a right to vote on union representation. Lee Saunders, the District Council 37 administrator, said, "This sends a clear message about the new direction we are taking. If the city is going to use public funds to privatize jobs that city workers could be doing, then we are going to respond by organizing and taking legal action." [21]

Elimination of Race-Based Contracting

The Giuliani administration awarded contracts without regard to the race or gender of bidders; that is, it did not use racial or gender preferences in contracting. This was a reversal of the policy introduced by Mayor Dinkins to award contracts to companies owned by minorities or women even if their bid prices were as much as 10 percent higher. Mayor Giuliani argued that such race-based discrimination was of questionable legality; several courts had declared such practices unconstitutional, and the policy exposed the city to millions of dollars in lawsuits. Besides, he argued, the program often helped businesses that did not need help and that employed few minorities or women.[22]

In 1992, the first year of Mayor Dinkins' program, the fraction of contracts awarded to this favored class almost doubled from 9 percent in 1990 to 17.5 percent. Prior studies showed that this group represented 25 percent of qualified bidders ("qualified" defined as being owned by women or minorities) but received less than 8 percent of contract dollars. Such studies may be flawed, however, and the results may be due to the small size of those firms: They were very likely to bid for (and win) small contracts but lacked the capacity to bid for large ones. Moreover, to the extent that such firms were relatively new and inexperienced, they may have been unable to prepare winning bids.

Rather than give preferences in contracting, Giuliani chose to improve minority businesses' ability to compete. He encouraged banks to lend to small, minority-owned businesses, and the city expanded bidding on smaller contracts as a way to include businesses located in poor communities. The city no longer recorded information on the sex and race of winning contractors, however, which brought complaints from some.

The First Competition

The first significant instance of competition between private firms and public employees in the Giuliani administration came in early 1995 when a *New York Times* headline reported that the unionized public employees of the Department of Transportation outbid private competitors for the job of installing "life-protecting devices." (These are stop signs, yield signs, one-way signs, and do-not-enter signs.) The full story below the headline painted a different picture, however. The city received bids from several private companies to do the work for about $1 million. Confronted with these bids, the union had to acquiesce to a large productivity increase to match the savings if it wanted to keep the work. The union agreed to install 54,000 signs in the coming year, an increase of 54 percent over the 35,000 installed the previous year. (Mayor Giuliani subsequently reported that productivity increased 50 percent and savings were $1 million a year.[23]) Moreover, the union agreed to accomplish that with only a twenty-seven-person workforce, down from forty-nine due to budget cuts.[24] In other words, the union outbid the private contractors but only by increasing its productivity from 714 signs per year per installer to 2,000, a whopping increase of 180 percent. To put it still another way, for years the city had been paying more than twice as much as it should have. Competition clearly worked in this case.[25]

When the union negotiated with the city the next year, it argued that the new productivity rate should not be used as a base; that is, the city should pay more if it wanted that productivity all the time! This was exactly the argument used in 1992 by the tree pruners in the Parks Department (See chapter 3). Another public-private competition no doubt would have forced the union to be at least as productive to keep the work in-house.

Summary

Upon winning election, mayor-elect Giuliani appointed a transition team to examine the potential for privatization, and the team produced a report listing thirty-two promising targets. In his first budget message, only a month after his inauguration, the mayor announced budget reductions of $500 million and asked each commissioner to develop more detailed plans for privatization or public-private (managed) competition projects.

The City Council was quick to block Giuliani's plans and passed a bill creating administrative obstacles. The mayor's staff then developed a cost manual and issued "Guidelines for Public/Private Competition" that followed the new city ordinance, Local Law 35.

By June 1994, six months after Giuliani took office, city agencies had produced privatization plans for twenty-six activities. Six months later the city had entered into numerous contracts (with more in the works), in addition to planned divestments and voucher programs.

No city workers were laid off, but the combination of a hiring freeze, normal attrition, and incentives for early retirement resulted in a decline of 18,000 employees (8 percent) in the first eighteen months of the administration. The positions were removed from the budget and could not be readily refilled. Because no workers were displaced, union opposition did not derail the privatizations.

The first significant instance of public-private competition—in which an employee union had to improve productivity to stave off private bidders—illustrates the power that Giuliani had gained through his privatization policy. This set the tone for privatization in the remainder of his administration.

Notes

1. Giuliani did this for many topics, as he notes in his book, *Leadership* (New York: Hyperion, 2002), 56.
2. Ibid., 57.
3. Ibid., 59.
4. *The Privatization Advisory Report for the Honorable Rudolph W. Giuliani, Mayor-Elect of the City of New York,* December 22, 1993.
5. Ibid.
6. Paul Tharp, "City's Execs Favor Privatized Services," *New York Post,* January 3, 1994.
7. Rudolph W. Giuliani, "Reforming New York City," in *Making Government Work,* ed. Paul J. Andrisani, Simon Hakim, and Eva Leeds (New York: Rowman and Littlefield, 2000), 163.
8. Henry Stern, campaign fund-raising letter, 1965.
9. Council of the City of New York, Committee on Governmental Operations, "Minority Report," April 28, 1994.
10. Geoffrey F. Segal, Adrian T. Moore, and Adam B. Summers, *Competition and Government Services: Can Massachusetts Still Afford the Pacheco Law?* (Boston: Pioneer Institute, 2002).
11. City of New York, Office of the Mayor, "Guidelines for Public/Private Competition," September 1994.
12. Steven Lee Myers, "Giuliani Moving Ahead to Put City Services in Private Hands," *New York Times,* December 5, 1994, A1.
13. Ibid.
14. "Privatizing City Services," *New York Times,* December 19, 1994; Melinda Henneberger, "Flat-Broke Washington Hears Giuliani's Advice," *New York Times,* March 9, 1995.

15. Adam Nagourney, "Messinger, to Pay for Proposals, Urges $1.1 Billion in Budget Cuts," *New York Times,* July 23, 1997, A1.
16. City of New York, "Mayor's Management Report," September 1997, 22.
17. Steven Lee Myers, "Giuliani and the Unions," *New York Times,* September 19, 1994, A1.
18. Steven Lee Myers, "Overtime Costs Eat Up Sanitation Savings," *New York Times,* July 25, 1995, A1.
19. David Firestone and Steven Lee Myers, "Despite Anti-Labor Oratory, Mayor Treats Unions Gently," *New York Times,* March 26, 1995, A1.
20. Steven Greenhouse, "Unions Push for Higher Minimum Wage on New York City Contracts," *New York Times,* January 2, 1996, B4; Vivian S. Toy, "Veto of 'Prevailing Wage' Bill Is Overridden by City Council," *New York Times,* September 12, 1996, B4.
21. District Council 37, "In Organizing Drive, District Council 37 Wins Right to Represent Computer Workers Employed by a City Consultant," press release, February 26, 1999.
22. Randy Kennedy, "Giuliani Defends Decision on Issuing City Contracts," *New York Times,* March 24, 1997, B3.
23. Giuliani, "Reforming New York City."
24. Steven Lee Myers, "Union Outbids Competitors for Work on Street Signs," *New York Times,* March 26, 1995, B2.
25. An interview with a department official yielded different figures than those reported in the *Times* or cited by the mayor. The installation goal was 47,207 and the productivity increase was calculated conservatively as 22 percent (Appendices A and B, line 80).

5 | The Extent, Pattern, and Outcomes of Privatization

By the end of Mayor Giuliani's eight years in office, he had established an extraordinary record of public-private initiatives. The city had used virtually all the methods listed in chapter 1: contracts, public-private (managed) competition, leases, franchises, vouchers, public-private partnerships, divestment, default, withdrawal, voluntarism, and deregulation.

It was not easy for the author to compile complete and accurate data on individual privatizations despite a thorough effort and full cooperation from city agencies. Information on proposed privatizations was obtained from official records and from media reports, but the results, costs, and benefits were not always available. Officials did not conduct before-and-after comparisons of effectiveness, responsiveness, and equity rigorously or routinely. Nor was it always possible to distinguish trial runs from serious implementation efforts or to establish rigid time boundaries. Several privatizations began under prior mayors, but Giuliani's administration changed or advanced them. In some cases it was unclear whether a planned privatization had been fully implemented. That is, bidding may have started and a contract may even have been awarded, but final implementation did not take place. Some of these cases were realized later under Mayor Bloomberg (See appendix B).

The Extent of Privatization

How do New York City's privatizations compare with national averages? Remember from chapter 2 that the average U.S. city contracts for 23 percent of sixty-four common municipal services. The average *large* U.S. city contracts 15 percent of its forty-seven common services, and private contractors deliver the average common municipal service in 27 percent of cities. By the end of the Giuliani administration in fiscal 2002, private firms (by contract or franchise) and private voluntary organizations (museums, libraries) provided about thirty-eight of sixty-six common services, or 58 percent. That is, New York appeared to be much more privatized than the average city, large or small. However, the shortcomings of the mail surveys used to estimate the national averages cast doubt on this comparison (See chapter 2).

Since 1991, as noted in chapter 3, the city has published an annual contract budget, which is a model of transparency in government. The 2002 document has 308 pages, classifies contracts in fifty-one categories, and lists the number of contracts in effect and their cost by category for each agency. New York City boasts a huge range and magnitude of contracting.

The contract budgets show that New York has "always" contracted with the private sector for many functions, but this is not privatization as understood in the field of modern public management. For example, in fiscal 1994, the final year of the Dinkins administration, 10,426 contracts were in effect with an annual cost of $2.8 billion.[1] In fiscal 2002, which encompassed the final six months of the Giuliani administration, city agencies entered into 4,630 new contracts costing $8.3 billion over the life of those contracts.[2] In total, more than 20,000 contracts were in effect that year, costing $6 billion—or 15 percent—of the city's $39.7 billion annual expense budget.[3] But two-thirds of the 20,464 contracts summarized in table 5.1 are for professional, technical, office, and personal services; bank and financial services; maintenance and repair of office and other equipment; cleaning; and subsidies to various institutions and to agencies for federally funded community programs. Although these contracts satisfy the technical definition of privatization from chapter 1, they are not introducing competition to public agencies or changing to more private service delivery.

In other words, table 5.1 is not a complete guide to privatization in New York—or any other city for that matter. Just because the Dinkins administration sponsored numerous contracts does not mean that much privatization took place then. As explained in chapter 4, Mayor Giuliani was the first mayor of New York to promote privatization; his four predecessors—dating back to the 1970s, when the idea first took hold nationally—had shunned it.

Table 5.1 **Private Contracts in New York City's Fiscal 2002 Budget**

Service	*Number of contracts*	*Amount ($ millions)*
Maintenance of telecommunications, office equipment, and data processing equipment	2,197	$90
Vehicle maintenance and repair	402	10
General maintenance and repair	1,599	92
Printing	474	16
Community consultants	258	25
Finance and investing	57	18
Security services	216	50
Office temporary services	600	61
Cleaning services	404	11
Maintenance for *in-rem* properties[a]	30	9
Transportation of pupils	430	568
Other transportation (for other than mass transit)	279	17
Protective services for adults	10	7
Children's charitable institutions	71	622
Child welfare services	302	133
Day care of children	583	492
Head Start	167	120
Home care services	129	223
Homemaking services	10	31
Homeless family services	308	196
Homeless individual services	146	139
Bank charges for public assistance accounts	19	2
Other social services	68	29
AIDS services	116	180
Mental hygiene services	309	497
Hospitals contracts for prison health care	14	156
Visiting nurse services	1	9
Economic development	65	7
Employment services for public assistance recipients	87	160
Legal Aid Society	2	63
Subsidies to cultural institutions	648	34

(table continues)

Table 5.1 (continued)

Service	*Number of contracts*	*Amount ($ millions)*
School contracts for handicapped children	291	383
Course development and training for city government employees	507	26
Maintenance and operation of infrastructure	433	118
Payments to private agencies for federal programs	2,369	356
Education and recreation services for youths	1,185	102
Professional services (legal, accounting, and so on)	4,502	330
Other personal and technical services	1,176	604
TOTAL	20,464	5,986

Source: Adapted from New York City's adopted budget, fiscal 2002, 4C–13C.

[a] *In rem* properties are those that have been foreclosed for nonpayment of property taxes.

Note: The data in this table are not complete due to the difficulty of counting services and distinguishing routine contracts from outsourcing initiated deliberately to improve government performance.

The Pattern of Privatization

The Giuliani administration proposed eighty-two privatizations, not including the numerous conventional and commonplace contracts discussed earlier. Of these proposed privatizations, sixty-six (80 percent) were realized and sixteen were not. These sixteen were either reconsidered, or encountered too much opposition and were abandoned (See chapters 6 and 7), or encountered implementation difficulties and were suspended, or were still pending and in process at the time of writing, or their status was ambiguous. Of the sixty-six realized privatizations, fifty-three were still in effect at the end of the Giuliani administration; that is, they were continuing in routine operation, whereas thirteen were completed—for example, as one-time divestments or completed contracts.

Table 5.2 lists each of the eighty-two initiatives by agency in alphabetical order and gives the outcome for each initiative. Table 5.3 presents the same information but lists the initiatives by method of privatization. Each initiative has a unique identification number. Appendix A summarizes information about each initiative; appendix B describes each in detail and also gives

Table 5.2 Privatization Initiatives, by Agency

Agency	*Number proposed*	*Not realized*		*Realized*			
				Completed		*Continuing*	
		No.	*ID #*	*No.*	*ID #*	*No.*	*ID #*
Buildings	3	1	#1			2	#2, 3
Business Services	1					1	#4
Administration for Children's Services	2					2	#5, 6
Citywide Administrative Services	5			2	#7, 10	3	#8, 9, 11
Consumer Affairs	1					1	#12
Corrections	1	1	#13				
Cultural Affairs	1					1	#14
Economic Development Corporation	7	2	#15, 18	5	#16, 17, 19, 20, 21		
Education	6	3	#22, 26–27	1	#25	2	#23, 24
Environmental Protection	3	2	#29, 30			1	#28
Finance	5					5	#31–35
Fire	3	1	#37			2	#36, 38
Health and Hospitals Corporation	5	2	#39, 42	1	#43	2	#40, 41
Homeless Services	1					1	#44
Housing Authority	3					3	#45–47
Housing Preservation and Development	5			1	#49	4	#48, 50–52
Human Resources Administration	4					4	#53–56

Table 5.2 continues

Table 5.2 (continued)

Agency	*Number proposed*	*Not realized*		*Realized*			
				Completed		*Continuing*	
		No.	*ID #*	*No.*	*ID #*	*No.*	*ID #*
Information Technology and Telecommunications	3	2	#57, 58			1	#59
Juvenile Justice	1					1	#60
Parks and Recreation	3			1	#63	2	#61, 62
Public Libraries	3					3	#64–66
Sanitation	6	1	#67			5	#68–72
Taxi and Limousine Commission	2			1	#73	1	#74
Trade Waste Commission	1					1	#75
Transportation	7	1	#81	1	#78	5	#76–77, 79–80, 82
TOTAL	82	16		13		53	

Source: Compiled by the author.

Note: The identification numbers correspond to entries in the appendices that provide more information about the privatization initiatives.

Table 5.3 Privatization Initiatives, by Method

Method of privatization	*Number proposed*	*Not realized*		*Realized*			
				Completed		*Continuing*	
		No.	*ID #*	*No.*	*ID #*	*No.*	*ID #*
One method only							
Contract[a]	40	8		2	#10, 63	30	
Managed competition	2	1	#81			1	#80
Lease	3	2	#27, 58			1	#77
Franchise	4			1	#73	3	#59, 69, 76
Voucher	1					1	#5
Public-private partnership (PPP)	2	1	#26	1	#43		
Divestment	15	4	#18, 29, 30, 39	8	16, 17, 19, 20, 21, 25, 49, 78	3	#6, 31, 50
Default	0						
Withdrawal	1					1	#55
Voluntarism	1					1	#64
Deregulation	1					1	#12

Table 5.3 continues

Table 5.3 (continued)

Method of privatization	*Number proposed*	*Not realized*		*Realized*			
				Completed		*Continuing*	
		No.	*ID #*	*No.*	*ID #*	*No.*	*ID #*
Multiple methods							
Contract +							
Managed competition	1					1	#62
Withdrawal + contract	1					1	#32
Withdrawal + divestment							
+ contract	1			1	#7		
Withdrawal + voluntary	2					2	#14, 65
Default (plus) voluntary	2					2	#4, 79
Default + vol. (plus)							
contract	1					1	#61
Default + deregulation	1					1	#74
Divestment + PPP	1					1	#48
Other							
Regulate to create a							
competitive market	1					1	#75
Forced private divestment	1					1	#52
TOTAL	82	16		13		53	

Source: Compiled by the author.

[a]Unrealized contracts comprise ID #1, 13, 15, 22, 37, 42, 57, 67. Realized contracts comprise ID #2, 3, 8, 9, 11, 23, 24, 28, 33, 34, 35, 36, 38, 40, 41, 44, 45, 46, 47, 51, 53, 54, 56, 60, 66, 68, 70, 71, 72, 82.

the date and method of privatization, the net benefits—both quantitative and qualitative, where available—and the implementation steps.

A word of caution. When the method of contract was ambiguous, the author's classification of initiatives as contract, franchise, and so on in table 5.3 was subjective. The boundaries between methods are not always sharply defined in the real world. For example, the Department of Sanitation has a contract with a private firm (#69) whereby the firm operates a gas emission-control system at the city's landfill and collects and sells the gas, paying the city an annual fee.[4] This is considered here as a franchise rather than a contract (outsourcing) because it is a commercial business that pays the city for the privilege. The fact that the legal instrument is a written contract does not change the basic nature of the arrangement; all franchises involve contractual agreements, as do leases, divestments, and grants, for that matter.

Some may question whether certain entries belong in this listing of privatizations at all. The basic principle applied here goes back to the definition of privatization in chapter 1: Privatization is an action that reduces the role of government or increases the role of the private institutions of society (markets, nongovernmental organizations, and the family) in delivering services. The public-private initiatives identified here fit this definition. For example, Mayor Giuliani's emphasis on adoption (#6) as better for children than foster care helped move 12,000 children out of city-sponsored foster care and secured adoptions for 21,000 children. This is privatization by divestment—by free transfer, no less! No doubt some will be appalled to think of adoption so heartlessly; others may be amused by this imaginative stretch. In any event, the children are generally better off in private families and the city saves money.

Most of the proposed initiatives, seventy of eighty-two, or 85 percent, used only one of the standard privatization methods, whereas the remaining twelve involved multiple methods. Similarly, of the sixty-six realized initiatives, fifty-four, or 82 percent, used only one privatization method. In no way were any of these simple or easy to implement. Most of the initiatives that used more than one method are particularly interesting and are examined in chapter 6. They illustrate the great flexibility and broad applicability of privatization and should stimulate creative thinking in New York and elsewhere.

Contracts were the most popular method of privatization (contracts alone, not in conjunction with other methods). They were proposed in 49 percent of the initiatives (forty of eighty-two) and accounted for 48 percent of the realized cases (thirty-two of sixty-six). In other words, contracts represented nearly half the initiatives and were realized in about the same proportion as they were proposed.

Their success rate—that is, the fraction of proposed contracts realized—was 80 percent (thirty-two of forty), exactly the same as the overall 80 percent success rate for all proposed privatizations regardless of method. One might have expected unions to oppose contracts more fiercely than other forms of privatization that have less of an impact on employees. But this was not the case, suggesting either that all forms of privatization are equally noxious to unions or that management handled the contracting adroitly.

The next most common form of privatization was divestment, proposed fifteen times and realized eleven times. Much less common were the other eight individual forms—managed competition, leases, franchises, vouchers, public-private partnerships, withdrawal, voluntarism, and deregulation, as well as other complex forms involving a combination of more than one of these methods. Default, of course, was not proposed; as chapter 1 defines it, default is perceived by the public as government failure, not a plan of action. Withdrawal, however, is a planned act and can achieve the same effect as default. In fact, withdrawal appears five times in table 5.3 and default appears four times; in all but one case these forms operate in conjunction with other forms, typically voluntarism or contracts. These interesting individual cases are discussed in the next chapter.

A comparison of the eighty-two proposed privatizations with the recommended privatizations in the 1993 Transition Report (See table 4.1) shows considerable overlap. Of the thirty-two recommended candidates, the Giuliani administration proposed eighteen and realized thirteen. Giuliani's transition team, long disbanded and scattered, should take satisfaction in this outcome.

The Outcomes of Privatization

The benefits commonly cited to justify privatization center on cost (lower cost, avoided cost, and increased revenue for government) and service (higher quality of service, more responsive service, and direct savings for the public). The sixty-six initiatives implemented in New York City, in the aggregate, produced all of these benefits, as well as nonmonetary benefits (See chapter 6), although some savings from individual privatizations were modest. Important caveats are in order, however. The cost of contracting or other privatization actions was not calculated. The savings and other financial benefits shown in the tables were not independently verified; they are from mayoral or agency reports or interviews. Different authoritative sources sometimes provided different estimates of savings, and in these cases the author's best estimates appear in the tables. In many cases no authoritative or reliable estimates of savings were available, and therefore none are given. For better or worse, this is the best extant record, and it is not likely to be improved.

There is no evidence of significant negative results. The city did not lose the capacity to monitor its contractors. No employees were laid off. There was no reported reduction in quality, effectiveness, or responsiveness of service. Nothing was lost by divesting the various city-owned assets: Even radio listeners who were unhappy when the city divested its stations (#20) were relieved to learn that their favorite programming would continue under private, nonprofit ownership. But there were few formal and thorough evaluations of contract performance. (See chapter 9 for one of the noteworthy exceptions.)

As for the monetary benefits of privatization, one-time revenues dominate; they total $2.3 billion. Almost all of that revenue is from divestments ($2.2 billion), and the remainder is from the sale of taxi franchises ($89.9 million; #73) and a combination of withdrawal and voluntary organizations ($12.5 million; See tables 5.4 and 5.5).

Savings (or avoided costs or more revenue) of $979 million are generated annually by the privatizations. If one assumes that the annual savings can be extrapolated for every year, in eight years the savings would be more than three times the divestment revenue, $7.8 billion versus $2.3 billion. Thus although the one-time divestments realized dramatically large revenues in single, finite steps, the many smaller initiatives that created savings arguably had a larger payoff. (This ignores any difference in the effort required to carry out the transactions.) In any event, sooner or later the city government will run out of assets to divest; there are many more opportunities for privatizing services using the other methods, as discussed in chapter 8.

The numbers in tables 5.4 and 5.5 seriously underestimate the true benefits of privatization and should be viewed as absolute minimums. In addition to the revenues and savings for the city government, there were also direct savings to the public—hundreds of millions of dollars—by reducing their costs. The last column in tables 5.4 and 5.5 lists some of these savings, as does table 6.2. Privatizing commercial solid waste disposal (#75) saved businesses some $400 million. Deregulating van services (#74) saved the public unknown millions of dollars and provided more convenient transportation. In many cases the savings, although obvious, were not quantified—such as greater convenience in

Table 5.4 Benefits from Realized Privatizations, by Agency

Agency	*No.*	*ID #*	*Savings or equivalent ($ million per year)*	*One-time revenue, ($ million)*	*Other benefits*
Buildings	2	#2, 3			
Business Services	1	#4	7.15		
Administration for Children's Services	2	#5, 6	44.0		
Citywide Administrative Services	5	#7–11	4.9		
Consumer Affairs	1	#12			Saved public $2.2 million per year
Corrections					
Cultural Affairs	1	#14	188.0		
Economic Development Corporation	5	#16, 17, 19–21		661.0	
Education	3	#23–25	3.8	45.0	
Environmental Protection	1	#28	1.0		
Finance	5	#31–35	1.0	1,450.0	
Fire	2	#36, 38	1.0		
Health and Hospitals Corporation	3	#40, 41, 43	8.61		
Homeless Services	1	#44	2.7		

Housing Authority	3	#45–47	2.45		
Housing Preservation and Development	5	#48–52	101.2	12.65	Saves housing stock
Human Resources Administration	4	#53–56	577.0		More jobs for welfare recipients
Information Technology and Telecommunications	1	#59			Greater convenience for the public
Juvenile Justice	1	#60	0.45		
Parks and Recreation	3	#61–63	17.24		
Public Libraries	3	#64–66	1.0	12.5	
Sanitation	5	#68–72	4.8		Closed landfill
Taxi and Limousine Commission	2	#73, 74		89.9	More van and taxi services for the public
Trade Waste Commission	1	#75			Saved public $400 million per year
Transportation	6	#76–80, 82	12.4	16.86	Better transportation, safer streets
TOTAL	66		$ 979	$2,288	

Source: Compiled by the author.

Table 5.5 **Benefits from Realized Privatizations, by Method**

Method of privatization	*No.*	*ID #*	*Savings or equivalent ($ million per year)*	*One-time revenue, ($ million)*	*Other benefits*
One method only					
Contract (12 of 32)[a]	32		54.0		See Table 6.2
Managed competition	1	#80			24% productivity rise
Lease	1	#77	6.1		
Franchise	4	#59,69,73,76	3.5	89.9	
Voucher	1	#5	44.0		Parental choice
Public-private partnership (PPP)	1	#43	(-0.39)		
Divestment[b]	11			2186.0	See Table 6.1
Default	0				
Withdrawal	1	#55	553.0		
Voluntarism	1	#64	1.0		
Deregulation	1	#12			$2.2 million in public savings
Multiple methods					
Contract + managed competition	1	#62	.54		Reduced vehicle down time by 62%
Withdrawal + contract	1	#32	1.0		Better service
Withdrawal + divestment + contract	1	#7			Cost reduction and revenue

Withdrawal + voluntary	2	#14, 65	188.0	12.5	
Default + voluntary	2	#4, 79	9.5		
Default + voluntary + contract	1	#61	17.0		
Default + deregulation	1	#74			Better service and savings for the public
Divestment + PPP	1	#48	95.4		
Other					
Regulate to create a competitive market	1	#75			$400 million annual savings for the public
Forced private divestment	1	#52	5.8		Avoid cost exposure for the city government
TOTAL	66		979	2,288	

Source: Compiled by the author.

[a]ID #2, 3, 8, 9, 10, 11, 23, 24, 28, 33, 34, 35, 36, 38, 40, 41, 44, 45, 46, 47, 51, 53, 54, 56, 60, 63, 66, 68, 70, 71, 72, 82.

[b]ID #6, 16, 17, 19, 20, 21, 25, 31, 49, 50, 78.

paying municipal bills (#32). In other cases the results, such as better performance by city government workers trying to stave off private competitors, were not readily calculable in dollars. Tax collection (#31), vehicle maintenance (#62), and street resurfacing (#81) are examples of services improved under these conditions. In fact, street resurfacing was an unrealized privatization precisely because the in-house unit, facing competition, agreed to reorganize and improve its performance, as happened also in Indianapolis.

To the author's knowledge, there have been no attempts to define and measure the financial impact of a city's privatization program in a way that invites comparison. This is worth attempting. To do this for New York, one could multiply the annual savings of Mayor Giuliani's privatization program ($979 million) by eight years and arrive at a theoretical total of $7.8 billion, as was done above. Assuming arbitrarily that the average privatization took effect halfway through Mayor Giuliani's term in office, the total savings over eight years amount to half that, or $3.9 billion. To this should be added the one-time divestment revenue, $2.3 billion, to arrive at a sum of $6.2 billion for the net benefits during the Giuliani administration. Dividing this sum by the number of years, eight, yields an average annual monetary benefit of $776 million from privatization. (Because of the one-time nature of divestment revenue, one cannot project these composite savings into the future, although some cynics feel that the city government has a virtually inexhaustible supply of assets that it could and should divest.)

Comparisons between cities, or between administrations in a single city, can be drawn by calculating this annual benefit as a fraction of the annual budget and also by expressing it on a per capita basis. The average yearly budget for New York City during the Giuliani administration was $34.7 billion.[5] Therefore the privatization benefits are estimated as 2.2 percent of the city's average annual budget. On a per capita basis, given that the city's average population during those eight years was 7,536,750, the privatization benefits were $103 per person per year, or $824 per person for the length of the administration, or $3,295 for a family of four.[6] Again, these are very conservative estimates. That said, these are impressive figures against which future administrations in New York and other cities can be measured.

Mayor Dinkins was right after all: Privatization is no panacea. Rather it is an opening wedge in adjusting the balance among society's principal institutions—government, the market, nonprofits, and the family—and perhaps, in time, enlisting a broader range of the city's human resources in building a better society.

Summary

The Giuliani administration proposed eighty-two privatizations in addition to the existing thousands of conventional and commonplace contracts. Sixty-six of these eighty-two privatizations were realized, and sixteen were not. Contracts were the most prevalent form of privatization. The next most common form was divestment, followed by franchises, leases, managed competition, public-private partnerships, vouchers, withdrawal, voluntarism, and deregulation. Even less frequent were combinations of two or more of these methods.

The average annual monetary benefit from privatization is about $776 million, and most of that is from divestments. Total privatization benefits for the duration of the administration are estimated as $6.2 billion. This was 2.2 percent of the city's average annual budget. On a per capita basis, privatization benefits were $824 per person for the eight years of the administration. However, these figures seriously underestimate the benefits and should be viewed as absolute minimums. In addition to the revenues and savings realized by the city government, there were also direct savings to the public of hundreds of millions of dollars in reduced expenditures and the benefits of higher quality and more responsive services.

Notes

1. City of New York, adopted budget fiscal 1993, 7C.
2. Dennis C. Smith and William Grinker, "The Promise and Pitfalls of Performance Based Contracting," paper presented at the 25th Annual Research Conference of the Association for Public Policy Analysis and Management, Washington, D.C., November 6, 2003.
3. City of New York, adopted budget fiscal 2002, 13C.
4. The numbers in parentheses are identification numbers for each privatization. These numbers direct the reader to the particular privatization in the tables and the appendixes.
5. Calculated from City of New York, "Comprehensive Annual Report of the Comptroller for the Fiscal Year Ended June 30, 2002," 251.
6. New York City population calculated from ibid., 272.

6 | Selected Successful Privatization Initiatives

The most interesting of Mayor Giuliani's successful privatizations are described in this chapter. They are divided for convenience into divestments, contracts, managed competition, and other arrangements. The next chapter describes the attempted privatizations that did not succeed. All the privatization initiatives are summarized in appendix A and described more fully in appendix B. The figures in parentheses identify individual privatizations and guide the reader to the appendices.

Divestments

Revenues from divestments amounted to $2.2 million in addition to ongoing revenues, namely, annual property taxes from properties now privately owned. This section discusses individual divestments and, with the exception of tax liens divestments, does not count revenue from increased property taxes (See table 6.1).

Principal Divestments

New York City's principal divestments were tax liens, the coliseum, radio and television stations, the United Nations Plaza Hotel, parking facilities, community gardens, and city-owned residential buildings.

Tax Liens (#31). New York City's most lucrative divestment was the sale of tax liens, which yielded $1.45 billion. Cities use the *in rem* process to foreclose

Table 6.1 Benefits from Realized Divestments

ID #	*Revenue ($ million)*	*Description*
6	0	Adoption instead of foster care for children
16	345.0	Sale of the Coliseum
17	4.0	Sale of community gardens
19	85.0	Sale of United Nations Plaza Hotel
20	20.0	Sale of WNYC-AM and FM radio stations
21	207.0	Sale of WNYC-TV station
25	45.0	Sale of Board of Education buildings
31	1,450.0	Sale of tax liens on buildings facing foreclosure; $895 million from the sale of bonds, $555 million from delinquent taxpayers fearing the loss of their property. The delinquency rate subsequently dropped by 20%.
49	12.65	Sale of tenant-occupied, city-owned buildings with market value
50	n.a.	Sale of vacant, city-owned, *in rem* buildings; creates housing[a]
78	16.9	Sale of city-owned parking lots and garages
TOTAL	2,186.0	

Source: Compiled by the author.

[a] *In rem* properties are those that have been foreclosed for nonpayment of property taxes.

properties that are delinquent in paying taxes. Because it is so time-consuming and expensive to take physical possession and then try to rehabilitate the decaying properties and sell them, the Giuliani administration abandoned that long-standing practice and adopted a very different policy pioneered in the late 1980s by Mayor Bret Schundler of Jersey City. Tax liens, the legal instrument permitting takeovers, were bundled in large blocks; that is, they were securitized—much like mortgages—and sold as bonds to investors. Eight such sales took place during the administration, generating $895 million without the city taking possession of the properties. Property owners, who saw that the city was no longer dragging its feet before starting the lengthy *in rem* procedure, hurriedly began paying their delinquent tax bills; the city collected $555 million from them. Some of these taxes were ongoing annual revenue. Now that the city had a good mechanism to enforce tax collection, the delinquency rate dropped. The sale of tax liens is replicable in the future; it is not a one-time sale, although presumably different delinquent properties would be involved. These multiple benefits could not all be monetized in table 6.1.

The Coliseum (#16). The sale of the Coliseum, an exhibition center, for $345 million made it the next-largest source of divestment revenue. Demolition was completed by 2001 and redevelopment of the site was well underway in 2002.

Radio (#20) and Television Stations (#21). A particularly interesting divestment, perhaps unique to New York, was the sale of the city-owned broadcasting empire, radio stations WNYC-AM and WNYC-FM (#20) and television station WNYC-TV (#21). The city got into the radio business in the 1930s, when there were few radio stations. But by 1993 the city had forty-nine radio stations and innumerable television channels and no good reason, according to Mayor Giuliani, to continue owning and operating them.[1] Once Giuliani took office he promptly started the sale process. The television station was sold to ITT Corporation and Dow Jones and Company for $207 million in 1996, and the radio stations were turned over to the nonprofit WNYC Foundation for $20 million.

United Nations Plaza Hotel (#19). The relatively straightforward sale of the city-owned land under the United Nations Plaza Hotel brought $85 million and an average annual increase in property taxes of $2.5 million. However, the city lost the rent that the hotel had been paying.

Parking Facilities (#78). The city also sold three parking garages and two parking lots for $16.9 million thereby shedding an activity that was far from a core function of municipal government. One garage was in Manhattan, and the other facilities were in Queens. The $16.9 million does not take into consideration the parking revenue that the city lost.

Community Gardens (#17). This was one of the city's most contentious divestments. The gardens were city-owned vacant lots that local residents, with hard work, had turned into "their" highly prized gardens and urban oases. Residents wanted the city to give the community groups title to those lots (divestment by free transfer) so they could continue their urban gardening. However, the gardeners were pitted against advocates of low-income housing, who had distinctly different ideas about the use of those lots, and the city, which wanted money. In the end the city sold 111 of the lots to two nonprofit organizations for $4 million with the agreement that they would maintain the gardens in good condition. Actress Bette Midler was the principal benefactor behind the purchase.

City-Owned Residential Buildings (#49 and #50). Mayor Giuliani inherited a huge inventory of city-owned residential buildings—5,458 of them with 52,000 housing units. He wanted to get rid of them, and for good reason. When the buildings were occupied the city lost a net of $2,900 in operating costs per year on each housing unit, after considering the rent collected. Vacant buildings were usable real estate to meet New York's perennial housing needs. The city sold occupied buildings with 583 housing units and 50 commercial units for $12.65 million (#49). It divested small (one to four families), run-down, vacant buildings by transferring them for a dollar each to experienced developers who were selected through a bidding process (#50). The city even provided tax abatements to stimulate private financing to rehabilitate the buildings and ultimately to sell them to eligible buyers as owner-occupied units.

Other Divestments

Two divestments—of city-owned buildings and privately owned housing—are not listed in table 6.1 because they were not pure divestments. Instead they are listed in table 5.5 as multiple-method or "other" divestments.

Public-Private Partnerships to Divest City-Owned Buildings (#48). The city realized substantial savings, but no revenue, by divesting additional tenant-occupied, city-owned, *in rem* buildings through complicated programs with different features depending on the nature of the buildings (See appendix B). The city entered into public-private partnerships with developers and, in effect, gave away buildings, sometimes with loans to encourage the private partners to rehabilitate them. This eliminated the annual cost of managing and operating those buildings, which amounted to annual savings of $95.4 million. Because this divestment involved partnerships, it is not the same as the process used to divest city-owned residential buildings (#50).

"Forced Divestment" of Privately Owned Housing (#52). A very different case is the forced divestment of private property to other private owners. This bold, unusual step arguably falls in the realm of public-private initiatives. The city was reluctant to take title to more properties in tax default. It was selling the stock already in hand (#48, #49, and #50) and forestalling abandonment (#51). In this case the city identified buildings that were in serious jeopardy of being abandoned and falling into the city's unwilling hands. Under local law and following a rigorous legal process the buildings were transferred to other owners. "Forced divestment" or "anticipatory divestment" (the author's coinage) applies because the properties would have come under city ownership sooner or later and probably would have required divestment by free transfer (#48 and #50). By acting sooner rather than later the city avoided a cost of $5.8 million, although it is not clear that this can be considered an annual saving.

Contracts

Contracting dominated the privatization methods in terms of sheer volume of activity. Of the sixty-six realized privatizations, thirty-two were "pure" contracts, meaning not a mixed or multiple method. However, only $54 million, or less than 5 percent, of the $1,148.8 million total annual savings from privatization are attributed to contracting. This figure is misleading because estimates of savings were available for only twelve of the thirty-two contracting initiatives, and many of the contracts had objectives other than savings (See table 6.2).[2] For example, contracts to transport solid waste to out-of-town disposal sites (#68) cost the city money but yielded a major environmental benefit: closure of the last landfill within city limits.

Most of the contracts were for such mundane services as data entry (#35), guard services (#66), elevator inspections (#2), reproduction and mailing (#36), boiler plant operation (#47), legal services for poor defendants (#54), administration of licensing examinations (#3), management of city-owned real estate (#10, #11, and #45), and more convenient bill-paying services for the public (#33). A few of the more interesting ones, however, are discussed in detail in the following sections on physical services and health and human services (See also appendixes A and B.)

Physical Services

Particularly noteworthy among the physical services that were contracted were vehicle-fleet maintenance, park maintenance, school custodial services, water-meter reading, delivery of office supplies, and red light cameras.

Table 6.2 Savings and Other Benefits from Realized Contracts

ID #	*Annual savings ($ million)*	*Other benefits*
2		More timely elevator inspections
3		More responsive administration of licensing examinations
8	4.7	Reduced vehicle out-of-service rates from 10% to 2.5%; released garage space
9		Lower cost, more choice, faster delivery of supplies; less storage space used
10[a]	0.2	Audit of leases paid to the city to assure correct payment
11		Better control of city-owned rental property; earlier deposit of rentals
23		Better instruction in summer school
24	3.8	Cleaner schools, faster and better maintenance, more community access
28	1.0	Lower cost of water-meter reading; can expand to save $2.15 million per year
33		More convenience for bill-paying public; lower costs for city
34		Lower staffing costs for processing bail receipts; quicker deposits
35		Lower cost of data entry for Department of Finance
36		Faster reproduction and mailing services for Fire Department.
38		Lower ambulance cost for private hospitals under contract with Health and Hospitals Corporation
40	6.0	Better health care for prison inmates at lower cost
41	3.0	Hospital laundry contract can be expanded to save $6 million per year
44	2.7	Higher quality of homeless shelters and better services
45		Savings, if any, unknown for private management of scattered public housing
46		Screens out ineligibles for public housing; not done regularly in the past
47	2.5	Savings in operation of boiler plants in five public housing projects

Table 6.2 continues

Table 6.2 (continued)

ID #	*Annual savings ($ million)*	*Other benefits*
51		Prevents abandonment of distressed residential buildings; avoids costs
53	24.0	Education and enrollment in managed care for Medicaid recipients
54		Introduces competition in legal services for poor defendants
56		Performance contracts to place welfare recipients in jobs; reduces welfare cost
60	0.5	Private facility operation and services for youths in detention
63[a]		Cleaner parks, park maintenance costs reduced by 30%
66		Lower cost of security service for library
68		Eliminated landfill operations within city limits
70		Reduces volume of waste that would otherwise require costly disposal
71	1.3	Continues recycling of waste paper but at lower cost
72		Avoids cost of solid waste collection
82	4.0	Increases public safety by reducing red-light running
TOTAL	54.0	

Source: Compiled by the author.

[a] Completed contract. The other initiatives are ongoing.

Automotive Fleet Management and Maintenance (#8). Before December 1995 the Department of Citywide Administrative Services (DCAS) maintained a fleet of approximately 734 vehicles using a city-owned garage in Brooklyn. Having one central facility posed problems. The garage was extremely crowded with vehicles awaiting maintenance, and so a substantial amount of the mechanics' time was spent jockeying cars in and out of available spots. The result was high costs and long periods when vehicles were out of service. Also, the garage had little ability to repair vehicles after hours or those on official business that broke down outside the city.

In 1995 DCAS contracted its fleet maintenance services, transferred the garage to the New York Police Department, and reassigned the mechanics to vacancies in other agencies. The contract is managed by the DCAS Office of

Fleet Administration, which maintains records substantiating the reduction in cost and out-of-service rates. In 1997 the Mayor's Office of Operations expanded the contract to four other city agencies, and still other agencies have requested permission to join the initiative, increasing the number of participating vehicles from 734 to about 1,900.

The program is very successful. The average annual cost of maintaining a vehicle has dropped from approximately $3,100 per year to $1,250 per year. Based on the number of vehicles in the program, the estimated annual total savings for the city are $3.5 million. The New York Police Department was able to take over the Brooklyn garage for its newly acquired Transit Police vehicles and thereby forgo a costly garage lease, saving $1.2 million per year. The total savings and cost avoidance for the city amounted to $4.7 million annually.

Additionally, the privatization initiative resulted in better service. The contractor has more than 200 associated garages in and outside New York City and can service vehicles around the clock and throughout the country. Vehicle out-of-service rates were reduced from more than 10 percent of the fleet to between 2 percent and 3 percent. And there were other benefits. DCAS cancelled an unreliable truck maintenance contract, and the Department of Transportation also followed the DCAS lead and established its own account, placing approximately 600 vehicles in its program. No dollar value was placed on these substantial benefits. For example, reduced out-of-service rates mean that vehicles return to service faster, and therefore agencies need fewer of them. This saves vehicle costs and garage space.

Park Maintenance (#63). Through competitive bidding, the city selected a contractor for an experimental one-year term to maintain forty-seven park properties in Queens. After this proved successful, the city awarded another contract a year later to another firm to maintain forty-five park sites in the Bronx. Together these contracts reduced costs by 30 percent and substantially improved cleanliness ratings (See chapter 9 for a detailed examination of this and other well done privatizations in this department.) The city terminated the program after two years because it could hire welfare recipients participating in the Work Experience Program, at no cost to the agency, to achieve similar results.

Custodial Services in Schools (#24). When Giuliani took office, the city's 1,100 public schools were in disrepair. They were dirty, repairs were not made promptly, and the school custodians did not keep the schools open for community use without extra payment. Nevertheless, the Department of Education proposed a contract with the school custodians that would have increased spending on a system riddled with inefficiencies. The mayor rejected this contract and instead pressured for a very different type of agreement. The final contract did away with long-standing but outlandish perquisites and privileges that the custodians had acquired over many decades, tied productivity to pay for the first time, and placed custodians under the control of the school principals.

A committee of experts from the private real estate industry helped develop a privatization program for custodial services in fifty-two schools; later the number was increased to seventy-nine. The city solicited competitive proposals from private firms to function as property managers. To avoid replacing a complacent public sector monopoly with a complacent private sector monopoly, no one firm could bid on all the schools. Contracts were awarded to the lowest responsible bidders; each one would maintain and repair a group of school buildings located in the same general area. The primary goal of this project was to provide quality custodial services.[3]

The contracted schools were indeed kept cleaner and repairs were better and completed more quickly. A cost comparison of contracted schools and schools maintained by in-house, school custodians indicated that the city was saving about $3.8 million per year for the seventy-nine schools; in-house work costs about 15 percent more. Another important benefit is that the contractor is required to keep the schools open, as needed, in the evenings and on Saturday mornings at no additional cost to the city. This greatly expands community access to school facilities. The satisfactory results led the Bloomberg administration to expand the program in stages to cover almost 500 schools, but vigorous opposition by teachers and custodians and their City Council allies continues.[4]

Water-Meter Reading (#28). The Department of Environmental Protection contracts with Con Edison to read water meters in the Bronx and Staten Island. Con Edison reads water meters every day, providing data for the city to issue quarterly bills for metered accounts. There are 98,000 meters in Staten Island and 65,000 meters in the Bronx. Con Edison has rerouted the meter readers so that the reading can be efficiently integrated into its own gas and electric meter-reading routes.

The city is paying $1.01 per reading to Con Edison. This saves $1.17 per reading in Staten Island relative to in-house costs and $2.07 per reading in the Bronx. Therefore, reading the 98,000 meters in Staten Island four times a year saves $458,640 per year, and reading the 65,000 meters in the Bronx four times a year saves $538,200 per year, for a total of almost $1 million per year. These savings recur each year and increase as the number of meters in these boroughs increases. If and when this contract is expanded throughout the city, the estimated annual savings would be $2.15 million per year.

Additionally, because department staff are now free for other problem-solving tasks (repairing or replacing meters and other equipment, verifying meter readings questioned by customers, inspecting for leaks, and so on), the number of bills based on estimated readings (because the meters were not read) has been reduced. This results in fewer customer inquiries and improved collections.

Delivery of Office Supplies (#9). Before privatizing the delivery of office supplies, the city purchased supplies in bulk through a competitive bidding process that took several weeks. Vendors awarded the supply contracts were obligated to use specific packaging or risk having the delivery rejected. The office supplies were stored in bulk at the New York City Central Storehouse pending receipt of agency orders. Agencies were obligated to purchase their office supplies from the storehouse. Only those items not stocked by the central storehouse could be purchased in the open market from local vendors. Further, the storehouse would deliver only those agency orders valued at $200 or more and only to one central location at each agency. If an agency wanted an order for less than $200, or needed the items in less than the standard six-week delivery time, the agency had to arrange its own pickup.

Privatization enabled the city to realize several economic benefits. Office supplies no longer occupied valuable city space permanently. In addition, agencies not only had more flexibility in their choice of products, they also received a 61 percent discount off list prices in the catalog. Moreover, the requestor received the order within five days rather than six weeks.

All New York City agencies are now eligible to receive direct delivery of office supplies. The discount has been increased from 61 percent to 66 percent and the delivery time reduced from five days to two. Delivery is free as long as the order is worth $50 or more.

Red-Light Cameras (#82). An advocacy group approached the Department of Transportation (DOT) about starting a program to remedy red-light running.

The state enacted a law authorizing the city to implement the Red-Light Camera program, in which cameras placed overhead at certain intersections automatically photograph the license plates of vehicles that drive through red lights. The city mails photographs and tickets to the owners of the vehicles.

DOT owns the cameras and contracts out the photographic processing component of this program, which includes maintaining all cameras, loading and unloading each camera, developing and delivering the films, and back-office tracking of each notice of liability. DOT is required by law to review the photographs of "events" and determine liability—a contractor cannot perform this function. DOT determines which event photos will result in tickets being issued; about half the events result in tickets.

The program's primary goal is to protect the safety of the traveling public by deterring red-light running. Between 1994 (the first year of operation) and 1997 red-light-running incidents dropped by 41 percent at intersections where cameras were operating. In 2000 the city issued about 200,000 tickets and collected about $9 million in revenue. The contract cost is about $5 million per year, so the net revenue increase is $4 million per year. There is no revenue sharing.

The only privatized part of this program is the operation of the photographic component. One could therefore question whether the savings—in lives and money—should be credited entirely to privatization, but there is no easy way to disentangle the contributions.

The program started in 1994 with twelve cameras, expanded to eighteen, then to thirty. DOT sought authority to expand to one hundred; however, civil rights groups concerned about privacy raised objections. In the meantime, the system was changing from conventional film photography to digital photography.

Health and Human Services

Whereas the physical services provided by contractors in New York can be found in both large and small cities, the health and human services illustrated in this section are more typical of larger cities and counties.

Private Ambulance Contracting by Private Hospitals (#38). The Fire Department (FDNY) operates 909 ambulance "tours" (eight-hour shifts) per day, either directly or indirectly. Of these, 325 (or 36 percent) are supplied by private, voluntary hospitals under contract with the city.

The city has long used private hospitals for emergency ambulance service; that is, the service has long been privatized, in this sense. What is new, however, is that some of these nonprofit hospitals started contracting with for-profit ambulance companies instead of or in addition to operating their own ambulances with their own employees. (This is a trend throughout the United States.) The hospitals do not need city approval to do this. Although this new practice does not represent municipal privatization and is not a direct city activity or contract or privatization, it is included here because the city is responsible for this vital emergency service system and it is being outsourced, indirectly, to private, for-profit firms.

National figures show that private emergency ambulance companies provide the same quality of service (or better) as municipal agencies but at a much lower cost. Therefore the lower cost of ambulance service for the private hospitals should result in a lower cost for the city in its contracts with those hospitals, but no data were available to support this presumption.

The contracting out of ambulance services encountered strong opposition from firefighters who work in the FDNY ambulances. They feared that if more hospitals reduced their costs, the city might contract with more private hospitals and use fewer FDNY ambulances. Some FDNY ambulance crews deliberately refused to bring patients to hospitals that were using private ambulance companies. Fire Department officials threatened to bring charges against any firefighters who did this, noting that patients' lives were endangered by such a boycott if patients were rerouted to more distant hospitals. This kind of opposition soon faded.

Health Care for Prison Inmates (#40). The Health and Hospitals Corporation (HHC) provides health care for the 13,000 inmates in twelve of the city's sixteen prisons. When media and government investigations exposed inmate health care as unsatisfactory, HHC contracted first with private voluntary hospitals—with unsatisfactory results—and then with a private, for-profit firm for this service. The contract was for three years at an average price of $99 million per year on a fee-for-service basis. The city expects to save $4–$8 million in the first year of the contract.

HHC monitors the contractor's performance and has also created an inspection and risk management committee. The contractor is measured on forty criteria such as asthma care, dental services, and HIV testing. The contractor encountered startup problems during the first three months of the contract and was penalized more than $100,000 for suboptimal performance. Problems persisted, however, in this troubled service.[5]

Hospital Laundry Service (#41). More than 200 employees in the Brooklyn Central Laundry plant were cleaning about 16 million pounds of laundry a year for the seventeen facilities of the HHC. The employees were members of the city's largest public employee union, District Council 37 (DC 37), which in turn is a member of the American Federation of State, County, and Municipal Employees (AFSCME), the nation's largest union of state and local government employees after the teachers' union. HHC planned to contract out all the work and close its laundry facility. In March 1999 HHC started discussions with Angelica Textile Services of New Jersey, a company that had submitted a bid and whose plant was located across the river in nearby New Jersey. Under city law, however, before being able to contract with Angelica, HHC had to allow the Municipal Hospital Employees Union (Local 420 of DC 37) to make a counterproposal.

The DC 37 administrator, Lee Saunders, attacked the plan in no uncertain terms. He argued that 200 modestly paid, unionized city employees in Brooklyn would lose their jobs and add to the already high unemployment rate in that borough. Much of his testimony before the City Council on January 28 focused on the city's alleged failure to provide more money for the municipal hospitals. He also claimed that the nearby plant could not handle the entire workload and that some of the work would have to be done in the company's other plants near Albany, Philadelphia, and Boston. He said, "The logistical problems of the Angelica contract is [sic] a prescription for disaster, arising from laundry not being delivered on time and from infectious waste (blood-soaked sheets) being transported on interstate highways and busy thoroughfares." [6] (He somehow failed to note that those materials were currently being transported on congested streets in a densely populated city.) Shortly thereafter, DC 37 and Local 420 mounted a radio advertising campaign to rally public support against the plan. The City Council weighed in with its economic analysis that the job losses would take away $8 million from the central Brooklyn economy. It assumed that hospital workers would not be placed in other city job openings and would be left unemployed (unlikely), and it ignored the benefit to hospital patients, namely, less money spent on laundry and more money available for health care.

In February 2000 workers at the Brooklyn Central Laundry won a compromise with HHC through a collective bargaining agreement. The compromise resulted in half of the HHC laundry work staying at the Brooklyn Central Laundry and the other half going to Angelica. As part of the compromise, the sixty-three Brooklyn Central employees whose jobs were in jeopardy were transferred to other positions within HHC. The union also won the opportunity to use new capital equipment purchased by HHC for $1 million, and another $600,000 was expended by HHC in additional capital expenses. HHC began using the new equipment on May 31, 2001.

A year later HHC conducted a one-year comparison of the contracted and the in-house work and found that, not counting the capital investment, operational savings by contract were $3 million, half the $6 million expected if all the work had been contracted out, and the quality of the work by Angelica and Brooklyn Central was equally good. The fact remains, however, that the city spent an extra $1.6 million to buy the union's acquiescence.

Homeless Shelters (#44). The Department of Homeless Services (DHS) became an independent agency in the beginning of fiscal 1994 and began contracting the operation of its homeless shelters. The number of privatized facilities in the adult and family systems gradually increased and by 2000, 109 of the 122 shelters were contracted out, mostly to community-based organizations.

The city aimed to transform the shelter system so that it provided emergency assistance to truly needy clients, assessed their needs within a limited time frame, and referred them, where appropriate, to services to meet those needs to end their homelessness. The city also planned to introduce performance measurements for those contracts.

The city saved an estimated $3.9 million during fiscal 1996, $2.7 million during fiscal 1997, and $2.7 million during fiscal 1998 while providing higher-quality shelters with better services to clients. This is best illustrated in the single-adult system, where the contracts called for converting general shelter beds with only basic services to program beds that provide more intensive programs and services, including employment training, mental health and substance abuse treatment, and programs for veterans and the elderly. In general, services have become more direct and personal.

Moreover best practices can be developed when several agencies provide services instead of just one, and they can be compared and evaluated. Thus privatization of homeless shelters became a tool that all agencies, including DHS and the contracted service providers, can use to discover best practices. An additional benefit was that contracted shelters could more easily remove violent and abusive men, drug dealers, and thieves, who were then sent to other shelters. After being shunted around among shelters, they learned that they had to obey the rules.

But DHS does not plan to contract out all of its services. By maintaining direct operation of some outreach, single adult, and family shelters, DHS sets a standard of care by which the contracted providers can be measured. Although privatization proved beneficial in many ways, it also posed such challenges as conflicting goals of contractors and DHS (referred to in chapter 1 as the principal-agent problem), difficulty in evaluating overall performance, and displacement of DHS staff.

Verifying Eligibility of Applicants for Public Housing (#46). Not all applicants for public housing are eligible. By screening out ineligible applicants, dwelling units are saved for eligible families, which is an effective and equitable policy. By the time Giuliani took office the New York City Housing Authority was no longer making routine visits to applicants to check on their eligibility. In 1995 the department conducted a pilot project with five or six vendors that involved talking with landlords, visiting homes, and checking for criminal backgrounds. The last check was too expensive and was dropped. After the pilot project the city entered into a contract with one vendor who proved unsatisfactory. So the department brought in a larger firm that could handle a variable workload and could bundle visits to an area for greater efficiency.

Investigators from the private contractor write, call, and arrange appointments to visit the homes of families applying for public housing. Working from a standard questionnaire and checklist, they confirm family composition, quality of housekeeping, and presence of pets and determine if the current housing is substandard. They attempt to speak to neighbors, landlords, and superintendents and to determine if anyone is working. It may take several visits to complete the investigation if the applicant is not home. The investigator completes a report and sends it to the Housing Authority, which pays only for completed visits. The investigator takes photos of the applicant during the home visit, so that when the applicant visits the housing office the photos can prove that the investigator visited the family and did not merely invent the report.

Based on a three-year average, the contractor completes 14,000 home visits per year. The department decides eligibility, and about 12 percent of applicants are rejected on the basis of the verification visit. Service by contract is less costly and more convenient than doing the work with in-house staff, which would require buying cars to visit applicants as well as other expenses. The cost per completed visit report for the winning bid is $45.50; other bids were slightly higher, $50–70. The department reports that service is excellent, and there was no significant union or other opposition because this was a new activity.

Performance-Based Contracting for Job Placement (#56). Before 1999 the Human Resources Administration (HRA) and the Department of Employment (DOE) contracted with almost a hundred vendors to place public assistance recipients in jobs. Contracts were essentially cost plus fixed fee. After the1996 welfare reform legislation, HRA focused on job placement for adults (mostly those on public assistance), while DOE focused on youths and older, displaced workers.

The city's welfare-to-work initiatives focused on the bottom line: getting participants into jobs so they could become self-sufficient. To this end, HRA designed two streamlined programs: Skills Assessment Program (SAP) and Employment Services and Placement (ESP). SAP is a short-term program, about four to six weeks for current public assistance recipients and new applicants who are deemed most ready for jobs. They spend two weeks in full-time training by the SAP vendor, then change to a schedule of three days a week at a Work Experience Program (WEP) work site and two at their SAP assignment. ESP is longer term, serving public assistance recipients and applicants who require significant training prior to attempted placement. The city pays the contractors only when people are placed in jobs.

The city used negotiated acquisition to arrive at the ESP and SAP contracts. Three-year contracts were signed with twelve vendors; eight did ESP only, one did SAP only, and three did both. Four of the twelve vendors, including America Works, are for-profit firms. These were prime contractors, and each had subcontractors, many of which were nonprofit, community-based organizations. Many of these subcontractors had direct contracts in the past with city agencies for similar work. These contracts are all performance based; that is, vendors are paid only for placing participants in jobs. This was a significant innovation in New York. HRA monitored the contractors at start-up and through frequent site visits to observe their processes and measure their performance.

The city realized several benefits from competitive contracting for these employment programs. First, the city reduced costs by paying only for positive outcomes, that is, job placement and retention; nonperforming vendors dropped out and no longer received line-item payments to run unsuccessful programs. Second, the city avoided costs when clients on public assistance got jobs, became self-reliant, and were dropped from the welfare rolls. Third, the change from cost-plus contracts to performance-based contracts led to a 56 percent increase in the job placement rate (from 16 percent placement to 25 percent), and an annual placement increase of 305 percent (from 3,875 clients to 15,697). By the end of fiscal 2000 ESP and SAP had placed 89,071 public assistance recipients in jobs. Fourth, the city improved the quality of placement services. To earn performance incentives from the city, vendors focused on finding high-paying jobs for participants to increase retention. Moreover, the prime contractor–subcontractor relationship encouraged vendors to help their smaller subcontractors perform better.

Privatization Using Multiple Methods or Unconventional Methods

Some privatizations took advantage of both a contract and public-private (managed) competition. Other privatizations combined contracts with withdrawal, default, and voluntarism.

Contracting and Managed Competition in the Department of Parks and Recreation

The Department of Parks and Recreation runs one of New York City's best-managed privatizations. (See chapter 9 for a full discussion of this interesting case.) The department has eight garages throughout the city where it maintains and fuels its 2,000 vehicles. The department contracted with a private firm to maintain the vehicles in the Bronx Garage. After a year of satisfactory results, the department contracted out the two Brooklyn garages to the same firm. In the end, contractors maintained 35 percent of the fleet at a cost 30 percent below in-house costs. Total automotive maintenance costs in fiscal 2001 were 16 percent less in current dollars than they were five years earlier despite inflation and labor agreements that raised per unit costs. The savings were 26 percent after adjusting for inflation.

Even more important, the department reduced its out-of-service rate by 62 percent, from 266 vehicles in 1994 to 104 vehicles in 2001. The contractor's rate reached a low of 2.6 percent of vehicles in the Bronx and 2.9 percent in Brooklyn in 1998. The results were so good that when the department started to contract out more garages, the union agreed to improve its operating practices and try to match the performance of the private contractors.

Although the union could not quite match the contractor in price and performance, it improved internal operations dramatically. Competition worked. The in-house out-of-service rate dropped from 14 percent to 5.5 percent in fiscal 2001, compared to the contractor's rate of 4.9 percent that year. The overall rate for all eight garages stayed between 5 percent and 6 percent from 1998 through 2001. Some 160 more vehicles are on the road each day due to better maintenance and management, resulting in better park maintenance and lower capital costs due to fewer vehicle purchases.

As a result of these improvements the department did not undertake further managed competitions, but it kept track of the performance in each garage and thus maintained a competitive spur on both the firms and its own units; each served as a yardstick to measure the performance of the other.

Withdrawal, Default, and Voluntarism

Withdrawal, default, and voluntarism—individually and in combination—contributed to many successful privatizations.

Welfare Reform (#55). Government withdrew support for welfare (that is, the privatization method was withdrawal as defined in chapter 1) because of a change in national legislation. Individuals left the public assistance rolls and went to work, primarily in the private sector; in effect, they were "privatized." As a result the city spent $553 million less on welfare in 2000 than it did in 1995. Although the number of public assistance cases could rise again, for now this money is a recurring annual savings.

Voluntary Support for Cultural Institutions (#14) and Libraries (#64 and #65). Voluntary contributions prompted by city government withdrawal or default account for $406.7 million in annual savings in New York City. Donors contributed $375 million to cultural institutions under a matching grant program initiated by the administration (#14) and $7.5 million to the New York Public Library under the administration's Adopt-a-Branch program (#65). Both of these initiatives are listed as "withdrawal + voluntary" in table 5.5. The administration also promoted contributions to the Brooklyn Public Library (#64), which increased by $1 million a year. Because this last campaign did not involve withdrawal or default, it is categorized in the table under voluntarism.

Business Improvement Districts (#4). Sometimes when people feel that city services or facility maintenance are inadequate, they decide to take matters into their own hands. For example, local property owners in a self-defined area can, with government approval, form a business improvement district. They levy a special tax on themselves that they use for extra cleaning, safety, or other services and for aesthetic improvements in street lights, architectural lighting, plantings, signage, litter baskets, newspaper boxes, newsstands, and the like. The result is a visibly improved neighborhood. This kind of privatization is labeled "default + voluntary" in table 5.5. The twelve new business improvement districts created during the Giuliani administration raise $7.2 million annually.

Adopt-a-Highway (#79). Another "default + voluntary" privatization is the Adopt-a-Highway program. Organizations or individuals can "adopt" a stretch of highway, pay for its periodic sweeping by private firms under one- or two-year contracts, and place signs on the road announcing their sponsorship. An estimated $2.3 million per year is contributed to this program. Unlike the Adopt-a-Branch library program, Adopt-a-Highway does not qualify as "withdrawal + voluntarism" because the city did not withdraw support; it did, however, recognize that the highways needed more frequent sweeping, and it promoted this voluntary program.

Central Park (#61). Central Park is perhaps the world's premier urban park. Many residents living nearby and users from all over felt that the park was neglected (that is, that the city was in "default"). In 1980 New Yorkers formed the Central Park Conservancy, a private, nonprofit group, and have since raised $250 million in private contributions to keep up the park, an average of $12.5 million a year. Today the conservancy raises about $17 million a year. Under Mayor Giuliani the city entered into a contract that allows the conservancy to manage the park. This public-private initiative for Central Park is labeled "default + voluntary + contract."

Commuter Van Industry (#74). Another important and highly visible instance of default is the emergence of the legalized commuter van industry. Poor bus service in parts of Brooklyn and Queens led to the appearance of van services providing low-cost, convenient surface transportation primarily in minority communities. Initially these services were quasi-legal, depending on where they operated and how they picked up passengers. (Among other constraints, they were not allowed to operate on streets that had bus routes, nor could they pick up passengers except by prearrangement. In other words, they were not allowed to operate where people wanted rides.) A vice president of the Transit Authority who vigorously opposed legitimizing the vans said, "The vans are stealing our passengers; those people belong to us!" [7] In any event, the Institute for Justice, a nonprofit law firm that often represents minority businesses suffering under perverse, inequitable regulations, brought suit on behalf of the van operators against the City Council for blocking their efforts to be licensed. Mayor Giuliani joined the suit on the side of the vans. The court ruled for the vans, and the system was deregulated with respect to licensing. This initiative is labeled "default + deregulation." No data are available on the cost savings for van passengers, but the vans (called "Dollar Vans" for good reason) continued to charge only $1 while city bus fares crept much higher, peaking at $1.50 at the end of the Giuliani administration.

Facilities for Paying City Bills (#32). The Finance Department had eight payment locations where individuals could go to pay such city bills as taxes, water, and parking fines. The department withdrew some staff from those payment centers yet improved service by contracting with a large check-cashing firm that has 402 convenient locations throughout the metropolitan area. Individuals can go to any location to pay their bills, and they pay the firm a $1 service fee. The city pays nothing to the firm. In 2000 the city collected $38 million from those locations for 299,490 parking summonses, 863 real estate transactions, and 1,245 water bills. This case is labeled "withdrawal + contract."

Closing City Fueling Stations (#7). The city owned and operated 500 gas stations where city vehicles, such as police cars, would get fuel. The city shut down and sold eighty-two of the stations and turned to the marketplace to supply fuel to its vehicles. It contracted to buy fuel at a discounted price from a major gasoline company and issued credit cards for each vehicle; the card could be used to fuel that vehicle at any of the company's many service stations in the city. This is listed as "withdrawal + divestment + contract."

Unconventional Methods

For most privatizations, the city used contracts alone or in combination with withdrawal, default, or voluntarism. These last three were often used alone, as well. However, less popular methods of privatization were also successful.

Vouchers for Child Day Care (#5). The city saved a lot of money through its voucher program for child day care, which replaced the city's program of contracting with day-care centers. In other words, the city now subsidizes the consumer instead of the producer. The program gives parents more choice by allowing them to choose among many day-care service providers. And the city saves $44 million a year.

Leasing Municipal Parking Garages (#77). The Bureau of Parking owns thirteen facilities operated and managed by private parking companies. The facilities were first privatized in 1982 by leasing them to private operators for a flat monthly fee. In 1995 the city changed the terms of the leases to include revenue sharing with incentive clauses. The city now receives a percentage of the parking revenue above a base target and pays a management fee. In fiscal 2000 gross revenue for the city from the parking garages and parking fields was $10.7 million; the city paid a management fee to the private operators of $4.6 million, yielding net revenue of $6.1 million.

Franchises (#73, #76, and #69). The city issued additional taxi (#73) and ferry (#76) licenses to franchisees. In another franchise, the Department of Sanitation implemented a landfill gas emissions control system for the collection and sale of methane gas generated by the landfill (#69), and a private firm was selected to manage this activity. The firm paid an initial fee of $875,000 and pays $1 million in combined annual payments for twenty years. Additional benefits include annual savings of $2–3 million in environmental compliance monitoring costs and greatly reduced emission of foul-smelling gases. The closure, capping, and post-closure monitoring of the Fresh Kills landfill provides substantial environmental benefits. These include the collection and reuse of methane gas, the collection and removal of impurities from leachate (fluids), and the long-term environmental monitoring of groundwater, surface water, and sediment (including tidal streams surrounding the landfill).

Public-Private Partnerships for Small-Business Health Insurance (#43). The Health and Hospitals Corporation (HHC) and a nonprofit insurance provider launched the Small Business Health Insurance Demonstration Project to make low-cost, comprehensive health insurance available to small businesses in parts of Manhattan, the South Bronx, and North Brooklyn. The project was intended as an economic development program, helping small businesses attract and retain good workers by offering health coverage. To qualify, a business must have between two and fifty employees and be located in certain areas.

The project charges a monthly premium of $100 for individuals and up to $235 for an employee, spouse, and children. Copayments for hospitalization are $250 for an in-network admission and $500 for an out-of-network hospitalization. The cost to employers is about half the average price paid for coverage in New York City.

The insurer initiated the plan and serves as the administrator. HHC provided health care. As of February 2000 the project had generated roughly $10,000 in revenue for HHC, but the hospital system spent more than $400,000 on staff, marketing, and advertising. The HHC expected up to 3,000 enrollees, but got only 378 enrollees in total from forty-nine small businesses. As of August 2000 only 166 members were still enrolled. Therefore HHC dropped out of the plan; the insurer is continuing but without HHC.

The lack of enthusiasm for the program has several sources. First, an employee may live and work in different locations and may not want to be restricted to a specified network location. Second, many uninsured employees are using the municipal hospital system already. Third, employers are reluctant to pay the monthly premiums.

Deregulation of Licensing (#12). In 1994 the Department of Consumer Affairs deregulated license categories for the following people and places:

- Billiard hall employees.
- Masquerade balls.
- Antique dealers without a place of business in the city.
- Operators and managers of antique expositions.
- Movie theaters.
- Sightseeing-bus drivers.
- Multiple-dwelling garages for tenants and exclusive (nonpublic) parking lots.
- Storefronts with up to three fixed-stand, coin-operated rides for kids.

The public saves money directly by eliminating these obsolete licensing requirements. Since 1994, 11,156 local businesses have been able to operate without licenses from the Department of Consumer Affairs; inasmuch as the cost of licenses was ultimately borne by the consumer, the public has saved approximately $2.23 million.

Regulation of Commercial Solid Waste Disposal (#75). Although the city handed over collection of commercial waste to the private sector in 1956, the government continued to regulate this activity as a matter of public health. Despite this involvement, the industry gradually became dominated by a collusive, anticompetitive cartel with involvement by organized crime.

When Rudolph Giuliani was a prosecutor he succeeded in getting dozens of mob figures convicted, and as mayor he attacked this cartel. He encouraged a large national firm to enter the New York market despite threats of violence, and then he worked with the firm to ensure its success. Legislation transferred regulation of this industry from the Department of Consumer Affairs to the newly created Trade Waste Commission, a regulatory and law enforcement agency, which removed corrupt individuals by denying them licenses. The commission reduced maximum allowed prices by 26 percent, but competition drove down actual prices by a staggering 48 percent. One large hospital saw its bill drop by several hundred thousand dollars a year. This was not a direct municipal service, but the city's regulatory action broke up a criminal conspiracy and created a competitive market for an important public service. This is a form of privatization, albeit an unusual one. The commercial waste collection industry was "cleaned up" and the city's businesses saved large sums of money, which ultimately benefited their customers to the tune of $400 million a year.[8]

Summary

The divestments, contracts, public-private (managed) competitions, and other more complex privatizations discussed in this chapter illustrate the wide range of applications and the imaginative flexibility of privatization.

The city scrutinized its inventory of assets and identified many that were not relevant to the core functions of government. Divestments relieved the city of these distractions and yielded not only direct and immediate revenue but other benefits as well, such as putting real estate on the tax rolls. And while divestments generally encounter little employee resistance, others may object. Lovers of classical music fought the sale of the radio stations, and community groups opposed the sale of neglected lots in which they had established lovely gardens. Another advantage of selling buildings and vacant land is that it obviates future demands for new city undertakings that would utilize this "free" property.

Sometimes it makes sense to divest by giving away the property and even to offer financial support to have someone take it. This was the case with occupied, city-owned residential buildings that cost the city a lot of money to maintain, with no hope of recovery. The city gave away the buildings, with loans and tax abatements, to private organizations that could rehabilitate and operate them.

Competitive sourcing is the objective, not privatization. An important benefit is that competition among contractors and between contractors and city employees leads to discovery, learning, transfer, and adoption of best practices.

The city engaged in competitive contracting (outsourcing) in those cases where there was little employee or public opposition. Savings are an obvious benefit but improved quality, effectiveness, and responsiveness of the service may be even more important. Cleaner schools and parks, better summer schools, safer elevators, better vehicle maintenance, and faster delivery of supplies mean more effective city services. Making streets safer (with "red-light cameras") and closing a landfill improve neighborhood life. The public likes the convenience of paying city bills without having to visit government offices. Eligible applicants for scarce public housing units are more likely to get them after a contractor screens out ineligible applicants.

Vouchers are used successfully for day care, housing, and job training. Could school vouchers be next in New York?

Withdrawal, default, and voluntarism are often overlooked as privatization tools. Major cultural institutions and parks that are getting shabby due to cutbacks in public funding can be revived by affluent devotees who are motivated to lend their leadership and support. Civic leaders adopt libraries, parks, and schools. Business leaders reclaim their commercial neighborhoods through self-imposed taxes in business improvement districts.

Market forces have been unleashed to improve services. Van services sprang up to provide underserved areas with responsive, low-cost transportation; they emerged as a result of inadequate public transit, immigrant entrepreneurship, and de facto deregulation. The city agency in charge of the vehicle fleet abandoned its fueling stations and relied instead, like millions of motorists, on ordinary gas stations. Breaking up the commercial waste-handling cartel allowed markets to work properly and saved the public hundreds of millions of dollars.

The principal lesson from these successes is that there are many arrows in the privatization quiver; many specific privatization techniques exist and can be custom tailored for the task at hand. The next chapter discusses failed privatization initiatives and offers a different, supplementary set of lessons learned.

Notes

1. Preelection discussion between the author and the candidate, 1993.
2. Note that savings are shown in table 6.2 as annual and are considered recurring, but they are not guaranteed for future years. One-time contracting costs were not available; the cost of ongoing contract monitoring and administration is assumed to be the same as for overseeing the performance of public employees.
3. Rudolph W. Giuliani, "Reforming New York City," in *Making Government Work,* ed. Paul J. Andrisani, Simon Hakim, and Eva Leeds (New York: Rowman and Littlefield, 2000), 164.
4. Elissa Gootman, "School Custodians Object as City Hires Private Firms," *New York Times,* September 26, 2003, B4; David M. Herszenhorn, "Unions and Lawmakers Attack Use of Private Custodial Services in Schools," *New York Times,* February 12, 2004, B4.
5. Paul von Zielbauer, "As Health Care in Jail Goes Private, 10 Days Can Be Death Sentence," *New York Times,* February 27, 2005, A1; Zielbauer, "Missed Signals in New York Jails Open Way to Season of Suicides," *New York Times,* February 28, 2005, A1.
6. District Council 37, "DC 37 Administrator Lee Saunders Opposes Contracting out the Work of Brooklyn Central Laundry in Testimony before the City Council Committee on Health," press release, January 28, 1999.
7. Statement made to the author at a meeting with the president of the Transit Authority at the agency's headquarters, 1991.
8. City of New York, *Mayor's Management Report, Fiscal Year 2001,* September 12, 2001, 57.

7 | Contested and Thwarted Privatization Initiatives

Not all of New York's privatization initiatives reached fruition. Opposition was the norm, particularly where current employees were members of strong municipal unions and felt that proposed contracts threatened their jobs. In those cases union members could usually rely on support from the City Council and other elected officials to block the privatization. Contracts for new services (those not currently provided by city government employees), such as catching red-light runners using cameras (#82), generally went smoothly. When a proposed privatization affected just a small number of employees who could be transferred easily to other city jobs, the unions made little fuss. This was true, for example, of the contract to allow people to pay their city bills at check-cashing sites around the city (#33). Least contentious was divestment of assets that involved few or no city employees, such as the sale of tax liens (#31), vacant buildings (#50), and radio (#20) and television stations (#21). This chapter looks at some of the city's most contested and contentious initiatives: selling municipal hospitals, contracting for hospital security, privatizing prisons, and selling the Off-Track Betting Corporation.

Municipal Hospitals (#39)

The number of hospitals operated by state and local governments in the United States declined by 23 percent from 1975 to 1995 (1,761 to 1,350), and the number of beds declined even more sharply, by 34 percent. This was a consequence of extensive privatization as public hospitals converted to private, nonprofit status or were sold or leased to investor-owned hospitals.[1]

Even before Rudolph Giuliani assumed office in New York City, the mayor-elect expressed his strong desire to change the city's unique and unsatisfactory municipal hospital system, beginning by privatizing at least three of the eleven hospitals.[2] The hospitals, under the Health and Hospitals Corporation (HHC), had a reputation for inefficiency and low quality and were smothered by a large, overcentralized bureaucracy. In Giuliani's view, privatization was to be the linchpin for changing health care for the poor.

No other city in the United States has a network of city-owned hospitals. Moreover New York's hospitals operate innumerable clinics and community outreach facilities. The city as a whole, however, has too many hospital beds, and health-planning experts believe that many should be eliminated. The administration chose Queens Hospital Center, Elmhurst Hospital Center (both in the borough of Queens) and Coney Island Hospital (in Brooklyn), as the initial targets for privatization with the aim of permitting decentralization and promoting creativity. Different privatization models were considered: creating subsidiary subcorporations of HHC; turning the hospitals over to private, nonprofit boards or to for-profit private management; and sale (or lease) to for-profit hospital companies.

The city announced in February 1995 that it would try to sell the three hospitals and reduce the number of beds in the system from 8,000 to 7,000. The occupancy rates of city hospitals had dropped from 91 percent in 1988 to 81 percent. The sale would save $1.7 billion over ten years and the city would gain an unknown amount of revenue.

Mayor Giuliani quickly found that the proposed privatization would be more complicated, politically and substantively, than anticipated. Nine of the sixteen HHC board members had been appointed by Mayor Dinkins and were opposed to privatization in any form. Fierce criticism from local elected officials, community groups, and unions quickly surfaced, arguing that hospitals would be in the hands of people with little experience or commitment to treating the city's poor. The community advisory boards of the hospitals were bitterly opposed. The doctors' union in the city hospitals ran a $300,000 scare-advertising campaign—on TV ads during Yankee games, among other places—predicting reduced access.[3] The administration delayed planning for privatization, and the project moved to the back burner. Stanley Hill, at the time the leader of District Council 37, which represented half the 45,000 HHC employees, said the sale would be totally insane.

Other cities—including Cleveland, Detroit, St. Louis, and Louisville—sold their public hospitals and became part of a national trend, and for-profit hospital companies grew by leaps and bounds.[4] New York was in the midst of a rapidly changing and competitive health-care environment, and HHC was trying to attract patients while suffering from a 25 percent budget cut.[5] A report by the Mayoral Advisory Panel for the HHC recommended abolishing the municipal hospital system, saying that it delivered inefficient health services whose low quality endangered health care for the poor. Moreover its various components were poorly prepared to compete in a marketplace dominated by managed care.[6]

Of the various privatization approaches, the mayor favored leasing rather than selling in order to retain ownership and more direct control and thereby to deflect some of the growing opposition on these grounds. The City Council now joined the opposition, expressing fear that the poor would have no place to go for health care. With the city planning to release the offering plan for the first privatization in October 1995, the Queens Hospital Advisory Board sought a restraining order from the state supreme court. The board asserted that it had been denied any information, contact, or advisory input, for which it had a legal right. It further asserted that the city generally sidestepped not only the individual hospital advisory boards but also the HHC board, and it claimed that the whole process was very secretive. The court issued the restraining order.

At this point Comptroller Alan G. Hevesi joined the fray and said that privatization should be delayed until a persuasive case could be made. He called for a more substantive review to answer several questions.[7] First, who will provide health care to those now served by HHC, particularly the uninsured? Now there is competition to serve Medicaid and Medicare patients, but if those programs are cut back, will private providers still compete to serve them? On the other hand, there is no competition to serve the 1.36 million uninsured people whose health care costs are only partially covered by the State Bad Debt and Charity pool. Who will serve them, and how will their care be paid for? What will happen to patients with AIDS, tuberculosis, and mental illness who are now served mostly by HHC but are not financially attractive?

Second, what are the financial consequences to the city of privatizing HHC? Will there be any savings? The advisory panel report makes no claims of savings and no city budget documents show any savings or revenue from the sale or lease of any HHC facility. In fact, some data indicate that HHC hospitals are less expensive than private facilities. How can the city privatize HHC without accurate knowledge of the current cost? If Medicaid care currently paid for by the city shifted to private hospitals, would city costs increase? HHC said that in fiscal 1996 the city will pay $230 million less than the full cost of the services HHC provides in treating police officers, firefighters, and other city personnel and prisoners; if the city has to buy those services from a private provider, will it have to pay a higher cost? Who will absorb the outstanding debt of $942 million used to build HHC facilities? Who will be responsible for the cost of medical malpractice claims? This cost of settling claims was $80 million in fiscal 1995, and another $4.2 billion in claims is awaiting adjudication.

Third, What legal issues must be addressed? State legislation created the HHC, yet the advisory panel report does not discuss the legal aspects of this plan. And finally, how will the city ensure an orderly transition? HHC is in a precarious financial position, and selling, leasing, or closing one or more facilities could create systemwide problems.

In late October 1995 Mayor Giuliani presented detailed plans to offer the three hospitals for long-term lease to private nonprofits that met the city's specific requirements for delivering health care to the poor. The plan, prepared for the city by its consultants, offered relief from labor contracts. HHC board members angrily denounced the plan, questioning whether the city had the right to do this without state authorization, inasmuch as the state created the HHC.[8]

In a surprising setback to the city's effort to dismantle the public hospital system, Mount Sinai Medical Center withdrew from the bidding to take over the Queens Hospital Center and the Elmhurst Hospital Center, two of the three hospitals in the mayor's leasing plan. Mount Sinai was expected to take over those hospitals because it had long-term affiliations with both. This decision left the entire privatization plan up in the air, much to the relief of the plan's many opponents.[9] Undeterred, the city identified three more hospitals to be privatized in 1996: Bellevue in Manhattan, and Jacobi and North Central Bronx hospitals in the Bronx. In the meantime, the City Council went to court to block privatization of the original three hospitals and submitted a bill to the state legislature that would make all of HHC independent of the mayor.[10] City Council Speaker Peter F. Vallone called for rebuilding, not dismantling, the city's hospital system.

Potential bidders had shown an embarrassing lack of interest in the city's hospitals since the mayor announced the privatization plan in October 1995, but by June 1996 Primary Health Systems (PHS), a for-profit company incorporated in Delaware and headquartered in Pennsylvania, came forward and offered to lease or manage Coney Island Hospital.[11] PHS operated five other hospitals in urban areas. While negotiations were continuing, the city signed a letter of intent indicating its desire to proceed with PHS. At this point three dissident members of the HHC board filed suit challenging the privatization plans on the grounds that city officials were bypassing laws governing the transfer to a private firm. Although for-profit hospital ownership and management were topics of increasing interest to public officials and the health-care industry nationwide, New York is the only state in the country that prohibits such companies from owning and operating hospitals. (About one-fifth of the nation's 6,500 hospitals are owned by publicly traded companies.)[12] The three HHC members alleged that the city was being very secretive, not releasing detailed information, and blocking open discussion and evaluation of the case. This suit was in addition to the suit by the City Council arguing that the mayor needed its approval to privatize the hospitals.[13]

The year-long negotiations with PHS bore fruit: It agreed to assume Coney Island Hospital's entire $48 million debt, make $25 million in capital investments, increase the financial commitment to indigent care by up to 15 percent over current levels, and pay for maintenance and insurance in a ninety-nine-year lease. The annual savings to the city were expected to be $100 million the first year and up to $30 million annually after that.[14] HHC executives visited PHS hospitals in Cleveland and came away more or less satisfied, although they were concerned that the company might be biting off more than it could chew.[15]

The HHC board was notified on a Monday that it would be voting on the lease that Friday. As late as a week before the board's vote on approving the lease, however, even Mayor Giuliani's appointees had privately threatened to reject the deal if more details were not forthcoming. Dissenting board members sought an injunction to prevent the vote, complaining that they were being hit with an avalanche of paper and being rushed to judgment. Unions held a candlelight vigil protesting the action. Politicians and community advocates held demonstrations and fired off angry letters to the mayor urging postponement. Critics warned of loopholes in the lease and said that PHS was an inexperienced young company with a meager track record and a poor record of caring for the poor. In a boisterous public meeting, with boos and jeers drowning out much of the discussion, the HHC board approved the lease by a ten to three vote. Supporters of the move said that it was a good deal for the community that could have been sold properly if not done seemingly by hook or crook.[16] Mayor Giuliani praised the board's actions and assailed the critics, saying they were engaged in political manipulation to subsidize jobs for their cronies and protect jobs in the labor unions.[17]

HHC President Luis Marcos presented a glowing report on the plans for the PHS takeover and reported on his visits to PHS hospitals in Cleveland. The hospitals had received excellent ratings from the state joint evaluation commission.[18] In New York PHS was planning major changes, modernizing the building and upgrading laboratory equipment and reducing the number of employees by 25 percent. The plan was on hold, however, awaiting the outcome of the two court challenges. In the meantime, negative stories began to circulate. PHS had no experience with large hospitals; its experience was limited to several very small facilities. Moreover, two of its hospitals scored the lowest of thirty-one hospitals in patient satisfaction according to a study by the Cleveland hospital-review panel.[19] Further reports from Cleveland suggested that PHS had been dumping poor patients on the remaining public hospital.[20]

Good news appeared elsewhere. Although Mount Sinai would not take over the Elmhurst and Queens hospitals, it agreed to much greater control by the city over its affiliation contract. In particular it agreed to link its payment for running the hospitals to how well it meets certain health care goals and to give the city more control over the assignment of doctors to the hospitals.[21]

In early 1997 a court ruled for the City Council in its suit against the mayor, agreeing that the new city charter required City Council approval for a lease to operate the city hospital. It further ruled that HHC had no authority to lease its facility to a private entity and required additional state legislation to do this. The mayor appealed this decision, but a four-judge panel of the appellate division of the state supreme court upheld the lower court ruling in September 1997. The judges said that if the city wanted to sell or lease the hospitals, it had to persuade the state legislature to amend the law. The City Council hailed its victory, but the city said it planned to appeal to the state's highest court, recognizing the near impossibility of gaining such authority from the legislature.[22] This ruling came in the middle of the 1997 campaign for mayor, and Giuliani's Democratic opponent, Ruth Messinger, blasted Mayor Giuliani for trying to privatize the hospitals, saying this would jeopardize health care for poor and immigrant New Yorkers who rely on the system.[23]

The city finally aborted the long, drawn-out process in March 1999, almost six years after it was conceived, when the state court of appeals, the state's highest court, decisively rejected the city's position and said that it had overstepped its authority in trying to lease Coney Island Hospital to a private firm; it needed new legislation. Given the political constellation in the state capital, this was an insurmountable obstacle for the mayor. The court did not comment on the City Council's claim that its approval was needed before privatization could occur. As Deputy Mayor Anthony P. Coles noted, the court decision meant that the city could only close a hospital; it could not sell or lease it to keep it running. In a final, ignominious ending to this story, PHS filed for bankruptcy protection that same month.[24]

What lessons can be learned from this failed privatization? Mayor Giuliani wanted to encourage efficiency and competition in the notoriously bureaucratic municipal hospital system by privatizing some or most of the public hospitals. His goal was entirely in keeping with the original goal of the legislature in creating the HHC thirty years earlier, an act intended to address the problems of high costs, money shortages, and inefficiency. The administration made a mistake, however, by enshrouding the process in secrecy and withholding information until the last minute. This enraged opponents and annoyed supporters.

Intense opposition arose from all sorts of special interests that felt threatened by the proposed changes; they believed that the poor were best served by the status quo. The hostility did not deter the administration, but it undoubtedly had an effect on any would-be bidders. They saw themselves walking into a buzz saw if they took over a hospital. Small wonder they showed so little interest. The only interested bidder—PHS—had few qualifications for the job.

More disturbing was the court's statement that it was troubled "by the inherent conflict between HHC's statutory mission and the profit-maximizing goals of a private, for-profit corporation. This clash of missions precludes the transfer of total operational control over a public hospital to a for-profit entity." [25] This is a myopic and stilted view of the matter. In the first place, suspicion of the profit motive seems a throwback to the antibusiness dogma of a half-century ago. The motives of public-employee unions— "rent-seeking" in economist terms—are equally suspect: Unions seek to protect well-paying jobs at taxpayer expense. Both the employee unions and private firms seek to maximize their income while doing their jobs. Second, the court apparently could not conceive of a contractor making money honestly by providing a public service well. But this happens all the time if contract specifications are clear and the public agency monitors the contractor's performance properly. Third, the number of hospitals operated by state and local governments in the United States had declined to about 1,350, while the number operated by publicly traded companies had grown to about the same number, 1,300, which might suggest that private profit-seeking hospitals are delivering satisfactory care. The court fell victim to another antiquated fallacy: Contracts or leases mean the loss of government control. "The statute clearly indicates that the municipal hospitals would remain a government responsibility . . ." the court said. But delegation of responsibility is not synonymous with abdication of responsibility. The government could retain responsibility by leasing, contracting, or other relationships besides direct operation by government employees. In fact, a prominent big-city mayor, Stephen Goldsmith of Indianapolis, came to the opposite conclusion from the court in a different setting:

> The truth is that we possess many more tools to control the quality and price of a private contractor . . . than we do those employees acting in a typical government bureaucracy . . . we can impose fines for poor quality . . . more easily reward performance, and if necessary simply cancel the contract. . . . In each of our competitive initiatives, the city retained and even enhanced its control over services. . . . In all too many American cities, mayors and city managers operating in monopolistic environments have very little control. Competition and marketization dramatically increased government control by giving policymakers more tools for putting their policies into effect and better yardsticks for measuring performance. The only control politicians lose is the ability to hire workers on the basis of patronage instead of productivity.[26]

On the other hand, former governor Michael Dukakis of Massachusetts claimed that contractors have more political leverage—through campaign contributions—on legislators than do public employees. Goldsmith, however, was speaking about the control that he, as an executive, can exercise; legislators lack such authority. (Moreover public employee unions make campaign contributions of both cash and manpower to legislators.)

Hospital Security (#42)

Opposition quickly surfaced when Mayor Giuliani tried to privatize another function in the municipal hospitals: security. To ensure the safety of patients, staff, and visitors, New York City's twenty-six hospitals and other health facilities are staffed with approximately 850 hospital police. These police officers are not part of the New York City Police Department, they are members of Local 237 of the International Brotherhood of Teamsters, classified as peace officers under New York state law and granted the power to use physical force, to make warrantless searches and arrests, to disarm individuals carrying unauthorized firearms, to investigate, and to issue summonses. They receive five weeks of state-mandated training in these areas. They are not permitted to carry firearms.

At an hourly wage of $13 to $17 plus all the fringe benefits and time off associated with city employment, the hospital police cost taxpayers $36 million a year. In early 2000, looking to reduce costs by privatizing noncore activities, HHC proposed hiring a private security firm to replace the hospital police. HHC believed that hospitals could save $10 million per year (collectively) with little or no impact on their facilities by using private guards; part of the savings would result from lower wages.

The labor agreement between HHC and its union allowed HHC to privatize, contract in, or contract out security services provided it observed the procedures requiring notification and discussions with the union, supplying sufficiently detailed information to enable the union to offer a counterproposal, and duly considering that counterproposal. The agreement recognized that involuntary separation should be considered as a last resort only when alternative or internal funding sources were not available. HHC agreed to try to redeploy any displaced Local 237 employees and to consider severance and early retirement options.

Despite the labor agreement, in August 2000 the union demonstrated in front of Bellevue Hospital and sued the HHC to keep its jobs. It also went to work on its friends in the City Council. The Council's Committee on Health held an oversight hearing on October 25 to allow for public airing of the HHC and union positions. Public officials and leaders of hospital unions and other special interests spoke against the move. The president of the union local testified that private guards would not be as well trained as his members, could not handle the crimes that occur in the hospitals, and could strike, which public employees could not do. (In fact, public employees in New York often threaten strikes and sometimes go on strike; the legal prohibition is relatively ineffective.) The committee's report supported the union:

> . . . private security officers that would replace current hospital police would not have peace officer status, should privatization occur. This lack of peace officer status would render the new security

personnel unable to discharge a number of functions currently rendered by hospital police, such as the ability to make arrests, conduct warrantless searches, and use deadly force where necessary. Thus, in seeking to contract with private security officers, HHC will receive a service essentially different from those it is currently receiving from Local 237.[27]

In February 2001 New York City's Office of Collective Bargaining, in an unprecedented step, granted the union permission to seek an injunction blocking a contract, asserting that there was reasonable cause to believe that the HHC had not bargained in good faith with the union prior to issuing a request for bid for the security contract. A week later the union persuaded the state supreme court to uphold a restraining order preventing the city from issuing the request for bid. That same month the City Council met and passed a bill requiring the city to use peace officers. The mayor vetoed the bill, but it was passed over his veto on March 28 by a vote of forty-three to three, with one member not voting. The state legislature passed a similar bill in June 2001. The city challenged these actions, the situation remained confused and unresolved, and the privatization initiative was left unimplemented as the administration's time ran out.

The lesson here is that notwithstanding an explicit agreement in the labor contract permitting privatization (obtained by the city in exchange for a costly concession in a past negotiation), bitter union opposition should be expected and will require significant effort to overcome.

Prisons (#13)

The concept of private prisons raises contentious debate. Some opponents argue that prisons are inherently governmental and that a private firm should not be allowed to exercise police powers over individuals. Moreover, to emphasize to a prisoner that he is being punished for his crime against society, his jailer should be a public employee whose uniform bears the emblem of a government agency, not a corporate logo. Proponents of prison privatization note that government courts are responsible for making the decision about sentencing someone to prison, but "the actual operation of a prison is much like running a full-service hotel, except that it is even more difficult than usual to check out in the morning," as a state corrections commissioner once said.[28] The U.S. Justice Department endorses this view inasmuch as it classified 7,256 federal prison guard positions as commercial jobs in the department's annual inventory of jobs, meaning that contractors could do them.[29]

The United States was home to some 151 private prisons in twenty-seven states with 143,000 beds in 2001.[30] These prisons housed about 3 percent of the nation's prison population. Generally speaking, the prisons were privately owned, and they had contracts with state or local governments to house their prisoners. Numerous studies showed that these were about 10–15 percent less costly than government-run prisons. Moreover their quality was at least as good, measured by such variables as health care, number of escapes, inmate and staff safety, and programs for education, work, counseling, and rehabilitation.[31]

It was not surprising therefore that in 1995 the Giuliani administration requested "expressions of interest" from private companies to take over part or all of the city's prison system, which had seventeen jails and 18,000 inmates. The city hoped to save part of the $746.3 million it was spending on labor costs for its 11,000 correction employees, in addition to reducing the cost of food, supplies, and building maintenance.[32] Eleven companies expressed interest in running anywhere from one to all seventeen jails. Mayor Giuliani said, "We may have to do a jail or two to create some competition with privatization. We need to shake up the ratios that presently exist between prison guards and inmates." [33]

The Correction Officers Benevolent Association and the Correction Captains Association angrily denounced the idea, saying it was union-busting and an insult to the correction workers. "One riot will wipe out all the savings the Mayor thinks he will get." [34] "Rent-a-cop," one state assembly member scoffed, and introduced legislation to bar the use of private firms to guard inmates in state or local custody.[35] Ultimately the city abandoned the idea.

Once again the public employee unions and their allies in the legislature blocked the initiative. The city failed to generate public support for its program, unlike Philadelphia mayor Ed Rendell who aggressively publicized the overly generous fringe benefits of public employees and won his battle to reduce them (See chapter 2).

Off-Track Betting Corporation (#18)

Bizarre as it may seem, the city of New York is a bookie: It owns and operates the Off-Track Betting Corporation (OTB), which takes bets on horse races. This decidedly odd municipal function began in 1971 during the Lindsay administration to raise money for education. Critics attacked it for being a featherbedded patronage sump and called it overstaffed, overpaid, and overcharged on long-term "sweetheart" leases for betting parlors in buildings whose landlords were politically connected.[36]

During Giuliani's 1993 campaign for mayor, he called it the only bookie in the world that loses money, and he promised to sell it. In the year before he took office, OTB lost $7.3 million on gross receipts of $742 million; its revenues had dropped from more than $1 billion in 1988.[37] Surely this agency, whose role was so far from a core function of government, should and could be sold.

In fact, Ladbroke, the well-known British bookmaker (bookmaking is legal in Great Britain), already operated racetracks elsewhere in the United States and expressed an interest in buying OTB. Ladbroke representatives met with the author (who was no longer in government), who directed them to the Corporation Counsel under Mayor Dinkins. The administration determined the value of OTB at $55 million, but nothing came of this contact.

Giuliani's strategy was first to improve OTB to increase its value, and then to sell it. The city closed some parlors, reduced staff by 7 percent, and offered in-home simulcasting of races on cable TV with telephone betting through an 800 number.[38] The very next fiscal year, 1995, OTB showed a profit of $4.5 million. By 1997 profits had grown to $11.9 million on revenues of $908 million, but Mayor Giuliani had yet to make a move to privatize. In the midst of his campaign for a second term, he received the endorsement of two unions that represented 1,850 workers at the seventy-six parlors.[39] With growing profits to be made by twenty-four-hour home televising of races from all over the world, OTB began looking like a growth business for the city.[40] People not actually at the track placed about 80 percent of racing wagers.

The New York Racing Association (NYRA) is a quasi-public corporation that owns and operates three racetracks, Belmont and Aqueduct in the city and Saratoga upstate. In 1999 NYRA negotiated with the city to buy OTB for a reported $240 million–$280 million but was unable to finance the purchase. By July 2000 OTB's annual revenues had climbed above $1 billion and OTB's value was estimated to be $300–$400 million. OTB was the largest such operation in the country and second only to Hong Kong's. It now had 68 betting parlors, three theaters with race video facilities, franchises in four restaurants, and telephone-account wagering. It had warehouse, distribution, and printing facilities, as well as an automotive and betting system repair center. In 2000 it paid $89 million to the racing industry, $36 million to the city, and

$12 million to the state. A buyer could take advantage of new technology that would allow racing fans to sit in their homes and place bets via the Internet or interactive television.[41]

Mayor Giuliani put a minimum asking price of $400 million for OTB.[42] The decision to improve it before selling it paid off; just a few years earlier under Mayor Dinkins the value was estimated at only $55 million. In July 2000 the city issued a request for expressions of interest for the sale of the franchise and operations of OTB. This time NYRA expressed its interest jointly with a partner, Television Games Network, which televises live racing from more than thirty tracks in the United States.[43] Altogether about ten organizations expressed interest, and in October 2000 the city advanced to the next step, issuing a request for proposals. The request stipulated that proposals must describe OTB's new relationship with the city and state and outline how the new owner would resolve union issues.

Four proposals were submitted: one by NYRA; one by a Japanese group; one by Churchill Downs, the Kentucky track that also owned five other racetracks; and one by a Canadian-based investor group that owned seven tracks and betting parlors. The state legislature had to approve the sale, and a fierce battle broke out. NYRA used all its political clout to block any outsider from buying OTB. The unions lobbied to prevent the sale, rightly fearing job losses, and filed a lawsuit. Other complex political crosscurrents muddied the track. Opponents were trying to "run out the clock" on the Giuliani administration, figuring that if a Democratic mayor were elected he or she would be less likely to sell OTB, as it was a recognized haven for party patronage.[44] Subsequently the Japanese group dropped out and NYRA joined the Churchill Downs group, leaving two big conglomerates in competition.[45]

In August 2001 Mayor Giuliani announced that the city was awarding the billion-dollar-a-year franchise to the Canadian-based conglomerate, GMR-NY LLC, and not to NYRA's conglomerate. He said the decision was a "no-brainer" because the NYRA group bid $284–$389 million, which was $113 million less than the Canadian group. (The exact price depended on the number of extra racetracks the state legislature would allow the company to add to OTB's simulcasting schedule.) The opponents—NYRA, District Council 37, and City Council Speaker Peter Vallone—all vowed to use their powers to prevent the sale, fully aware that the legislature still had to approve it.[46] On the other hand editorials heartily endorsed the sale.[47]

The legislature did not approve the sale—nor did it disapprove. Giuliani left office and the plan to sell OTB remained on the table, dormant and unconsummated. Well into the administration of Mayor Michael Bloomberg, Giuliani's successor, the question of what to do about OTB resurfaced with a state plan to allow slot machines and video lottery terminals in OTB betting parlors. In other words, far from getting city government out of the gambling business, OTB was now proposed as the nucleus of a city-operated casino industry. This was the state legislature's contribution to the latest municipal budget crisis, but Mayor Bloomberg objected on both economic and moral grounds.[48] OTB was still in play in 2005.

Summary

The attempted privatizations of hospitals, hospital security, prisons, and the Off-Track Betting Corporation failed. The principal lessons to be learned are tenfold.

1. The privatization process must be open and transparent.
2. Every imaginable special interest—with public employee unions at the forefront—will emerge and wield its influence.
3. Forceful employee opposition to privatization will deter firms from bidding on privatization contracts.
4. The public must demonstrate strong support to overcome local legislators' natural deference to organized municipal unions.
5. Government must vigorously campaign to gain public support by explaining the benefits of the proposed privatization and answering opposing arguments.
6. Reflexive public hostility to business as an institution has to be overcome; the self-interest of private companies is no different than that of employee unions.
7. Another fallacy to be overcome by educating the public is that delegating operational responsibility to a contractor means a loss of government control; on the contrary, competition increases government control.
8. An explicit clause in a labor agreement permitting privatization is no guarantee of labor's cooperation in a privatization effort.
9. Private firms competing for contracts will fight to win with no holds barred.
10. Sympathetic judges make a big difference in the outcome of a privatization battle.

Notes

1. California Hospital Association, *California Health Care: 1996–2005: A View of the Future* (Sacramento: 1996).
2. Steven Lee Myers, "Giuliani Moves on 'Privatization' Pledge," *New York Times,* December 26, 1993, 33.
3. Mark Mooney, "Doctors Fighting Hosp Privatization with a Media Blitz," *New York Post,* July 28, 1994.
4. Steven Lee Myers, "Giuliani Seeks to Sell 3 Hospitals and Shrink Public Health System," *New York Times,* February 24, 1995.
5. Elisabeth Rosenthal, "Hospital Agency Is Striving to Adapt in Competitive Era," *New York Times,* February 27, 1995.
6. Elisabeth Rosenthal, "A Mayoral Panel Urges Dismantling of City Hospitals," *New York Times,* August 16, 1995.
7. Alan G. Hevesi, speech to the Citizens Budget Commission on the proposed privatization of the Health and Hospitals Corporation, New York, October 12, 1995.
8. Elisabeth Rosenthal, "Mayor Offers 3 Hospitals for Lease," *New York Times,* October 27, 1995, B1.
9. Elisabeth Rosenthal, "Mount Sinai Rejects Plan to Run Public Hospitals," *New York Times,* March 13, 1996, B3.
10. Mark Mooney, "City Wants 3 Hosps Cut Loose This Year," *New York Post,* March 26, 1996, 10.
11. Vivian S. Toy, "Deal Is Near with a Company to Run Coney Island Hospital," *New York Times,* June 26, 1996, B2.
12. Esther B. Fein, "Move to Hospitals-for-Profit Gaining Support in New York," *New York Times,* July 5, 1996, A1.
13. Mike Pearl and Sue Rubinowitz, " 'Private' Concerns Prompt Hosp-Board Bigs to Sue City," *New York Post,* October 8, 1996.
14. "Healthy Idea," *Daily News,* October 25, 1996.
15. Elisabeth Rosenthal, "Approval Seen for Giuliani Plan to Privatize a City Hospital," *New York Times,* November 8, 1996, B1; Esther B. Fein, "Agency Approves Private Control of Coney Island Hospital," *New York Times,* November 9, 1996, 25.
16. Fein, "Agency Approves Private Control."
17. Rosenthal, "Approval Seen for Giuliani Plan."
18. Luis Marcos, "Coney Island Hospital Needs to be Privatized," *New York Post,* November 9, 1996, 19.

19. Susan Rubinowitz, "Cleveland Flunks Pa. Firm Taking over Coney Is. Hosp," *New York Post,* November 27, 1996, 20.
20. Susan Rubinowitz, "Study Hints Privatized Hospital Dumped Poor," *New York Post,* December 14, 1996.
21. Esther B. Fein, "In Reversal, Mount Sinai Signs Pact With Agency," *New York Times,* January 29, 1997.
22. David Firestone, "City Hospital Lease Exceeds Law, Appeals Panel Rules," *New York Times,* September 10, 1997, B3.
23. David M. Herszenhorn, "Messinger Assails Plan on Hospitals," *New York Times,* September 25, 1997, B4.
24. Alan Finder, "Court Deals Blow to Giuliani's Hospital Privatization Plan," *New York Times,* March 31, 1999, B1.
25. Ibid.
26. Stephen Goldsmith, *The Twenty-First Century City: Resurrecting Urban America* (Washington, D.C.: Regnery, 1997), 70.
27. New York City Council, "Report of the Committee on Health," December 7, 2000.
28. Personal communication with the author, 1972.
29. Reason Public Policy Institute, *Privatization 2002* (Los Angeles: 2002), 35.
30. Charles W. Thomas, "A 'Real-Time' Statistical Profile," September 4, 2001, www.crim.ufl.edu/pcp.
31. Adrian T. Moore, *Private Prisons: Quality Corrections at a Lower Cost* (Los Angeles: Reason Public Policy Institute, 1998).
32. Thomas J. Lueck, "Giuliani Is Gauging Companies' Interest in Operating Jails," *New York Times,* August 12, 1995, A1.
33. David Seifman, "Rudy May Privatize Jails," *New York Post,* January 18, 1996, 3.
34. Statement by Peter Meringolo, president of the Correction Captains Association, in Vivian S. Toy, "Idea of Private Jail Operations Angers Unions," *New York Times,* August 13, 1995.
35. Statement by state assembly member Daniel Feldman in Mara Mornell and Tom Topousis, "Rudy Takes Heat over Private Jails," *New York Post,* March 25, 1996, 12.
36. Jerry Flint, "Horsefeathers," *Forbes,* October 24, 1994, 169.
37. Ibid.
38. Tom Lowry, "OTB Finishing in Money," *Daily News,* May 21, 1995, 8.
39. Robert Hardt Jr., "Union-Boosted Rudy Goes to Bet for OTB," *New York Post,* July 12, 1997.

40. Neal Travis, "City May Bet Future on OTB," *New York Post,* October 7, 1997, 13.
41. Paula Young, "Rudy's Asking $400M for OTB," *Daily News Express,* October 5, 2000.
42. Paula Young, "Rudy's Asking $400M for OTB," *Daily News Express,* October 5, 2000.
43. Ed Fountaine, "Joint Bidders to Place Bets on OTB buyout," *New York Post,* September 2, 2000, 15.
44. James C. McKinley Jr., "Racing Association in Fierce Fight to Own City OTB Parlors," *New York Times,* March 3, 2001, B1.
45. Eric Lipton, "Conglomerates in Horse Racing Compete to Buy OTB Parlors," *New York Times,* June 4, 2001, B1.
46. City of New York, "Mayor Giuliani Announces Sale of Off-Track Betting Corporation Projected to be up to $389 Million," press release, August 2, 2001; David Seifman and Ed Fountaine, "Racing Ass'n Rips Rudy on OTB 'Buyer,' " *New York Post,* August 3, 2001, 22.
47. "The City's Best Bet," *New York Post,* August 6, 2001, 30; "Let's Make a Deal," *Daily News,* August 7, 2001.
48. Kenneth Lovett and Frederic U. Dicker, "Mike Wary of Plan for OTB $lots," *New York Post,* April 7, 2003.

8 | Summing Up and Looking Ahead

The world lauded Rudolph Giuliani for his valiant leadership after the terrorist attack on New York City on September 11, 2001. In the last months of his eighth and final year as mayor, Giuliani won *Time* magazine's highest honor: person of the year. But Giuliani had already firmly secured his reputation as an effective leader during his administration.

In Summary

Mayor Giuliani's most widely heralded accomplishments in city management were in welfare reform and crime reduction. In 1994, the first year of his administration, 1.16 million people received welfare assistance—one out of seven New Yorkers. By the end of Giuliani's administration, this figure had dropped precipitously by 60 percent to 467,000, the smallest number in thirty-five years.[1] He initiated welfare reforms aggressively even before the federal government passed legislation in 1996 that "ended welfare as we know it." About 250,000 welfare recipients went through the city's workfare program, working in city agencies in exchange for their welfare checks.

Crime was also reduced dramatically. Murders fell from a peak of 2,245 in 1990 (two years before Giuliani took office) to 642 in 2001, down 71 percent. Shootings were down by 69 percent, grand larceny by 46 percent, auto theft by 73 percent, robbery by 67 percent, burglary by 69 percent, rape by 39 percent, and assault by 44 percent. New York rose above its reputation as a crime-ridden megalopolis to become by far the safest big city in the United

States, ranked 192nd in crime rate on the Federal Bureau of Investigation list of 222 cities with populations greater than 100,000.[2] The result was to attract visitors by the millions and to liberate residents formerly trapped in crime-ridden neighborhoods. The other side of the coin was anger in minority communities about overly aggressive police behavior and what many community leaders felt was an uncaring response by the mayor to their legitimate complaints.

Other notable accomplishments include the following:[3]

- Improving quality of life by reducing graffiti, street-level drug dealing, street-level prostitution, aggressive panhandling, and squeegee men. Previously, graffiti on sanitation trucks and subway cars had been rolling advertisements proclaiming that vandalism was flourishing in New York.
- Crippling the role of organized crime in construction, wholesale markets, and gambling cruises, in addition to eliminating its activity in commercial waste handling.
- Revitalizing the housing market by divesting city-owned residential properties.
- Restructuring the emergency medical response system by transferring it from the quasi-independent hospital agency to the Fire Department for more rapid response.
- Overcoming a $2.3 billion budget deficit.
- Reducing or eliminating twenty-three taxes in eight years.
- Promoting and supporting charter schools.
- Raising standards and eliminating remedial education programs in the senior colleges of the city university system. The result: SAT scores of entering students higher by 100 to 200 points, higher high school grades and Regents' exam scores, higher enrollments, and greater numbers of African American, Hispanic, and Asian students.[4]

Mayor Giuliani demonstrated that New York City was governable after all, overturning the conventional wisdom. He abandoned New York's failed policies and infused new values, making government work for the benefit of the public in a city long ruled by narrow interests.[5] He was one of the city's most successful mayors of the twentieth century, perhaps even eclipsing the popular and colorful Fiorello LaGuardia of the 1930s and 1940s, and he is widely considered to be a promising candidate for higher office in the future.

This is remarkable because the mayoralty is viewed politically as a dead-end job: No mayor of New York has advanced to higher office despite the prominence and visibility of the position. (Theodore Roosevelt went from New York City police commissioner to president.)

Leadership

In his book, *Leadership,* Giuliani identifies and discusses the principal elements of his leadership style, several of which were particularly evident in his privatization program.[6]

"Study. Read. Learn Independently." Giuliani read about privatization and questioned academic experts, authors, and successful mayors. He visited a private, for-profit company that trained welfare recipients and placed them in jobs; he spoke there with welfare recipients and learned firsthand the nature of the welfare problem and the bureaucratic obstacles within city government that hindered recipients from becoming self-reliant. In this he glimpsed a privatized path to success. He adopted privatization as his policy based on his own firm knowledge; he did not merely rubber-stamp a subordinate's advice.

"Surround Yourself with Great People." The major actors in the mayor's privatization program were Senior Adviser Richard J. Schwartz; Deputy Mayor Anthony P. Coles; Human Resources Administrator Jason A. Turner, who directed the welfare reform program; Parks Commissioner Henry J. Stern; and Commissioner William J. Diamond of the Department of Citywide Administrative Services. Each of these people was outstanding in his role and advanced the program effectively. Many other officials appointed by the mayor pressed the program in their agencies despite internal opposition.

"Organize around a Purpose." No special unit had to be created to pursue privatization. By and large, the mayor used the city government's existing organizational structure to carry out the program and, through Richard Schwartz, kept it on track directly from City Hall.

"Develop and Communicate Strong Beliefs." Mayor Giuliani describes in his book how he developed his basic principles and core beliefs concerning political and religious freedom, the importance of private property, a free economic system, and the dignity of the individual human being. No doubt his decision to pursue privatization came from this set of values. But it is not enough to adopt policies and set goals and directions. They must be communicated in a way to bring people aboard, excite them, and get them to share the leader's vision. This is perhaps the most important attribute of a leader. Ronald Reagan was such a leader; so is Rudy Giuliani.

"First Things First." Frequent communication and constant coordination was a hallmark of Giuliani's management approach, as he says in his book. He recognized the importance of starting fast and setting and controlling the agenda. A morning meeting every day with top staff assured that everyone got the message and stayed on the same page. His transition team delivered a privatization report, and he launched his program within a month of taking office.

"Stand Up to Bullies." "Some of the biggest bullies I faced as mayor were a few of the heads of New York City's powerful labor unions," says Giuliani.[7] They were a constant obstacle to his privatization program and used litigation to block his plans. The City Council, often considered subservient to the unions, was also overwhelmingly opposed to the mayor's plans. Rather than be intimidated, Giuliani fought back. He was tough, but he picked his battles carefully.

Privatization

Many of Giuliani's accomplishments were highly visible—reduced crime, reformed welfare—but privatization was not one of them. Nevertheless, in a city as liberal as New York, privatizing some city services was a huge achievement never before attempted. Mayor Giuliani summarized his privatization accomplishments in these words:

> We now have a broad array of privatization programs that impact nearly every aspect of the city government. We have privatized custodial services for public schools, job placement services, security guards, vehicle fleet maintenance, data entry services, tax billing services, medical labs, road resurfacing, office supply delivery, and reproduction and mail room services and numerous other city services.
>
> As part of our privatization program, we divested ourselves of businesses that more appropriately belong in the private sector. In addition to the sale of our two radio stations and a television station, we

have sold a city-owned luxury hotel and several municipal parking garages. Now these properties generate tax revenues and private-sector jobs.[8]

Table 8.1 presents a concise overview of the privatization program and its results.

Many of the services the city sourced competitively were new. For example, welfare reform created a greater demand for specialists to check the eligibility of those receiving public assistance, evaluate their skills, prepare them for real jobs, place them in private-sector employment, and provide day care for their children. Both for-profit and nonprofit organizations came forward to bid for contracts to perform these services.

In addition, modern technology created an opportunity to provide new and improved services to the public, and the administration quickly took advantage of the technical advances: more convenient paying of municipal bills and fees through intermediaries and by phone, and access to the Internet through public pay phones.

New functions and new services such as these are politically attractive not only because they are good public policy and offer new conveniences for grateful voters, but because no current employees perform that work or fear the loss of their jobs; therefore no union has a vested interest in the service and privatization is generally unopposed.

With respect to existing services, agency heads responded with alacrity (not surprising) to the mayor's instruction that they scan their organizations for services that could be privatized. The result was many small outsourcing projects but no large ones. These would have aroused strong union opposi-

Table 8.1 Summary of Privatization Results

Number of proposed privatizations	82
Number realized	66
Total estimated savings by the city government	$6,204 million
Sum of one-time revenues	$2,288 million
Estimated sum of recurring savings	$3,916 million
Average annualized savings	$776 million
Annual savings as percentage of average annual budget	2.2%
Savings for a family of four over eight years	$3,296

Source: Compiled by the author.

tion, as we saw in chapter 7 for the attempted privatization of hospitals and prisons. The successful privatizations were for services with fewer employees and weaker unions. Normal attrition among existing employees and reassigning redundant workers into vacant positions helped avoid layoffs.

Asset sales ($2.3 billion) may have reduced the pressure for more contracting out, more fundamental reforms, and other difficult changes that would have further improved operating efficiency in city agencies. Indeed, some say that Mayor Giuliani failed to curb the excessive power of the public employee unions in New York.[9] Generous employee benefits remained intact, and the unions made no significant concessions, nor did they increase worker productivity. "[Giuliani] came to terms with the unions and offered voluntary severance with financial incentives instead of layoffs without productivity concessions by the union." Most unions supported him for reelection in 1997.[10]

Despite Giuliani's privatization program, municipal expenditures and employment increased substantially in his second term, with the result that although he slashed the city payroll by 15,000 jobs in his first term, the city ended up with 6,000 more employees when he departed. This tarnished his image as a tight-fisted manager and fiscal conservative and left a large budget gap for his successor—not even counting the costs of the 2001 terrorist attack.[11] Like Mayor Giuliani, Mayor Michael Bloomberg has talked aggressively about the need for "givebacks" from public employees as their benefits continued at well-above-market levels—far above what most taxpayers receive at their jobs in the private labor market.

Mayor Bloomberg has continued to outsource and otherwise privatize activities but, unlike Giuliani, he has done so without a strong push or an explicit mayoral directive. Bloomberg outsourced substantially more custodial work in the public schools, sold more taxi franchises, sold the century-old residence of the school chancellor (for $2.4 million), and contracted with an innovative entrepreneurial firm to auction off via the Internet the huge array of unclaimed lost and stolen goods in the bulging warehouses of the Police Department property clerk.[12] (The website, www.propertyroom.com, has contracts with some 300 police departments across the country and gets 12 million hits a month. The New York Police Department received $55,000 in four months, far more than it traditionally recovered from its own poorly attended in-person auctions.[13])

In one respect privatization might have gone too far. An explosion of social service contracts with community-based and other nonprofit organizations has created a powerful lobby for more government spending on services that are inherently difficult to monitor and evaluate. Steven Malanga warns that networks of neighborhood organizations, fueled by government funds, have become local patronage mills and political powerhouses rivaling the bosses' machines of a bygone era.[14] Remarkably, "deprivatization" is also taking place. The Bloomberg administration turned over private bus service to the Metropolitan Transportation Authority in an attempt to reduce city subsidy payments; if the MTA were a city and not a state agency, this would be called "municipalization." Mayor Giuliani promoted a city plan to construct another sports stadium, and Mayor Bloomberg is pursuing it; its primary beneficiaries would be the well-heeled owners of sports teams and their well-paid athletes. This, too, is reducing the role of the private sector.

What Might Have Been

There is no question that Mayor Giuliani tackled two overwhelming public concerns, crime and welfare, and succeeded beyond New Yorkers' wildest dreams. One wonders, however, what else he might have done. More visibly displaying his respect and concern for minorities would be high on such a list. Although liberals disliked him because he was a Republican, conservatives withheld their warm embrace because he was too liberal: Government grew during his watch. Giuliani never seriously challenged union power, as did Mayor Rendell in Philadelphia. No major "givebacks" or civil service reforms were negotiated. Unlike Rendell and Mayor Goldsmith in Indianapolis, Giuliani did not undertake a public relations campaign to educate the public and rouse its support for privatization. Nor did he appoint and empower a task force of civic leaders to examine city operations, recommend reforms, and identify privatization candidates, as did Goldsmith and Mayor Vinroot of Charlotte. He barely touched the large services where privatization can make a monumental difference. He was part Hercules, cleaning out the Augean stables, and part Sisyphus, straining to push a boulder uphill only to watch it roll back down. He accomplished a lot, yet much remains to be done.

A Look Ahead

New York City can and should do much more in the future by following the privatization trail that Giuliani pioneered. With the city again teetering on the brink of fiscal breakdown, all promising opportunities for privatization need to be examined despite inevitable opposition from public employee unions and their faithful allies in public office. The city has tried all other options: raising taxes, pleading for more money from taxpayers elsewhere (that is, state and federal aid), and earnestly requesting "givebacks" from city workers. They have been unavailing, and the city continues to lurch from crisis to crisis.

One can always rely on the city to make the right decision—but only after it has exhausted every other conceivable alternative. Privatization is the last alternative. One starting point is to look at the most commonly privatized functions elsewhere (See table 2.1) and target those functions in New York. Another is to examine the list of 122 activities contracted out in Anaheim, California, as noted in chapter 2, and select candidates for feasibility studies. The following sections will discuss some of the many opportunities that an aggressive program would explore after gaining enough public support to overcome the political power of unionized public employees.

Sanitation Services

Mayor Fiorello LaGuardia, promoting bipartisan government, once said, "There is no Democratic or Republican way to clean the streets." Actually, that is not true. In New York the Democratic way is to use a public-employee monopoly, whereas the Republican way is to do competitive sourcing. Indeed street sweeping is an ideal candidate for competition. Just across the Hudson River, the city of Newark contracted with a New York firm to sweep the streets in one-third of the city, in competition with Newark's own Sanitation Department that swept a matched area. This was an all-too-rare example: a one-year, head-to-head experiment closely monitored by the city's Engineering Department. Both areas were equally littered; that is, the amount of material swept up by the mechanical brooms was identical in the two areas, 0.19 tons per curb mile, but the contractor's price was 62 percent less than the city's cost.[15]

With respect to garbage collection, Mayor Giuliani broke up the crime-infested private monopoly in *commercial* waste collection, saving businesses and their customers an estimated $400 million annually, but he failed to take on the public monopoly in *residential* waste collection, the Department of Sanitation. (He did wield the threat of privatization but settled readily for some concessions in labor negotiations.) This is one of the most commonly contracted municipal services, as shown in table 2.1, and one of the most studied. It presents an opportunity to introduce competition and achieve large savings; careful evaluations show that municipal collection is 14–43 percent more costly than contract collection.[16]

Recycling should be reviewed critically, as it is not necessarily cost effective, and the putative environmental benefits may be illusory. Recycling aluminum cans and paper is usually beneficial, both economically and environmentally, but that is not generally true of other materials. For example, recycling glass uses about as much energy as making new glass, which explains its low rate of recovery.[17] Moreover the energy consumed to collect, transport, and process recyclables is both costly and pollution generating. Market forces may dictate that it is more cost effective to dispose of materials directly at landfills, with no discernable harm to the environment.[18] The city should adopt this form of privatization for a sound recycling program. (Environmentally sound landfill space is readily available in physical terms, but is politically unavailable—"not in my back yard.")

Transportation

Bus service offers one of the best opportunities for competitive contracting. The Metropolitan Transportation Authority (MTA), a state agency with city representation on the board, operates the bus system. In addition to absorbing taxes and toll revenues that are dedicated to the system, bus operations consume at least $340 million in state and city operating subsidies. Competitive contracting in big-city bus systems in the United States and Europe reduced operating costs 20–51 percent, with savings in excess of 35 percent the norm. If even the least impressive of these results, 20 percent, is replicated in New York's bus system, $340 million would be saved, enough to nearly eliminate the city and state operating subsidies.[19]

Competitive contracting can work in a high-wage environment like New York's. For example, bus routes put up for competitive bidding by the New Jersey Transit Authority have expenses 35 percent lower than the routes the authority operates itself. With large savings available, the fare should be set to cover the full cost—a desirable permanent operating principle.[20]

London and Copenhagen introduced excellent bus systems that New York should emulate. In Copenhagen a public authority runs the entire system but contracts competitively with eight private firms—three foreign and five domestic—to operate the buses. No contractor is allocated enough routes to become dominant, and the public agency carefully monitors contractor performance. Savings amounted to about 23 percent. London has a similar system and achieved even greater savings.

A promising immediate target in New York is the late-night bus routes that have few passengers. A study several years ago found that the cost of those routes was as high as $36 per passenger. The obvious solution is for the MTA to contract with van operators to serve those routes. They can provide more frequent service—an important safety feature for late-night users—at substantially lower cost.

Vans serve an important role in providing efficient transportation alternatives in parts of the city that otherwise lack adequate public transportation. Entry into the van and taxi business should be deregulated; the city should issue more licenses along with safety regulations for drivers and vehicles and requirements for passenger insurance. In other words, the city should couple economic deregulation of van services with safety regulation.

The city's ferry operation should also be competitively sourced; poor management and a careless, inattentive crew caused a disastrous accident that killed eleven passengers in 2003. Private operators of popular ferry services in the area can be expected to bid for the routes and to provide safe, efficient commuter service if selected. Fares should be market based and unsubsidized.

Subways, too, can get a dose of privatization. Contractors can clean and maintain subway stations (if not transit operations themselves). This was done in Tokyo. Alternatively, stations can be franchised with the franchisee responsible for cleaning and maintenance and with the right to advertising revenue.

High-occupancy toll lanes (HOT lanes) should be introduced on major highways entering the city. Market forces affecting automobile usage should be strengthened by imposing time-of-day tolls on all bridges and tunnels; the user should pay for the congestion he or she causes during rush hours and should be encouraged with lower tolls to drive in off-peak hours. Those facilities could be sold to the MTA or even to private owners with the right to collect tolls according to a formula that adjusts for inflation and the responsibility to maintain the bridge or tunnel according to established, enforceable standards. Proud New Yorkers may even consider the unthinkable, such as selling naming rights to famous landmarks. Anyone want to buy the Brooklyn Bridge?

Finally, the city operates tow pounds to which illegally parked cars are towed, and the owner has to appear to claim the car and pay a stiff fine and fee. A competitively selected contractor could operate these pounds.

Education

Mayor Giuliani's exasperation with the Board of Education helped lay the groundwork for Mayor Bloomberg to take over the public school system through enabling state legislation and to operate it as a municipal department. Privatization in New York's schools is sorely needed and can be applied in instructional services, through competition and choice via vouchers and charter schools, and in support services, such as food and custodial services and school bus transportation. The school-bus cartel may require the same firm approach that Mayor Giuliani needed to break up the cartels in commercial waste collection, construction, and wholesale markets. Education is a priority of Mayor Bloomberg's, and he moved aggressively to outsource custodial and repair services. The biggest challenge is to overcome teacher resistance and improve the faltering education system through parental choice.

Health Care

The city government owns too many hospitals, and the city as a whole has too many hospital beds. The municipal government should close or sell some of its hospitals and utilize the excess capacity of the private, nonprofit hospitals in the city. As we saw in chapter 7, a major public education campaign is needed to gain public support.

One of the biggest financial burdens on the city is the cost of Medicaid, whose coverage is controlled by the state government. The program is far more generous in New York than in other states: proportionately more people are eligible, more optional procedures are covered, and payments are larger. The state spends almost twice as much per beneficiary as the national average, and spends much more in total than California and Texas together, which have many more people. In recent years eligibility in New York was expanded to include people far above the poverty line. New York City should join other cities and counties in the state to reduce the cost of the program. The beneficiaries should be sharply limited to those under the poverty line, and the range of conditions covered should be narrowed. Additionally, a promising approach is to introduce health-insurance vouchers and thereby bring cost consciousness into this runaway program.

Housing

Housing is a perfectly ordinary economic good that is conventionally provided by the market; it does not require the heavy hand of city government, aside from building and safety codes. In fact, in New York the city government contributes greatly to housing shortages, high rents, and derelict and abandoned housing because of inappropriate regulations and other involvement. The city should deregulate rents; abandon rent control; sell off the remaining city-owned, *in rem* housing; issue housing vouchers to public housing tenants; sell off some Housing Authority buildings that can attract buyers; prune unnecessary regulations and cumbersome processes that inhibit housing construction and conversions; make more city-owned land available for private housing; and stop building and financing new and rehabilitated homes. (A recent finding reinforces the last point: State-subsidized low-income housing costs 9–32 percent more to build than private housing projects.[21]) In short, New York should restore a housing market, one that is relatively free, as exists in most of the rest of the country.

Public Works

The city's wastewater treatment plants are attractive candidates for contract operation. The City Council showed some interest in selling three of the city's fourteen facilities (See chapter 4) but failed to pursue the matter. Indianapolis and Milwaukee contract for the operation of their plants, with very satisfactory results: high quality operation and large savings. Similarly, water supply lends itself to contract operation as well. Privatization of water systems is a growing industry in the United States and abroad. Given the magnitude and cost of New York's water operations, competitive procurement can be highly beneficial. All plants and all parts of the water supply system should be considered eligible for contracting.

Divestments and Asset Sales

The city should sell air rights over schools, firehouses, police precincts, and other city buildings, allowing those rights to be transferred to other sites whose zoning would otherwise not allow larger buildings to be built. It should finally sell the Off-Track Betting Corporation (OTB), and try again to sell one or more prisons. As of 2001, private firms operated 151 prisons in twenty-seven states, accommodating 143,000 inmates.[22] This is no longer an appalling and inhumane concept, as some strident opponents once proclaimed, but a routine and satisfactory practice. New York should take advantage of the experience gained in these other states.

Conclusion

Privatization is not a panacea, nor even an end in itself, but part of a multipronged effort to improve government performance. As Mayor Giuliani said,

> The lesson we have learned is that there is no simple answer to the challenges we face, and herein lies New York City's unique approach. Privatization and workfare programs, downsizing, and reengineering all comprise a means toward our larger goal: to deliver quality services at a reasonable cost and to eliminate functions better performed by the private sector.[23]

Additional means toward that goal must include reexamining budget priorities. Advancing toward the even greater goal of a better society requires basic rethinking of the proper roles of government and society's private institutions: markets, voluntary organizations, and families. The cities' experiences highlighted in this book demonstrate the evolution of privatization and the emerging new shape of the public sector. Simple outsourcing led to competitive sourcing and to innovative public-private partnerships in Indianapolis and New York. For example, fifty-one of the realized privatization initiatives in New York City were simple—contracts, divestments, and the like—but eleven were more complex, involving multiple methods and partnerships (See chapter 5).

Former mayor Goldsmith of Indianapolis and William Eggers describe this new governance model, in which networked government replaces hierarchical government.[24] The new model requires a different role for public managers, calling for the talents of facilitators, conveners, and brokers who can engage the community. Reliance on partnerships, innovative business relationships, joint funding, and leveraging nongovernmental organizations are hallmarks of networked government.

> In the twentieth century, hierarchical government bureaucracy was the predominant organizational model used to deliver public ser-

> vices and fulfill public policy goals. . . . Today, increasingly complex societies force public officials to develop new models. . . . Rigid bureaucratic systems that operate with command-and-control procedures, narrow work restrictions, and inward-looking cultures . . . are particularly ill-suited to addressing problems that often transcend organizational boundaries. . . . [N]ew tools . . . allow innovators to fashion creative responses [to ever more complicated problems] . . . Government agencies . . . are becoming less important as direct service providers, but more important as generators of public value within a web of multiorganizational, multigovernmental, and multisectoral relationships that increasingly characterize modern government.[25]

President Reagan's 1982 *National Urban Policy Report,* mentioned in chapter 1, anticipated this evolution, however dimly:

> The basis for a more stable future for a city is . . . a sound strategy, incorporating flourishing partnerships among government, private, and neighborhood interests. . . . Urban leaders, in tandem with their residents, civic organizations, and [businesses], can find the means to rebuild, revive, and renew confidence in the future of their city. . . . Local governments and their states are bringing new and invigorating approaches to problems of finance, service provision, community involvement, and neighborhood revitalization. In addition, local governments and private corporations are far in the lead in developing public-private partnerships to accomplish social goals.[26]

Notes

1. E. S. Savas, ed., *Managing Welfare Reform in New York,* (Lanham, Md.: Rowman and Littlefield, 2005).
2. Rudolph W. Giuliani, "Efficiency, Effectiveness, and Accountability: Improving the Quality of Life through E-Government," conference proceedings, Temple University Second Annual Conference of Mayors, New York City, June 26–27, 2001, 8–16; Dennis C. Smith and William J. Bratton, "Performance Management in New York City: Compstat and the Revolution in Police Management," in *Quicker Better Cheaper? Managing*

Performance in American Government, ed. Dall W. Forsythe (Albany: Rockefeller Institute, 2001), 453–482.

3. City of New York, *Reengineering Municipal Services, 1994–2001, Mayor's Management Report, Fiscal 2001 Supplement.*
4. Benno Schmidt, "CUNY's Progress," *New York Post,* December 30, 2003.
5. Fred Siegel, *The Prince of the City: Rudy Giuliani and the Revival of New York* (New York: Encounter Press, 2005).
6. Rudolph W. Giuliani, *Leadership* (New York: Miramax Books, 2002).
7. Giuliani, *Leadership,* 272.
8. Rudolph W. Giuliani, "Reforming New York City," in *Making Government Work,* ed. Paul J. Andrisani, Simon Hakim, and Eva Leeds, (New York: Rowman and Littlefield, 2000), 163.
9. David Firestone and Steven Lee Myers, "Despite Anti-Union Oratory, Mayor Treats Unions Gently," *New York Times,* July 25, 1995, A1.
10. Lynne A. Weikart, "The Giuliani Administration and the New Public Management in New York City," *Urban Affairs Review* 36, no. 3 (2001): 359–381.
11. Michael Powell, "For N.Y., Giuliani's Legacy Is Leadership—And a Very Big Bill," *Washington Post,* January 29, 2003, A3.
12. Carl Campanile, "School Bosses' House Is Sold," *New York Post,* July 24, 2003, 27.
13. Michael Wilson, "Police-Seized Loot Is Online, and Yes, It's a Steal," *New York Times,* January 4, 2004, A1.
14. Steven Malanga, "Who Runs New York?" *City Journal* 13, no. 4 (autumn 2003): 46–54.
15. Contemporaneous interview with Newark's director of engineering, Alvin Zach, 1980
16. E. S. Savas, "Public vs. Private Refuse Collection: A Critical Review of the Evidence," *Urban Analysis* 6 (1979): 1–13.
17. "The Economics of Recycling," *CQ Researcher,* March 27, 1998.
18. Jane S. Shaw, "Recycling," *The Concise Encyclopedia of Economics,* www.econlib.org/library/Enc/Recycling.html, January 27, 2005.
19. E. S. Savas and E. J. McMahon, *Competitive Contracting of Bus Service: A Better Deal for Riders and Taxpayers,* Civic Report No. 30 (New York: Manhattan Institute, 2002).
20. Ibid.
21. Sarah Dunn, John M. Quigley, and Larry A. Rosenthal, "The Effects of Prevailing Wage Requirements on the Cost of Low-Income Housing,"

working paper W03-003, Institute of Business and Economic Research, University of California, Berkeley, September 2003.

22. U.S. Department of Justice, Bureau of Justice Statistics, *Census of State and Federal Correctional Facilities, 2000* (Washington, D.C.: 2000).
23. Giuliani, "Reforming New York City," 166.
24. Stephen Goldsmith and William D. Eggers, *Governing by Network: The New Shape of the Public Sector* (Washington, D.C.: Brookings, 2004), 3–24.
25. Ibid., 7–8.
26. U.S. Department of Housing and Urban Development, *The President's National Urban Policy Report* (Washington, D.C.: 1982), 59, 65.

9 | Case Study: The Department of Parks and Recreation

One of the highlights of Mayor Giuliani's privatizations was the introduction of managed competition for fleet maintenance in the Department of Parks and Recreation (DPR). This case study describes in detail the origin, evolution, and results of the program.[1]

Introduction

In a memo to First Deputy Commissioner Alan M. Moss of DPR in early 1994, mayoral assistant Lynne Murray stated that "the Mayor is very anxious to put together several privatization or managed competition programs throughout the city, and the Parks proposal is integral to that plan." [2] The mayor directed his commissioners to use managed competition to do more with less. By "managed competition," he referred to the process that allows public and private agencies to compete for a contract to provide public services.[3]

Since then DPR implemented managed competition in many areas, including automotive repair, park maintenance, trades (plumbing, masonry, carpentry, electrical, and the like), organic recycling, night security, and building maintenance. According to DPR's Chief of Operations Keith T. Kerman "there have been no layoffs as a result of privatization. Affected employees have been transferred to other districts or redeployed to other agencies. In many cases, new technologies, improved internal management and process reengineering, not privatization, have resulted from managed competition–related analysis." [4]

Fleet maintenance turned out to be the department's most successful managed competition. Starting in June 1995 DPR introduced privatization and managed competition to improve the maintenance and repair of its diverse fleet of nearly 2,000 vehicles and eight automotive repair garages. DPR established an innovative arrangement in which a private fleet-management firm maintained part of the agency's fleet while in-house staff maintained the remainder. The program increased efficiency and effectiveness in all fleet repair operations, not just in the privatized garages.

The privatization process that led to these results was not smooth, however. As early as June 5, 1995—almost eight months before the awarding of the first contract—First Deputy Commissioner Moss cautioned Richard J. Schwartz, Mayor Giuliani's senior policy adviser, about expected hurdles. Moss wrote: "While the operational and cost benefits of privatizing the Bronx Garage are compelling, we should not minimize the union and funding problems." [5]

> The process of privatization in the DPR was intensive and time consuming. It required substantial amounts of analysis along with a complicated process of proposals, counter proposals, hearings, and meetings. For instance, DPR had to get the Request for Bid (RFB) approved by the comptroller's office as per Section 312A of the City Charter. It also had to redeploy all displaced employees as per Section 11 of the Municipal Coalition Agreement. The union had the right to counter-propose. It was also greatly affected by political considerations at citywide, union and intra-organizational levels.[6]

Nonetheless, DPR overcame these obstacles and implemented a highly successful program of managed competition and partial privatization of its fleet maintenance. This case study illustrates how methodical persistence can bring about change in the most stagnant environments and how managed competition can be profitable for all parties. The study begins with a brief review of the evolution of privatization and managed competition in park maintenance.

Managed Competition in Park Maintenance

In 1994 and 1995 DPR privatized park maintenance and repair services in some boroughs to stimulate competition, focus citywide efforts on improving Parks Inspection Program ratings, and save money. In a memo to Commissioner of Labor Relations Randy L. Levine, DPR Commissioner

Henry J. Stern stated that the purpose of DPR's introduction of managed competition was twofold: "(1) to determine whether the private sector can provide maintenance services more efficiently than the public sector and (2) to stimulate a competitive environment." [7]

Privatization of Park Maintenance in Queens

In December 1994 DPR launched its first experiment with managed competition for basic park and playground maintenance. Staff spent six months studying the in-house maintenance operations, developing a request for bid (RFB), designing a contract, and securing legal and institutional approvals. At the conclusion of this start-up period, DPR issued an RFB for a one-year contract for the maintenance of forty-seven parks and playgrounds in Queens Community Board Districts 5 and 6. Bidding was open to the private sector and the union representing DPR's employees in Queens 5 and 6, but the union did not submit a bid.[8]

On December 5, 1994, DPR awarded a one-year contract to Reliable Cleaning Systems, a private janitorial firm based in Peekskill, New York. The forty-seven sites in the contract comprised sixteen playgrounds, five parks, and twenty-six small triangular parks. DPR set standards for cost effectiveness and other performance indicators. Its Operations and Management Planning Office (OMP) examined the results of contract operation after one year and prepared a report that addressed cost, performance, and productivity.[9]

Cost. The contract price was $356,244. DPR saved $287,287 by contracting out this repair work, a 44.6 percent savings over the precontract cost of $643,531.

Performance. The contractor was able to lower the total cost of park and playground maintenance while improving the cleanliness of DPR's properties. The most reliable indicators of performance in cleaning and performing minor repairs in parks and playgrounds are site inspection ratings compiled by OMP. Under the Parks Inspection Program, OMP inspectors survey DPR's properties throughout the city and rate them according to twelve criteria; five cleanliness features (glass, graffiti, lawns, litter, weeds) and seven structural features (sidewalks, safety surfaces, paved surfaces, play equipment, trees, benches, fences). The twelve ratings are aggregated to produce the overall condition rating for each site. The work performed by Reliable Cleaning in

Queens directly affected only the cleanliness features, not the structural features. Before the start of the contract, 67 percent of the contract sites had an acceptable rating for cleanliness; at the conclusion of the contract, 100 percent of the sites had such a rating.

Productivity. DPR saved money under the contract not because Reliable paid its workers less than DPR, but because the contractor was able to do the work with only half the staff that DPR had deployed the preceding year. The report credited the increase in productivity to three factors. First, the contract tied DPR's payments very closely to the contractor's performance. At the end of each week, DPR's contract administrator met with the contractor and reviewed all the work that had been completed that week and all the corresponding payments that were scheduled. If the contract administrator was dissatisfied, she ordered Reliable to return to the site and withheld payment until the work was completed to her satisfaction. Even if the contractor had to clean a site two or three times, DPR paid for the work only once. Thus Reliable had a straightforward incentive to perform the work properly the first time. In contrast, DPR's employees were paid as long as they were on duty, regardless of performance.

Second, the contractor was relatively free from bureaucratic constraints on hiring and firing, setting pay, defining job duties, and purchasing supplies. A DPR manager rarely has the luxury of custom building a staff from scratch. Once Reliable hired its employees, their tenure depended on their work performance, not on whether they fell into "permanent," "provisional," or "seasonal" employment categories, as DPR used. Moreover, Reliable got more work done because its staff were not restrained by title and therefore not limited to only certain types of work, as DPR employees were. If a job called for materials the contractor did not have on hand, Reliable employees could go directly to a store and purchase the needed items with cash or could easily enter into open contracts with suppliers and obtain the needed items the same day. In contrast, DPR must go through an arduous, paper-intensive process that can result in months of delay between the time a request is made and the time supplies actually reach the field.

Third, Reliable was also free to shop around for the best deal and contract out repair work to a private garage of its own choosing. By using the competitive market, Reliable was able to repair and return disabled vehicles to the field quickly. A DPR manager, on the other hand, had no choice but had to use his own garage for auto repairs and therefore did not have the leverage to press for more responsive service.

Encouraged by these results, DPR issued a bid for a new Queens contract for 1996. The renewal contract was in most aspects identical to the 1995 contract. The two-year contract was advertised on November 1 and awarded to another bidder, McGuire Landscape, on December 21, 1995; the work began in early 1996.

Privatization of Park Maintenance in the Bronx

In light of the successful Queens privatization, DPR decided to expand the program to the Bronx. On May 18, 1995, after a competitive bidding process, DPR awarded a contract to the lowest bidder, Parente Landscape Corporation, to maintain forty-five park sites in Bronx Districts 1 and 2 during fiscal 1996. Parente began work on July 24, 1995. The contract had three distinct components. The first called for general cleaning of the parks to restore them to acceptably clean and safe conditions. The second component called for miscellaneous repairs to be performed at the direction of DPR's area inspector. Miscellaneous repairs included but were not limited to replacing damaged or worn swings, repairing holes in fences, replacing vandalized or deteriorated bench slats, and unclogging sinks and drains. The third component of the contract included such items as comfort-station cleaning, grass mowing, line trimming, and graffiti removal, which were performed on a seasonal basis and only at a few facilities.[10]

DPR assigned an area inspector to oversee the contractor's performance. His main responsibilities were preparing monthly work schedules, identifying necessary repairs, and verifying payments. Unfortunately, unlike the Queens contractor, the Bronx contractor failed to satisfy DPR with respect to maintenance and repairs. DPR conducted an exhaustive investigation of the contractor's performance and began default hearings on January 18, 1996. On February 16, 1996, DPR notified the contractor that it was deemed to be in default due to performance shortcomings and that the contract would be terminated effective March 1, 1996. On March 2, 1996, DPR replaced Parente with Reliable Cleaning Systems, the next lowest bidder and the successful contractor in Queens.

The New York City Comptroller's Office conducted an audit of the contract covering the period from July 24, 1995 (the date the contractor began providing services), to March 1, 1996 (the date DPR terminated the contract). The audit stressed that the failed contract in Bronx Districts 1 and 2 proved that privatization is no panacea and highlighted the need for more effective supervision of contractors. The audit found that these park sites were not being cleaned and maintained satisfactorily, and that DPR failed to plan, direct, and evaluate the contractor's work adequately and to enforce the contract's terms aggressively. DPR did not notify the contractor, in writing, that it was dissatisfied with its overall performance or impose liquidated damages (payment for harm caused). Finally, in the sixth month of the contract, DPR took strong action by initiating default proceedings. According to the audit, DPR's ineffective supervision of the contractor led to the continuing existence of unhealthy, hazardous, and unpleasant conditions in the parks.

DPR agreed with the auditor's contention that privatization is no panacea, but it did not agree that the process was a failure. In fact, in a press release regarding the termination of the Bronx contract, Commissioner Henry J. Stern said, "One of the best aspects of managed competition is that if a private contractor doesn't do the job, we can terminate the contract."[11] He might have added, "which we can't do if our own workforce fails to perform satisfactorily."

Overall Results of Park Maintenance Privatization

DPR regarded its privatization and managed competition initiative as a great success, despite the failure of the competitive contract in Bronx Districts 1 and 2. The department reported that over the fifteen-month period, managed competition had saved nearly $500,000 in district maintenance costs and was expected to produce additional savings of over $1 million in 1996 and 1997.[12] Reliable Cleaning Systems maintained forty-seven parks and playgrounds in Queens, resulting in savings of 44.6 percent, or almost $300,000. Moreover, cleanliness ratings improved from 79 percent to 100 percent, and overall condition ratings improved from 44 percent to 67 percent, as measured by the newly installed Park Inspection Program. Subsequently, McGuire's Service Corporation won a two-year contract to maintain Districts 5 and 6 in Queens for an annual price of $349,000, representing savings of almost $600,000 over the two years. In Districts 1 and 2 in the Bronx, Reliable's bid price of $469,000 was expected to produce savings of more than $150,000. On July 10, 1996, Jeke Cleaning assumed maintenance of the Olmsted Center, DPR's capital projects headquarters in Flushing, Queens, saving more than $46,000. In fiscal 2000 DPR began contracting for sign production and anticipated savings of more than 35 percent in fiscal 2002.

Despite these excellent results, over time the contracts were not renewed: Management improvements, capital expenditures, and especially the expanded Work Experience program (WEP) helped DPR raise site condition ratings elsewhere in Queens and citywide to the level achieved in the privatized districts. Under WEP, part of the welfare reform program, many welfare recipients were assigned to work on routine maintenance and cleaning in the parks, and it was no longer cost effective to hire contractors.[13] In other words, DPR could match the contractor's performance only by using labor that was cost-free to the department. The program had the added social benefit of inculcating a work habit in this population.

The major benefits of the privatization initiatives, however, went far beyond the dollar savings. DPR created a competitive environment that pervaded the department and persisted into the next mayoral administration. "Breaking the monopoly" was the signal accomplishment. DPR also elevated and established the Park Inspection Program (PIP) as an important management tool. The early success in improving park ratings was widely touted and presented as a benchmark that other districts must achieve to avoid similar privatization contracts. Prior to the managed competition effort, PIP had limited influence on park workers. After this two-year experience, PIP was the order of the day and governed behavior at all levels, from borough commissioner to city park worker. PIP remained in effect into the Bloomberg administration. Finally, DPR gained valuable experience and knowledge by studying the managerial, operational, and monitoring methods used in the privatized districts. It was also able to assess operational improvements that might be transplanted to in-house districts.

Managed Competition in Fleet Maintenance

After the park maintenance privatization program ended, the mayor chose fleet maintenance and repair as the next major focus for managed competition. Before privatization, DPR had a fleet of approximately 2,000 vehicles and equipment units plus numerous pieces of small, engine-powered equipment used primarily in horticultural work. To service this fleet, the department had a network of eight maintenance facilities located at Bronx Park, Prospect Park, Coney Island, Staten Island (Cloves Lakes), Cunningham Park, Flushing Meadows, Rockaway Beach, and Randall's Island (the "5-Boro Shops"). The department performed about 98 percent of its vehicle maintenance in house. The facilities in the boroughs were responsible for maintaining and repairing the vehicles and equipment units stationed in their respective boroughs. The 5-Boro Shops were responsible not only for servicing Manhattan-based vehicles but also for providing maintenance and repair support to the other facilities, especially for heavy equipment and body repairs. The 5-Boro Shops also housed the administrative offices for vehicle maintenance operations.

Stone and Webster Report

DPR hired an outside consultant, Stone and Webster, in December 1994 to analyze its fleet maintenance services. This extensive study focused on several indicators of maintenance resources and performance and compared them to similar indicators in other government and utility fleets. The study had several primary findings.[14]

Maintenance Resources. Stone and Webster examined the adequacy of DPR's maintenance in several areas. The consultant compared the number of DPR fleet employees, 125, to the average for government fleets and fleets of various public utility companies of the same size and found that the staff size was comparable not only in number but also in distribution. The report found that the overall number of work bays compared favorably with other government and utility fleet organizations. The spare-parts inventory was also found to be sufficient compared to government and utility fleet organizations (but see the next section).

Maintenance Performance. Stone and Webster used several performance ratios to compare the effectiveness of DPR's fleet-maintenance operation to that of other governments and utilities.

- Preventive maintenance inspections: DPR completed only 0.09–0.10 inspections per month per vehicle, on average, in contrast to the 0.19 average of government fleets and the 0.22 average of utility fleets; in other words, DPR was only about half as productive as other fleets. Whereas government fleets completed 97 percent of scheduled inspections and the utility fleets 96 percent, DPR completed only 60–70 percent of scheduled inspections.
- Out-of-service rate: DPR's officially reported out-of-service rate for its fleet ranged between 10 percent and 14 percent but was estimated

by the supervisory staff to be 16 percent. In contrast, government and utility fleets averaged 5 percent and 3 percent respectively. Furthermore, Stone and Webster's inspection of the manually produced out-of-service reports in each borough indicated that many vehicles were out of service for weeks—and in some cases, months—at a time.

- Percent direct time charged by mechanics: Direct time is the time mechanics spend in "turning a wrench." This report estimated that DPR's mechanics charged only 51 percent of their time to direct labor activities in contrast to 70 percent in government shops and 66 percent in utilities. That is, DPR mechanics spent too much time unproductively.
- Spare parts turnover ratio: In contrast to the average spare parts turnover ratio of 3.5 per year for government fleets, DPR averaged a turnover ratio of 1.4, indicating that DPR had an unnecessarily large inventory of spare parts.

Conclusions and Recommendations. Overall, Stone and Webster concluded that the general performance of DPR's fleet maintenance needed significant improvement through better resource and workforce management practices. Whereas DPR's total staffing resources were comparable to other government agencies for the fleet size, and the number of work bays and spare parts volume were adequate to maintain the fleet, departmental performance was below average in preventive maintenance, downtime, direct hours charged by mechanics, and spare parts turnover ratios. Although some of this could be attributed to certain structural impediments, such as outdated information systems, limited funding for purchases, outdated maintenance facilities, and impediments associated with procuring parts, vendor services, and other items, the report asserted that most of the underperformance was attributable to poor resource and workforce management.

To improve DPR's fleet maintenance, the report recommended more training and improved workforce management and scheduling but said that these would not be sufficient. It considered large-scale outsourcing of the entire fleet operation as another possibility; however, it suggested a less radical approach: partial privatization. DPR would retain the best performing third to half of its fleet supervisors, redeploy the remainder to other functions, and hire a contractor with the expertise to turn around the fleet operation. The contactor should have nationwide fleet-management experience. The privatization contract should have incentive clauses for the private firm and for supervisory personnel. The contract should last three to four years but be viewed as a temporary arrangement. The contract firm should be obligated to provide training to the DPR fleet supervisory staff during the contract period, but then gradually the training would be phased out. The report predicted that if productivity levels could be raised by 10 percent under this approach, savings of more than $700,000 per year could be achieved. Furthermore if out-of-service rates could be cut roughly in half to 7 percent, DPR would need 150 fewer vehicles and equipment units.

Privatization of the Bronx Garage

In light of the Stone and Webster report's findings and the earlier success with managed competition and privatization of park maintenance in several districts, DPR decided to initiate a similar program for fleet maintenance, starting with the Bronx Garage. In the proposal for this project, DPR stated three goals:

> 1) to determine if the private sector can provide automotive services more efficiently and cost effectively than the public sector; 2) to assess the management and technical practices and methods a private automotive maintenance company would utilize to maintain the Bronx fleet, and especially, to operate the Bronx Garage facility; and 3) to stimulate an environment of competition and innovation throughout Park's other automotive repair and maintenance operations.[15]

Before issuing a request for bid, DPR conducted a thorough market analysis to understand the vehicle repair and maintenance industry. The findings were encouraging. Both national fleet-management companies and local, medium-size garages had the capacity and interest to maintain DPR's large and diverse fleet in the Bronx. The large number of garages and management companies suggested the existence of a competitive environment. In addition, the various management companies and garages that provided fleet maintenance had different abilities, work strategies, and technical sophistication. Some companies, for example, stressed preventive maintenance.

DPR decided to start the process of managed competition by issuing a contract for maintenance and repair of the nearly 300 vehicles in the Bronx and for operation of the Bronx Garage located at 1 Bronx River Parkway. The

Bronx had the most serious fleet repair concerns: a high out-of-service rate, a disorganized facility, and unmotivated civil service employees.

Before privatization, fourteen DPR employees worked full-time at the Bronx Garage, including one supervisor of mechanics, one senior auto service worker, nine auto mechanics, and three city park workers who assisted in the operation and maintenance of the garage. Some major repairs, such as transmission or engine replacements, were performed at the 5-Boro Shops on Randall's Island. Management support, parts procurement, and parts handling services were also provided from the 5-Boro Shops. DPR's trades people performed work on the Bronx Garage building and utilities and there was a towing crew that reported to the Bronx dispatcher. The Flushing Auto Body Shop in Queens also worked on Bronx vehicles.

DPR established a managed competition team directed by Keith Kerman to develop and monitor this program. Working with the managers of the in-house garages, Kerman drafted the contract, and the city issued the request for bid on January 5, 1996. The important features of the bid were the following:

- Scope of work: As of October 1995 the Bronx fleet consisted of 301 vehicles and large pieces of equipment. (The actual number of vehicles in the fleet fluctuated because of vehicle acquisitions and relinquishments.) The bid called for the general repair and maintenance of all the vehicles and large pieces of equipment that were permanently assigned to the Bronx, as well as one-time emergency repairs of vehicles from other boroughs. The contractor would use and maintain the Bronx Garage. The work included but was not be limited to fleet management, preventive maintenance inspections, quick repairs and overhauls, routine maintenance, mobile service and road calls, towing, tire replacement and repair, coordination of all repairs, reports and record keeping, coordination of the work of external contractors, trades work, and maintenance of the Bronx Garage.
- Remuneration: The contract had two main sections: a fixed-rate section and an allowance section. The fixed-rate section called for a fixed price for each vehicle rather than separate billings for each repair: The contractor bid a per-month price for complete maintenance and repair of a vehicle in each of nine classes. The contractor was required to perform any necessary repairs and maintenance of the vehicles and equipment in all nine classes, including sedans, utility vehicles, heavy

trucks, and off-road vehicles. The request for bid estimated the fleet size for bidding purposes; the actual number of vehicles would vary during the life of the contract depending on fleet additions or subtractions. The allowance section permitted the contractor to bill DPR separately for labor and parts for certain types of repairs on a per-repair basis: facility repairs and maintenance, accident repairs and glass replacement, and repairs and service on non-Bronx vehicles. In an earlier cost analysis, DPR estimated annual expenses of $25,000 for facility repairs and maintenance, $25,000 for accident repairs and glass replacement, and $10,000 for service on non-Bronx vehicles. DPR specified these figures in the bid documents. The vendors were not asked to estimate or to bid on these allowance costs when bidding for the contract.

- Performance standards: DPR outlined in the contract a set of standards to which all bidders must adhere. The first standard was to establish and maintain an overall fleet out-of-service rate of no more than 5 percent, with the rate in any vehicle class not to exceed 7 percent. The second standard was to provide preventive maintenance inspection services and repair work. The third standard was to track the out-of-service rate by a new daily out-of-service rate report. This report was different from and in addition to the twenty-four-hour out-of-service calculation used by the city's fleet management system. This was expected to improve DPR's ability to manage the out-of-service rate.
- Contract guarantees: The city contract required the contractor to post a performance bond of 50 percent of the total bid price to ensure adequate performance of the contract. After the first six months of the contract, the contractor would be penalized $250 per day if the out-of-service rate for the entire Bronx fleet were over 5 percent. The contractor would also be penalized $250 per day for each class of vehicles that had an out-of-service rate over 7 percent.

Comptroller's Review of the Request for Bid and DPR's Response

Pursuant to Section 312A of the city charter, DPR sent the request for bid to the New York City Comptroller's office for review. The comptroller congratulated DPR on its approach—seeking a fixed-price "package deal" for each vehicle per month rather than paying for parts and labor on each repair—but he noted some potential problems with the draft request for bid.[16] The comptroller was concerned that DPR had not tried to correct deficiencies of poor workforce and resource management before conducting cost comparisons and deciding to issue a request for bid; if the efforts to correct the problems were insufficient it might be unfair to displace city workers through privatization. DPR responded that in the previous years it had tried many initiatives to improve fleet operations, such as reorganizing management, updating the training of DPR's mechanics through private-sector training courses, and strengthening oversight in such problem areas as inventory and purchasing. DPR added that the request for bid was an additional and important part of these efforts to improve its fleet-repair operation. Through observing and studying a private company's approach to operating the Bronx Garage, DPR would be able to determine whether a private firm could perform automotive repairs and related work more efficiently. If so, it would have benchmarks for evaluating and improving its internal operation.

DPR further stressed that the union would have a chance to offer a counterproposal as outlined in section eleven of the Municipal Coalition Agreement, the agreement between the city and its unions concerning privatization (See chapter 4), and would be able then to offer a program for reorganization. DPR would closely analyze and compare this proposal to the bids of the private contractors before making its decision.

The review also questioned the requirement for the contractor to maintain and use the city's fleet management system, because the system suffers from "inaccurate and incomplete cost data, inaccessible information, unintelligible and misleading reports." [17] DPR responded that the contractor would be required to submit daily, weekly, and monthly reports on several important performance indicators. The contractor would produce these reports in addition to the conventional reports, thereby allowing the city to maintain continuity of records on the Bronx fleet.

Another concern was DPR's intent to exclude from the contractor's base bid the cost of accident and glass-related repairs, which would be paid from a separate $25,000 fund to be drawn upon on a case-by-case basis. Comptroller Hevesi stated, "In my opinion, that rather significant loophole will guarantee that if you go forward with the current contract, the contractor—in an effort to maximize his revenues and minimize the number of repairs he has to perform under the contract's fixed price-per-vehicle allowance—will make every attempt to categorize as many repairs as possible as accidents." [18] DPR explained that the contract specified that DPR's project manager must approve all repairs charged to the allowance for accident repairs and glass replacement. DPR would monitor the use of this allowance closely and guard against any abuse. In addition, the contract required the private contractor to report daily on any suspected misuse or carelessness by DPR employees.[19]

DPR did not make any changes to the request for bid, which was finally issued to vendors for competitive contracting.

Contract for the Bronx Garage. On May 16, 1996, DPR entered into a two-year contract with J. L. Associates (JLA), a management firm in Hampton, Virginia, that specialized in privatized government services. JLA is a minority- and women-owned firm that had successful contracts throughout the United States, including a five-year, $17.2 million contract with the U.S. Army. DPR made the decision to award this contract to JLA only after extensive study of its history of performance, its financial status, and its reputation for integrity. In the course of the prequalification review, DPR checked the company's references, reviewed the Vendex (a city register of minority- and women-owned companies) and Dun and Bradstreet reports on the company, interviewed its representatives, and carefully studied its proposal to operate the Bronx Garage.[20]

JLA's bid price was 38 percent below the existing in-house cost. More than three-quarters of these savings were expected to result from the reconfiguration, reorganization, and consolidation of personnel and other resources and more flexible use of personnel—broadened job descriptions to permit staffers to perform work they were capable of performing but could not perform under present work rules. For example, procurement functions and other management and administrative functions for the Bronx Garage that were performed at the 5-Boro Shops would be performed by fewer people on site at the Bronx Garage. Automotive repair work would be performed at one site—the Bronx Garage—instead of being split between three sites, as it was at present. JLA staff responsible for tire repair—unlike city tire repairers—would also perform minor automotive repairs and preventive maintenance inspections, as well as helping to clean and maintain the garage.[21]

Union Issues. Pursuant to section eleven of the Municipal Coalition Agreement, labor representatives from the Service Employees International Union (SEIU), Local 246 and 621, were notified prior to the bid because this contract would involve the displacement of city personnel. (Local 246 represents auto mechanics; Local 621 represents repair supervisors.) The union resented the idea of privatization yet failed to submit a bid on time. It tried, however, to stall the privatization. Richard W. Cordtz, international president of the AFL-CIO, wrote a letter to DPR complaining on behalf of Locals 621 and 246. He stated that DPR was wrongly privatizing the Bronx Garage when the inefficiencies stemmed from bloated management bureaucracy and terribly inadequate systems for managing the work. He also complained that DPR managers were not willing to sit down to discuss how the work could be done more cost effectively. According to DPR, however, DPR management and union leaders had held extensive meetings, letter writings, and other exchanges.

Despite the union's failure to submit a bid on time, DPR allowed it to counterpropose before the awarding of the contract. The union's counterproposal was not as fully developed as the private firm's and did not provide evidence that certain important contract criteria would be met. DPR responded to the counterproposal by saying that, although there may be instances in which the union can outperform a private contractor, in this case DPR had decided to award the contract to JLA.

DPR rejected the union proposal on several grounds. First, the union counterproposal did not address service issues and did not present a program for improving service while reducing expenses. The counterproposal reduced staffing to nine, two fewer than JLA planned to use, and four fewer than were currently being used. DPR was not convinced that the union could improve service amid this reduction in staff and costs. The Bronx automotive operation used facilities in other boroughs and staff in other divisions of DPR. The counterproposal did not explain how the functions performed by these personnel would be addressed.

JLA, on the other hand, demonstrated that it had successfully performed the same work at similar costs in other locations and provided detailed information about its organization, its title specifications, its performance and morale improvement initiatives, and its operating procedures. For example, JLA made clear its intention to spend two weeks thoroughly cleaning and reorganizing the garage, to subcontract work that could not be performed at the garage, to use a commercial fleet-management system in addition to the city's fleet management system to monitor and report on garage operations, to hire mechanic helpers for daily maintenance of the facility, and to have two staff available by pager at all times.

Second, DPR rejected the union counterproposal because, unlike the contractor, the union did not offer any performance guarantees. (The contract required the contractor to provide a performance bond of 50 percent of the total bid price.) DPR did not see how the union could guarantee a 5 percent out-of-service rate with a smaller staff when the garage had averaged an 18 percent out-of-service rate for the past three years.

Third, the counterproposal did not indicate that additional fleet management reports would be produced. The contract required the contractor to provide daily, weekly, monthly, and annual reports, in addition to fully administering the city's fleet management system and tracking information specific to the contract, such as current expenditures under the three kinds of allowances and monetary penalties due to excessive out-of-service rates. JLA informed DPR that it had used a commercial fleet-management system in other jurisdictions that would produce these reports and provide other performance indicators.

Fourth, the counterproposal did not provide a detailed explanation of the costs as required by the contract and provided no grounds for DPR to evaluate the union's $1.2 million base bid, which was similar to JLA's base bid of $1.212 million and was approximately $929,000 (net expected savings, after factoring in the proposed allowances for both bids) under the current in-house cost of $2.346 million. Nor did the union comply with the contract requirement that all proposals separate costs for each of the eight vehicle classes. JLA's bid included specific prices to maintain each of the eight classes of vehicles specified in the contract and also provided estimates for staffing, parts, and subcontract costs.

Fifth, the counterproposal failed to include the cost of repairs due to employee misuse in its base bid of $1.2 million even though the contract stipulated that the contractor would be responsible for these repairs, but that DPR would investigate these cases and take appropriate action to prevent future misuse. The counterproposal stated that repairs due to negligence or driver abuse would be charged to DPR for parts and labor. This brought into question the reliability of the $1.2 million estimate, for which there was no detailed breakdown. The counterproposal also had a $75,000 increase in the accident repair allowance to pay for serious incidents, such as multicar collisions or broken windows, from $25,000 to $100,000.

Finally, by requesting a third party arbiter and a committee to oversee day-to-day operations, the counterproposal disregarded standard practice in New York City contracts, which empowers DPR's contract manager to make final decisions on the contractor's operations, including the use of allowances and the subcontracting of work over $500. JLA agreed to these provisions in submitting its bid. DPR believed that the counterproposal would not only add costs but would also be impractical.

Results of Privatization of the Bronx Garage. The contractor began work in June 1996. DPR performed an internal audit of the Bronx privatization in April 1997 that confirmed the generally positive opinions of the borough commissioner, the chief of operations, and the deputy chief of operations in the Bronx. The audit found that JLA's out-of-service rate was "well below [the prescribed] 5 percent rate" during the sample month of January 1997.[22] It was reduced from more than 16 percent to 4 percent using the same twenty-four-hour downtime calculation used in other boroughs (See figure 9.1).

In the first year JLA thoroughly cleaned, reorganized, and reequipped the garage, even purchasing a vehicle lift. Each vehicle received an exhaustive preventive maintenance inspection within the first seven months. Vehicle repairs were turned around more quickly thanks in large part to the single source that JLA used for parts, most on same-day delivery. JLA also subcontracted for tire repair, auto-body repair, and certain specialized functions such as engine overhauls.

Figure 9.1 Out-of-Service Rates for Vehicles in the Bronx, 1995–1998

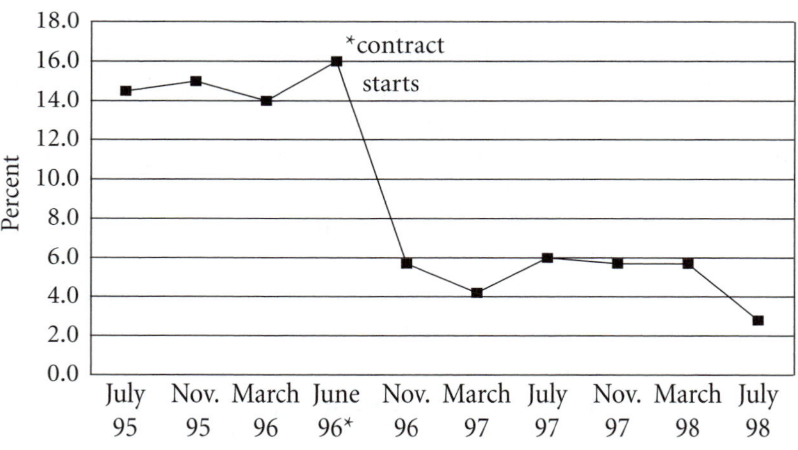

Source: Keith T. Kerman, "Managed Competition in Vehicle Repair at Parks," New York City Department of Parks and Recreation, March 2001.

JLA used fewer workers than DPR had used, contributing to the cost savings. JLA also brought a spirit of cooperation and customer service to an operation that had historically been poorly received by borough operations. JLA gave a presentation on their efforts at the garage for more than one hundred agency senior managers, including the managers and senior supervisors of the remaining in-house garages.

The project remained on budget. DPR spent approximately $728,000 in the first year, compared to $1.17 million for the previous operation, a savings of nearly $442,000 or 38 percent.[23] DPR realized these savings through voluntary redeployment of auto mechanics to fill vacancies in the Department of Sanitation; there were no layoffs.

Comptroller's Audit of the Bronx Privatization. An audit by the Comptroller's Office in 2000 estimated that DPR achieved savings of $700,340 over the first two years of contracting the Bronx Garage operations (32 percent), but this was less than the $899,338 in savings (38 percent of in-house costs) reported in the 1997 and 1998 Mayor's Management Reports. According to the report, this difference resulted from DPR overstating its in-house costs and understating its contract costs.

The audit also commended the privatization process, saying that DPR

> has achieved material savings from its fleet maintenance privatization initiatives while achieving an increase in efficiency at all garages remaining under its in-house operation. In the context of privatization, the competition that currently exists within fleet operations (because some garages remain under an in-house operation while other garages were privatized) has probably led to improved efficiency in all garages.[24]

The audit confirmed the performance improvements achieved at all garages. Out-of-service rates at the in-house garages reached a level similar to that of the contracted garages. In fact, from March 16 to July 10, 1998, four of the five in-house garages had monthly average out-of-service rates below 5 percent, as did two of the three privatized garages.

However, the audit also expressed some concerns regarding the contract and DPR's operations.[25] During the first two-year contract term, the contractor exceeded amended out-of-service rate limitations. DPR's discretionary assessment of $70,125 for liquidated damages was not charged because DPR changed the liquidated damage clause in a contract amendment signed July 17, 1997, retroactively effective from January 1997. This amendment lowered the required performance levels. The audit questioned contract changes made after the award of the contract, especially for monetary requirements on which potential bidders might have based their bid or no-bid, as these affected the fairness and integrity of the competitive sealed bid process. DPR disagreed with the recommendations regarding liquidated damages, stating that it should not apply discretionary damages against a contractor providing excellent service.

Another concern regarded repairs improperly charged; DPR paid an estimated $42,737 to the contractor for allowance repairs that should have been covered in the fixed-rate portion of the contract, according to the audit. The majority of improperly charged repairs were under the accident allowance. The comptroller's review of repairs paid for in the allowance section of the contract from June 1996 through December 1997 revealed that 88 of 363 repairs did not match the definitions of the allowance sections or the DPR deputy commissioner's definition of "accident." DPR disagreed that $42,737 had been improperly charged to the allowances. It said that that the majority of payments were correct.

The audit noted that the contractor did not always comply with the preventive maintenance inspection schedules set forth in the contract. JLA did not inspect 77 (30 percent) of the 255 vehicles that required it during the first six months of the contract and did not perform the required minimum number of inspections for 121 (41 percent) of the vehicles in the first year. These vehicles were missing 157 (25 percent) of the 622 required minimum number of total preventive maintenance inspections. In fact, the contractor did not perform any inspections in the first year of the contract on 14 (5 percent) of the vehicles.

The audit's analysis of repairs per vehicle in 1997 revealed frequent vehicle returns to the garage within thirty days to repair the same problem, which indicated that some repairs made by JLA fixed the problem only temporarily. Repeat repairs accounted for 402 (15.9 percent) of the 2,525 repairs listed in the log for 1997. These frequent return trips reduce the number of vehicles in service. The return trips will not affect the computed out-of-service rate, since vehicles are not counted as out of service during trips to and from the garage or the time waiting to be transported to the garage. DPR stated that in many cases vehicles return to a garage more than once because of good service, not poor service. Sometimes JLA repaired a vehicle temporarily to have it in service over the weekend, with the intention of completing the repair on Monday. Whereas every garage has the occasional need to repeat repairs, this has not been a regular complaint at the Bronx Garage, and DPR had no reason to believe it was more prevalent than at the in-house garages.

Although DPR and the Comptroller's Office disagreed slightly on the magnitude of the savings—32 percent by the auditors' methodology and 38 percent by DPR's analysis—overall, both agreed that privatization saved money and improved performance.

Privatization of the Brooklyn Garage

In light of the early success of the Bronx privatization, DPR turned its attention to the Brooklyn garages—Prospect Park Garage and the Coney Island Garage. These garages serviced 336 vehicles. The Prospect Park Garage maintained approximately 270 vehicles, and the Coney Island Garage maintained approximately 66, including the vehicles and equipment used to clean and maintain the beaches. The facilities performed preventive maintenance inspections and most repairs for the Brooklyn fleet, which included sedans, vans, utility vehicles, packers, bulldozers, beach cleaners, tractors, chippers, packers, forklifts, and dump trucks. They also performed "one shot" work on vehicles from other boroughs and divisions.

Thirteen city employees worked full-time at the Brooklyn Garages, including two supervisors of automotive mechanics, one senior auto service worker, seven auto mechanics, one clerical associate, and two city park workers. Two of the mechanics were at the Coney Island facility, and the remaining staff were at Prospect Park. Some major repairs, such as transmission or engine replacements, were performed at the 5-Boro Shops, which also provided management support, parts procurement, and parts handling. The Flushing Auto Body Shop in Queens worked on Brooklyn vehicles, and a private company performed preventive maintenance inspections and small repairs on Brooklyn's light vehicles, such as vans and pick-ups.

As part of DPR's analysis of the Brooklyn operation, the Brooklyn borough operations staff in early January 1997 completed a thorough inventory of their vehicle fleet and compiled an out-of-service rate list. Staff and supervisors were called to provide the status of the vehicle(s) they drove or for which they were responsible. Borough operations staff determined that the out-of-service rate as of January 13, 1997, was 23 percent. The rate was 16 percent if seasonal vehicles such as beach equipment and grass tractors were excluded. The Brooklyn rates were the highest of any borough or division in DPR at that time.

By expanding the managed competition program to Brooklyn, DPR intended to promote competition while testing this initiative in a second borough with different challenges and needs, including a larger fleet, two garages, and an extensive beach-cleaning operation.[26]

Brooklyn Bidding Process. In December 1996 DPR met with representatives from Local 246 to discuss the problems in Brooklyn and requested a proposal to replicate the Bronx experience. The union did not submit a proposal, so DPR issued a request for bid for these services in mid-February. The important clauses of the bid were similar to the Bronx contract in terms of the scope of work, remuneration, performance standards, and contract guarantees. The work under this contract included general repair and maintenance of the approximately 336 vehicles and 23 attachment pieces, such as mowers and plows, which were assigned to Brooklyn, as well as one-time repairs of vehicles from other boroughs. The contractor was to make use of and maintain the Prospect Park and Coney Island garages. The Comptroller's Office reviewed the request for bid, and then DPR sent it out.

Contract for the Brooklyn Garage. DPR received bids in late March and ultimately awarded the contract to JLA, the same company that had performed well in the Bronx. In August 1997 JLA assumed operation of the Brooklyn garages.

Union Issues. Although the union locals had not submitted a proposal before the bidding of the contract, they participated actively in the bidding process and submitted a counterproposal in late May 1997. According to President Jack Friedman of Union Local 246, this proposal differed significantly from the prior union proposals in several ways. First, the proposal was developed in conjunction with DPR's management. The union discussed all elements in this proposal with the department team and resolved any problems. Second, the proposal was very specific in the details of the operation and stated what would be necessary for a successful project. (Prior proposals had been rejected for being too general.) Third, the proposal met all the rules and regulations stipulated in the request for bid.[27]

However, DPR decided to award the contract to the private firm, which in DPR's estimation had offered a superior proposal and the best guarantee of improved service and lower cost. It reassured the union, however, that the mechanics would be assigned to other DPR garages or redeployed to other city agencies.

As in the Bronx privatization, DPR provided a full assessment to the union of its counterproposal in comparison to the private bid.[28] The union's proposed shop organization reduced total staff to eight full-time and one seasonal worker, which was below JLA's staff levels of ten in the Bronx and eleven in Brooklyn. However, the union proposed to use auto mechanics only—rather than a mix of mechanics, as JLA did—for all work at the garages. This would require auto mechanics to dedicate a substantial fraction of their time to nonmechanical work, which they had not performed in the past. If this work could not be completed within normal working hours, overtime and compensatory costs would be charged. DPR stated that it was unrealistic to believe that the union would be able to improve service and stay on budget under this staffing plan.

DPR required a performance bond of 50 percent from the contractor to ensure compliance with the contract. The contract allowed liquidated damages to be assessed for excessive out-of-service rates and noncompletion of other contract requirements. In place of the performance bond, the union proposed to waive its contractual rights under section eleven of the Municipal Coalition Agreement relating to this project. DPR had already complied in full with the section eleven requirements, however, by giving the union a fair chance to bid and then counterpropose; waiving the process at this point did not constitute a performance guarantee for routine operation.

When liquidated damages are charged to the private contractor, the city's total payments to the contractor are reduced. This could result in lower profits or require the contractor to access other financial resources to complete the work. Therefore, the contractor has a strong incentive to avoid these penalties. The union proposed that liquidated damages for excessive out-of-service rates be taken out of the budget for parts, contracts, and so on. DPR observed that this would be penalizing DPR itself.

The proposed contract with JLA gave DPR's contract manager, who would report to the Brooklyn chief of operations, the authority to make final decisions on all aspects of the contractor's operations. The union proposal called for establishing a labor-management committee to oversee daily operations and third-party resolution of all contract issues, including the decision to terminate the project. DPR concluded that this would prove impractical and unworkable and also impose an additional cost that was not included in the proposed budget.

The union proposed to charge $50 per labor hour for accident repairs and charge 90 percent of the retail price for parts. The $50 per hour would be approximately double JLA's current price in the Bronx. Also, the contract required that accident work be bid out and that parts and contracts be obtained at the lowest possible prices, with DPR paying the actual cost of the parts and contracts. By paying 90 percent of retail price under the union proposal, DPR would be paying more than the actual purchase price.

JLA determined its bid price using a costing model that had been used for fixed-price contracts throughout the country; in other words, the bid price had a solid basis. Moreover, JLA guaranteed its work with the resources of its large company. The union proposal cost $24,592 less than JLA's over a two-year period; however, DPR's analysis indicated that the union would have great difficulty staying within these costs. Furthermore, the union proposal did not include approximately $77,000 for work by the 5-Boro Shops and Flushing Auto Body Shop.

Although the union reduced staff size significantly, it gave little detail of how the work would be organized and the efficiencies achieved. The proposal called for decentralization of operations and purchasing. DPR accepted that decentralization could provide greater flexibility and accountability if the project were well supervised, but the union proposal cut the number of supervisors in half. The union also failed to indicate who would order and deliver parts or monitor external contracts. Moreover, the proposal did not discuss how the mechanics would divide the work previously performed by support staff.

Results of Privatization of the Brooklyn Garages. JLA began work in the Brooklyn garages in August 1997. As in the Bronx, out-of-service rates dropped (from 17 percent to 3 percent in seven months), facilities improved, and customer satisfaction increased, all at a cost nearly 30 percent lower than the previous in-house costs (See figure 9.2).[29] In 2000 DPR rebid the Bronx and Brooklyn garage programs and a new company, First Vehicles Services, assumed the contract at very similar bid prices as in 1996, four years earlier, despite inflation.

Figure 9.2 Out-of-Service Rates for Vehicles in Brooklyn, 1997–1998

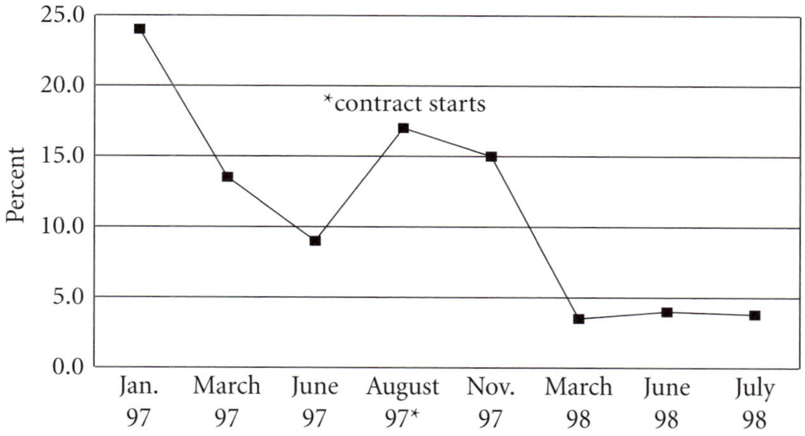

Source: Keith T. Kerman, "Managed Competition in Vehicle Repair at Parks," New York City Department of Parks and Recreation, March 2001.

Reorganization of In-House Vehicle Maintenance

To improve the performance of the in-house garages, in 1997 DPR issued small contracts with local repair shops for preventive maintenance and minor repairs of light-duty vehicles in each of the boroughs with in-house garages. This improved the turnaround on those vehicles and permitted DPR mechanics to focus on repair of the agency's diverse and aging heavy-duty fleet. The contracts cost $227,000 and resulted in savings of $140,000, or 38 percent.

As an alternative to further privatization, DPR reiterated its willingness to implement—with the cooperation of the unions—an ambitious program of change and improvement in the remaining in-house garages, where the out-of-service rates remained high. The intent was to enable in-house garages to compete with private contractors and, if successful, to obviate the need for further privatization (and, incidentally, to maintain a permanent public-private competitive environment). This effort would be completed before DPR bid contracts for the other facilities. DPR assigned responsibility to the managed competition unit for coordinating these efforts and assisting the union. DPR's in-house supervisors and staff began to display increased commitment to performance and customer service. This response to competition had also occurred in Brooklyn, where the out-of-service rate decreased while the union still hoped that it would win its bid for the contract (See figure 9.2).

In January 1997 DPR and Local 246 agreed to changes modeled after the changes in the Bronx and Brooklyn. The program first focused on the Queens garages but quickly expanded to all five remaining in-house garages: Flushing Meadow, Cunningham, and Rockaway in Queens; Staten Island; and the Randall's Island Garage in Manhattan. In March 1998 the director of managed competition, Keith Kerman, who had spearheaded the privatization program, assumed full responsibility for DPR's citywide fleet, including both the in-house and privatized garages.

The initiatives implemented under the reorganization program include the following:

- Establishment of the citywide daily out-of-service rate report used to monitor performance and improve customer service. Borough operations receives this report by 9:00 a.m. each morning. The state government established a similar performance report to monitor its inspections.
- Regular distribution of charts comparing the performance of the private and public garages in DPR.
- A weekly meeting of all garage supervisors, including the privatization project managers. This was a regular opportunity to compare approaches in various areas and to share information.
- Introduction of new computers; replacement of the city's fleet management system with a new one, the Maintenance Management Control System; purchase of new light- and heavy-duty inspection equipment; and introduction of Mitchell on Demand (CD-ROM) diagnostic equipment to all garages.
- Establishment of new subcontracts in house including a contract with a large national parts supplier to provide daily delivery of parts to all five in-house garages and to assist with storehouse inventory management. This initiative is directly modeled on JLA's parts arrangement. In-house subcontracts were established for auto waste removal, engine and transmission repairs, tire repairs, and body repairs.

- A focused effort to clean and modernize the in-house garages, purchase new equipment, and reduce parts inventories. In-house parts inventories were reduced by more than 40 percent. Staff were reassigned to garage cleanliness, and facility inspections were made routine. More than $425,000 was invested in three years on in-house facilities and equipment.
- New systems for tracking motor vehicle and preventive maintenance inspections, resulting in elimination of the large in-house backlogs in these areas.

In the three years after the reorganization effort, DPR saw considerable improvement in the in-house operation along with even better results at the privatized garages. The out-of-service rate for Manhattan vehicles decreased from 13.2 percent in June 1997 to 5.6 percent in 2001 (See figure 9.3). The average out-of-service rate for all in-house garages decreased to 5.9 percent in 2001, whereas the contractors' garages saw a decrease to 5.1 percent. The sense of competition and rivalry that DPR brilliantly created spurred both the contractors and the in-house units to improve their performance.

Figure 9.3 Out-of-Service Rates for Vehicles in Manhattan, 1997–1998

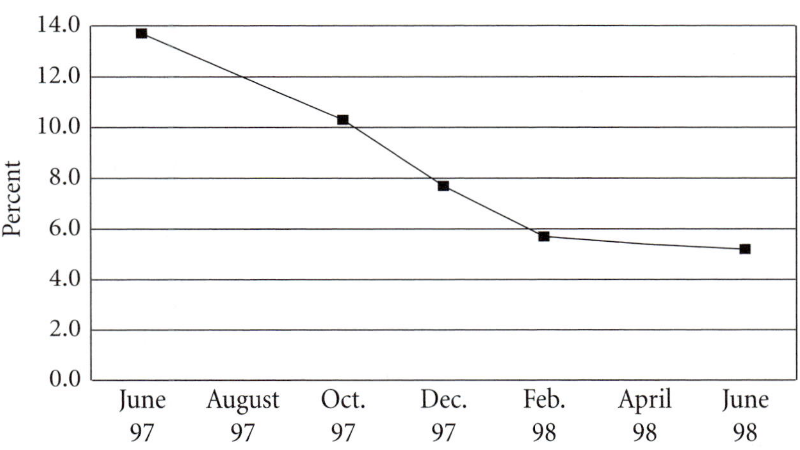

Source: Keith T. Kerman, "Managed Competition in Vehicle Repair at Parks," New York City Department of Parks and Recreation, March 2001.

Overall Results of Privatization

DPR had three goals for privatizing its fleet maintenance. The first was to see if private management of fleet repair could work. The second was to learn from the private sector. And the third was to establish competition and a spirit of achievement. The process of privatization and managed competition was intensive and time consuming, requiring proposals, bids, union counter-proposals, hearings, and meetings, and it was influenced by political considerations. Through constant high-level commitment, DPR achieved its goals, vastly improved this vital support service, and effectively balanced two complementary models for maintaining the municipal fleet: privatization and the resulting spur of competition to improve internal performance.

Over six years DPR used privatization as a management tool to create effective competition and thereby greatly improve fleet services, which had been underperforming for a long time. Although in-house performance improved dramatically, DPR kept the operations partially privatized to maintain a competitive environment and a spirit of achievement. Since almost anyone can bid for private maintenance contracts, managed competition has encouraged contractors to deploy new, innovative work techniques, thereby making employees more flexible, efficient, and effective. Managed competition agreements were task-based, allowing contractors to concentrate their resources on performing specific duties as needed rather than assigning employees by civil-service title and restricting their job functions. In addition, DPR's in-house supervision and staff grew more committed to performance and customer service in response to the competition. Most important, the contracted and in-house garages provided yardsticks to measure each other.

In summary, privatization and managed competition achieved results little short of spectacular both in park maintenance and in fleet maintenance. During the two years that park maintenance was contracted out in four districts, costs fell by 30 percent, and conditions improved significantly. Although DPR abandoned contract maintenance of the parks when it assigned welfare recipients (at no cost to the DPR budget) to do the work, lessons from the privatization were put to good use in vehicle maintenance. DPR also contracted for maintenance of one of its buildings, reducing its cost from $173,000 to $72,000, saving $101,000, or 58 percent, and getting a 20 percent improved performance according to the building's users.

For vehicle maintenance DPR established an innovative arrangement in which the private sector maintained 35 percent of the fleet in three garages in two boroughs, while in-house staff maintained the remaining 65 percent in the other five garages in three boroughs. The contractors reduced costs by 35 percent. This is consistent with numerous studies of municipal services throughout the world, which show that savings due to contracting average about one-third.[30] As for the in-house garages, the competition brought about an 8 percent cost reduction and a 28 percent reduction in staffing. In those garages DPR entered into small contracts for preventive maintenance and minor repair of light-duty vehicles; this produced savings of 38 percent and a rapid return of those vehicles to service. As a result, total automotive costs in fiscal 2001 for all vehicle maintenance operations, both contracted and in-house, were $1.27 million (16 percent) less in current dollars than they were five years earlier, in fiscal 1996, despite inflation and labor agreements that raised per-unit costs (See table 9.1). (The savings were 26 percent after adjusting for inflation.)

Moreover, DPR reduced its overall out-of-service rate by 62 percent, from 14 percent, or 266 vehicles, in 1994 to 5.3 percent, or 104 vehicles, in

Table 9.1 Cumulative Savings from Privatization in the Department of Parks and Recreation

Area and period	*In-house cost*	*Contract cost*	*Savings ($)*	*Savings (percent)*	*Service improvements*
Building maintenance, 1995–1997	$172,841	$72,256	$100,585	58%	Customers report 20% improvement
Park maintenance, 1994–1997	2,133,153	1,497,984	635,169	30	Cleaner parks, im proved conditions
Small vehicle repairs, 1996–1997	366,950	226,854	140,096	38	Faster turnaround
Vehicle maintenance, 1996–1999	6,193,445	4,050,036	2,143,409	35	Out-of-service rate reduced from 17% to 5%
TOTAL	8,866,389	5,847,130	3,019,259	34	

Source: Compiled by the author.

2001. The contractor's rate reached a low of 2.6 percent in the Bronx and 2.9 percent in Brooklyn in 1998. The in-house rate was 5.5 percent in fiscal 2001 and the contractor's rate was 4.9 percent. The overall rate for all the garages stayed between 5 percent and 6 percent for four years, from 1998 through 2001. More than 160 additional vehicles are on the road each day due to better maintenance and management, resulting in better park maintenance and lower capital costs (fewer vehicles have to be purchased).[31] In short, privatization increased both efficiency and effectiveness.

Through these successful efforts, DPR proved to be the star performer in Mayor Rudolph Giuliani's privatization program, and it can serve as a model that other cities with strong public-employee unions can follow. Among other things DPR's efforts demonstrated the point made at the start of the privatization movement, namely, that the issue is not public versus private but monopoly versus competition.[32]

Notes

1. This case study was prepared by Professor E. S. Savas and Vanita Gangwal, based on reports and materials from Keith Kerman, chief of operations of the Department of Parks and Recreation. Mr. Kerman's extensive help is greatly appreciated, as is the cooperation of Commissioner Henry J. Stern.
2. Memo from Mayoral Assistant Lynne Murray to First Deputy Commissioner Alan Moss, February 4, 1994.
3. E. S. Savas, *Privatization and Public-Private Partnerships* (New York: Chatham House, 2000), 196–199.
4. Keith T. Kerman, "Managed Competition in Vehicle Repair at Parks," New York City Department of Parks and Recreation, March 2001.
5. Memo from First Deputy Commissioner Moss to Mayoral Policy Advisor Richard Schwartz, June 30, 1995.
6. Kerman, "Managed Competition."
7. Memo from Commissioner Stern to Commissioner of Labor Relations Randy L. Levine, June 3, 1994.
8. Josh Anderson, Tom Piller, and Suany Chough, "Managed Competition in Queens Districts 5 & 6, December 1994–December 1995, Evaluation: Parts 1–4," partial draft for review, New York City Department of Parks and Recreation, May 1996.
9. Ibid.

10. Office of the Comptroller, Bureau of Management Audit, "Audit Report on the New York City Department of Parks and Recreation Contract with Parente Landscape Corporation," June 17, 1996.
11. DPR press release no. 60, March 29, 1996.
12. Ibid.
13. Steven Greenhouse, "Many Participants in Workfare Take the Place of City Workers," *New York Times*, April 13, 1998.
14. Stone and Webster Management Consultants, "City of New York Department of Parks and Recreation Fleet Competitiveness Review," March 1995.
15. Memo from First Deputy Commissioner Moss to the Competition Coordinating Committee, September 8, 1995.
16. The information presented here on the comptroller's concerns and DPR's response comes from two documents: "Comptroller's review of draft RFB for Bronx vehicle maintenance," letter from First Deputy Comptroller Steve Newman to Commissioner Stern, January 30, 1996; "DPR response," letter from First Deputy Commissioner Moss to First Deputy Comptroller Newman, February 28, 1996.
17. City of New York, "Mayor's Private Sector Survey," September 1989.
18. Letter from Deputy Comptroller Roger D. Liwer to First Deputy Commissioner Moss, March 20, 1996.
19. Response to Deputy Comptroller Liwer from First Deputy Commissioner Moss, April 1, 1996.
20. Testimony of Alan M. Moss, Deputy Commissioner of Parks and Recreation, before the City Council Committee on Governmental Operations, April 26, 1996.
21. Ibid.
22. "Internal Audit of Bronx Garage," memo from John Ifcher, senior advisor to the commissioner, to First Deputy Commissioner Moss, April 8, 1997.
23. Kerman, "Managed Competition."
24. Office of the Comptroller, Bureau of Management Audit, "Audit Report on the New York City Department of Parks and Recreation's Use of J. L. Associates to Privatize the Maintenance of Its Bronx Vehicle and Equipment Fleet," March 3, 2000.
25. Ibid.
26. Memo from First Deputy Commissioner Moss to the Competition Coordinating Committee, January 15, 1997.
27. Letter from Jack Friedman to First Deputy Commissioner Moss, May 29, 1997.

28. Reply from First Deputy Commissioner Moss to Jack Friedman, June 2, 1997.
29. Kerman, "Managed Competition."
30. Savas, *Privatization,* chap. 6.
31. Kerman, "Managed Competition."
32. E. S. Savas, "Municipal Monopoly," *Harper's Magazine,* November 1971, 55–60.

Appendix A | Summary of Privatization Initiatives in New York City, 1993–2001

No.	*Department or Administration*	*Program*	*Method of privatization*	*Date of privatization*	*Status*	*Magnitude*	*Quantitative benefits*	*Qualitative benefits*	*Description/Comments*
1	Buildings	Collection of fees	Contract	Pending in 2001	Drafting contract	$2.25 million per year		More accurate data; more prompt and efficient	Collect fees and data for elevator and boiler inspections
2	Buildings	Elevator inspections	Contract	1998	Ongoing	3 contracts totaling $2.5 million per year		More timely inspections; greater public safety	Inspect elevators and certify for compliance
3	Buildings	Licensing examination service	Contract	2000	Ongoing			More responsive and prompt	Develop and administer exams for site safety managers and private elevator agency directors and inspectors
4	Business Services	Business improvement districts (BIDs)	Default and voluntarism	1994–2000	Ongoing	12 new BIDs added to preexisting 29	$7.15 million per year raised by BIDs for better local services	Better security, sanitation, amenities, local promotion	Voluntary formation of BIDs and self-imposed taxes result in better services and quality of life in their areas
5	Children's Services	Child day care	Voucher	Late 1990s	Ongoing	12,710 children in care using vouchers	$44 million in 2000	Greater parental choice	Number of children cared for through vouchers increased from 3,103 in 1993 to 12,710 in 2000, a 310% increase; voucher cost is 42% less per child than contract cost
6	Children's Services	Foster care	Adoption (divestment)	Late 1990s	Ongoing	Number adopted up by 21,000		Children placed in permanent homes instead of remaining as city wards	Giuliani administration emphasizes adoption over continuation in foster care; children in foster care down by 12,000 and number adopted up by 21,000

Appendix A | continued

No.	Department or Administration	Program	Method of privatization	Date of privatization	Status	Magnitude	Quantitative benefits	Qualitative benefits	Description/Comments
7	Citywide Administrative Services	Vehicle fueling facilities	Withdrawal, divestment, and contract	1994	Ongoing	Began by closing 85 sites	Significant cost reduction	Faster, more convenient fueling	City closed its fueling sites and issued credit cards for city vehicles to refuel at chain of contracted service stations
8	Citywide Administrative Services	Fleet maintenance	Contract	1995	Ongoing		$4.7 million per year, including $1.2 million for released space	Out-of-service rates reduced from 10% to 2–3%	More vehicles available for daily service; less need to buy additional vehicles; more responsive city services by agencies that use autos
9	Citywide Administrative Services	Delivery of office supplies	Contract	1996	Ongoing		66% discount off list price	2-day delivery; more product choice; less warehousing	This is a conventional commercial activity that enables direct delivery of office supplies in just 2 days and at discounted prices
10	Citywide Administrative Services	Audit of leases	Contract	1993–2000	Completed	7-year contract	Reduced landlord overcharges by $2.8 million	In-house staff learned efficient methods from contractor	City employees learned from contractor how to manage leases and were able to do the work at lower cost; contract was not renewed
11	Citywide Administrative Services	Real-estate broker services	Contract	1995	Ongoing		Increased rental revenue	Better control of city property	Contractor manages city's leases and rentals; assures timely receipt of rents
12	Consumer WhaAffairs	Occupational licensing	Deregulation	1994		9 occupations	$2.2 million savings		Direct savings to the public by dropping nine obsolete licensing requirements

13	Corrections	Prisons	Contract	1995	Abandoned				Attempted but abandoned because of strong political opposition
14	Cultural Affairs	Cultural institutions	Withdrawal and voluntarism	1994	Ongoing	$5 million per year, $26.5 million total	Challenge resulted in at least $36.2 million in new money		Cultural institutions apply for challenge grants but must match every city dollar with new private dollars; total private giving more than doubled to $675 million
15	Economic Development Corporation (EDC)	JFK and LaGuardia airports	Contract	1994	Dropped in 2003		Much higher rent paid by Port Authority	Airport development	Port Authority to operate under lease extended to 2050; city used privatization plan to get more rent
16	Economic Development Corporation (EDC)		New York Coliseum	Divestment	1999	Completed		$345 million	Joint project: EDC and Metropolitan Transportation Authority
17	Economic Development Corporation (EDC)	Community gardens	Divestment	1999	Completed		$4 million revenue	Satisfied local communities	Vacant lots throughout the city were purchased by benefactors and kept as community gardens for local groups
18	Economic Development Corporation (EDC)	Off-Track Betting Corporation	Divestment	2000	Being considered		$250–389 million price, depending on number of racetracks to be added	Get out of noncore business	Sale requires state approval; strong opposition from unions and New York Racing Association, which submitted a losing bid
19	Economic Development Corporation (EDC)	United Nations Plaza Hotel	Divestment (asset sale)	1997	Completed		$85 million revenue; taxes up by $6.5 million per year by 2010	Got out of noncore business	No reason for the city to be in the commercial real estate business
20	Economic Development Corporation (EDC)	WNYC-AM and WNYC-FM radio	Divestment	1995	Completed		$20 million revenue	Got out of noncore business	No reason for the city to be in the radio business

Appendix A | continued

No.	Department or Administration	Program	Method of privatization	Date of privatization	Status	Magnitude	Quantitative benefits	Qualitative benefits	Description/Comments
21	Economic Development Corporation (EDC)	WNYC-TV	Divestment	1996	Completed		$207 million revenue	Got out of noncore business	No reason for the city to be in the TV business
22	Education	Contracts for charter schools	Contracts	2001	Not realized	$60.8 million (budgeted)		Better education, more parental choice	Contractor for 5 schools was selected but parents rejected the concept in a referendum
23	Education	Summer school	Contract	2000	Ongoing	$32 million (budgeted)		Better educated students	46 vendors awarded contracts in 20 districts for professional development, direct student services, instructional materials, test preparation, programs to increase parental involvement
24	Education	Custodial services	Contract	1995	Ongoing	Covers 79 of 1,100 (7%) schools.	Saving 15%, or $3.8 million per year	More flexible and responsive service; schools kept in better condition and kept open more hours for community activities	In 2003 an additional 133 schools were outsourced
25	Education	Department of Education buildings	Divestment	2001	Sold in 2003		$45 million revenue		Buildings are 110 Livingston St. and 2 other nearby buildings and chancellor's residence
26	Education	Construction of new school buildings	Public-private partnership	2001	Suspended		Private financing to build 3 new schools.		Private foundation will float $200 million in tax-exempt bonds and will pay debt service from lease payments by Board of Education; financing is outside city debt limit
27	Education	WNYE-FM and WNYE-TV	Lease	2001	Not realized		Revenue from sale or lease; eliminate all operating costs	Better programming; get out of noncore business	Founded in 1938, radio station would be turned over to WNYC public radio station for operation and TV to WNET-TV

28	Environmental Protection	Water-meter reading	Contract	1997	Ongoing; expansion pending		Recurring savings of $997,000 per year for Staten Island and Bronx	Fewer inquiries; higher collection rate; better service due to faster repairs	Net annual savings should be $2.15 million per year when expanded throughout city
29	Environmental Protection	Water system	Divestment to public agency	1995	Not realized		Would raise $2.3 billion		City would sell its entire water system to the quasi-independent Water Board; perceived as a budget gimmick
30	Environmental Protection	Wastewater treatment plants	Divestment	1994	Not realized	Sell 3 plants	Would raise $750 million	Would improve effluent water quality	Proposed by City Council to raise funds for other purposes
31	Finance	Tax liens on delinquent properties	Divestment	1996	Ongoing	35,410 properties sold in this manner.	$1.45 billion revenue, tax delinquency rate dropped from 3.67% in 1996 to 2.96% in 2000	Housing restored to market and to good condition, much sooner than if city had taken title	Instead of taking title to delinquent properties, city sells the tax liens directly by bulk sales of securitized liens; when city took title in the past, it owned and managed the buildings for an average of 19 years before selling them
32	Finance	Neighborhood payment centers and website	Withdrawal and contract	1998	Ongoing	More than 25,000 transactions per month	Greatly reduced cost of operation, roughly $1 million per year; 20 fewer clerks	Greater customer convenience, less waiting time	City closed most of its payment centers and allows private firm to receive payments for the city; public can pay at 402 locations at check-cashing stores; customer pays for the service; city is setting up website for further convenience and savings to the public
33	Finance	Bill payment by credit card	Contract	1998	Ongoing	Nearly 200,000 transactions	Reduced processing cost and collection cost on bad checks	Greater convenience to public	People can pay their city bills by credit card in person or by phone
34	Finance	Bail processing	Contract		Ongoing		Less staff needed; quicker deposit of receipts		Contractor (bank) receives bail receipt and check, verifies amount, deposits check, and transmits data to city

Appendix A | continued

No.	Department or Administration	Program	Method of privatization	Date of privatization	Status	Magnitude	Quantitative benefits	Qualitative benefits	Description/Comments
35	Finance	Data entry	Contract	1999	Ongoing; being expanded	Most data entry has been outsourced	Cost reduction		Also eliminated microfilming; exploring privatization of few remaining data entry functions, except property-owner registration
36	Fire	Reproduction and mail management	Contract	1994	Ongoing		$1 million savings in 1998, mostly in reduced vehicle costs	Customized and faster print, copy, delivery, and distribution services	Fire Department used competitive bidding to privatize these services
37	Fire	Billing for ambulance calls	Contract	2001	Pending		Expect at least $10 million more annual revenue		Department transports about 600,000 people to hospitals every year
38	Fire Department and Health and Hospitals Corporation	Emergency ambulance service	Private subcontracts by city's prime contractors	2001	Ongoing		Lower cost for hospitals	More hospital ambulance service for the same amount of money	Not a direct city activity or contract. Of the 909 ambulance tours per day, 325 (36%) are by private hospitals; some of these are by private ambulances under hospital contracts
39	Health and Hospitals Corporation (HHC)	Sale of municipal hospitals	Divestment	1995	Abandoned		Would generate large savings in expenditures and revenue from sales	Better health care for low-income people	Unsuccessful effort to sell Coney Island Hospital; further efforts dropped
40	Health and Hospitals Corporation (HHC)	Health care for prison inmates	Contract	1995		13,000 inmates	Approximately 10% lower cost than previous contract	Better staffing and health care than HHC is able to provide, but there were performance problems	Three-year contract based on fee for service to inmates of 12 of the 16 city jails; average daily inmate population of the contracted facilities is 13,000; problems in first 3 months resulted in $100,000 penalty assessed against contractor

41	Health and Hospitals Corporation (HHC)	Laundry service	Contract	2000	Ongoing	Half of the 16 million pounds of laundry annually	$3 million in the first year, cost reduced from 68 cents to 28 cents per pound. Will save $6 million per year under full contract	Quality of work at least as good	Strong union opposition; after HHC spends $600,000 in 2001 for new laundry equipment, in-house work will be compared with contract work in one-year experiment.
42	Health and Hospitals Corporation (HHC)	HHC security guards	Contract	Not realized	In litigation; negotiating with bid finalists	Replace 850 security guards at 26 hospitals	Estimated $10 million per year savings		Contract cost is expected to be about $22 million per year; strong opposition by union to contracting for private guard services; ten firms submitted bids
43	Health and Hospitals Corporation (HHC)	Small business health insurance	Public-private partnership	1999	GHI is continuing but without HHC	Expected 3,000 enrollees, only got 378	Was intended to be profitable for HHC		GHI initiated plan; GHI was insurer and administrator; HHC provided health care; only 378 enrollees from 49 small businesses; HHC dropped out of plan
44	Homeless Services	Shelters for homeless adults	Contract	1994	Ongoing	109 of 122 shelters	3-year average savings of $3.1 million per year	Higher quality shelters, better services, faster facility siting	Also provides individually specialized services and leads to dissemination and adoption of best practices
45	Housing Authority	Management of scattered housing sites	Contract	1997	Ongoing	4,100 units	Unknown, being studied	Better housing conditions	Though not clear if cost effective, a positive indicator is that no contractors have been terminated or eliminated
46	Housing Authority	Verifying eligibility of applicants for public housing	Contract	1994	Ongoing	Average of 14,000 home visits per year	Avoids using housing for ineligibles	Reserves housing for eligible persons	Service considered excellent by New York City Housing Authority
47	Housing Authority	Boiler plant privatization	Contract	1997	Ongoing	At 5 Housing Authority projects	Savings of $2.45 million per year		Contractor is Brooklyn Union Gas, a local utility

Appendix A | continued

No.	*Department or Administration*	*Program*	*Method of privatization*	*Date of privatization*	*Status*	*Magnitude*	*Quantitative benefits*	*Qualitative benefits*	*Description/Comments*
48	Housing Authority	Tenant-occupied, city-owned, *In-rem* buildings	Divestment and public-private partnership	1994	Ongoing	Sold 2,000 buildings with 32,000 units (2/3 of such buildings)	Cost avoidance and savings of $95 million per year	Return properties to private housing market and city tax rolls	Net cost avoidance for operations was $2,900 per unit oer year; staff reduction was $2.55 million per year
49	Housing Authority	Tenant-occupied, city-owned buildings with market value	Divestment	1996	Ongoing	Sold 74 buildings and 2 rental properties	Revenue of $12.65 million; avoided operating costs	Return of properties to private housing market and city tax rolls	City sold 74 buildings with 286 housing and 50 commercial units and 2 rental properties with 297 housing units acquired through mortgage foreclosures
50	Housing Authority	Vacant, city-owned, *in-rem* buildings	Divestment	1994	Ongoing	Sold about 1,200 buildings	City subsidizes this program	Creates market-based, owner-occupied housing	Vacant 2–4 family buildings turned over to developers; after private financing and HPD subsidy for rehabilitation, sold at market price to qualified buyers
51	Housing Authority	Preventing abandonment of buildings	Contract	1997	Ongoing	1,000–1,500 buildings per year	Avoids cost of city ownership, management, and operation	Keeps buildings in private hands, paying taxes	Troubled buildings are identified and efforts are made to keep them in the hands of current owners and not be taken over by the city for tax arrears
52	Housing Authority	Preventing abandonment of buildings	Forced private divestment and ownership transfer	1998	Ongoing	134 buildings transferred to qualified new owners	Avoided cost of $5.8 million	Keeps buildings in private hands, paying taxes	Buildings in arrears are diverted prior to tax-lien sale; city forces transfer of ownership to a third party; avoids cost of city ownership, management, and operation
53	Human Resources Administration	Education and enrollment for Medicaid managed care	Contract	1999	Ongoing	3 year contract for $18.5 million	Savings of $24 million in the first year		Delayed due to union opposition; contract finally awarded after court decision

54	Human Resources Administration	Legal aid for welfare recipients	Contract	1995	Ongoing	12 contracts		Process substantiated pricing information	Competitive solicitation was conducted
55	Human Resources Administration	Welfare reform (Work Experience Program)	Withdrawal	1995	Ongoing	Public assistance cases reduced from 1.16 million in March 1995 to 0.47 million in December 2001; 151,376 Work Experience Program participants in 2001	Tax -levy spending for public assistance reduced from $984 million in 1995 to $431 million in 2000, for $553 million per year savings	Cleanliness of parks rose from 73% to 96%; of streets from 74% to 87%	Reduction in the number of public assistance cases; useful public work being performed; greater self-reliance and less dependency
56	Human Resources Administration	Employment preparation and job placement	Performance- based Contracting	2000	Ongoing		89,071 public assistance recipients were placed in jobs by end of fiscal 2000	Greater sense of self worth for former public assistance recipients and better life prospects	Change from cost-plus contracts to performance contracts led to 61% increase in placement rate and 305% increase in number of placements
57	Information Technology and Telecommunications	Kiosks for interactive "e-government"	Contract	2001	Request for proposal issued February 2001; proposals received	3 year contracts with 12 vendors		Better and faster service to citizens and businesses	More convenient access for citizens and businesses to obtain information, file applications, make payments
58	Information Technology and Telecommunications	Pneumatic tube network to be used for fiber optic cables	Lease	2001	Request for proposal issued 2001				City has unused underground water lines and abandoned pneumatic tubing
59	Information Technology and Telecommunications	Webphones as public pay telephones	Franchise	2001	Implemented in 2003			Expand services at no cost to city	Allow convenient public access to the Internet
60	Juvenile Justice	Nonsecure detention facilities for youth	Contract	1998–2001	Ongoing	3 new facilities	Saved $450,000 per year with no change in service level		Agency obtained nonsecure detention services from a community-based organization by competitive, sealed- proposal procurement

Appendix A | continued

No.	Department or Administration	Program	Method of privatization	Date of privatization	Status	Magnitude	Quantitative benefits	Qualitative benefits	Description/Comments
61	Parks and Recreation	Central Park	Default, voluntarism, and contract	1998	Ongoing		Conservancy raises $7 million to qualify for $2 million city contract	Better condition of one of the world's premier urban parks	Central Park Conservancy provides 85% of the park's operating budget of $20 million per year
62	Parks and Recreation	Vehicle maintenance	Managed competition and contract	1996	Ongoing	Three of eight garages are contracted out	Bronx savings: 38% ($1.17 million to $728,000), and 30% in Brooklyn	Out-of-service rate reduced from 14% to 5% on average	Classic example of well managed privatization process with excellent results; agency's own workforce now competes well with contractor; both have improved
63	Parks and Recreation	Park maintenance	Contract	1994	Completed and terminated	92 park sites in Queens and Bronx	30% cost reduction	Higher cleanliness ratings	Successful contract, but welfare recipients subsequently performed the work at lower cost
64	Public Library, Brooklyn	General support	Voluntarism	1995	Ongoing		$2 million per year		Amount given has doubled during the Giuliani administration
65	Public Library, New York	Library renovation	Withdrawal and voluntarism	1996	Ongoing	15 branches	$12.5 million raised		$0.5 million to renovate each of 15 branches in Manhattan and Bronx, plus $5 million for a Bronx branch through private funding
66	Public Library, New York	Security guards	Contract	1996	Ongoing		Lower cost		

67	Sanitation	Residential solid-waste collection	Contract	1994	Not implemented		20% gain in productivity reported		The threat of managed competition led to productivity improvement
68	Sanitation	Solid-waste transfer and disposal	Contract	1997	Ongoing	Gradual growth of program; all solid waste to be exported by end of 2001	City incurs net cost although contractor cost is less than in-house cost	Closed Fresh Kills; higher quality of life; higher property values and tax receipts in the long term	City closed the last landfill within city limits; solid waste is now collected and brought to privately operated transfer stations and is then sent out of state by the contractor
69	Sanitation	Control of gas emission at Fresh Kills landfill	Franchise	1998	Ongoing		Franchisee paid initial fee of $875,000, pays $1.0 million per year. City saves $2–3 million per year in cost of compliance monitoring	Reduced emission of greenhouse gases	Franchisee controls gas emissions and collects, processes, and sells landfill gases
70	Sanitation	Fresh Kills landfill composting	Contract	2000	Ongoing			Volume reduction, better maintenance of site without odor problems	Contractor sells compost product but operation is not self-sustaining; city pays contractor
71	Sanitation	Wastepaper recycling	Contract (with risk sharing for market variation)	1996	Ongoing		Eliminates OTPS cost (was up to $6 million in bad year); minimum of $1.3 million per year in new revenue ($5 per ton guarantee)	Creates city infrastructure for recyclables, jobs for limited- skill workers, and new revenue stream	5- to 20-year contracts with 5 recycling processors; city will reduce costs by up to $120 million and gain revenue of at least $26 million in 20 years (at least $1.3 million per year); revenue was $7.5 million in 2000, a very good year for paper prices
72	Sanitation	Stuff exchange program	Contract	2000	Ongoing		Saves cost of collecting and disposing of material, which would be much greater than cost of system	Satisfies environmental concerns	City pays $250,000 per year for 64 phone lines and to keep information up to date; also pays $1.5 million per year for advertising; serves as broker matching donor with recipient; city does not handle materials
73	Taxi and Limousine Commission	Taxicabs	Franchise	1996	Ongoing	Number of medallions increased by 400, from 11,787 to 12,187	$89.9 million revenue from auction of medallions	More service and greater convenience for public	First increase in number of medallions since 1937; in 2003 Bloomberg administration said it planned to sell 900 more for about $250,000 each; fares would be raised 25% to assuage current owners

Appendix A | continued

No.	Department or Administration	Program	Method of privatization	Date of privatization	Status	Magnitude	Quantitative benefits	Qualitative benefits	Description/Comments
74	Taxi and Limousine Commission	Commuter vans	Default and deregulation	1999	Ongoing	Number of licensed vans incre-ased from 262 to 397	Direct savings to riding public due to lower fares	More frequent and convenient transportation for the public	Local surface transit was inadequate in parts of the city; responding to market demand, private vans filled the void; they were legitimized by easing the regulations after a court challenge
75	Trade Waste Commission	Commercial solid-waste collection	Regulating to create a competitive market	1995	Ongoing	Affects all commercial establishments	Direct savings to businesses of nearly $400 million per year		City cleaned up racket-influenced commercial solid-waste industry, allowing legitimate companies to enter the market.
76	Transportation	Private ferry operations	Franchise	1986	Ongoing	Four firms operate 15 routes, averaging 35,000 trips each day		More and better transportation options for public	Half the routes were initiated during the Giuliani administration; DOT and EDC provide terminals to promote ferry usage and reduce congestion
77	Transportation	Municipal parking garages	Lease	1982, 1995	Ongoing	All 13 city-owned garages	$6.1 million in fiscal 2000		Leasing started in 1982, but revenue control was poor, since 1995 city has had a revenue sharing agreement
78	Transportation	Parking garages and parking fields	Divestment	1996	Sold 5 of 13 facilities	3 garages and 2 parking fields	$16.86 million in revenue	Got out of a noncore activity	Sold one garage in Manhattan and 2 parking fields and 2 garages in Queens
79	Transportation	Adopt-a-highway	Default and voluntarism	1995	Ongoing	334 (92%) of the 362 eligible miles of arterial highways adopted	Contribution is $6,000 to $10,000 per mile per year depending on service, i.e., only sweeping, or more	Weekly mowing, sweeping, landscape maintenance, and removal of litter and graffiti	Sponsors who want cleaner roadways can contribute to this program and get recognition on highway signs; they can choose among six qualified firms to perform the work

80	Transportation	Installation of street signs	Managed competition (work kept in house)	1995	Ongoing	About 50,000 signs installed annually	22% increase in productivity	Better signage for public	Union agreed to greater productivity to avoid outsourcing by the city
81	Transportation	Street resurfacing	Managed competition	1995	Not implemented		Large savings were expected		Bids were received but no awards were made; union agreed to increase productivity
82	Transportation	Red-light cameras	Contract	1993	Ongoing	30 cameras, going to 50 in 2001; seeking to go to 100	200,000 tickets were issued in 2000; city collected $9 million in fines; contract price is $5 million per year	Improve safety; 41% reduction in red-light running at covered intersections	Cars driving through red lights at selected intersections trigger cameras and sensing equipment; violators are identified and are issued tickets by mail

Appendix B | Privatization Iniatives in Detail

This appendix describes each of New York City's eighty-two privatization initiatives in detail, including the agency, the specific function or activity, the year and method of privatization, the benefits—both quantitative and qualitative, where available—and the implementation steps. The benefits indicated for each initiative might include any or all of the following: reduced cost, avoided cost, increased revenue, higher quality of service, greater responsiveness of service, and direct savings for the public.

Because the initiatives were part of routine municipal business rather than a controlled experiment, the data are not completely reliable. Savings and other benefits came from mayoral or agency reports or interviews and were not independently verified. Different authoritative sources sometimes provided different estimates of savings, and in these cases the author's best estimates appear here. In many cases no authoritative or reliable estimates of savings were available, and therefore none are given. The cost of contracting or other privatization actions was not calculated.

AGENCY: Department of Buildings 1

FUNCTION, SERVICE, OR ASSET PRIVATIZED: Collection of fees

FORM AND DATE OF PRIVATIZATION: Contract, pending in 2001

DESCRIPTION: The Department of Buildings is in the process of drafting a contract for collecting the mandated fees and reports for elevator and boiler inspections. The expected cost of the contract is $2.25 million per year.

BENEFITS: The private contractor will provide a more efficient, accurate and cost-effective method to collect fees and prepare data-entry reports. Revenue collections will also be accelerated. The Department of Buildings will then be able to improve quality control in this area, meet processing deadlines, and accelerate depositing of revenues.

Payments would be made to a post-office box that would be serviced by the contractor. He would deposit the funds immediately, thereby earning maximum interest for the city, and prepare the necessary payment records. The common term for this is "lock-box service."

IMPLEMENTATION: Due to the dismal results of an internal review of the overall condition of collection of fees and data entry of annual mandated reports of Local Law 10/81 (Elevators) and Local Law 62/91 (Boilers), the Department of Buildings is privatizing these services. The Department of Finance is assisting with the terms of this contract.

AGENCY: Department of Buildings 2

FUNCTION, SERVICE, OR ASSET PRIVATIZED: Elevator inspections

FORM AND DATE OF PRIVATIZATION: Contract, 1998

DESCRIPTION: The Department of Buildings privatized its elevator inspections through a contract in 1996 in which the private contractors are responsible for inspecting elevators and certifying that the devices are in compliance with Subchapter 18 of the New York City Building Code and Reference Standard 18.1.

BENEFITS: The decision to hire private contractors to inspect elevators in New York City was made in order to have more timely inspections, thereby ensuring greater public safety.

IMPLEMENTATION: In August 1996 forty-one elevator inspectors and support staff of the Department of Buildings had been fired following a federal and city investigation. Therefore, the Department of Buildings initiated three emergency contracts in fiscal 1998 at the cost of $2.5 million per year to prevent delays in the mandated inspection of elevators and escalators. The department continues to use private inspections instead of adding staff. The decision to continue with these contracts is reviewed annually.

AGENCY: Department of Buildings 3

FUNCTION, SERVICE, OR ASSET PRIVATIZED: Licensing examinations

FORM AND DATE OF PRIVATIZATION: Contract, 2000

DESCRIPTION: This is an ongoing program in which a private contractor is responsible for developing, administering, and rating professional examinations for the Department of Buildings' site safety managers, private elevator agency directors, and inspectors.

BENEFITS: The department decided to hire a private contractor to develop and administer licensing examinations in order to increase the responsiveness of this service to the public and also to reduce the turnaround time from date of exam to approval of qualification. The Department of Buildings selected these licenses due to the increasing demand for these services.

IMPLEMENTATION: The Department of Buildings originally had the Department of Administrative and Citywide Services Peform this function but soon changed to a private contractor.

AGENCY: Department of Business Services 4

FUNCTION, SERVICE, OR ASSET PRIVATIZED: Business improvement districts

FORM AND DATE OF PRIVATIZATION: Default and voluntarism, 1994–2000

DESCRIPTION: From 1994 to 2000, twelve new business improvement districts (BIDs) were added to the already existing twenty-nine in New York City. The new BIDs include the Hospitality Alliance for Downtown NY, 60-86 Madison Avenue, Lincoln Square, Village Alliance, Noho, 47th Street, 125th Street, Mosholu-Jerome-East Gun Hill Road, Sunset Park 5th Avenue, Montague Street, White Plains Road, and 180th Street.

BENEFITS: In their areas, BIDs provide such services as:

- Security services, including the provision of security officers, lighting programs, and crime prevention activities.
- Sanitation services, including street sweeping and refuse and snow removal.
- Maintenance of horticulture, street pavements and furniture, and graffiti removal.
- Hospitality, including promotional activities, informational services, and cultural events.

Voluntary formation of BIDs and self-imposed taxes have resulted in better services and quality of life in BID areas. These new BIDs raised approximately $7.15 million for better maintenance, security, sanitation, and hospitality in 2000.

IMPLEMENTATION: Some people feel that the city is failing to provide adequate services or to maintain certain facilities satisfactorily, and these people decide to take voluntary action to remedy the situation. For example, local property owners in a self-defined area can form a BID with government approval. They levy a special tax on themselves that they use for extra cleaning, safety, or other services and for aesthetic improvements in street lights, architectural lighting, plantings, signage, litter baskets, newspaper boxes, newsstands, and the like. The result is a visibly improved neighborhood.

Communities seeking to establish a BID must submit a Memo of Intent to the Department of Business Services (DBS) and receive authorization from the mayor to proceed with BID planning. Once a preliminary plan—including services to be provided, budgetary and assessment formulas, and BID boundaries—has been adopted by the BID sponsors, at least one public hearing must be held, and documented support for the proposed BID from at least 60 percent of property owners must be obtained. The finalized BID plan, supporting documentation, and hearing evidence must be reviewed by DBS and receive approval from the local Community Board, the City Planning Commission, and the City Council.

BIDs must comply with all rules and regulations governing the establishment and operation of BIDs. BID contracts are reviewed by DBS during renewal. Renewal decisions are based on a formal evaluation by DBS of the BID's performance, including financial integrity, compliance with contract terms, and constituent surveys conducted by the BIDs.

AGENCY: Administration for Children's Services 5

FUNCTION, SERVICE, OR ASSET PRIVATIZED: Child day care

FORM AND DATE OF PRIVATIZATION: Voucher, late 1990s

DESCRIPTION: The Administration for Children's Services operates no child care programs directly; it does, however, provide child-care services for more than 50,000 children and their families through contracts with several hundred private for-profit and nonprofit sponsoring organizations and through the distribution of vouchers to parents that enable them to place their children with the child-care program or provider of their choice.

Vouchers are a payment mechanism that parents can use for any modality: day-care centers or family day-care homes that are under contract; licensed or regulated family day-care homes or licensed day-care centers that the city does not have under contract; unlicensed informal care; or legally exempt care (such as care provided by certain religious institutions that are exempt from some state regulations). In other words, vouchers allow parents to select any legal day-care provider in New York City, including private nurseries and day-care centers, family day-care homes, and informal providers, thereby maximizing customer choice and ensuring that individual child care needs are met.

The great majority of vouchers are issued to children in low-income families with high-priority reasons for child care such as child-welfare cases, public assistance recipients, and low-income working families who need child care to participate in work and work activities.

BENEFITS: One major benefit of vouchers is that they cost the city much less than contracts. The average other-than-personnel services (OTPS) expenditure per contract slot is $8,324. The corresponding average per voucher is 42 percent less, or $4,853, resulting in a savings of $3,471. For fiscal 2000 this amounted to a total savings of $44 million. The two main reasons for this difference are that vouchers cover no more than the market rate, whereas the price of a contract is up to the cost of care, and that vouchers may not be accepted in more expensive facilities. The difference may be greater or less if one takes into account any difference between contracts and vouchers in the mix of ages served and the mix of part-time vs. full-time care. Another benefit of vouchers is that they offer greater parental choice and ensure that individual childcare needs are met.

IMPLEMENTATION: The Administration for Children's Services provides subsidized childcare for eligible children and families using contracts and vouchers. Contracting dates back to the agency's inception in 1970; the agency has contracted with hundreds of private organizations since then. Vouchers were introduced on a very limited basis in the 1980s, but they have been used far more extensively in the late 1990s. The number of vouchers issued in fiscal 2000 was 12,710, compared to 3,103 issued in fiscal 1993, an increase of 310 percent.

AGENCY: Administration for Children's Services 6

FUNCTION, SERVICE, OR ASSET PRIVATIZED: Foster care

FORM AND DATE OF PRIVATIZATION: Adoption ("Divestment"!), late 1990s

DESCRIPTION: The Giuliani administration emphasized adoption over keeping children in foster care. From 1996 to 2001, this resulted in a decrease in the number of children in foster care by 12,000 (a 40 percent decrease compared to the previous six years), and an increase in the number of children adopted by 21,000 (an increase of 66 percent over the past six years). Although it may seem odd to think of it this way, a shift from foster care toward adoption is a move toward privatization. That is, children in foster care are wards of the city, but adopted children are the responsibility of private citizens, their adoptive parents. The big secret of many child welfare programs is that foster care is, to a great extent, a jobs program (or a welfare program) for those who become "career" foster parents.

BENEFITS: The increase in the number of children adopted from 1,784 in 1992 to 3,148 in 2000 means a direct monetary saving to the city, namely the elimination of payments for foster care for these children. The more important benefit, however, is for the children themselves, who are placed in permanent homes instead of being temporarily placed in a foster family.

IMPLEMENTATION: The new policy also provided more children with at-home preventive services than with foster care. This was accomplished by hiring more caseworkers with higher qualifications and salaries and lowering their caseloads to ten children each, a drop of 41 percent.

AGENCY: Department of Citywide Administrative Services 7

FUNCTION, SERVICE, OR ASSET PRIVATIZED: Vehicle fueling facilities

FORM AND DATE OF PRIVATIZATION: Withdrawal, divestment, and contract, 1994

DESCRIPTION: The Department of Citywide Administrative Services owned and operated 500 fueling facilities, with underground storage tanks, for city-owned vehicles. It consolidated many sites and closed 85 of them; that is, it withdrew from providing this service and sold the properties. The department turned instead to the marketplace by contracting to buy fuel at a discounted price from a major gasoline company, and it issued credit cards for each vehicle; the card could be used to fuel that vehicle at any of the company's many service stations in the city.

BENEFITS: Costs were reduced significantly, and the department was no longer responsible for complying with environmental regulations for underground tanks.

IMPLEMENTATION: The closures were done in stages, department by department, starting with the facilities serving the Police and Fire Departments and the municipal hospitals.

AGENCY: Department of Citywide Administrative Services 8

FUNCTION, SERVICE, OR ASSET PRIVATIZED: Fleet maintenance

FORM AND DATE OF PRIVATIZATION: Contract, December 1995

DESCRIPTION: Prior to December 1995, the Department of Citywide Administrative Services (DCAS) maintained a fleet of approximately 734 vehicles using a city-owned garage in Brooklyn. Having one central facility posed significant problems. The garage was extremely crowded with vehicles awaiting maintenance, and the mechanics spent considerable time jockeying cars in and out of available spots. The result was high downtime and cost. Also, the garage had little ability to repair vehicles after hours or outside city limits.

In 1995 DCAS contracted out its fleet maintenance, transferred the garage to the New York Police Department, and had its mechanics reassigned to vacancies in other agencies. The contract is managed by the DCAS Office of Fleet Administration, which maintains records substantiating the reduction in cost and downtime. In 1997 the Mayor's Office of Operations expanded the contract to four other city agencies. Since 1997 many other city agencies have requested permission to join this initiative, increasing the number of participating vehicles from 734 to about 1,900.

BENEFITS: The program continues to be very successful. The average annual cost of maintaining a vehicle was reduced from approximately $3,100 per year to $1,250 per year. Based on the number of vehicles in the program, the estimated annual total savings for the city are approximately $3.5 million. The NYPD was able to take over the Brooklyn garage for its newly acquired Transit Police vehicles and was able to forgo a costly garage lease, saving $1.2 million per year. The total savings and cost avoidance therefore amounted to $4.7 million annually.

Additionally, the privatization initiative resulted in better overall service. The contractor has more than 200 associated garages in the city of New York and can service vehicles around the clock and throughout the country. Out-of-service rates were reduced from over 10 percent to 2–3 percent. There were other benefits as well. DCAS cancelled an unreliable truck maintenance contract, opting instead to use this maintenance and management contract. The Department of Transportation also followed DCAS's lead and established its own account, placing approximately 600 vehicles in its program. No dollar value was placed on these substantial benefits. For example, reduced out-of-service rates mean that fewer vehicles are needed to carry out the work, and so fewer have to be bought and less garage space is required.

IMPLEMENTATION: This initiative began in 1993 when Commissioner Diamond proposed the privatization of all city light-duty fleet maintenance (autos, vans, and pickups). A consultant was hired and concluded that substantial reductions in cost and out-of-service rates could be realized using the services of a maintenance management contract. The mayor asked DCAS to institute a pilot program. The DCAS Office of Fleet Administration (OFA) and the consultant performed a cost-benefit analysis and forwarded it to OMB. OMB endorsed it and the proposal gained the support of Operations and the Office of Labor Relations (OLR). OLR then instituted a series of meeting with the affected unions, allowing them to voice their concerns.

The two major obstacles to implementing the program were the unions and the lack of a contract. The unions spent over a year questioning the proposal and offering several counterproposals, none of which substantially lowered either out-of-service rates or cost. New York state was also developing a similar initiative and established a contract with GE Fleet Services, Inc. Once the final decision to privatize the city's fleet maintenance was made, DCAS utilized the state contract.

AGENCY: Department of Citywide Administrative Services 9

FUNCTION, SERVICE, OR ASSET PRIVATIZED: Delivery of office supplies

FORM AND DATE OF PRIVATIZATION: Contract, March 1996

DESCRIPTION: In March 1996 the Department of Citywide Administrative Services began its pilot program to privatize the delivery of office supplies to New York City agencies. Before the implementation of the direct delivery of office supplies, the city of New York purchased office supplies in bulk through a competitive bidding process, which took several weeks. Awarded vendors supplying the items were obligated to use specific packaging or risk having the delivery rejected. The office supplies were stored in bulk at the New York City Central Storehouse, pending receipt of agency orders. Agencies were obligated to purchase their office supplies from the storehouse. Only those items not stocked by the storehouse were eligible for open market purchases from local vendors. Further, the storehouse would deliver only those agency orders valued at $200 or more and only to one central location at each agency. If an agency placed an order for less than $200, or needed the items in less than the standard six-week delivery time, the agency would be required to arrange its own pickup of the supplies.

BENEFITS: Privatization of the delivery of office supplies enabled the city to realize several economic benefits. Specifically, office supplies no longer occupied valuable city space on a long-term basis. In addition, agencies were not only afforded more flexibility in their choice of products, but also received a 61 percent discount off list prices in the catalog. Moreover, the requestor received the order within five days rather than the several weeks it took storehouse deliveries to reach the user.

IMPLEMENTATION: All New York City agencies are now eligible to enjoy direct delivery of office supplies. Since the beginning of this program, the discount has been increased from 61 percent to 66 percent, and the delivery time reduced from five days to two days. Delivery is free, as long as the order is valued at $50 or more. The vendor delivers orders that are less than $50; however, a delivery charge applies in those cases. Agency response to this initiative has been satisfactory, and informal research indicates that no agency supports returning to the old system of requisitioning office supplies from the central storehouse.

AGENCY: Department of Citywide Administrative Services 10

FUNCTION, SERVICE, OR ASSET PRIVATIZED: Audit of leases

FORM AND DATE OF PRIVATIZATION: Contract from fiscal 1993 through fiscal 2000

DESCRIPTION: The Department of Citywide Administrative Services (DCAS) leases space from private landlords for such city uses as offices, garages, warehouses, and senior citizen and day-care centers. The city pays the landlord for its proportionate share of real estate taxes and operating expenses, in addition to monthly rent. DCAS auditors review the financial records of the landlords to determine if the city has been correctly charged for its share of those costs. As a result of the audits, the landlords have been more accurate in charges to the city, thereby greatly reducing the number of leases to audit.

In fiscal 1993 the city engaged private contract auditors to supplement DCAS's internal audit staff. Over the course of the contract period, while the private contractors have netted cost reductions to the city of approximately $1.5 million, DCAS's in-house audit staff of two full-time and one part-time auditor netted cost reductions of approximately $6.8 million. Considering the above, and the high fee paid to the private contractors, DCAS has decided that it is not cost effective to continue with the contract and will rely strictly on the in-house audit staff to review the remaining leases under consideration for audit. The privatization contracts expired in fiscal 2000, and the agency decided not to issue a new request for proposal and contract.

BENEFITS: Over the contract period, DCAS contracted with two firms, which identified approximately $2.8 million in overcharges by landlords to the city. As a fee for this service, the contractor is paid between 40 percent and 50 percent of the overcharged amount. The net cost reduction to the city over the course of the contract period, therefore, has been approximately $1.5 million spread over the contract period.

IMPLEMENTATION: The city first contracted out the review and audit of the leases in fiscal 1993. Assignments were given to the contractors throughout the contract period at the decision of DCAS. The contracts were successful because the auditors were able to identify considerable overcharges by the landlords. Although the results were successful, at the end of the contract period DCAS decided not to issue a new request for propsal in fiscal 2001. This decision was based on the reduction in the number of leases to audit, the high fee paid to the contractors, staff time required to administer the contracts, and the fact that in-house staff was able to achieve better results at a lower cost after observing and learning the methods of the private sector.

AGENCY: Department of Citywide Administrative Services 11

FUNCTION, SERVICE, OR ASSET PRIVATIZED: Real-estate broker services

FORM AND DATE OF PRIVATIZATION: Contract, 1995

DESCRIPTION: The Division of Real Estate Services (DRES) of the Department of Citywide Administrative Services (DCAS) manages the inventory of city-owned commercial real estate, both buildings and vacant lots. In many cases, leasing is available for limited time periods while city agencies work on development plans for the property. DRES does not have responsibility for residential buildings or apartment units.

Short-term leases have month-to-month terms. Typically, tenants rent these properties for parking for an adjacent home or business. In most cases, leases can be arranged directly with the DRES Lease In-Take Unit with rents ranging from under $100 to $5,000 per month through a public lease auction. Leases with terms longer than one year are available on selected properties. Longer terms allow tenants to make improvements to the property. Long-term lease sites must be offered through a public lease auction, which is held several times each year. Sites are offered with terms and special use requirements specific to the unique nature of each property. Public parking lots, retail spaces, office spaces, and vacant lots can be offered for lease. DRES has contracted out the management of its real-estate leases and rentals.

BENEFITS: The private contractor is expected to have better control of city property and assure timely receipt of rentals.

IMPLEMENTATION: Not applicable.

AGENCY: Department of Consumer Affairs 12

FUNCTION, SERVICE, OR ASSET PRIVATIZED: Occupational licensing

FORM AND DATE OF PRIVATIZATION: Deregulation, 1994

DESCRIPTION: In 1994 the Department of Consumer Affairs (DCA) deregulated license categories in the following areas:

1. Billiard hall employees.
2. Masquerade balls.
3. Antique dealers without a place of business in the city.
4. Operators and managers of antique expositions.
5. Motion picture theaters (movie theaters).
6. Sightseeing-bus drivers.
7. Multiple dwelling garages for tenants and exclusive use of parking lots.
8. Up to three fixed-stand, coin-operated rides for kids in storefronts.
9. Less than five common show coin-operated amusement devices, common show attendants, common show name games, and common show skating rinks.

BENEFITS: There are direct savings to the public by dropping these obsolete licensing requirements. Since 1994, 11,156 local businesses have been able to operate without being required to obtain licenses from DCA; the public has saved approximately $2,230,890 inasmuch as the cost of licenses was ultimately borne by the consumer.

IMPLEMENTATION: In 1994 DCA began the process of deregulating license categories that had not historically generated consumer complaints. DCA has subsequently taken on additional licensing responsibilities through the management of the consolidated Citywide Licensing Center, which includes 45,000 Department of Health licenses, and the transfer of 16,285 tobacco retailer licenses to DCA from the Department of Finance.

AGENCY: Department of Corrections 13

FUNCTION, SERVICE, OR ASSET PRIVATIZED: Prisons

FORM AND DATE OF PRIVATIZATION: Contract (considered and abandoned)

DESCRIPTION: The city has seventeen prisons with about 18,000 prisoners. In 1995 the administration issued a request for expressions of interest (RFEI) to determine if private prison firms would bid for contracts to operate the city's entire prison system, individual jails, dining halls, social services, or prisoner transport.

About 120,000 prisoners in the United States, or six percent of the total, are in more than 120 private prisons. These prisons are generally owned by state or local governments but operated under contract by specialized private firms. (Some prisons were built and are owned by private firms.) Almost twenty American firms provide these services. The two largest, Corrections Corporation of America and Wackenhut Corrections Corporation, in total operate 59 prisons in the U.S., Puerto Rico, Great Britain, and Australia.

BENEFITS: When the RFEI was issued, the city was spending $746.3 million for the 11,000 employees of the prison system. The reason for testing the private market was to explore the possibility of contracting out all or some of the prisons or services and thereby reducing the cost of the system without reducing the quality. Expected sources of savings were not only labor costs but also the cost of food and supplies, building maintenance, and other operations. Other states and local governments that had contracted out prison operations showed generally good results—with some exceptions—and savings of about 10–15 percent.

IMPLEMENTATION: Eleven firms responded and indicated their interest in operating all or part of the city's prison system. The affected municipal unions objected fiercely to this plan, however, and they were supported by various elected city and state officials. Legislation was introduced in the state legislature to bar the use of private firms to guard inmates in state or local custody. Ultimately the city had to abandon this idea.

AGENCY: Department of Cultural Affairs 14

FUNCTION, SERVICE, OR ASSET PRIVATIZED: Cultural institutions

FORM AND DATE OF PRIVATIZATION: Withdrawal and voluntarism, 1994

DESCRIPTION: The Department of Cultural Affairs (DCA) of New York owns the land and buildings of thirty-four major cultural institutions and leases them to trustees of the institutions. These institutions include the Metropolitan Museum of Art, American Museum of Natural History, New York Botanical Garden, and Wildlife Conservation Society (for the Bronx Zoo and the Aquarium).

Since 1870 the city had been paying all expenses to run these institutions. The Giuliani administration changed this in 1994 by introducing incentives for more voluntary donations to these institutions through its newly created Cultural Challenge Program. The city and the state of New York put up $5 million each in the first year to be matched one to one, two to one, or three to one by new private donations to cultural institutions. This program was not restricted to the thirty-four city-supported institutions. Any institution could apply for a challenge grant on a dollar-for-dollar matching basis; that is, the institution must raise a dollar for every dollar for amounts less than $10,000; and $3 for every city dollar over $100,000. The state dropped out after the first year but the city continued, providing $26.5 million total. The city also gives 10 percent of capital funds for major construction. For instance, it gave $65 million to the Museum of Modern Art toward its new $650 million building, while private donors provide the remaining 90 percent.

BENEFITS: The institutions raised at least $36.2 million in new private funds in response to the challenge presented by the city's $26.5 million. This figure understates the result, however, as institutions did not report gifts in excess of the target. The program was very effective in that 90 percent of applying organizations made the match.

The city budget for institutional support stayed about the same, but challenge and private matches resulted in more money for the institutions. DCA funding as a fraction of all other income for the institutions dropped steadily from 19.3 percent in 1994 to 12.2 percent in 2000. Private donations more than doubled, increasing from $299 million in 1994 to $675 million in 2000, an average increase of $188 million per year over the pre-Giuliani era.

IMPLEMENTATION: The Bloomberg administration continued and promoted this program even more strongly, arguing that some institutions dependent on city funding should focus even more effort on private contributors.

AGENCY: Economic Development Corporation 15

FUNCTION, SERVICE, OR ASSET PRIVATIZED: John F. Kennedy and LaGuardia Airports

FORM AND DATE OF PRIVATIZATION: Contract management, proposed in 1994, dropped in 2003

DESCRIPTION: John F. Kennedy and LaGuardia Airports are owned by the city but leased to the Port Authority of New York and New Jersey until 2015. The city maintains that the lease payments are much too small. Negotiations to increase the payments to the city were unavailing. In May 2000 Mayor Rudolph W. Giuliani announced that the city and the New York City Economic Development Corporation (EDC) had decided to enter into negotiations with BAA USA, Inc. over the terms of a contract for the long-term management, operation and development of the city's two airports—John F. Kennedy Airport (JFK) and LaGuardia Airport (LGA).

If an agreement can be reached, the city and EDC intend to enter into a contract with BAA under which BAA would initially provide oversight and consulting services for the airports. BAA would assume management and operation of the airports when the city's lease with the Port Authority of New York and New Jersey, the current operator, expires in 2015 or earlier if the lease is terminated before then.

BENEFITS: Potential benefits from this contract include a portion of the approximately $180 million that are currently redirected by the Port Authority to nonairport projects. If the operation of these airports were contracted out, the city would get more money than it is getting now from its lease to the Port Authority. Additional benefits may also include recurring revenues from operating budget savings. Besides these monetary savings, the most important benefit of this competitive contract would be for the public in the form of better management of the airports.

IMPLEMENTATION: Giuliani first proposed privatizing these airports while he was still a candidate in early 1993. As mayor in 1994 he repeated the proposal and received support from Governor George Pataki. In 1996, the city contracted for a feasibility study. Negotiations with the Port Authority continued unsuccessfully for an increase in the lease payments from the Port Authority to the city. In February 2000, in response to a request for proposal (RFP) seeking a qualified airport management firm to improve quality and competitiveness at JFK and LGA, the city and EDC received proposals from four firms with considerable experience operating and managing world-class international airports: BAA USA, Inc.; Schiphol USA, Inc.; Hochtief Airport GmbH; and Unique Zurich Airport.

The city and EDC established an evaluation committee to consider the proposals. After considering the written proposals and interviewing all four proposers, the Evaluation Committee decided that the city and EDC should begin negotiations with BAA USA, Inc. to see if an agreement could be reached on the terms of a contract for consulting services and, at the termination of the existing Port Authority lease, management of the airports. If an agreement with BAA could not be reached, the Evaluation Committee would then consider whether to proceed with one of the other three proposers.

Many considered this effort to be a negotiating strategy aimed at receiving more money from the Port Authority. After the September 11, 2001, terrorist attack, a discussion ensued about trading the World Trade Center site (owned by the Port Authority) for the airports. In October 2003 Governor George E. Pataki and Mayor Michael R. Bloomberg announced that the Port Authority and city of New York had reached an agreement that means approximately $700 million to the city when the deal closed, and significantly raises annual payments for John F. Kennedy International and LaGuardia airports through 2050. The $700 million includes a $500 million lump sum and a $90-million-per-year increase over the present annual lease payment of $3.5 million. This is a minimum of $5 billion in minimum total value of the lease to the city through 2050. The Port Authority Board of Commissioners still must approve the agreement before it is finalized

AGENCY: Economic Development Corporation/Metropolitan Transportation Authority 16

FUNCTION, SERVICE, OR ASSET PRIVATIZED: New York Coliseum

FORM AND DATE OF PRIVATIZATION: Divestment, June 1999

DESCRIPTION: In June 1999 the city's Economic Development Corporation (EDC) and the Metropolitan Transportation Authority (MTA), a state agency, sold the Coliseum, an exhibition center, to a private entity for $345 million.

BENEFITS: Two hundred million dollars of the total $345 million sale price was allocated to the MTA for its 1995–1999 capital program and the remaining $145 million for its 2000–2004 capital program. Under a memorandum of understanding between the MTA and the city, the proceeds from the sale will be given to the city, which will sell bonds in the same amount to pay for NYC Transit capital projects through a letter of agreement.

IMPLEMENTATION: The sale of the Coliseum was undertaken in 1999. Demolition was completed by 2001 and redevelopment of the site was well underway in 2002.

AGENCY: Economic Development Corporation 17

FUNCTION, SERVICE, OR ASSET PRIVATIZED: Community gardens

FORM AND DATE OF PRIVATIZATION: Divestment, May 1999

DESCRIPTION: One of the most contentious divestments was the bitter battle over the "community gardens." These were city-owned vacant lots that local residents, with hard work, had turned into "their" highly prized gardens and urban oases. They wanted the city to give the community groups title to those lots (divestment by free transfer) so they could continue their urban gardening activity. The residents were, however, pitted against advocates of more low-income housing, who had distinctly different ideas about the use of those lots. The city wanted money. In the end, the city reached an agreement to sell Greenthumb Gardens to the Trust for Public Land and the New York Restoration Project. A total of 111 lots were sold for approximately $4 million in revenue with the agreement that they would maintain the lots as community gardens in good condition.

BENEFITS: The city earned $4 million in revenue from the sale of the vacant lots. Other benefits include the direct advantage to the communities in which these lots will be maintained as gardens.

IMPLEMENTATION: The sale of lots to the Trust for Public Land was completed in December 1999, and the sale to the New York Restoration Project was completed in December 2000.

AGENCY: Economic Development Corporation 18

FUNCTION, SERVICE, OR ASSET PRIVATIZED: Off-Track Betting Corporation (OTB)

FORM AND DATE OF PRIVATIZATION: Divestment, 2000, under consideration

DESCRIPTION: The New York City Off-Track Betting Corporation consists of sixty-eight betting parlors, three tele-theaters, and four restaurant-sports pubs, with plans to add up to eight additional sports restaurants. OTB owns warehouse, distribution, and printing facilities, as well as an automotive and betting system equipment repair center. In addition, it has more than 1,000 full-time employees, 500 part-time employees, and 300 per diem employees.

In 2001 Mayor Giuliani announced that New York City had accepted an offer from GMR-NY, LLC, for the sale of OTB in one of the largest and most profitable privatization deals in the city's history. GMR-NY, LLC, was to pay up to $389 million in current dollars (net present value basis).

This was the last step in the turnaround of OTB, once considered the only money-losing bookmaker in town. When Mayor Giuliani took office in 1994, OTB had an operating deficit of $5.3 million. It experienced great success since then as the Giuliani administration ran it like a private business rather than a quasi-government agency. In 2000 OTB exceeded $1 billion in gross wagering and its revenues totaled $246 million, with $35 million going directly to the city coffers. OTB has gained dramatically in market value, making it a prime candidate for a timely and profitable sale. As of early 2003, however, the sale had not yet been approved and consummated.

BENEFITS: The city expects $250–389 million in revenue from the sale of OTB depending on the number of racetracks to be added. Under the terms of the deal, the city will also receive an annual cash flow expected to be in millions, based on a percentage of OTB's annual gross handle (to be determined in the provisions of the final sale). Additional savings will be gained from the elimination of operating expenses of nonessential services (also to be determined in the sale contract). Besides the attractive revenues, it was beneficial for the city to sell OTB because a private entity is in a better position to adapt to the rapid market and technological changes that affect the racing industry.

IMPLEMENTATION: The New York City Off-Track Betting Corporation was formed in 1971. The operations at OTB were frequently the source of controversy because of mismanagement and profit shortfalls. In an effort to get out of noncore businesses, Mayor Rudolph W. Giuliani announced on October 5, 2000, that the New York City Economic Development Corporation (EDC) will issue a request for proposal (RFP) for the sale of the franchise and operations of the OTB.

In August 2001 Mayor Giuliani announced that the city was awarding the billion-dollar-a-year franchise to the Canadian-based firm conglomerate, GMR-NY, LLC, However, this transaction was subject to the New York state legislature's approval and authorization of enhanced business capacity. If the legislature approves this sale but does not authorize the business capacity enhancements, then GMR-NY, LLC, will pay a purchase price of $284 million, which will include an immediate payment of $150 million, another $50 million paid out over five years, and an additional ongoing annual cash flow. If only some business enhancements are authorized, then GMR-NY, LLC, will pay an amount greater than $284 million and up to $389 million, in proportion to the enhancements granted.

The legislature never did approve the sale—nor did it disapprove. The sale of OTB also faced strong opposition both from labor unions and the New York Racing Association, which submitted a losing bid. The Giuliani administration came to an end and the plan to sell OTB remained on the table.

AGENCY: Economic Development Corporation 19

FUNCTION, SERVICE, OR ASSET PRIVATIZED: United Nations Plaza Hotel

FORM AND DATE OF PRIVATIZATION: Divestment, May 1997

DESCRIPTION: In May 1997 the city of New York reached an agreement to sell the United Nations Plaza Hotel to a Hong Kong–based hotel chain. The city earned $85 million from the sale. Due to this divestment, annual city taxes will increase to $9 million by 2010, compared to the annual average of only $2.48 million during the ten years preceding the sale.

BENEFITS: The benefits from this divestment include the one-time revenue of $85 million and a yearly increase in tax revenues for the city of approximately $6.5 million by 2010. The average annual tax between the date of sale and 2010 is $5 million, an increase of $2.5 million over the prior average annual tax.

IMPLEMENTATION: Not applicable.

AGENCY: Economic Development Corporation 20

FUNCTION, SERVICE, OR ASSET PRIVATIZED: WNYC Radio 820 AM and 93.9 FM

FORM AND DATE OF PRIVATIZATION: Divestment, March 1995

DESCRIPTION: The city started in the radio business in the 1930s, when there were few radio stations. But with forty-nine radio stations and innumerable TV channels in 1993, Mayor Giuliani realized that there was no good reason for the city to continue owning and operating these stations. In March 1995 the city of New York reached an agreement with the not-for-profit WNYC Foundation for the sale of WNYC radio 820 AM and 93.9 FM for $20 million.

BENEFITS: The benefits from this divestment include the one-time revenue of $20 million. In addition, the city is no longer responsible for this commercial activity; there is no reason for government ownership, subsidy, or operation of these radio stations.

IMPLEMENTATION: Not applicable.

AGENCY: Economic Development Corporation 21

FUNCTION, SERVICE, OR ASSET PRIVATIZED: WNYC-TV

FORM AND DATE OF PRIVATIZATION: Divestment, August 1996

DESCRIPTION: In August 1996, WNYC-TV was sold to ITT Corporation and Dow Jones & Company Inc. for $207 million.

BENEFITS: The principal benefit of this divestment was the one-time revenue of $207 million. In addition, the city is no longer responsible for this commercial activity; there is no reason for government ownership, subsidy, or operation of this television station.

IMPLEMENTATION: Not applicable.

AGENCY: Department of Education 22

FUNCTION, SERVICE, OR ASSET PRIVATIZED: Low-performing schools

FORM AND DATE OF PRIVATIZATION: Contracts for charter schools, 2001, not realized

DESCRIPTION: Some New York City public schools have consistently ranked very poorly in student achievement. The State Education Department annually identifies schools that fail to meet state criteria in reading or mathematics. Schools furthest from state standards are identified as Schools Under Registration Review (SURR) and are divided into two categories for intervention and supervision. Category 1 schools fall under the direct jurisdiction of the Chancellor's District and Category 2 fall under the joint management of the chancellor and the local districts, the Chancellor-District Partnership.

Mayor Giuliani called for transforming these failing schools into charter schools and selecting-by competitive contract-private education firms to manage these schools.

BENEFITS: Throughout the country, private management has shown generally good results in improving school performance and could help improve New York's worse schools. The mayor's proposed program for private management of SURR schools would provide financial incentives to firms that succeed in removing schools from the SURR list. The creation and privatization of charter schools would give parents alternatives and allow them and the public to compare the results of for-profit firms against those of the city's (then) Board of Education.

IMPLEMENTATION: The mayor put $60.8 million into the board's 2000–2001 budget to privatize the management of at least 20 percent of the ninety-nine schools identified by the State Education Department as SURR schools. In order to convert some of the schools within the Chancellor's District into charter schools, the chancellor sought proposals from education firms experienced in converting and managing charter schools. These organizations, upon the approval of the charter schools, would act as Educational Management Organizations for the newly created charter schools.

The board proposed that private organizations be paid a fee up to $600,000 per school as a progress payment basis upon completion of a charter application, infrastructure building, and transition to a charter school. On average, each student in the Chancellor's District of failing schools received $10,019 in funding during the 1999–2000 school year, compared with $9,573 allocated per student in the rest of the school system. The chancellor hoped to maintain this higher level of funding for the privatized schools.

A request for proposal was sent to about a hundred private education companies. Fourteen firms and nonprofit organizations from around the country submitted proposals. In October 2000 the Board narrowed the list of candidates to four for-profit companies. The board planned to focus on five to twenty of the fifty-one Chancellor District's schools in its first year, depending on the number and quality of applications received. The converted schools, if approved by the Board of Education and the State Board of Regents, would open in September 2001. A contractor for five schools was selected but under the Board of Education's plan at least 51 percent of the parents at each school had to approve a conversion to a charter school. Parents, however, rejected the concept in a referendum.

AGENCY: Department of Education 23

FUNCTION, SERVICE, OR ASSET PRIVATIZED: Summer school

FORM AND DATE OF PRIVATIZATION: Contract, 2000

DESCRIPTION: The success of (then) Board of Education's (BOE) promotion policy hinges on early identification of "at-risk" students and the quality of instructional "interventions" and support services provided to them. As a result of the 2000 school year's policy to end social promotion, all students at risk of failing were expected to attend summer school. To assist BOE in managing an enlarged summer program, the mayor proposed that at least 20 percent of the program should be delivered through contracts with private education companies, private schools, and colleges. These providers generally worked with and trained BOE personnel to administer intensive remedial course work.

In summer 2000 some districts used private providers in their summer-school programs. Twenty districts utilized the services of private providers; in seven of these districts private vendors were used for more than one service. Fifteen districts contracted for professional development services, four for direct services to children, and five for parent involvement activities. Five districts utilized the vendors for districtwide professional development and direct services to students, including test preparation and guidance support. The private contracts, serving 64,000 students, were valued at $32 million.

BENEFITS: Through improved instructional interventions and support services, BOE aims to increase the percentage of students passing summer school. For summer 2000 services of private vendors were made available to superintendents, providing them with more resources than ever before to conduct summer school.

IMPLEMENTATION: For summer 2000, in support of the promotion policy and the summer program, the BOE issued a request for proposal (RFP) and conducted a vendor fair to help superintendents identify organizations that could assist in providing summer-school services for students in grades three through twelve at risk of not being promoted. Vendors were queried about their capacity to provide professional development for teachers and other staff, curriculum or instructional materials, direct services to students, programs to increase parental involvement, and test preparation for examinations.

Each district was required to submit a summer program instructional plan in which they were to address any planned services provided by private vendors. The Division of Instructional Support reviewed instructional plans for their comprehensiveness and appropriateness of design, and, where necessary, assisted districts in the development or revision of their plans.

For summer 2000, forty-six vendors were awarded contracts in twenty districts. An independent evaluation of summer school 2000 looked at the effect of private providers on student achievement.

AGENCY: Department of Education 24

FUNCTION, SERVICE, OR ASSET PRIVATIZED: Custodial services

FORM AND DATE OF PRIVATIZATION: Contract, 1995

DESCRIPTION: There was dissatisfaction with the condition of the school custodial services; too many of the schools were dirty, repairs were not made promptly, and the custodians did not keep the schools open for community use without extra payments. Under great pressure from the mayor, the decision was made to award competitive contracts for the work in seventy-nine of the system's 1,100 schools. The primary goal of this project was to provide quality custodial services and keep the buildings in better repair than the (then) Board of Education's Division of School Facilities (DSF) was doing.

BENEFITS: The contracted schools were kept cleaner and were better maintained; repairs were completed much more quickly and to a higher standard. A comparison of costs of contracted schools and schools maintained by in-house, school custodians indicates that the board is saving about $3.8 million per year for the seventy-nine schools; in-house work costs about 15 percent more.

Another important benefit is that the contractor is required to keep the schools open, as needed, in the evenings and on Saturday mornings at no additional cost to the board. This greatly expands community access to school facilities.

IMPLEMENTATION: In 1995 the Chancellor's Commission on School Facilities and Maintenance Reform, working in conjunction with mayoral staff, developed a request for proposal (RFP) to utilize private contractors for facilities management of school buildings. A committee of experts from the private real-estate industry helped develop a privatization program for fifty-two schools; later the number was increased to seventy-nine. The city solicited competitive proposals from private firms to function as property managers. No one firm could bid on all the schools, thereby avoiding the complacency that might be expected if a private-sector monopoly simply replaced the existing public monopoly. Contracts were awarded to the lowest responsible bidders; each one would maintain and repair a group of school buildings located in the same general area. The primary goal of this project was to provide quality custodial services and keep the buildings cleaner and better.

After more than five years of having private contractors maintain and operate seventy-nine facilities satisfactorily, a new RFP was issued to replace the first cycle of contracts that were expiring on December 31, 2000. RFP notices were mailed to 110 prospective vendors and advertised in the City Record. Two mandatory preproposal conferences were held in August and September 2000 and were attended by nineteen interested parties. DSF received five proposals. Of the five, three met the minimum functional and technical requirements. The three finalists were rated on preestablished criteria developed by a selection committee composed of eight staff members of DSF.

In making its selections, the committee considered experience, price, workplan approach, and staffing commitments in evaluating the proposals. Johnson Controls and Temco Service Industries were deemed by the evaluation committee to be responsive to the needs outlined in the RFP. The contracts were for the calendar year 2002 and may be extended, after careful review and evaluation, for up to six additional one-year periods. The cost of the contracts is $11.1 million. The satisfactory results led the Bloomberg administration to expand the program significantly. In 2003 it outsourced custodial services in an additional 133 schools. Also in 2003 it hired outside contractors for painting, carpentry, plumbing, and electrical work, displacing 486 in-house jobs (60 percent of the 830-person work force) and saving at least $20 million per year. The union promptly sued DOE.

AGENCY: Department of Education 25

FUNCTION, SERVICE, OR ASSET PRIVATIZED: Board of Education buildings

FORM AND DATE OF PRIVATIZATION: Pending in 2001, sold in 2003

DESCRIPTION: In March 2000 Mayor Giuliani announced the city's intention to sell three buildings used by the Board of Education: the headquarters buildings at 110 and 131 Livingston Street and at 65 Court Street, Brooklyn. Ten firms responded to a request for expressions of interest (RFEI). They would buy the buildings and convert them into apartment complexes, office towers, or college facilities.

BENEFITS: The revenue from the sale of these buildings would be used to build a new headquarters building for the Board of Education. Estimated revenue from the sale of 110 Livingston Street alone was announced as more than $45 million.

IMPLEMENTATION: A request for proposal was finally issued in 2003, and the sale was consummated that year.

AGENCY: Department of Education 26

FUNCTION, SERVICE, OR ASSET PRIVATIZED: Construction of new school buildings

FORM AND DATE OF PRIVATIZATION: Public-private partnership, 2001 (suspended)

DESCRIPTION: The School-House Foundation, a nonprofit group, proposed an innovative plan to build new schools without using any of the construction budget of the Board of Education (BOE) as it was called then. The School-House Foundation plans to raise $200 million by selling tax-exempt bonds to private investors through the city's Industrial Development Authority to build three schools. The foundation would then lease the schools to the BOE for the term of the bonds, probably fifteen–twenty years using the lease payments of $12–14 million a year to pay the interest and principal on the bonds. After the bonds are retired, the buildings will be sold to the board for $1 and will pay debt service from lease payments by BOE. Financing is outside the city debt limit.

The proposal was scheduled to be presented to the board on March 15, 2000, but it was canceled and the project has yet to be approved for the lack of $170 million needed to start construction.

BENEFITS: Given the Board of Education's shortage of funds, this is an excellent idea to privately finance construction of three new schools. The advantage is that the BOE could use its annual expense budget to pay the cost of leasing the schools, producing schools that could accommodate 2,300 students but leaving the troubled capital budget unencumbered.

IMPLEMENTATION: The proposal remained on the drawing board at the end of the Giuliani administration, apparently caught up in a budget dispute between the schools chancellor and City Hall.

AGENCY: Department of Education 27

FUNCTION, SERVICE, OR ASSET PRIVATIZED: Radio Station WNYE-FM and TV Station WNYE-TV

FORM AND DATE OF PRIVATIZATION: Proposed lease, 2001, not realized

DESCRIPTION: The Board of Education owns a radio station, WNYE-FM, and a TV station, WNYE-TV. The schools chancellor, recognizing that this activity is not a core function of the board, proposed selling both. The radio station, a little-known outlet, would be sold to WNYC-FM, which was privatized by Mayor Giuliani. The TV station would be sold to WNET-TV, the national public television channel. There is strong opposition within the board to the TV sale, although the chancellor believes that WNET-TV would provide better programming for the schools. Sale of the radio station, on the other hand, has strong internal support but is being protested by others. Leasing the radio station instead of selling it has been proposed.

BENEFITS: The potential benefits include revenue from the sale or lease, reduction or elimination of the annual operating costs, and better educational programming. It also gets the Board of Education out of a distracting noncore business.

IMPLEMENTATION: Established by the board in 1938, WNYE-FM began leasing its air time to ethnic program producers in the late 1970s during the city's fiscal crisis. In November 2000 the schools chancellor announced his intention to sell the radio and TV stations to WNYC and WNET respectively, arguing that they could run the stations more effectively and improve the programming. He contended that few people listened to the radio station and that selling it would increase the audience and upgrade the educational content.

The proposed sale is being protested by ethnic program producers and their audience who worry that WNYC would raise the price of their marginal, non-primetime slots and therefore eliminate some ethnic programming.

According to a proposed new management contract, the board could continue to own the WNYE-FM station license, while the operator, WNYC, would present programming primarily of classical music. Existing contracts with the ethnic-radio producers would be canceled. WNYC would assume all operating expenses and pay for new educational programming for ten years. This organizational arrangement corresponds to a lease.

AGENCY: Department of Environmental Protection 28

FUNCTION, SERVICE, OR ASSET PRIVATIZED: Water meter reading

FORM AND DATE OF PRIVATIZATION: Contract, 1997

DESCRIPTION: The Department of Environmental Protection (DEP) contracts with Con Edison to read water meters in the Bronx and in Staten Island. Con Edison reads water meters every day, providing the data the department uses for the quarterly billing of its metered accounts. There are 98,000 meters in Staten Island, and 65,000 meters in the Bronx. Con Edison has rerouted the meter readers so that the water meter reading can be efficiently integrated into its own gas and electric meter reading routes.

BENEFITS: The city is paying $1.01 per reading to Con Edison. This saves $1.17 per reading in Staten Island relative to in-house costs, and $2.07 per reading in the Bronx. Therefore, reading the 98,000 meters in Staten Island four times a year saves $458,640 per year, and reading the 65,000 meters in the Bronx four times a year saves $538,200 per year, for a total citywide savings of approximately $1 million per year. These savings recur each year, and increase as the number of meters in these boroughs increases. If and when this contract is expanded throughout the city, the estimated annual savings would be $2.15 million per year.

Additionally, since DEP staff is now free to perform various problem-solving tasks (repairing or replacing meters and remotes, verifying meter readings questioned by customers, inspecting for leaks, and so on) the number of estimated bills has been reduced. This results in fewer customer inquiries and improved collections.

IMPLEMENTATION: DEP pilot-tested the process in Staten Island, where the first contract was awarded, and work began in 1997. The success of the Staten Island contract was followed by the bidding for a contract to read the meters in the Bronx, where the different types of buildings were expected to yield different bid prices and additional tests of the contractual relationship. The Staten Island work was also rebid and again won by Con Edison. Work under the two new contracts began in the spring of 2000. The contracts have a duration of three years with options to renew for two more years.

The department submitted specifications for a contract to the Office of Management and Budget for reading all the meters in all five boroughs, and anticipates soliciting bids and initiating contract reading in the remaining three boroughs during fiscal 2001.

AGENCY: Department of Environmental Protection 29

FUNCTION, SERVICE, OR ASSET PRIVATIZED: Water system

FORM AND DATE OF PRIVATIZATION: Divestment (to public agency), 1995, not realized

DESCRIPTION: The mayor proposed selling the city's entire water system—nineteen upstate reservoirs, pipes, and sewers—to the quasi-independent New York Water Board for $2.3 billion. The board currently leases the system from the city and pays rent. In effect, the board would end the stream of annual rental payments and buy the system in one transaction. The city would pay water fees to the board, as it does now. The mayor appoints the board, and the workers are city employees.

BENEFITS: The funds would be used to pay off the city's long-term water and sewer bonds and would leave $800 million that the city could spend for various long-term (nonwater) construction projects. Critics note that water rates would go up and water users, instead of taxpayers, would end up paying for nonwater capital projects.

IMPLEMENTATION: This was criticized as a budget gimmick and was not implemented.

AGENCY: Department of Environmental Protection 30

FUNCTION, SERVICE, OR ASSET PRIVATIZED: Wastewater treatment plants

FORM AND DATE OF PRIVATIZATION: Divestment, 1994, not realized

DESCRIPTION: The city owns and operates fourteen wastewater treatment plants in the city. The City Council proposed selling three of them to private firms. Other cities have taken similar steps. The firm or firms would maintain and operate the plants and sell the treatment services for a predetermined user fee. The firm would be held responsible for satisfying Environmental Protection Agency standards for effluent water quality.

BENEFITS: Sale price for the three plants is estimated to be $750 million, which would help close budget gap. Total value of all the plants is said to be $2.28–3.40 billion.

Moreover, private operation of municipal wastewater treatment plants is widespread and growing in other large cities throughout the world because large savings of the order of 40 percent are being realized due to much more efficient operation, fewer but better trained employees, better use of chemicals, and computer monitoring of conditions to detect incipient equipment failure. Generally speaking, effluent water quality has improved under private operation.

IMPLEMENTATION: Mayor Giuliani reacted positively to the City Council initiative. The City Council held a hearing and many speakers, including the author, spoke favorably of the idea. Union spokespersons argued against it, fearing job losses. Ultimately, the idea was not pursued.

AGENCY: Department of Finance 31

FUNCTION, SERVICE, OR ASSET PRIVATIZED: Tax liens on delinquent properties

FORM AND DATE OF PRIVATIZATION: Divestment, 1996

DESCRIPTION: Under previous administrations, the city of New York used the *in-rem* process and took title to delinquent properties, that is, properties that had not paid their real-estate taxes. The result of this policy was that by 1994 the city owned 5,458 buildings with 52,000 housing units, almost all of which were occupied. It was extremely expensive for the city to own, manage, and operate these buildings. The net cost of operation was $2,900 per housing unit per year after allowing for rent receipts; this figure does not include personnel costs or in-house support and overhead expenses.

The city owned these buildings for an average of nineteen years before disposing of them. In 1994 the city estimated that it would cost $10.6 billion to manage, maintain, and prepare these buildings for sale, an astronomical figure. The huge expense was not the only detrimental consequence of this policy. The buildings were in poor condition to begin with and the delay in executing the *in-rem* transfer to city ownership resulted in even greater deterioration of the buildings, a further loss of the city's housing stock, and no tax revenue from these properties.

As a new policy under the Giuliani administration, the city decided not to take possession of any more tax-delinquent properties. Instead, it decided to sell new tax liens in the marketplace. Using a financial process pioneered by Mayor Bret Schundler in Jersey City only a few years earlier, the tax liens were bundled in large blocks, that is, securitized—much like mortgages—and sold as bonds to investors. Eight such sales took place between 1996 and 2001.

Distressed properties are not included among the tax-lien sales, and therefore the properties sold in this manner generally do not return to the New York City Housing and Preservation Department's attention. The few that do are foreclosed and sold at open auction on the courthouse steps.

BENEFITS: The city generated $1.45 billion by selling delinquent real-estate tax liens on 35,410 properties, without taking title to any property. The real threat of loss of their property forced many of the affected owners to pay up after receiving notices that their property was to be taken. Of the $1.45 billion, $895 million was from the bond sale and the remaining $555 million was from back taxes paid to prevent the sales.

Greater discipline was engendered in all property owners. Seeing that the city now had a good mechanism to enforce tax collection, and that owners could no longer count on the city to drag its feet before starting the lengthy *in-rem* procedure to take over a delinquent property, delinquency rates declined—from 3.67 percent in 1996 to 2.96 percent in 2000, a reduction of 20 percent.

Instead of foreclosing on the properties and taking them over, as in the past, and keeping them for an average of nineteen years and losing money every day on each building, the buildings were back in private hands within two years and paying taxes. Moreover they were rehabilitated by the new owners where necessary and returned to the housing stock in satisfactory condition much sooner than if the city had taken title.

IMPLEMENTATION: The Department of Finance has conducted these sales annually since May 1996.

AGENCY: Department of Finance 32

FUNCTION, SERVICE, OR ASSET PRIVATIZED: Neighborhood payment centers and Web site

FORM AND DATE OF PRIVATIZATION: Withdrawal and contract, 1998

DESCRIPTION: The Department of Finance (DOF) of the city of New York is a collection agent for water bills, real estate taxes, parking summonses, and so on. It has eight payment locations, one or two in each borough, staffed by full-time city employees.

Starting in 1998 DOF entered into a contract with the city's largest check-cashing conglomerate, Cashpoint, which serves "the unbanked"—those without bank accounts or credit cards. People can go there in person to cash their paychecks and to pay their various private bills (such as utility bills), city fees, fines, water bills, and taxes. The customer pays Cashpoint one dollar per transaction, the city pays nothing, and the collected money is deposited promptly to the city's interest-bearing account. There are 402 such locations in the metro area, including the outlying suburbs: Long Island; Bergen County, NJ; Westchester County, and Rockland County. They are referred to as Neighborhood Payment Centers (NPCs).

The city of New York is also setting up a Web site to enable people to pay their city bills (such as traffic tickets, water bills, and real-estate taxes) through the Internet. The city will have a contract with two firms working together, American Management Systems and Government Works, which currently process 12,000 parking tickets per month, for a fee of $1.50 paid by the customer. They will start with water bills and real-estate tax.

BENEFITS: This program reduced the number of customers at the eight borough offices and served them at Cashpoint locations, resulting in improved efficiency at the offices, shorter lines, shorter waiting times, and therefore better customer service. Twenty percent of the walk-ins use the NPCs. In addition, the average processing time at Parking Violations Office Help Centers has decreased from forty minutes in fiscal 1996 to twenty-eight minutes in fiscal 2000 due to lower volume in the help center. This lower volume is directly attributable to the increase in NPCs.

DOF has also been able—by attrition—to reduce staff by three or four per office, or about twenty employees in total, thereby reducing personnel costs by roughly $1 million per year.

This service is very popular, with more than 25,000 city transactions per month. A national automobile organization awarded DOF its Silver Summons Award for the program, and a local magazine recognized the program as the best in New York for cutting through red tape.

IMPLEMENTATION: The number of NPCs rose from 91 in fiscal 1998 to 205 in fiscal 1999 and to 402 in fiscal 2000. During fiscal 2000, NPCs processed 299,490 parking summons transactions, 863 real estate transactions, and 1,245 water bill transactions. The department collected more than $38 million through these centers.

AGENCY: Department of Finance 33

FUNCTION, SERVICE, OR ASSET PRIVATIZED: Payment of bills by credit card

FORM AND DATE OF PRIVATIZATION: Contract, 1998

DESCRIPTION: The Department of Finance now offers another way to pay parking fines and tickets—by credit card. The city provides three options to its customers for credit card payment. The first option is to pay onsite at one of eight payment centers. The city pays a merchant fee of 1.66–2.12 percent to Payment Technology. In fiscal 2000, there were 52,000 credit card transactions, and $9.5 million in revenue was collected through this mode of payment. The second option is the Interactive Voice Response System (IVR). This system has also been subcontracted to Payment Technology for processing. The city pays 4 percent including the merchant fee. In fiscal 2000, 112,000 credit card transactions were processed and $7.2 million in revenue was collected. The third option is to pay via the Internet. The city started its own Web site in January 2000, but volume was too low. The city contracted the site out to Government Works to design and run and collect fees at no cost to the city. Users pay Government Works. The initial volume for the four-month period between July and October 2000 was 10,900 transactions and $1.38 million in revenue.

BENEFITS: In fiscal 2000 the department's eight payment centers completed more than 52,000 credit card transactions and collected a total of $9.5 million in revenue. Customers also made 112,000 payments through the IVR system, totaling $7.2 million. The use of credit cards reduces processing costs and the cost of collection on bad checks. Moreover, it offers significantly greater convenience to the public.

IMPLEMENTATION: The credit card processing contract went operational in July 1998. Since then the payment modalities have been expanded, such as IVR in February 1999 and the Web site in January 2000.

AGENCY: Department of Finance 34

FUNCTION, SERVICE, OR ASSET PRIVATIZED: Bail processing

FORM AND DATE OF PRIVATIZATION: Contract, date unknown

DESCRIPTION: The processing of bail receipts has been outsourced to Chase Manhattan Bank. The actual bill receipt along with a check is sent to Chase. Chase verifies that the bail receipts and check are in balance, deposits the check, enters data on the bail receipt, and submits a tape to the Department of Finance (DOF) to upload into its system.

Other bail processing functions, such as transactions accounting, the generation of refund checks, and the processing of forfeitures, are handled in house by DOF.

BENEFITS: This contract benefits the department by not having to allocate staff to enter data on the receipt and to deposit the funds physically. Another benefit is quicker deposit of receipts into the city's interest-bearing account.

IMPLEMENTATION: All remaining bail processing functions will be outsourced in the future.

AGENCY: Department of Finance 35

FUNCTION, SERVICE, OR ASSET PRIVATIZED: Data entry functions

FORM AND DATE OF PRIVATIZATION: Contract, 1999

DESCRIPTION: Most of the Department of Finance (DOF) data-entry functions, such as parking tickets, have been outsourced to private vendors.

BENEFITS: The primary benefit from these contracts is cost reduction for DOF. For instance, outsourcing of data entry eliminated the need for microfilming.

IMPLEMENTATION: DOF is undergoing an agencywide inventory of remaining data entry functions and is exploring privatization options. The main data-entry function still performed in house, property owner's registration, was recently put online, eliminating the need for an outside vendor.

AGENCY: Fire Department 36

FUNCTION, SERVICE, OR ASSET PRIVATIZED: Reproduction and Mail Management Services

FORM AND DATE OF PRIVATIZATION: Contract, 1994

DESCRIPTION: Since January 1994 the Fire Department of New York (FDNY) has outsourced its reproduction and mail management services. The outsourced services include printing; binding; servicing copiers; managing convenience copiers; and pick up, delivery, and distribution of all external and internal mail between the post office, FDNY headquarters, and 250 facilities throughout the five boroughs. The private vendor provides customized service, with the capability to satisfy printing requests within one to three days in a cost-efficient manner.

BENEFITS: In fiscal 1998 a cost analysis study indicated an overall saving of approximately $1,039,875 by contracting for the services. Had the reproduction and mail management services not been privatized, the total direct and indirect costs for FDNY would have been $2,559,172. The total direct and indirect costs for outsourcing the services during fiscal 1998 amounted to $1,519,298. Outsourcing these services reduced spending on vehicle services including maintenance and fuel costs as well as materials and machinery costs, including equipment leasing. Moreover, FDNY now has a customized and much faster reproduction and mail delivery service.

IMPLEMENTATION: The Fire Department privatized its reproduction and mail management services in January 1994, using competitive bidding.

AGENCY: Fire Department 37

FUNCTION, SERVICE, OR ASSET PRIVATIZED: Billing for ambulance calls

FORM AND DATE OF PRIVATIZATION: Contract, 2001, pending

DESCRIPTION: In March 2001 the Fire Department of New York (FDNY) issued a request for proposal (RFP) to outsource billing for ambulance calls. The department charges $350 a ride for basic life support and $425 for advanced life support. It transports about 600,000 people a year to hospitals.

A study by the New York State Comptroller concluded that the department failed to collect millions of dollars in ambulance bills each year because of a poorly organized and poorly managed collection effort. Contracting with a collection agency is expected to bring in more money.

BENEFITS: The FDNY expects a net revenue increase of at least $10 million per year or 45 percent more than the 1999 revenue of $22.1 million. Of this latter figure, $8.4 million is from Medicare, which is collected by another city agency from the state of New York. Another $10.7 million is from private insurance companies, and $3 million is from individuals.

IMPLEMENTATION: Responses to the RFP were scheduled for early 2001. Review and award of the contract is expected by the end of 2001. The success rate of collections from this population and the fee to be retained by the contractor are not yet known.

AGENCY: Fire Department 38

FUNCTION, SERVICE, OR ASSET PRIVATIZED: Emergency ambulance service

FORM AND DATE OF PRIVATIZATION: Private contracts by subcontractor, 2001

DESCRIPTION: The FDNY operates 909 ambulance tours (a tour is an eight-hour shift) per day, either directly or indirectly. Of these, 325 or 36 percent are supplied by private voluntary hospitals under contract with the city. Private ambulance companies under contract to the private hospitals operate some of these 325 ambulance tours.

The city has long used private hospitals for emergency ambulance service; in other words the service has long been privatized in this sense. What is new, however, is that some of these nonprofit hospitals started contracting with for-profit ambulance companies instead of or in addition to operating their own ambulances with their own employees as crews. (This is a trend in the United States.)

Although this new practice does not represent municipal privatization and is not a direct city activity or contract or privatization, it is included here because it is a vital city emergency service being outsourced, indirectly, to private, for-profit firms.

BENEFITS: National figures show that private emergency ambulance companies provide service at least as good service as municipal agencies do but at a much lower cost. Therefore, the lower cost of ambulance service for the private hospitals should result in a lower cost for the city in its contracts with those hospitals, but no data were available to support this presumption.

IMPLEMENTATION: City approval is not needed by the private hospitals to outsource their work. This new practice, however, encountered strong opposition from firefighters who man the ambulances operated by the NYFD. They fear that if more hospitals do this and reduce their costs, the city may contract with more private hospitals and use fewer FDNY ambulances.

In fact some FDNY ambulance crews deliberately refused to bring patients to hospitals that were using private ambulance companies. Fire Department officials threatened to bring charges against any firefighters who did this, noting that patients' lives were endangered by such a boycott if patients were taken instead to more distant hospitals.

AGENCY: Health and Hospitals Corporation 39

FUNCTION, SERVICE, OR ASSET PRIVATIZED: Municipal hospitals

FORM AND DATE OF PRIVATIZATION: Divestment, 1995, not implemented

DESCRIPTION: Even before Mayor Giuliani assumed office he expressed his strong desire to change New York's unique and unsatisfactory municipal hospital system, beginning by privatizing at least three of the eleven hospitals. The Giuliani administration introduced a plan to sell the city's municipal hospitals, beginning with Coney Island Hospital and Elmhurst Hospital. The hospitals, under the Health and Hospitals Corporation (HHC), had a reputation for inefficiency and low quality, smothered by a large, overcentralized bureaucracy. Privatization was to be the linchpin for changing health care for the poor.

The city announced in February 1995 that it would try to sell the three hospitals and reduce the number of beds in the system from 8,000 to 7,000. The effort to sell Coney Island Hospital was unsuccessful. The courts aborted the plan, and further efforts were dropped.

BENEFITS: New York city is virtually unique in having a municipal hospital system. Many believe that low-income New Yorkers can get better health care through a privatized hospital system than through continued operation of the municipal hospital system. Moreover, privatization would generate large savings in city expenditures for health care as well as revenue from the sales. The sale would have saved $1.7 billion over ten years and the city would have gained revenue.

IMPLEMENTATION: The affected municipal unions displayed intense opposition to the plan, and other elected officials including members of the City Council supported them.

AGENCY: Health and Hospitals Corporation 40

FUNCTION, SERVICE, OR ASSET PRIVATIZED: Health care for prison inmates

FORM AND DATE OF PRIVATIZATION: Contract, 1995

DESCRIPTION: The Department of Correction (DOC) operates sixteen prison facilities with about 15,000 inmates who have many health-care needs. Beginning in November 1994, the Health and Hospitals Corporation (HHC) was responsible for providing comprehensive medical, dental, mental health, and ancillary services to the inmates. HHC staff is unable to perform the work because inmates display a wide range of acute and chronic medical conditions, dental disease, and mental health disorders. HHC sought outside entities to provide professional health care; recruitment and retention of qualified staff is less difficult through a contracted provider.

HHC contracted with Montefiore Medical Center and St. Vincent's Medical Center for service from 1995 through 1997 for $112 million per year. This contract covered 13,000 inmates in twelve of the sixteen facilities. From 1998 through 2000 another private voluntary hospital, St. Barnabas, provided that service for $342 million or $114 million per year. In January 2001 Prison Health Services, Inc., a for-profit firm, entered a three-year $297.5 million contract (an average of $99 million per year) for these services to the inmates at those facilities.

Previously, contracted services were paid on a capitated basis, that is, a fixed amount per inmate per day; the new contract is based on a fee-for-service basis. HHC is responsible for monitoring the contractor's performance, including assessment, analysis, and the creation of an inspection and risk management committee. PHS will be measured on forty criteria such as asthma care, dental services, and HIV testing, an increase of five performance measures over the St. Barnabas contract.

BENEFITS: The main objective of contracting was to improve health care for the inmates, which was exposed as unsatisfactory by media attention and by government investigations.

In addition the city expects to save $4–8 million in the first year of the contract compared to the prior year's cost. The contractor, however, encountered startup problems during the first three months of the contract and was therefore penalized more than $100,000 for suboptimal performance.

IMPLEMENTATION: St. Barnabas contract allowed the vendor to submit projected spending patterns instead of actual patterns, therefore it was difficult for HHC to know exactly how much profit the hospital was making or how much care it was providing. In 1999 HHC put in place strengthened processes of oversight, taking into account the new infrastructure needed to support an outcome-oriented contract.

As a result, in 2000 HHC issued a new RFP that added five new performance measures to the existing thirty-five and stricter guidelines measuring quality and speed of critical health assessments. In November 2000 the HHC Board of Directors approved a three-year term contract with Prison Health Services. This agreement, the largest jail-care contract in the country, differs substantially from the contract the city had with St. Barnabas Hospital.

AGENCY: Health and Hospitals Corporation 41

FUNCTION, SERVICE, OR ASSET PRIVATIZED: Laundry Service

FORM AND DATE OF PRIVATIZATION: Contract, 2000

DESCRIPTION: The Brooklyn Central Laundry is located on Kingston Avenue in Brooklyn behind Kings County Hospital. The plant was cleaning about 16 million pounds of laundry a year for all seventeen Health and Hospitals Corporation (HHC) facilities. Half of that amount is now being cleaned by Angelica Textile Services, a New Jersey company that won a competitive bid for a two-year contract.

BENEFITS: According to HHC, if all the work had been contracted out, as originally planned, the corporation would have saved $30 million over five years as a result of closing the Brooklyn Central Laundry and contracting with Angelica Textile Services of New Jersey. As only half was contracted out, savings were only $3 million in the first year. HHC spent 68 cents per pound to have hospital laundry cleaned, processed, and delivered. Angelica Textile submitted a bid to do the same work for 28 cents a pound. The number of employees dropped from 200 to 100, but the quality of the work is equally good.

IMPLEMENTATION: In 1998 HHC started discussions with Angelica Textile Services of New Jersey as a result of a bidding process to clean the soiled linens of HHC's seventeen facilities. More than 200 unionized employees were performing the work. Under city law, however, before being able to contract with Angelica, HHC was required to allow the worker's union (Local 420 of DC 37) to make a counterproposal.

In February 2000 workers at the Brooklyn Central Laundry won a compromise with HHC through a collective bargaining agreement. The compromise resulted in half of the HHC laundry work staying at the Brooklyn Central Laundry and the other half going to Angelica. The union was also granted the opportunity to use new capital equipment. The latter has been purchased by HHC for $1 million, and another $600,000 has been expended in additional capital expenses. The new equipment was put in place by May 31, 2001. A one-year comparison of the contracted and the in-house work will be carried out after that. HHC will evaluate both the Brooklyn and Angelica costs of cleaning.

As part of the compromise, the sixty-three Brooklyn Central employees whose jobs were in jeopardy were transferred to other positions within HHC.

According to the workers' union, the neighboring area of Brooklyn would have lost approximately $8 million in taxes, jobs, and spending if the Brooklyn Central Laundry had closed.

AGENCY: Health and Hospitals Corporation 42

FUNCTION, SERVICE, OR ASSET PRIVATIZED: Security guards

FORM AND DATE OF PRIVATIZATION: Contract, not realized

DESCRIPTION: In fiscal 2000 the Health and Hospitals Corporation (HHC) planned to replace all 850 HHC police officers with private security guards at twenty-six HHC facilities. The goal of a special officer/hospital police officer is to protect life and property by providing a safe and secure environment for patients, staff, and visitors. HHC police officers receive annual training on protocol and procedures. An officer may eject or arrest persons violating New York state laws or the laws of the city of New York. In addition, HHC police officers have the power of arrest and the power to confiscate weapons, but contracted security guards would not have these powers. The officer must be familiar with a variety of New York state and city laws, HHC policies, and individual facility rules and regulations.

The contract cost was expected to be about $22 million per year. Factors necessary for success in performing this work include adequate training and pay scale and a relatively low attrition rate. All of these factors must be examined if private guards are used.

BENEFITS: According to HHC, it would save about $10 million annually by contracting for guard services in its facilities. The savings would accrue because the city employees receive higher wages, more generous fringe benefits, and more paid time off than workers in private firms.

IMPLEMENTATION: In August 2000 Local 237 filed suit to prevent the mayor and the HHC president from privatizing security at municipal medical centers. The union believed that HHC efforts were in retaliation because the union sought state legislation to carry firearms. The union obtained permission to arm officers during a pilot program at Lincoln and Kings County Hospitals beginning in 1993, but it was cancelled in January 1999. The suit charged that the cancellation was punishment for its lobbying, which the union said was an expression of free speech. Police at other hospitals, such as Veterans Affairs hospitals and hospitals in Chicago and Atlanta, are permitted to carry guns. (Note: Carrying weapons justifies higher salaries and more liberal pension and fringe benefits.)

The union persuaded the State Supreme Court to uphold a restraining order prventing the city from issuing the request for bid. That same month the City Council met and voted a bill requiring the city to use peace officers. The mayor vetoed the bill, but it was passed over his veto on March 28 by a vote of forty-three to three, with one member not voting. It may have been overkill, but the state legislature passed a similar bill in June 2001. The city challenged these actions, the situation remained confused and unresolved, and the initiative was left unimplemented as the administration's time ran out.

AGENCY: Health and Hospitals Corporation 43

FUNCTION, SERVICE, OR ASSET PRIVATIZED: Small business health insurance

FORM AND DATE OF PRIVATIZATION: Public-private partnership, 1999, terminated

DESCRIPTION: In February 1999 Health and Hospitals Corporation (HHC) and a nonprofit insurance provider, GHI, launched the Small Business Health Insurance (SBHI) Demonstration Project, which makes low-cost, comprehensive health insurance available to small businesses located in parts of Manhattan, the South Bronx and North Brooklyn. To qualify, a business must have between two and fifty employees and be located in certain areas. Participants can gain access to services from HHC's Generations+ and North Brooklyn Networks. In addition, there are more than 750 affiliated physicians.

As of August 2000 there were 166 members enrolled in the SBHI program. Seventy-three members selected providers from the Generations+ Network and ninety-three members selected the North Brooklyn Health Network as their provider.

GHI initiated the plan and was the insurer and administrator. HHC provided health care. The HHC expected up to 3,000 enrollees, but got only 378 enrollees from forty-nine small businesses. HHC dropped out of the plan; GHI is continuing but without HHC.

BENEFITS: SBHI was intended as an economic development program, helping small businesses retain and attract good workers by offering health coverage. The cost of SBHI to employers is about half the average price paid for coverage in New York City.

The program charges a monthly premium of $100 for individuals and up to $235 for an employee, spouse, and children. Copayments for hospitalization are $250 for an in-network admission and $500 for an out-of-network hospitalization.

As of February 2000 SBHI had generated roughly $10,000 in revenue for HHC, but the hospital system spent more than $400,000 on staff, marketing, and advertising for a net loss of $390,000.

IMPLEMENTATION: The lack of enthusiasm for the program may be due to several reasons. First, an employee may live and work in different locations and may not want to be restricted to a specified network location. Second, many uninsured employees are using the municipal hospital system already. Third, employers are reluctant to pay the monthly premiums.

AGENCY: Department of Homeless Services 44

FUNCTION, SERVICE, OR ASSET PRIVATIZED: Shelters for homeless adults

FORM AND DATE OF PRIVATIZATION: Contract, 1994

DESCRIPTION: In 1992 the city's capital budget allocated approximately $200 million for the development of 2,500 units of transitional housing for homeless adults to replace some barracks-style shelters in use at that time. The New York City Commission on Homelessness subsequently recommended that the city use the nonprofit sector to develop these units, for two reasons. First, to capitalize on private-sector efficiencies, thereby enabling the units to be developed for much less than $200 million and allowing additional development with those funds. Second, the nonprofits were thought to be better able to work with communities to determine appropriate sites for new facilities and thereby to expedite development. The perceived advantages of private sector development depend on the ability of not-for-profit developers to maintain greater flexibility than the city in hiring practices and location decisions.

In May 1994 Mayor Giuliani presented a plan to implement those recommendations. In addition to the development of replacement sites, the city was also to contract out most of its directly operated adult shelters to community-based organizations. The city aimed to transform the shelter system so that it provided emergency assistance to those who truly needed it, assessed their needs within a limited time frame, and referred them, where appropriate, to services to meet those needs to end their homelessness. The city also planned to introduce performance measurements for those contracts.

BENEFITS: The city saved an estimated $3.9 million during fiscal 1996, $2.7 million during fiscal 1997, and $2.7 million during fiscal 1998 while providing higher quality shelters with better services to clients. This is best illustrated in the single-adult system where great progress was made in converting general shelter beds that provide only basic services to program beds that provide more intensive programs and services, including employment training, mental health and substance abuse treatment, and programs for veterans and the elderly.

As a result of this privatization, service providers are now able to provide more direct and personal services instead of the impersonal services in the armories that served as shelters previously. Finally, a broader benefit of privatization is that it became a "best practices" tool that all agencies, including DHS and the contracted service providers, can use in providing services. "Best practices" can be developed only when several agencies provide services instead of just one, and they can be compared and evaluated.

While privatization benefited DHS, the city, and clients, DHS does not plan to contract out all of its services. By maintaining direct operation of some outreach, single adult, and family shelters, DHS can set a standard of care against which the contracted providers can be measured.

IMPLEMENTATION: The Department of Homeless Services became an independent agency in the beginning of fiscal 1994. Since then the number of privatized facilities in the adult and family systems has gradually been increased. By 2000, 109 of the 122 shelters were contracted out, mostly to community-based organizations.

While privatization proved beneficial in many ways, it also posed some challenges to DHS, such as conflicting goals of contractors and DHS, difficulty in evaluating overall performance, and displacement of DHS staff.

AGENCY: New York City Housing Authority 45

FUNCTION, SERVICE, OR ASSET PRIVATIZED: Management of scattered housing sites

FORM AND DATE OF PRIVATIZATION: Contract, 1997

DESCRIPTION: The New York City Housing Authority (NYCHA) privatized the management of scattered housing sites, especially small buildings with seventy-five to one hundred housing units in the building. Called the Alternative Management Program, it uses property management companies from the private sector to manage specific developments on behalf of NYCHA. Currently 4,100 units are under private management.

BENEFITS: A minor study was done in 1998, but no quantifiable results were obtained because NYCHA was not able to allocate its internal costs to individual housing sites (for example, for bulk purchases of supplies). Another study is underway. Therefore, it is not yet clear if privatization is cost effective for this function. It may be a positive indicator is that no contractors have been eliminated nor have contracts been terminated.

IMPLEMENTATION: The NYCHA is in the process of reviewing all U.S. Department of Housing and Urban Development (HUD) and NYCHA procedures and policies to identify ways of streamlining and reducing paperwork requirements while maintaining its capacity to meet all reporting and regulatory requirements imposed by the U.S. Congress, HUD, and the city and state of New York.

AGENCY: New York City Housing Authority 46

FUNCTION, SERVICE, OR ASSET PRIVATIZED: Verifying eligibility of applicants for public housing

FORM AND DATE OF PRIVATIZATION: Contract, 1994

DESCRIPTION: Investigators from private contractors write, call, and arrange appointments to visit the homes of families applying for public housing. Working from a standard questionnaire and checklist, they confirm family composition, quality of housekeeping, presence of pets, and determine if the current housing is substandard. They attempt to speak to neighbors, landlord, and superintendent and to determine if anyone is working. It may take several visits to complete the investigation if the applicant is not home. The investigator takes photos of the applicant. (During a subsequent office visit by applicants, the photo serves in part as a check that the investigator did in fact visit the family.) The investigator completes a report and sends it to the New York City Housing Authority. Payment is for a completed visit only (that is, a submitted report), regardless of the number of visits required.

Based on a three-year average, the number of completed home visits per year is 14,000. The agency decides eligibility, and about 12 percent of applicants are rejected on the basis of the verification visit.

BENEFITS: Before this contract, checking by home visits was rarely done. By screening out ineligible applicants, dwelling units are saved for eligible families; public housing is therefore provided more effectively and equitably. The service is considered excellent by the NYCHA.

Service by contract is less costly and more convenient than doing the work with in-house staff, which requires automobiles and other equipment. The cost per completed visit report for the winning bid is $45.50; other bids were higher, ranging from $50 to $70.

IMPLEMENTATION: The NYCHA did no routine home visits in the past, except possibly decades ago. In 1995 it conducted a small pilot project with five or six vendors that involved talking with landlords, visiting homes, and checking for criminal backgrounds. The last was too expensive and was dropped. The first contract was started but the vendor was unsatisfactory and was terminated; Wells Fargo was brought in on an emergency contract. Because the workload is irregular, a large contractor is needed who can handle a variable workload. The bundling of visits to an area leads to efficiency. Subsequently, Wells Fargo won a competitive bid and later changed its name to Burns International. Its two-year contract is expiring and the agency is getting ready to renew for another year. There was no significant union or other opposition because this was a new activity.

AGENCY: New York City Housing Authority 47

FUNCTION, SERVICE, OR ASSET PRIVATIZED: Boiler plant privatization

FORM AND DATE OF PRIVATIZATION: Contract, 1997

DESCRIPTION: In February 1997 the New York City Housing Authority (NYCHA) entered into a contract with Brooklyn Union Gas (BUG), now a subsidiary of Key Span, for the operation of the boiler plants at five public housing projects with a total of 5,410 apartments. BUG has sole responsibility for producing and maintaining all heat and hot water at the five developments: Coney Island, Haber, Boulevard, Linden, and Bronx River. Although privatization services have been transferred to KeySpan Energy Management, another subsidiary of KeySpan, BUG continues to have sole responsibility for the operation of the five heating plants. It provides the management, supervision, labor, tools, materials, supplies, and parts necessary to operate, maintain, and repair all equipment at each service location.

BENEFITS: The benefits from this contract include rate reductions and both operational and maintenance savings. An evaluation conducted at the conclusion of the first two contract years determined that NYCHA achieved savings of $3,532,883 from rate reductions and $539,267 in operational and maintenance costs, a total of $4,072,150.

Based on these savings and recommendations from the Brooklyn and Bronx Management Departments, NYCHA extended the contract for a third year beginning February 1, 1999, through January 31, 2000. This represented the first of eight one-year extensions. The third contract year showed savings of $2,120,836 from rate reductions and $325,185 on operational costs, bringing the total contract savings to over $2.45 million for that year.

IMPLEMENTATION: The agreement between NYCHA and BUG was signed on December 1, 1996, and commenced February 1997. The contract stated that at the completion of a two-year evaluation, NYCHA would have the option of extending the agreement annually for up to eight years, providing that both parties agreed. Under the agreement, BUG shall meet the following "Operating Standards" regarding the provision of heat and hot water services: Between the hours of 6:00 a.m. and 10:00 p.m., the heating plants must maintain a temperature of at least 68 degrees Fahrenheit in all occupied areas when the temperature outside falls below 55 degrees. When the temperature outside falls below 40 degrees between the hours of 10:00 p.m. and 6:00 a.m., a temperature of at least 55 degrees Fahrenheit must be maintained in all occupied areas. In the evening between 10:00 p.m. and 11:00 p.m. during the winter season, BUG must provide an additional hour of 68 degrees Fahrenheit in all occupied areas when the temperature is 20 degrees Fahrenheit or lower.

Brooklyn Union must supply 130 degrees Fahrenheit hot water, 24 hours a day, 365 days a year, to all occupied areas.

AGENCY: Department of Housing Preservation and Development 48

FUNCTION, SERVICE, OR ASSET PRIVATIZED: Tenant-occupied, city-owned, *in-rem* buildings

FORM AND DATE OF PRIVATIZATION: Divestment and public-private partnerships, 1994

DESCRIPTION: On January 1, 1994, the city owned 5,458 residential buildings with 52,000 housing units. These included both occupied and vacant buildings. They were delinquent properties that had been acquired by previous administrations through the *in-rem* process for nonpayment of taxes. The city's policy under Mayor Giuliani was to dispose of these buildings and to avoid taking over any more. Public-private partnerships carry out this policy using both public and private funds to rehabilitate the housing. Many different disposition programs—some old, some new—were used to sell the tenant-occupied buildings that the city owned and managed.

"Building Blocks!" is a particular disposition strategy for city-owned, tenant-occupied residential property and is a comprehensive approach to rebuilding communities. Under this program, the city sold the buildings in clusters instead of as individual buildings in order to develop an entire neighborhood. This approach permitted comprehensive redevelopment of entire blocks in a community rather than the uncoordinated approach to rehabilitation that is driven by separate programs.

Buildings are sold under three different programs. Under the Neighborhood Entrepreneurs Program (NEP) the buildings are sold first to the New York Partnership, which rehabilitates them using city and federal loans plus private funds from syndicators. The buildings are subsequently sold to for-profit developers and are eligible for J-51 tax abatement, but they pay water and sewer charges; the loans are converted to mortgages. Under the Neighborhood Redevelopment Program (NRP) buildings are sold directly to community-based nonprofit organizations under similar financial arrangements. Under NEP and NRP the buildings are sold for $1 each. Under the Tenant Interim Lease Program (TIL) buildings are rehabilitated by the city and leased to low-income tenant cooperatives for $250 each with no ongoing city subsidy.

BENEFITS: As of June 2001, approximately 2,000 of the original 3,300 occupied *in-rem* buildings, with 32,000 housing units, had been sold. For every unit sold, the city saved $2,900 per year in operating costs (OTPS). The cost avoidance therefore amounts to $92.8 million per year. In addition, $2.55 million per year was saved in personal services, as eighty-five full-time positions used to manage and operate those buildings were eliminated. The number of area offices was reduced from ten in fiscal 1994 to three.

Another obvious benefit is that neighborhoods are being rehabilitated, the stock of modern housing is being increased, and the buildings have been restored to the private housing market and are returning to the tax rolls.

The buildings that passed into private hands now pay more than $8 million annually in taxes.

IMPLEMENTATION: "Building Blocks!" was started in 1994. Through this program, HPD sold 984 buildings (14,737 units) by June 2000. Through all its disposition programs, the city reduced the number of *in-rem* buildings it owns by 85 percent between 1994 and 2003. The inventory of city-owned buildings is expected to be depleted by the end of fiscal 2007. The average fiscal year budget for "Building Blocks!" through 2007 is $204 million.

AGENCY: Department of Housing Preservation and Development 49

FUNCTION, SERVICE, OR ASSET PRIVATIZED: Tenant-occupied, city-owned buildings with market value

FORM AND DATE OF PRIVATIZATION: Divestment, 1996

DESCRIPTION: The city sold seventy-four buildings with 286 housing units and fifty commercial units (for example, street-level stores). These buildings had market value, unlike the occupied buildings that were disposed of through "Building Blocks!" and other such programs. This was also unlike the sale of vacant, city-owned *in rem* buildings that could only be sold with subsidies. The city also sold two former Mitchell-Lama rental properties—with 297 housing units—acquired through mortgage foreclosures..

BENEFITS: The city realized $11.4 million from the sale of the seventy-four buildings and $1.25 million from the sale of the two former Mitchell-Lama rental buildings.

IMPLEMENTATION: Not applicable.

AGENCY: Department of Housing Preservation and Development 50

FUNCTION, SERVICE, OR ASSET PRIVATIZED: Vacant, city-owned *in-rem* buildings

FORM AND DATE OF PRIVATIZATION: Divestment, 1994

DESCRIPTION: On January 1, 1994, the city owned 5,458 buildings, acquired by the *in-rem* process; 1,862 were vacant. More than half of these were sold and restored to the private housing market through various disposal programs, some old and some new. Three notable new programs were HomeWorks, StoreWorks, and Vacant Building 2000.

The HomeWorks program sells small, vacant, city-owned residential buildings that are suitable for one to four families for one dollar each to experienced developers selected through a request for proposal (RFP). The developers obtain private financing for gut rehabilitation, but the city can provide partial financing and loans. The developers resell the buildings at market rates as owner-occupied dwellings to qualified individuals who must be city residents and satisfy other criteria. The buildings have five-year tax abatement. The city subsidy is, therefore, somewhere between the cost of development and the sale price. Approximately 454 buildings with 1,230 units were disposed of through this program.

StoreWorks applies to mixed-use properties, typically buildings with storefronts and one to eight apartments above the stores. This program has been conducted with Neighborhood Housing Services of New York, a nonprofit group. It is similar in operation to HomeWorks.

Vacant Building 2000 is a program that sells vacant multifamily buildings by RFP to developers; there is no subsidy. Developers were selected for thirteen clusters of buildings in Manhattan and one in the Bronx.

BENEFITS: Of the 1,862 vacant, city-owned buildings in 1994, only 633 remained in 2000; 66 percent had been sold. Although the HomeWorks Program costs the city money, its principal benefit is the creation of moderately priced, owner-occupied housing. This keeps working class and lower middle-class families in the city. Because the housing is owner occupied, this program stabilizes the neighborhoods. StoreWorks helps revitalize commercial strips in neighborhoods.

Vacant Building 2000 is intended to continue selling off the large reservoir of buildings that the city had accumulated through the *in-rem* process during prior administrations. This generates sales revenue, eliminates the cost of city maintenance and management, and restores the buildings to the private market where they will pay property taxes.

IMPLEMENTATION: Not applicable.

AGENCY: Department of Housing Preservation and Development 51

FUNCTION, SERVICE, OR ASSET PRIVATIZED: Preventing abandonment of buildings

FORM AND DATE OF PRIVATIZATION: Contract, 1997

DESCRIPTION: The Division of Anti-Abandonment (DAA) was established in the Department of Housing Preservation and Development (HPD) to prevent buildings from being abandoned by their owners and falling into the hands of the city for tax arrears. The division identifies buildings in distress by examining data on tax arrears, housing code violations, and emergency repairs. About 5,000–6,000 suspect buildings are examined in this way annually. The division operates out of four borough offices. Building evaluators from these offices visit, inspect, and assess the identified buildings, rating them as good, fair, or poor.

Part of this work is contracted out. The division pays $48,000 to each of forty-five local organizations (mostly or all nonprofit) for Neighborhood Preservation Consultants (NPCs) to help carry out the large number of onsite inspections.

About 20–25 percent of the buildings (1,000–1,500) are rated as "poor" and attention is focused on them. Owners are provided three paths to help preserve and maintain their properties: education, investment, and enforcement. The NPCs and DAA offer workshops, disseminate information on HPD programs, and work with owners on various short-term interventions to keep the buildings from being abandoned. Repair agreements with owners are the principal tool used by the division. Low-interest loan programs are also available. HPD's goal is to provide an array of tools to aid owners working in good faith and to intervene aggressively where owners remain in noncompliance despite HPD's efforts.

BENEFITS: The net other-than-personal-services (OTPS) cost of city ownership, management, and operation of troubled, occupied, residential buildings is approximately $2,900 per unit per year, after subtracting the rent that is collected. This cost is avoided by a successful antiabandonment effort. This program also keeps buildings in private hands, which means more taxes for the city.

HPD provided antiabandonment assistance to a total of 6,167 buildings in fiscal 1999 and 2000. Hard data on the number of buildings saved from abandonment are not available, although the DAA is currently developing a computer-based system that is intended in part to measure the success of this program. Data are available on such secondary measures as the number of owners attending information sessions, signing repair agreements, and the like.

IMPLEMENTATION: Not applicable.

AGENCY: Department of Housing Preservation and Development 52

FUNCTION, SERVICE, OR ASSET PRIVATIZED: Preventing abandonment of buildings

FORM AND DATE OF PRIVATIZATION: Forced private divestment and ownership transfer, 1998

DESCRIPTION: This is one of the programs undertaken by the Department of Housing Preservation and Development (HPD) to prevent abandonment of residential buildings and subsequent takeover by the city. Private buildings that are in danger of becoming eligible for *in rem* takeover by the city are transferred to other private owners under Local Law 37 after a specified period of tax arrears and a court judgment. This can be considered the next step if the first steps to prevent abandonment are unsuccessful. The transfer may be to a qualified for-profit or nonprofit organization or to the tenants; a competitive RFQ process has identified 132 qualified entities.

Forty-eight properties were transferred temporarily to the nonprofit Neighborhood Restore, which helped rehabilitate the buildings before final transfer to qualified third parties. This pilot program was followed by another round involving 86 buildings, or a total of 134 buildings transferred under this program. In the Department of Housing Preservation and Development, this is called "the third-party transfer program."

BENEFITS: The large cost of city ownership, management, and operation of troubled, occupied residential buildings is avoided. Based on the cost avoidance of over $2,900 per unit in the Building Blocks Program and an average of fifteen units per building, the transfer of these 134 buildings resulted in estimated cost avoidance of $5.8 million.

IMPLEMENTATION: Not applicable.

AGENCY: Human Resources Administration 53

FUNCTION, SERVICE, OR ASSET PRIVATIZED: Education and enrollment for Medicaid managed care

FORM AND DATE OF PRIVATIZATION: Contract, 1999

DESCRIPTION: The purpose of this contract was to reach out, educate, and enroll at least 800,000 Medicaid-eligible recipients into managed care plans in order to reduce the cost of the Medicaid program. The pre-existing Medicaid program in the city was primarily a fee-for-service program that served 1.8 million eligible city residents with health care. Only 381,000 of them were enrolled in managed-care plans, however. More than thirty different managed care programs, with various features, were available to city residents. Whereas individual plans marketed their own programs to eligible residents, only in an experimental area was there objective education available to the eligible public about different plans.

BENEFITS: The gross cost of the city's Medicaid program was $12.6 billion, of which the cost to the city was approximately $2.6 billion. State legislation in 1991 required the city to meet minimum levels of enrollment in managed care plans over a five-year period. The more residents that could be enrolled in managed care programs, the greater the savings to the city. The city estimated that savings would amount to $24 million in the first year.

IMPLEMENTATION: In late 1991 an experimental program was launched in southwest Brooklyn to enroll eligible residents in managed care programs. This was done with 38 city employees organized into four "Education and Enrollment Units." In 1995 the city issued a request for proposal to ninety-nine providers for vendors to perform education, enroll individuals in managed care programs, develop systems, develop a client complaint tracking system, and operate a helpline. Following the established process, four proposals were received and the city selected HealthChoice, Inc., for a three-year contract costing $18.5 million.

The City Council held a hearing about this proposed privatization, but the public employee union objected strongly to such a contract. It wanted the thirty-eight employees to continue doing this work and the city to expand the program citywide, using public employees. After a delay of several years punctuated by allegations of improper procedures, a contract was finally approved and went into effect. Ultimately the winning contractor was Maximus.

AGENCY: Human Resources Administration 54

FUNCTION, SERVICE, OR ASSET PRIVATIZED: Legal Aid Services for Welfare Recipients

FORM AND DATE OF PRIVATIZATION: Contract, 1995

DESCRIPTION: A competitive solicitation was held to obtain legal services for welfare recipients who were in danger of eviction. In the past the Legal Aid Society (LAS) did all the work without any competitive process. The Human Resource Administration opened up the service to competitive contracting and seven of the eight bidders were awarded contracts. Previously these organizations had been subcontractors to LAS.

BENEFITS: Although no significant savings were realized, and, in effect, it was the same organizations doing the work, the Human Resources Administration officials felt that the process was both healthy and useful because it substantiated and solidified pricing information and gave them confidence that they were dealing with the best service providers.

IMPLEMENTATION: The competitive procurement ended the automatic renewal of the LAS contract and forced it to compete against other providers. Separate competitions were held for twelve contracts, each one restricted to a single borough, instead of one single monopolistic contract for the entire city awarded without competition. LAS fought against this competitive procurement process and accused Mayor Giuliani of trying to reduce its influence because it went on strike against the city in 1994 ten months after he became mayor.

AGENCY: Human Resources Administration 55

FUNCTION, SERVICE, OR ASSET PRIVATIZED: Welfare reform (Work Experience Program)

FORM AND DATE OF PRIVATIZATION: Withdrawal, 1995

DESCRIPTION: The Work Experience Program (WEP) is an innovative welfare reform initiative that requires public assistance recipients to engage in work, work-related activities, work assessment, or the work assignment process for their benefits. Those who are unable or unwilling to find private sector jobs are assigned to work in city agencies or nonprofit organizations. This can be considered privatization because individuals who were essentially dependents of the city moved into the world of work. Another perspective is that the city withdrew from a function—it stopped issuing welfare checks—and utilized market incentives instead.

BENEFITS: Welfare reform reduced tax-levy spending for public assistance and enhanced the city's quality of life by employing WEP workers to perform useful public work. The number of public assistance recipients declined 60 percent, from 1,160,600 in March 1995 to about 470,000 in December 2001, and public assistance city tax-levy expenditures declined from $984.2 million in June 1995 to $431.0 million in June 2000, resulting in savings of $553 million; adjusting for inflation would show even greater savings.

The initiative benefits the former welfare recipients as they become more self-reliant and less dependent on public assistance, and it reduces the likely number of future dependent people. In fiscal 2001, the number of public assistance recipients placed in jobs was 151,376, sixteen times the number (9,215) placed in 1993. In total, some 330,000 disadvantaged New Yorkers earned benefits and gained work experience while performing important work for the city, such as raising the cleanliness level of city streets and parks. Many WEP workers were assigned to jobs in the private nonprofit sector.

IMPLEMENTATION: In fiscal 1995 the city's welfare reform initiative, the New York City Work, Accountability, You (NYCWAY), began with requirements for eligibility verification and job search activities from applicants' first contact with the Human Resources Administration (HRA). Public assistance recipients were directed to work assignments after their applications were accepted. HRA also instituted the Intensive Case Control (ICC) process, which combined case tracking with intensive case monitoring. ICC caseworkers were responsible for overseeing all aspects of a case and ensuring that the participants moved through required activities in compliance with program standards and regulations.

In fiscal 1996 HRA expanded NYCWAY to include employable Aid to Families with Dependent Children (AFDC) recipients (with children three years of age or older), who were determined to be appropriate after assessment, and placed in structured quality-of-life work assignments in city agencies. The federal Personal Responsibility and Work Opportunity Reconciliation Act of 1996 replaced AFDC with Temporary Assistance to Needy Families (TANF).

The philosophical change was signaled by transforming the city's so called "Welfare Offices" into "Job Centers." By August 1999 HRA had converted nineteen Income Support Centers into sixteen Job Centers to provide public assistance applicants with assistance in arranging child care, referrals for assistance with home and family problems, and employment-related activities such as help with job search, resume preparation, and interviewing techniques. In December 1999 HRA achieved the mayor's goal of engaging all public assistance clients by 2000 in work, work-related activities, work assessment, or the work assignment process or appropriately exempting them from work requirements. In 1999 the union challenged the program in court on the grounds that welfare workers were replacing unionized employees, in violation of state law, but they lost, finally, in 2003.

AGENCY: Human Resources Administration 56

FUNCTION, SERVICE, OR ASSET PRIVATIZED: Employment preparation and job placement

FORM AND DATE OF PRIVATIZATION: Performance-based contracting, 2000

DESCRIPTION: Prior to 1999 HRA and the Department of Employment (DOE) contracted with almost one hundred vendors to place public assistance recipients in jobs. Contracts were essentially cost plus fixed fee. With welfare reform, HRA turned to job placement; it focused on adults (mostly those on public assistance) while DOE focused on youths and older displaced workers.

Two new streamlined programs were designed: Skills Assessment Program (SAP) and Employment Services and Placement (ESP). Private contractors operate these programs. The city's welfare-to-work initiatives focus on the bottom line: getting participants into jobs and becoming self-sufficient. SAP is short term, about four to six weeks for public assistance applicants and recipients who are deemed most ready for jobs. Accepted applicants spend two weeks full time with the SAP vendor, then change to a schedule of three days a week at their WEP worksite and two at their SAP assignment. ESP is longer term, for public assistance recipients and non–public assistance individuals who require significant training prior to attempted placement. Contractors are paid only when people are actually placed in jobs.

BENEFITS: The city realized several benefits due to competitive contracting for these employment programs.

- Cost reduction: Payment only for positive outcomes; nonperforming vendors drop out and no longer receive line-item payments to run unsuccessful programs.
- Cost avoidance: Reduced payments for public assistance as individuals become self-reliant and their public assistance cases are closed.
- Success in job placement: Improved performance by vendors in job placements; the change from cost-plus contracts to performance-based contracts led to an increase in the placement rate by 61 percent (from 16 percent to 25 percent) and an annual placement increase of 305 percent (from 3,875 to 15, 697). By the end of fiscal 2000, 89,071 public assistance recipients had been placed in jobs through these two programs.
- Increased quality or responsiveness of service: Greater focus by vendors on finding higher-paying jobs for participants in order to earn performance incentives; greater focus by helping participants keep their jobs in order to earn performance incentives. Moreover, the prime contractor–subcontractor relationship encourages vendors to help their smaller subcontractors perform better.

IMPLEMENTATION: Negotiated acquisition was used to arrive at the ESP and SAP contracts in 1999. Three-year contracts were signed with twelve vendors; eight did ESP only, one did SAP only, and three did both. Startup was delayed because the comptroller held up the contracts. The city went to court and won. Effective startup therefore was July 2000. Four of the twelve vendors, including America Works, are for-profit firms. These contracts are all performance based; that is, vendors are paid only for placing participants in jobs. HRA monitored the contractors at startup through frequent site visits to observe their processes.

In fiscal 2000 HRA entered into performance-based contracts for employment preparation and employment services for all public assistance clients, including those with special needs and substance abuse problems. The fifteen new Skills Assessment and Placement (SAP) and Employment Services and Placement (ESP) programs maximize participant services by combining funding sources such as the Job Training Partnership (JTPA), Welfare-to-Work, TANF, and SNA. HRA plans to achieve 100,000 job placements by the end of fiscal 2001. HRA's fiscal 2001 budget for employment-related programs was $247 million.

AGENCY: Department of Information Technology & Telecommunications 57

FUNCTION, SERVICE, OR ASSET PRIVATIZED: Kiosks for interactive "e-government"

FORM AND DATE OF PRIVATIZATION: Contract, 2001, planned

DESCRIPTION: CityAccess is New York City's kiosk project designed to provide important city services conveniently. The demonstration phase of CityAccess, which was first deployed in August, 1996, officially ended on December 31, 2000 with the old kiosks being removed. Because CityAccess was overwhelmingly approved of through satisfaction surveys, the city decided to broaden the program to place at least one kiosk in each of the fifty-nine Community Districts. The city is working with each Community Board to find the best permanent locations in each neighborhood. These locations may be different from the ones in the demonstration project.

BENEFITS: This service provides a more convenient way for citizens and businesses to obtain information, file applications, make payments, and so on.

IMPLEMENTATION: After the successful demonstration project, the Department of Information Technology and Telecommunications issued a request for proposal in 2001 to solicit bids for the CityAccess contract.

AGENCY: Department of Information Technology & Telecommunications 58

FUNCTION, SERVICE, OR ASSET PRIVATIZED: Pneumatic tube network or water pipe network that could be used for fiber-optic cables

FORM AND DATE OF PRIVATIZATION: Lease, request for proposal issued in 2001

DESCRIPTION: This is a remarkable and exotic case. In 1897 the U.S. Post Office put into use an underground network of pneumatic tubes in Manhattan and part of Brooklyn. It was used to move mail quickly and effectively through the city at thirty miles per hour. It was famous for delivering important mail on time during snowstorms.

Technological innovation has made the system obsolete, but it was recently rediscovered and its possible use for modern communications was suggested. A fiber-optical network could make use of the existing, almost forgotten, network. Similarly, an unused water main system of 175 miles could be used in the same way. It was originally designed in the early twentieth century to provide high-pressure water to fire hydrants, but it became superfluous when fire engines were designed to develop their own high pressures.

For more on this intriguing story, see Robin Pogrebin, "Underground Mail Road," *New York Times*, May 7, 2001, B1.

BENEFITS: The city could earn rent if either network found a user, and it would serve as a useful element of communication infrastructure to support the New York economy.

IMPLEMENTATION: The city issued a request for proposals for the water system in 2001 but prospective bidders showed no interest.

AGENCY: Department of Information Technology and Telecommunications 59

FUNCTION, SERVICE, OR ASSET PRIVATIZED: Web phones as public pay telephones

FORM AND DATE OF PRIVATIZATION: Franchise, planned in 2001, implemented in 2003

DESCRIPTION: Public telephones on the streets of New York are owned by private firms but are franchised by the city. It was proposed that the owners of these telephones be required to upgrade at least some of them so that the public could use them for access to the Internet as well as for voice communication. The franchise was awarded and the first twenty-five Web phones, providing high-speed access to the Internet, were installed in 2003.

BENEFITS: These phones improve the quality of life for the public and expand services at no cost to the city; users pay for the service.

IMPLEMENTATION: Initiated near the end of the Giuliani administration, it was implemented under Mayor Bloomberg.

AGENCY: Department of Juvenile Justice 60

FUNCTION, SERVICE, OR ASSET PRIVATIZED: Nonsecure detention facilities for youth

FORM AND DATE OF PRIVATIZATION: Contracts, fiscal 1998–2001

DESCRIPTION: The Department of Juvenile Justice (DJJ) provides detention, postdetention, and delinquency prevention services to juveniles, ages seven through fifteen, in New York City. The department operates secure and nonsecure detention facilities throughout the city. DJJ operates its detention facilities under oversight by the New York State Office of Children and Family Services and is required to adhere to regulations governing the care and custody of youth in detention.

Three secure and two nonsecure facilities are directly operated by DJJ. The agency contracts with community-based providers for additional nonsecure detention services. From July 1998 to June 2001 DJJ added three nonsecure detention (NSD) facilities to meet population-driven needs. The three additional facilities were acquired through the competitive bidding process and are operated by community-based organizations.

The services provided by NSD facility contractors include residential services; custodial supervision; case management; medical, dental, and mental health services through DJJ's onsite medical contractor; group and individual counseling; transportation to and from court appointments; recreational activities; the provision of clothing and personal hygiene supplies; and educational services.

BENEFITS: The average cost of a nonsecure detention facility operated directly by DJJ is $1 million per year. The average cost to DJJ to contract with a community-based organization to operate a nonsecure detention facility is $850,000 per year. As a result of contracting out the additional three nonsecure detention facilities, DJJ was able to achieve approximately $450,000 per year in savings by fiscal 2001 with no change to the level of services.

IMPLEMENTATION: The agency obtained nonsecure detention services from the community-based organization by the competitive, sealed proposal procurement method (request for proposal).

AGENCY: Department of Parks and Recreation 61

FUNCTION, SERVICE, OR ASSET PRIVATIZED: Central Park

FORM AND DATE OF PRIVATIZATION: Default, voluntarism, and contract, 1998

DESCRIPTION: Perhaps the world's most famous urban park, Central Park is an 843-acre jewel in the center of Manhattan Island. It was designed by the famous landscape architects Frederick Law Olmsted and Calvert Vaux. It was not simply a fenced-off piece of land; it was manmade, built between 1856 and 1873. Not only were the bridges, paths, and buildings manmade, but virtually all the topsoil, lakes, trees, shrubs, and lawns were placed or built by human hands.

Despite its illustrious past and international recognition, Central Park was suffering from decay. The park receives nearly 20 million visitors a year, a level of traffic that causes significant damage to lawns, vegetation, benches, buildings, paths, fountains, and playgrounds if maintenance fails to keep up. This was indeed the case: The city seemed unable to maintain the park in satisfactory condition. A quarter of Central Park was barren of vegetation. In addition, its infrastructure exhibited clear signs of decay: bare lawns, broken benches, graffiti, and deteriorated paved surfaces.

Deploring the park's decline, concerned citizens (Richard Gilder and George Soros) commissioned a comprehensive management study in the mid-1970s that cataloged the problems and suggested solutions. Local citizens then organized an effort to rescue and maintain the park. Elizabeth Barlow Rogers founded the Central Park Conservancy (CPC) in 1980. It is a private, not-for-profit organization that raises monetary and other support for the restoration and preservation of Central Park. Rogers published a master plan in 1987 that was instrumental for repairing and sustaining the park. CPC now manages Central Park under a contract with the city of New York's Department of Parks and Recreation.

BENEFITS: Over the past twenty years, the conservancy raised approximately $250 million for the park through private donations from individuals, foundations, and corporations. The conservancy funds major capital improvements, provides horticultural care and management, and offers programs for volunteers and visitors. Conservancy staff and resources beautified the park for public enjoyment in a myriad of ways. The conservancy provides more than $17 million, or 85 percent, of Central Park's annual operating budget of nearly $20 million.

IMPLEMENTATION: In February 1998 the conservancy signed an eight-year management agreement with the city of New York. The management agreement requires the conservancy to raise support from corporations, foundations, and private citizens in order to qualify for additional funds from the city. For example, during fiscal 2001 the conservancy had to raise and spend $7 million on the park to qualify for $2 million from the city.

AGENCY: Department of Parks and Recreation 62

FUNCTION, SERVICE, OR ASSET PRIVATIZED: Vehicle maintenance

FORM AND DATE OF PRIVATIZATION: Managed competition and contract, 1996

DESCRIPTION: For a comprehensive report, see the case study in Chapter 9. The Department of Parks and Recreation (DPR) has eight garages located throughout the city where its 2,000 vehicles are maintained and fueled. Utilizing the city's new competitive bidding process and in conformance with Local Law 35 concerning contracting for services, the department contracted with a private firm to maintain the vehicles in the Bronx Garage. After a year of satisfactory results, the department contracted out the two Brooklyn garages as well to the same firm. In the end, contractors maintained 35 percent of the fleet while in-house forces maintained 65 percent.

BENEFITS: Savings in the Bronx were 38 percent (the cost dropped from $1.17 million to $0.728 million); in Brooklyn, 30 percent. Overall, contract costs were 35 percent less than in-house costs. Total automotive maintenance costs (public and private) in fiscal 2001 were $1.27 million (16 percent) less in current dollars than they were five years earlier, in fiscal 1996, despite inflation and labor agreements that raised per-unit costs. (Inflation-adjusted costs were 26 percent less.)

Moreover, DPR reduced its overall out-of-service rate by 62 percent, from 14 percent, or 266 vehicles, in 1994 to 5.3 percent, or 104 vehicles, in 2001. The contractor's rate reached a low of 2.6 percent in the Bronx and 2.9 percent in Brooklyn in 1998. The in-house rate was 5.5 percent in fiscal 2001, and the contractor's rate was 4.9 percent. The overall rate for all eight garages stayed between 5 percent and 6 percent for four years, from 1998 through 2001. Over 160 more vehicles are on the road each day due to better maintenance and management, resulting in better park maintenance and lower capital costs because fewer vehicles have to be purchased.

IMPLEMENTATION: The results of competitive contracting were so good that when the department started the process of contracting out more of the garages, the union agreed to improve its operating practices and try to match the performance of the private contractors. In fact, although the agency did not do quite as well, it improved the internal operation dramatically and almost matched the private firm in some respects. As a result, the department did not undertake further managed competitions but it kept track of the performance in each garage and thus maintained a competitive spur on both the firms and its own units; each served as a yardstick to measure the performance of the other. See Chapter 9 for details of this and other privatizations in the department.

AGENCY: Department of Parks and Recreation 63

FUNCTION, SERVICE, OR ASSET PRIVATIZED: Park maintenance

FORM AND DATE OF PRIVATIZATION: Contract, 1994, completed and terminated

DESCRIPTION: For a comprehensive report, see Chapter 9. Through competitive bidding, a contractor was selected on an experimental one-year basis to maintain forty-seven park properties in Queens. Because of the success of this experiment, another contract was awarded a year later to another firm to maintain forty-five park sites in the Bronx.

BENEFITS: Costs were reduced by 30 percent, and cleanliness ratings improved substantially.

IMPLEMENTATION: The contractor awarded the work in the Bronx was deemed unsatisfactory and in default after several months and was replaced satisfactorily by another one. Despite its success, the program was terminated after two years because the department was able to use welfare recipients participating in the Work Experience Program, at no cost to the agency, to achieve similar economies.

AGENCY: Brooklyn Public Library 64

FUNCTION, SERVICE, OR ASSET PRIVATIZED: General support

FORM AND DATE OF PRIVATIZATION: Voluntary action, 1995

DESCRIPTION: The Giuliani administration promoted the idea of voluntary contributions from the patrons of the Brooklyn Public Library for its development, rehabilitation, and maintenance.

BENEFITS: Many separate contributions add up to about $2 million per year, an increase from about $1 million per year before the Giuliani administration.

IMPLEMENTATION: Not applicable.

AGENCY: New York Public Library 65

FUNCTION, SERVICE, OR ASSET PRIVATIZED: Library renovation

FORM AND DATE OF PRIVATIZATION: Withdrawal and voluntarism, 1996 (Adopt-a-Branch)

DESCRIPTION: The Giuliani administration started an initiative in 1996 to fund the renovation of fifteen neighborhood public library branches in the Bronx, Manhattan, and Staten Island by securing private contributions to cover part of the cost.

BENEFITS: Fifteen branches in Manhattan each received $500,000 of private funding, totaling $7.5 million for major capital renovation. Each branch had a different donor. A Bronx branch, the Bronx Borough Center Library at 310 East Kingsbridge Road, received $5 million. It will be the largest Latino and Puerto Rican resource center of its kind in the United States. Total funding amounted to $12.5 million.

IMPLEMENTATION: The following is a list of local branches participating in the New York Public Library Adopt-a-Branch Program:
(Dollar amounts reflect total project renovation costs.)

1. Aguilar (Manhattan) full renovation $2.68 million. Renovation completed, branch reopened April 30, 1996.
2. West Farms (Bronx) major renovation $2.06 million. Renovation completed, branch reopened June 11, 1996.
3. Tompkins Square (Manhattan) full renovation $2.34 million. Renovation completed March 1996.
4. Sedgwick (Bronx) new construction $1.77 million. Construction completed June 1994.
5. Morrisania (Bronx) interior renovation $2.02 million. Renovation completed July 1997.
6. Chatham Square (Manhattan) full renovation $3.42 million. Scheduled completion March 2001.
7. George Bruce (Manhattan) full interior and partial exterior renovation $3.65 million. Scheduled April 2001.
8. Inwood (Manhattan) interior renovation and expansion of branch $3.75 million. Scheduled April 2001.
9. Mott Haven (Bronx) interior renovation $3.17 million. Scheduled completion May 2001.
10. Muhlenberg (Manhattan) interior renovation $3.12 million. Scheduled completion January 2001.
11. Ottendorfer (Manhattan) interior renovation $2.48 million. Scheduled completion May 2001.
12. Seward Park (Manhattan) interior renovation $3.98 million. Construction not yet started.
13. Stapleton (Bronx) full renovation and expansion $4.52 million. Construction not yet started.
14. Harlem (Manhattan) full interior and exterior renovation $3.5 million. Construction not yet started.
15. 115th Street (Manhattan) full interior and exterior renovation $3.15 million. Construction not yet started.

AGENCY: New York Public Library 66

FUNCTION, SERVICE, OR ASSET PRIVATIZED: Security guards

FORM AND DATE OF PRIVATIZATION: Contract, 1996

DESCRIPTION: The New York City Public Library contracts out the service to provide security guards at its various locations.

BENEFITS: The primary benefit of this contract is a lower cost for the library.

IMPLEMENTATION: Not applicable.

AGENCY: Department of Sanitation 67

FUNCTION, SERVICE, OR ASSET PRIVATIZED: Residential solid waste collection

FORM AND DATE OF PRIVATIZATION: Contracting, 1994, not implemented

DESCRIPTION: For many years the city's collection of residential waste was considered very inefficient. Collection routes had not been changed even though the residential patterns, and hence the pattern of waste generation, had changed, and the introduction of recycling—with separate pickups—meant that the amount of waste generated per route had been reduced significantly. As a result, some collectors completed their workday after only three or four hours. Labor agreements coupled with the political strength of the relevant unions prevented previous mayors from making the changes that were obviously needed.

From the beginning, the Giuliani administration insisted on productivity improvements and an end to those practices. It threatened to hold competitive bids and bring in private contractors to do some of the work.

BENEFITS: In a labor settlement reached in September 1994, the union representing sanitation workers agreed to increase the length of their collection routes by 20 percent, collect nearly two tons more per truck per day, and cut the size of the work force by 600 people. For example, a two-person crew that used to collect 8.5 tons of refuse in an eight-hour shift on a twenty-block route would have to collect 10.1 tons from a twenty-four- or twenty-five-block route. This amounted to a 20 percent gain in productivity. Crews that failed to meet this productivity standard would have their pay docked. The agreement also allowed the city to contract out if it so wished.

IMPLEMENTATION: The productivity improvement was achieved and maintained, and therefore the city did not invoke its right to contract with private firms.

AGENCY: Department of Sanitation 68

FUNCTION, SERVICE, OR ASSET PRIVATIZED: Solid waste transfer and disposal

FORM AND DATE OF PRIVATIZATION: Contract, 1997

DESCRIPTION: All city-collected refuse was being brought to the Fresh Kills landfill in Staten Island for disposal. Space there was running short, and residents of that borough—important political supporters of Mayor Giuliani—strongly opposed continuing operations. Therefore, in July 1997 the Department of Sanitation (DOS) decided to close the Fresh Kills Landfill and start exporting refuse. Waste-export vendors provide waste transfer stations and transport the waste to environmentally approved landfills in other states.

BENEFITS: The city incurs net costs for exporting its solid waste and disposing of it, although using contractors to transport the waste is much less costly than having the department do it using its own personnel, transfer stations, and transport vehicles. Property values, however, can be expected to rise along with property taxes in the vicinity of Fresh Kills landfill.

IMPLEMENTATION: In 1997 DOS awarded a short-term contract for exporting 1,700 tons per day of Bronx-generated waste from an existing private transfer station located in the Port Morris area of the Bronx. An additional 2,400 tons per day of Brooklyn-generated refuse began to be exported in 1998. In 1999 the department began to export refuse generated in Manhattan and Staten Island. In 2000 the department began exporting the remaining refuse generated in Brooklyn and Queens in 2000 and 2001 respectively.

AGENCY: Department of Sanitation 69

FUNCTION, SERVICE, OR ASSET PRIVATIZED: Control of gas emission at Fresh Kills landfill

FORM AND DATE OF PRIVATIZATION: Franchise, 1998

DESCRIPTION: The DOS implemented a landfill gas emissions control system for the collection and sale of methane gas generated by the landfill. The operation and maintenance of the system is contracted to GSF Energy L.L.C.

BENEFITS: The firm paid an initial fee of $875,000 and pays $1 million in combined annual payments for twenty years. Additional benefits include annual savings of $2–3 million in environmental compliance monitoring costs and a great reduction in emissions of foul-smelling gases. The closure, capping, and post-closure monitoring of the Fresh Kills landfill provides substantial environmental benefits. These include the collection and reuse of methane gas, the collection and removal of impurities from leachate (fluids), and the long-term environmental monitoring of groundwater, surface water, and sediment (including tidal streams surrounding the landfill). The Department of City Planning is investigating potential uses for the site after closure.

IMPLEMENTATION: The first stage (Part I) of this process consisted of completing the gas-collection system at the landfill and installing and operating enclosed flares during 1998. Part II involved the upgrading and expansion of an existing energy recovery system so that landfill gas can be recovered and used beneficially.

AGENCY: Department of Sanitation 70

FUNCTION, SERVICE, OR ASSET PRIVATIZED: Fresh Kills landfill composting

FORM AND DATE OF PRIVATIZATION: Contract, 2000

DESCRIPTION: The Department of Sanitation (DOS) hires and pays a contractor who has the professional expertise to operate the Fresh Kills landfill compost site. (Composting using food waste is also being carried out at the Rikers Island prison, where prisoners grow vegetables.)

BENEFITS: The operation is not self-sustaining and therefore the contractor is paid by the city. The cost is lower than it was when DOS employees operated the facility. The contractor sells the compost product, which has little market value, with no income to the city, but it helps lower the operating cost. There are also several qualitative benefits: The contractor generates more annual compost product at a lower operating cost, which reduces the volume of waste to be disposed of at the landfill and therefore reduces disposal costs. The site is also maintained in better condition without odor problems.

IMPLEMENTATION: The Department privatized all DOS composting operations at the Fresh Kills landfill compost site in 2000.

AGENCY: Department of Sanitation 71

FUNCTION, SERVICE, OR ASSET PRIVATIZED: Wastepaper recycling

FORM AND DATE OF PRIVATIZATION: Contract, 1996

DESCRIPTION: The city contracts with six firms that process and recycle wastepaper that is collected at curbside by the Department of Sanitation.

BENEFITS: The DOS calculated that $1.3 million in revenue was generated in fiscal 1998 due to the contract with Visy Paper. As a $150 million project, Visy Paper employed a 1,000-person construction workforce at its peak, and as an operating facility it employed 115 workers. This contract provided continuing benefits to the Department's curbside program and to the city by:

- Establishing a long-term supplier relationship with a local market for the city's wastepaper.
- Reducing the truck traffic for transporting curbside-collected paper in the five boroughs.
- Assisting the development and expansion of the city's infrastructure for processing recyclables.
- Providing entry-level employment for those with limited job skills.
- Eliminating all other-than-personal services (OTPS) expenditures for wastepaper processing and creating a new revenue stream (a minimum of $1.3 million per year).

In 2000 the city successfully eliminated all OTPS expenditures for wastepaper processing through unique contractual arrangements whereby the city shares risk with the individual contractors. This arrangement allows the contractor in turn to commit to paying the city $5–10 per ton regardless of market conditions.

Estimated cost reduction over twenty years is $20–120 million. Estimated revenue is $30 million over twenty years (at least $1.3 million per year). The revenue in fiscal 2000 (a very good year for paper prices) was an impressive $7.5 million. The estimated revenue of $1.3 million per year is even more impressive considering that DOS used to pay up to $6 million in a bad year (that is, low value for recycled paper) for in-house processing.

IMPLEMENTATION: In 1996 the city successfully negotiated a contract to supply recyclable paper to Visy Paper (N.Y.) Inc., the U.S. subsidiary of Pratt Industries, Inc., an Australian liner-board manufacturer. Visy directly received Staten Island's recyclable paper by truck and Manhattan's paper by barge. At full operation, the Visy Plant was estimated to receive up to almost 50 percent of all the paper the department collected through curbside collection.

In 2000 the department entered into competitive contracts with five additional wastepaper processing vendors. The department now has established contracts with five local wastepaper processors for a term of five to twenty years to process the city's wastepaper. (These are five-year contracts with up to three automatic five-year renewals.)

The contracts are geared to the changing market price for wastepaper and the quality of the collected paper.

AGENCY: Department of Sanitation 72

FUNCTION, SERVICE, OR ASSET PRIVATIZED: New York City Stuff Exchange Program

FORM AND DATE OF PRIVATIZATION: Contract, 2000

DESCRIPTION: New York City Stuff Exchange serves as a broker connecting donors and receivers of discarded textiles and hard goods. The Department of Sanitation has set up a telephone and computer-based system to give businesses and consumers detailed information on locations in their areas where they can drop off or obtain reusable products (clothing, rugs, and the like) that would otherwise be discarded into the waste stream. The system matches donors and recipients of these materials and works much like ordering movie tickets by phone: The user calls in, gives his zip code, and what he wants to give away or obtain, and the system matches him with a nearby donor or recipient of that material.

BENEFITS: The city avoids millions of dollars in costs by not having to collect the material at curbside before reuse or disposal. It spent $1.5 million for advertising to launch this program, and it spends $250,000 per year for telephone lines and to keep the information up to date. Moreover, the program appeals to those who are very concerned about the environment.

IMPLEMENTATION: The department is expanding this program to provide more detailed information on exchange locations citywide.

AGENCY: Taxi and Limousine Commission 73

FUNCTION, SERVICE, OR ASSET PRIVATIZED: Taxicabs

FORM AND DATE OF PRIVATIZATION: Franchise, 1996

DESCRIPTION: The Taxi and Limousine Commission (TLC) regulates and licenses the medallion taxi and for-hire vehicle industry. State legislation authorized the city to sell up to 400 new medallions. The City Council authorized the sale of these medallions through Local Law 16 beginning in February 1996. This was the first increase in the number of medallions in fifty-nine years, that is, since 1937. The number of medallions had been constant at 11,787 and is now 12,187. Increasing the number of taxi franchises is a form of privatization.

BENEFITS: The auction of 133 new medallions in May 1996 generated $26 million. An auction of 133 more new medallions generated $28.9 million in revenue in fiscal 1997. The final auction of 134 new medallions generated $35 million in fiscal 1998. The total revenue was $89.9 million for 400 new medallions, or about $225,000 for each one. The benefits to the public are more service and greater convenience by having more taxis available.

IMPLEMENTATION: In 2003 the Bloomberg administration planned to issue 900 more franchises, beginning with a sale of 300 in June 2004. Estimated sale price is $250,000 each. Fares would be raised 25 percent to mollify existing owners.

AGENCY: Taxi and Limousine Commission 74

FUNCTION, SERVICE, OR ASSET PRIVATIZED: Commuter vans

FORM AND DATE OF PRIVATIZATION: Default and deregulation, 1999

DESCRIPTION: The Taxi and Limousine Commission (TLC) licenses commuter-van companies originally granted licenses by the state to operate vehicles in designated areas. During Mayor Giuliani's administration, market forces were recognized and the number of licensed vans was increased from 262 to 392, almost 50 percent, to provide service in underserved parts of the city. There are now sixty-four licensed commuter-van companies operating those vehicles, and they have the newly won authority to operate 712 vehicles.

BENEFITS: The major benefit is to the riding public due to lower fares ($1.00 vs. $1.50) and better, more convenient (no standees), and more frequent service during the limited operating hours. No direct savings accrue to public agencies from this form of privatization, that is, from allowing market forces to operate. In fact, there is a net cost to the city for licensing and enforcement. However, vans provide service to underserved areas of the city. If the public bus agency, New York City Transit (a unit of the Metropolitan Transportation Authority, a New York state agency), had to serve those areas, the public cost would be much greater. This corresponds to an avoided cost for the higher level of transportation service available to riders.

IMPLEMENTATION: Implementation was not easy. Associations of van operators in the city long sought the right to increase the number of vans and to be allowed to operate along more routes. There is significant resistance, however, to role of the private sector from the transportation union that represents the city's transit workers. The City Council supported the union and blocked the commission from granting more licenses despite the obvious popularity of the vans and the need for more service in parts of the city.

It required a lawsuit brought by the Institute for Justice, a Washington, D.C.–based public-interest law firm, to force the City Council to allow TLC to expand the number of licenses. Mayor Giuliani joined the suit on the side of the van operators. The court ruled in favor of the institute, the van operators, and the mayor.

AGENCY: Trade Waste Commission 75

FUNCTION, SERVICE, OR ASSET PRIVATIZED: Commercial solid waste collection

FORM AND DATE OF PRIVATIZATION: Regulating to create a competitive market, 1995

DESCRIPTION: The city ended the municipal collection of commercial waste in 1956 and left it up to the private sector to provide this service, but the city remained responsible and regulated this activity as a matter of public health. This industry gradually became dominated by a collusive, anticompetitive cartel with involvement by organized crime.

When Rudolph Giuliani was a prosecutor, he succeeded in getting dozens of mafiosi convicted, and as mayor he attacked this cartel. He worked with a large national firm that entered the New York market despite threats of violence. Legislation transferred regulation of this industry from the Department of Consumer Affairs to the newly created Trade Waste Commission (TWC), a regulatory and law enforcement agency that initiated stringent regulation of the industry and removed corrupt individuals by denying them licenses. Maximum allowed prices were reduced by 26 percent, but competition drove down actual prices by a staggering 48 percent. One large hospital saw its bill drop by several hundred thousand dollars a year.

This was not a direct municipal service, but the city's regulatory action broke up a criminal conspiracy and created a competitive market for an important public service. This is a form of privatization, albeit an unusual one.

BENEFITS: The commercial waste-collection industry was cleaned up and the city's businesses saved large amounts of money, which ultimately benefited their customers, the public, to the tune of an estimated $400 million a year.

IMPLEMENTATION: Not applicable.

AGENCY: Department of Transportation 76

FUNCTION, SERVICE, OR ASSET PRIVATIZED: Private ferry operations

FORM AND DATE OF PRIVATIZATION: Franchise, 1986

DESCRIPTION: The Department of Transportation (DOT) Private Ferry program exemplifies privatization in that it relies on the private sector and market forces. The city is not contracting out services that were formerly publicly provided, and the city does not pay the private ferry operators. The operators receive no direct operating subsidies from the city, state, or federal governments. More than half the current fifteen ferry routes carrying 35,000 passenger trips each weekday were initiated after 1993, that is, during the Giuliani administration.

DOT licenses private companies to operate ferry services in New York and works to encourage increased investment in new services to promote ferry usage and reduce congestion. The city also invests in infrastructure by creating ferry landings at strategic city-owned locations. Currently, DOT is involved in the management of ferry landings at Wall Street (Pier 11), East 34th Street, East 62nd Street, East 90th Street, and near Yankee Stadium. DOT is participating with EDC on the creation and replacement of landings at West 39th Street, South Ferry (Slip 5/6), St. George (Slip 7), and East 75th Street.

BENEFITS: The private ferry program gives the public more and better transportation options. Four private companies now operate approximately fifteen routes. This helps to relieve pressure on bridges, tunnels, and roadways—especially for travel between New Jersey and New York. Ridership on privately operated ferries has increased every year since 1986.

IMPLEMENTATION: Privately operated ferry services returned to New York Harbor in 1986 after a twenty-year absence. New York is now home to the largest and fastest growing network of commuter ferries in North America. DOT is responsible for granting operating permits to all ferry routes and for issuing landing licenses to those routes using city-owned piers. These piers are jointly administered by DOT and EDC under the terms of a memorandum of understanding between the two agencies. All landing fees payable by ferry operators under the DOT licenses are collected by EDC and placed into a fund to be used for the upkeep of the piers.

EDC and DOT are jointly developing a new West Side Central Ferry Terminal at West 39th Street, as well as a new system of ferry landings along the East River. The DOT Office of Private Ferry Operations works closely with ferry operators, as well as the Port Authority, the New York Metropolitan Transportation Council, and federal transportation agencies.

In 2004 the largest ferry operator requested financial aid from the city or state because of a decline in the number of passengers, a decline attributable to the loss of jobs in downtown Manhattan caused by destruction from the terrorist attack of September 11, 2001. As of early 2005, no decision on the aid request had been made.

AGENCY: Department of Transportation 77

FUNCTION, SERVICE, OR ASSET PRIVATIZED: Municipal parking garages

FORM AND DATE OF PRIVATIZATION: Lease, 1982, 1995

DESCRIPTION: The Bureau of Parking has thirteen facilities operated and managed by private parking companies. The first proposal for privatization, in 1982, was to lease the facilities to private operators for a monthly flat fee that the operator would pay to the city. In 1995, under Mayor Giuliani, the city changed the terms of the leases to include revenue sharing with incentive clauses. The city receives a percentage of the parking revenue above a base target.

BENEFITS: In fiscal 2000 gross revenue for the city from the parking garages and parking fields was $10.7 million; the management fee paid by the city to the private operators was $4.6 million. The net revenue to the city was therefore $6.1 million.

IMPLEMENTATION: The initiative to privatize the management and operation of the municipal garages was originally driven by the 1975 fiscal crisis. The Bureau of Parking was forced to seek alternatives to reduce the operating cost.

In late 1981 the Bureau of Parking finalized the first lease agreement, which took affect in February 1982 for the 3rd Avenue and E 149th Street garage, in the Bronx. The city was not satisfied with the control of revenue and the inability to dictate the experience and accountability of the operators. This led to the evolution of the management and operation contracts. Over the next five years the contracts grew into their current form. Private parking companies using a three-year management and operation contract now operate the facilities. These contracts are competitively bid under a sealed-bid process. As of June 1987 all thirteen of the garages owned by the Bureau of Parking were managed and operated privately under contract.

In 1995 the city changed the contracts to include revenue sharing with incentive clauses. Based on targets set by the city, a percentage of monies above the target would be shared with the operator.

AGENCY: Department of Transportation 78

FUNCTION, SERVICE, OR ASSET PRIVATIZED: Parking garages and parking fields

FORM AND DATE OF PRIVATIZATION: Divestment, 1996

DESCRIPTION: In an effort to get out of this noncore business, a city-owned garage on West 54th Street in Manhattan and two garages and two parking fields in Jamaica, Queens, were sold between 1996 and 2001.

BENEFITS: The Manhattan site was sold for $14.11 million in 1996. One Jamaica garage was sold to the Greater Jamaica Downtown Development Corporation for $1 million in 1996. The other three facilities were sold for $1.75 million in 2001. The total revenue was $16.86 million. The city will also receive annual property taxes.

IMPLEMENTATION: Not applicable.

AGENCY: Department of Transportation 79

FUNCTION, SERVICE, OR ASSET PRIVATIZED: Adopt-a-Highway

FORM AND DATE OF PRIVATIZATION: Default and voluntarism, 1995

DESCRIPTION: Under this program, sponsors who want cleaner roads adopt a one-mile segment of the city's 362 adoptable arterial highway miles by contracting with one of the six DOT-approved maintenance providers. Sponsors can be individuals, companies, or organizations. They may contract for one or two years depending on the level of service they choose. The maintenance providers are selected and approved by DOT based on their marketing and highway-maintenance experience. This support is acknowledged by posting a sign with the sponsor's name and logo.

The performance of the maintenance providers is monitored by DOT through a system of daily inspections. A numerical rating of quality is assigned to each segment, and the ratings are analyzed to determine the quality of the service.

BENEFITS: The Adopt-a-Highway program provides maintenance on both the main line and all corresponding exit and entrance ramps of the city's 362 adoptable arterial highway miles. These services include litter removal, trimming, sweeping, mowing, and graffiti removal. Before the implementation of Adopt-a-Highway in 1995, DOT used the Community Service Program (CSP) to provide litter removal once every two months on the main line. The other services were provided only when the availability of resources permitted. Under this program, an estimated $2.31 million per year is contributed, which results in more frequent sweeping and cleaner, less hazardous roads.

IMPLEMENTATION: In May 1995 the Adopt-a-Highway program was implemented. DOT identified 362 miles of arterial highway as eligible for adoption by corporate and individual sponsors. DOT compiled a list of qualified and responsive maintenance providers from which sponsors could choose. Litter removal, trimming, sweeping, mowing, and graffiti removal were identified as tasks that could benefit from privatization. DOT and the maintenance providers solicited corporate sponsors. At that time, 23 percent of the total adoptable miles were adopted.

Now more than 91 percent of the total adoptable miles (330 of 362) are adopted. This was accomplished through a rigorous marketing strategy undertaken as a joint effort by DOT and the maintenance providers. Marketing materials were developed jointly and distributed to prospective sponsors.

The most formidable obstacle was the union's initial concern that this would eliminate jobs. DOT was able to alleviate that concern by demonstrating that jobs were not being threatened as workers would still be needed to do the more skilled tasks on the arterial highways such as grass cutting and seeding, guide-rail repair, attenuator repair, pothole repair, and repairing of chain-link fencing.

The primary factor in the success of the program is the quality control and maintenance provider evaluation system. As stated above, each mile is evaluated periodically and rated according to the quality of work performed. Ongoing communication among DOT, the maintenance providers, and the sponsors is essential. Both positive and negative evaluations are discussed and strategies are developed to deal with deficiencies in service. Additionally, sponsors are commended for their participation in the program.

AGENCY: Department of Transportation 80

FUNCTION, SERVICE, OR ASSET PRIVATIZED: Installation of street signs

FORM AND DATE OF PRIVATIZATION: Managed competition (work retained in house), May 1995

DESCRIPTION: The city sought to increase the number of signs installed each year. Various options were considered, including increasing the amount of work contracted out. Ultimately it was decided that the most cost-effective option was to "contract in." Negotiations then ensued with the union to improve, through incentives, the productivity of the existing workforce. The Sign Maintenance Managed Competition is an agreement entered into by District Council 37, representing traffic device maintainers (TDMs), and the city of New York. Under this agreement, TDMs receive bonus payments for meeting and exceeding a productivity rate of 10.5 signs per person per day. The bonus payments are based on productivity rate, defined as signs installed on regular time per day per TDM. The amount increases for every increase of an increment of 0.10 in the productivity rate. The current agreement is valid for fiscal 2000 and 2001.

BENEFITS: The Productivity Rate for the installation of street signs has increased steadily for the four periods the program has been operating:

Pre-competition	May 1994–April 1995	9.92 signs/day/TDM
Year 1	May 1995–April 1996	12.11 signs/day/TDM
Year 2	September 1997–June 1998	11.12 signs/day/TDM
Year 3	July 1998–June 1999	11.32 signs/day/TDM
Year 4	July 1999–June 2000	12.29 signs/day/TDM

The program achieved an immediate productivity increase of 22 percent in the first year and then declined to only 12 percent in the second year because the contract had expired after the first year and was not renewed until two months into the new fiscal year. Productivity then increased slowly under the incentive system until it reached 24 percent in the fourth year.

IMPLEMENTATION: In May 1995 the Department of Transportation and District Council 37, representing TDMs, entered into an agreement to increase the installation of traffic signs. The target was set at 47,207 signs for 27 TDMs, for a twelve-month period from May 1, 1995, through April 30, 1996. At the end of the twelve-month period, the actual number of signs installed was 49,582. This represented an increase of 5 percent in signs installed over the revised target. This was accomplished by a 22 percent increase in the productivity rate over the rate for the twelve-month period preceding the project.

AGENCY: Department of Transportation 81

FUNCTION, SERVICE, OR ASSET PRIVATIZED: Street resurfacing

FORM AND DATE OF PRIVATIZATION: Managed competition, 1995, not implemented

DESCRIPTION: Plans were developed to carry out a simultaneous experiment comparing the performance of a private firm with city employees for resurfacing comparable streets. Documents were prepared to receive bids and to conduct such an experiment, but the competition was not carried out.

BENEFITS: Large savings were expected if contracts were to be awarded to the winner of a managed competition for street resurfacing. It appears that privatization was perceived as a threat, however, and the in-house unit agreed to reorganize its work practices to increase productivity.

IMPLEMENTATION: No contract was awarded because the department changed its operating procedures and increased its productivity to counter the threat of privatization.

AGENCY: Department of Transportation 82

FUNCTION, SERVICE, OR ASSET PRIVATIZED: Red-light cameras

FORM AND DATE OF PRIVATIZATION: Contract, 1993

DESCRIPTION: The red-light camera program automatically photographs and issues notices of liability to vehicles that drive through certain red lights. The Department of Transportation (DOT) owns the cameras and contracts out the photographic processing component of this program, which includes back-office tracking of each notice of liability, maintenance of all cameras, loading and unloading of each camera, and development and delivery of film. DOT is required by law to review the photographs of "events" and determine liability—this function cannot be performed by a contractor. DOT determines which event photos will result in tickets being issued; about half the events result in tickets.

The annual number of "events" photographed is as follows:

1994 440,000 events
1995 380,000
1996 320,000
1997 260,000 (the decrease from 1994 to 1997 is 41 percent)
1998 418,000 (number of cameras increased from eighteen to thirty)
1999 392,000
2000 414,000

BENEFITS: The primary goal of the red-light camera program is to protect the safety of the traveling public by deterring red-light running. A 41 percent decrease was observed between 1994 (the first year of operation) and 1997 in the total number of red-light-running incidents at intersections where the cameras are operating. The decrease was even larger if one assumes that the number of violations was even greater the year before the cameras went into operation.

In 2000 about 200,000 tickets were issued and the city collected about $9 million in revenue. The contract cost is about $5 million per year, so the net revenue increase is $4 million per year. There is no revenue sharing.

IMPLEMENTATION: An advocacy group, "STOP," approached DOT about starting a program to remedy the problem of red-light running. A state law was enacted authorizing the city to implement the red-light camera program.

The program began as a pilot demonstration in December 1993 and was the first full-time photographic, red-light enforcement program in the country. The program started with twelve cameras, expanded to eighteen, then to thirty in 1998. DOT plans to increase the number of operating cameras to fifty citywide by summer 2001. It can do this within its existing legislative authorization. It is seeking authority to expand to one hundred; however, there is opposition by civil-rights groups concerned about privacy.

A new contractor, Mulvihill Electric, is taking over from the previous contractor, EDS. The system is being changed from conventional film photography to digital photography.

Index

Citations of Authors